The Constitution and America's Destiny

In this ambitious study, David Brian Robertson explains how the U.S. Constitution emerged from an intense battle between a bold vision for the nation's political future and the tenacious defense of its political present. Given a once-in-a-lifetime chance to alter America's destiny, James Madison laid before the Constitutional Convention a plan for a strong centralized government that could battle for America's long-term interests. But delegates from vulnerable states resisted this plan, seeking instead to maintain state control over most of American life while adding a few more specific powers to the existing government. These clashing aspirations turned the convention into an unpredictable chain of events. Step by step, the delegates' compromises built national powers in a way no one had anticipated and produced a government more complicated than any of them originally intended. Their Constitution, in turn, helped create a politics unlike that in any other nation.

David Brian Robertson is Professor of Political Science at the University of Missouri–St. Louis. He is the author of *Capital, Labor, and State: The Battle for American Labor Markets from the Civil War to the New Deal*, *The Development of American Public Policy: The Structure of Policy Restraint* (with Dennis R. Judd), and numerous journal articles, and he is the editor of *Loss of Confidence: Politics and Policy in the 1970s*. He is associate editor of the *Journal of Policy History*, and he edits *CLIO*, the newsletter of the Politics and History section of the American Political Science Association. Professor Robertson has received the Governor's, Chancellor's, and Emerson Electric Awards for Teaching Excellence. He is the political analyst for KSDK Television (NBC in St. Louis) and is frequently quoted on political issues.

The Constitution and America's Destiny

DAVID BRIAN ROBERTSON
University of Missouri–St. Louis

CAMBRIDGE UNIVERSITY PRESS
Cambridge, New York, Melbourne, Madrid, Cape Town, Singapore, São Paulo

Cambridge University Press
40 West 20th Street, New York, NY 10011-4211, USA

www.cambridge.org
Information on this title: www.cambridge.org/9780521845557

First published 2005

Printed in the United States of America

A catalog record for this publication is available from the British Library.

Library of Congress Cataloging in Publication Data

Robertson, David Brian, 1951–
The Constitution and America's destiny / David Brian Robertson.
p. cm.
Includes bibliographical references and index.
ISBN-13: 978-0-521-84555-7 (hardback)
ISBN-10: 0-521-84555-6 (hardback)
ISBN-13: 978-0-521-60778-0 (pbk.)
ISBN-10: 0-521-60778-7 (pbk.)
1. Constitutional history – United States. 2. United States –
Politics and government – 1783–1789. I. Title.
KF4541.R63 2005
342.7302′9 – dc22 2004029683

ISBN-13 978-0-521-84555-7 hardback
ISBN-10 0-521-84555-6 hardback

ISBN-13 978-0-521-60778-0 paperback
ISBN-10 0-521-60778-7 paperback

To two inspiring mentors
Alfred Diamant
and
Dennis R. Judd

Contents

Tables and Figures

TABLES

FIGURES

Preface

I did not set out to write a book about the U.S. Constitution. I set out to write about the obstacles that American political institutions have placed in the way of American businesses, workers, and other economic interests. But to write that book, I had to start by working out the institutional foundations of American government. I had to understand the design of the Constitution as thoroughly as I could. I knew the Constitution was a solution, but precisely what was it a solution *to*? What pressing policy problems were the founders trying to solve? How did they think the Constitution's provisions would address these problems? What policy results did they expect the government to achieve? Whose interests did they expect policy makers to serve?

I expected to find answers in the many books written about the Constitution, but I was disappointed. None of these books had tried to provide a systematic political explanation for all the Constitution's provisions. Instead, many authors seemed to be bogged down in a hopeless effort to determine the relative impact of abstract principles and personal interests on the Constitution's design. Few books seriously examine the politics of provisions that now seem relatively unimportant, although the delegates to the Constitutional Convention considered many of them important enough to fight about at length. I was especially surprised to find that, with a couple of exceptions, social scientists in the field of American political development had largely ignored questions about the Constitution's original design. This field is my intellectual home. Many scholars in the field dedicate themselves to understanding the way durable political institutions shape politics and policy. Yet virtually none had tried to understand methodically the most basic and enduring choices about the design of America's political institutions.

Meanwhile, the more I read about the Constitutional Convention, the more mysterious it seemed. James Madison, already an experienced and shrewd politician in his mid-thirties, had prepared more than anyone for the meeting in Philadelphia that began in late May 1787. He developed an ingenious agenda to steer its deliberations. I was surprised by the scope of the remarkably strong central government he planned and his determination to exclude the state governments from influencing national policy. Although Madison often is credited as the primary architect of the Constitution, the document finally signed on September 17, 1787, did not include those provisions he considered the most indispensable. This inconsistency helped me clarify my basic questions. Exactly what problems did Madison and other supporters of a new constitution face? Exactly why did they consider these to be problems that necessitated a new constitution? How did Madison think his initial agenda would answer these problems? How did other delegates react to his proposal, and why? What made them change so many fundamentals of his plan, and exactly how did the changes they made affect the final constitution?

Before I knew it, I was deeply invested in writing a book about the politics of the Constitution's design. I began by arranging each one of the original Constitution's provisions into three categories: agency (*who* governs), authority (*what* is governed), and the policy process (*how* is the nation governed). With this map in hand, I set out to understand the way the delegates worked through these issues by studying closely the accounts they left behind. I read the records of the Constitutional Convention over and over, at first chronologically, then by categories of decisions, then provision by provision, and then chronologically again. I puzzled through votes, speeches, legislative tactics, and rhetorical devices. I used insights from recent political research to understand better the political logic playing out in Philadelphia. I returned again and again to the problem of understanding the sequence of events. Small riddles began to take on more meaning. Why, for example, did Madison fight so hard for a national government power to veto state laws? Precisely what caused two of the New York delegates to walk away from the convention for good after July 10, instead of earlier, or later, or not at all? The solutions to such puzzles provided clues to the meeting's bigger mysteries. Gradually, the convention's politics grew clearer to me.

As I see it, politicians wrote the Constitution for politicians to use. The most active delegates knew their fellow politicians' thinking intimately.

They sought to shape the future strategic calculations of the politicians who were going to populate and use the government they were building. The delegates' central dilemma was to create a government that could produce beneficial policies while at the same time ensuring that its policies would not harm the nation, or their own constituents, or interests that they considered vital. They especially wanted a government whose policies would cultivate commerce and protect property. My interpretation emphasizes the framers' political interests and long-term goals for economic policy, rather than their philosophical beliefs, their personal economic interests, or the short-term financial interests of the nation's wealthy elite. Most of the politicians who shaped the Constitution had won elections and many evidently intended to win more. They had to make economic development acceptable to a reasonably large political constituency. These delegates had considerable confidence in their own public-spiritedness and in their own understanding about the kinds of long-term economic policies that could balance the turbulent political dynamics of postrevolutionary America.

Madison's opponents influenced the Constitution's design in more far-reaching ways than scholars recognize. The Constitution emerged from a battle between Madison's vision for the nation's political future and his opponents' defense of much of the nation's political present. Connecticut's delegates in particular challenged Madison and his allies from start to finish. Madison met his political match in Connecticut's wily and accomplished Roger Sherman, who opposed Madison more often and more effectively than any other delegate. While Madison and his allies were trying to maximize national authority to nurture the American economy as a whole, Sherman and his allies were fighting for a more restricted set of specific national powers that would better enable the states to manage their own economies and societies. Connecticut's delegates and their allies gained major concessions and won more frequently as the convention wore on. The underlying battle between the Madison and Sherman positions shaped the Constitution's most controversial provisions: the apportionment and power of the Senate, dual state and national sovereignty, and the selection and powers of the president. Step by step, the delegates narrowed down national authority and fortified those policy institutions they believed most responsive to their interests. The delegates produced a government that was much more complicated and difficult to use than any of them originally intended. They reached compromises that gave different institutions the power to impede national policy, and they forced these institutions to collaborate to get things done.

The framers placed obstacles in the way of political cooperation in the United States, and those obstacles profoundly affect American politics today. As the delegates left the convention, perhaps the most perceptive of them grasped that their Constitution made it easier for politicians to win elections than to use government to change the world. The Constitution gives American politicians remarkable power but at the same time makes it remarkably difficult to use that power. Those who want to use American government today must have a realistic understanding of the fundamental political dilemmas at the core of the Constitution. Putting American government to work on major problems requires much effort to construct and maintain large political coalitions. Building such coalitions is difficult, and the Constitution makes it even more difficult than it ordinarily would be. But it can be done, and it has been done. Many of my students and friends have a deep reservoir of idealism about the use of government. I sincerely hope that such idealists find my interpretation challenging and inspiring, rather than discouraging. By better understanding how Americans made their Constitution and expected it to work, I hope more will feel inspired to dedicate the substantial energy needed to put their government to work in the service of a better world.

Acknowledgments

Let's start at the beginning. A late 1997 conversation with Linda Kowalcky about our respective research projects on the early republic gave me enduring fortitude to turn this project into a book; without a doubt, that valuable exchange became a necessary and probably sufficient condition for bringing this book into being. I tried out many a half-formed idea on Rich Pacelle and Bryan Marshall while they were colleagues at the University of Missouri–St. Louis; these good friends gave me much-needed support, and in the bargain they taught me a lot about American politics, courts, and Congress. Several other wonderful colleagues at UM–St. Louis also were helpful sounding boards and supporters for me; they include David Kimball, Bob Bliss, Dennis Judd, Lana Stein, Terry Jones, Lyman Sargent, and Brady Baybeck.

I subjected numerous graduate and undergraduate students to iterations of this argument, and their feedback immensely benefited the results. I am deeply indebted to Professor Susan Mason, who read the entire manuscript with care and provided extensive, exceptionally helpful comments. Steve Gardner read two versions, one early, one virtually complete; a former state legislator and a current Ph.D. student, Steve unfailingly shared incisive comments, and they greatly improved the manuscript in countless ways. Matthew Sherman also provided many comments on several chapters. Adam Murray shared provocative and helpful interpretations, and Jeremy Yowell found some egregious typographical errors. Will Winter deserves credit for assembling a mountain of information about business and American policy development. Thanks to students in my graduate seminars on American Political Development and on Political Economy, and to the undergraduates who participated in an honors class on the Constitution and American Political Development. All of them forced me to articulate my ideas more clearly, and if ambiguities remain, it's not because they failed to help.

In the early stages of the project, I tried out some interpretations on Cal Jillson and Rick Wilson. Both provided enormously helpful feedback on these early ideas, and both encouraged my efforts. Since then, both also have provided very valuable additional suggestions. Jim Morone has been a terrific professional and personal friend whose encouragement helped even more than he knows. Richard Franklin Bensel's sensitive reading of the strong and weak spots in my arguments – and encouragement to back away from bottomless pitfalls – made this a much better manuscript. Don Critchlow has been a good friend, supporter, and cheerleader for the many years we've worked together on the *Journal of Policy History*. Colleagues at Syracuse University, including most notably Suzanne Mettler, Rogan Kersh, and Kristi Andersen, provided extremely helpful ears for my evolving ideas. On a couple of important occasions, early and late, Keith Whittington gave me very useful comments on the project. Several individuals at the 2003 conference of the Society for the History of the Early Republic – especially David T. Konig and Jack Rakove – shared excellent, pointed criticisms that sharpened the argument considerably. A plethora of others merit thanks for comments and encouragement, including Bat Sparrow, Eileen McDonagh, Howard Reiter, Charles Kromkowski, Sam Kernell, Dan Wirls, Frances Lee, Emery Lee, Calvin Johnson, and Gerald Gamm. Two anonymous reviewers at Cambridge University Press engaged the manuscript in such a careful, painstaking analysis that it could not help but turn out better for their efforts. Lew Bateman was the perfect editor for the project, and I much appreciate his help and support. Brian R. MacDonald's careful editing greatly improved the final manuscript.

Thanks to Jan Frantzen, Lana Vierdag, Brenda West-Ammons, Linda Miller, Paula West, Sandra Beins, the staff of the Political Science Department who made it possible for me to serve a term as department chair and still make steady progress on this project. Thanks to library staff, particularly at the University of Missouri–St. Louis and also at St. Louis University and Washington University in St. Louis. Thanks to the University of Missouri Research Board for early support, the Institute for Political History for later support, and a special thanks to the Public Policy Research Center for support since I arrived at UM–St. Louis. I appreciated the opportunity to try out various pieces of these findings at the 2003 and 2004 American Political Science Association meetings, the 2004 Midwest Political Science Association meetings, the 2003 Society for the History of the Early Republic meetings, the 2002 Social Science History Association meetings, the 2003 conference on Evolving Federalisms in the Maxwell School at Syracuse University, the 2001 conference on the occasion of James Madison's 250th birthday at the University of California–San Diego, and the 1999 Western Political Science Association meetings. Three anonymous reviewers for the *American Political Science Review*, as well as *APSR* editor Lee Sigelman, made helpful comments on a separate paper that also strengthened this book. This article, "Madison's Opponents and Constitutional Design," appeared in the *American Political Science Review* 99:2 (May 2005). Material in Chapter 3 was adapted from *James Madison: The Theory and Practice of Republican Government*, edited by Samuel Kernell, © 2003 by the Board of Trustees of the Leland Stanford Jr. University, by permission of the publisher.

Anyone who reads the book must be made to understand how coffee and music pervasively influenced the research and writing from start to finish. A string of coffee shops from Boston to Seattle provided congenial settings for many ideas to percolate and for caffeine to accelerate reflection. Many a composer unknowingly helped me bridge a terrific sticking point, artfully polish a sentence, and force my fingers to the keyboard for an extra hour. I'm especially grateful to Brahms (Fourth Symphony), Saint-Saëns (Third Symphony), Holst (*The Planets*), Beethoven (Seventh, Sixth, and Third Symphonies), Copeland (*Appalachian Spring*), Rimsky-Korsakov, Chopin, Satie, Grieg, Bach, and Howlin' Wolf. None of these contributors to the soundtrack ought to be held responsible for the result.

Six unforgettable people deserve especially warm thanks for the circumstances that made the book possible. First, Carol Robertson and the late Allan Robertson provided a good deal of support many years ago when it mattered most, and this book could never have happened without that support. I'm just one of many, many people who can't express enough gratitude to Carol for all her kindnesses. Second, I've been so lucky to have not one but two inspiring mentors, each a gifted and humane scholar: Alfred Diamant, my dissertation chair, and Dennis Judd, my coauthor and colleague. These exemplary scholars always will have an unshakable influence on me. Finally, much appreciation goes to my family. Bryan Robertson has kept me on my toes, physically, emotionally, and intellectually. He doesn't know how much I care about him and thank him for it. By putting up with my intense fervor to write this all down, by being caring and patient and understanding, Cathie Robertson has made it impossible to thank her enough. She's appreciated eternally for all that and so much more.

Abbreviations

DHFFC	*Documentary History of the First Federal Congress of the United States of America*, ed. Linda Grant De Pauw et al., (Baltimore: Johns Hopkins University Press, 1972–)
ED	*The Debates in the Several State Conventions, on the Adoption of the Federal Constitution*, ed. Jonathan Elliot, 5 vols. (New York: Burt Franklin, 1968; orig. 1836–45)
JCC	*Journals of the Continental Congress, 1774–1789*, ed. Worthington C. Ford et al., 34 vols. (Washington, DC: Government Printing Office, 1904–37), http://memory.loc.gov/ammem/amlaw/lwjc.html
LDC	*Letters of Delegates to Congress, 1774–1789*, ed. Paul H. Smith et al., 25 vols. (Washington, DC: U.S. Library of Congress, 1976–2000)
PJM	*The Papers of James Madison*, ed. William T. Hutchinson et al., 17 vols. (Chicago: University of Chicago Press; Charlottesville: University of Virginia Press, 1962–91)
PRM	*The Papers of Robert Morris, 1781–1784*, ed. E. James Ferguson et al., 9 vols. (Pittsburgh: University of Pittsburgh Press, 1973–99)
RFC	*The Records of the Federal Convention of 1787*, ed. Max Farrand, 4 vols. (New Haven: Yale University Press, 1937), http://memory.loc.gov/ammem/amlaw/lwfr.html

1

Politics and the Constitution

[T]here can be no doubt but that the result [of the Constitutional Convention] will in some way or other have a powerful effect on our destiny.

– James Madison to Thomas Jefferson, June 6, 1787

What problems were the U.S. Constitution's authors trying to solve? How did they imagine their Constitution would answer these problems? We know the framers intended to change America's destiny, and we know they succeeded. But how did they intend to transform the way American government uses its power and the way Americans use their government? What kinds of politics were the delegates to the Constitutional Convention trying to make – and what kinds of politics *did* their design make? For all that has been written about the Constitution, we do not have satisfactory answers to these questions.

Practicing politicians wrote the Constitution, and they expected politicians to use it. To understand the enduring effects of the Constitution on America's destiny, we need to know what its designers thought they were doing. We need to understand the circumstances that convinced these politicians that they could and should reconstitute the nation's government. We need to understand precisely how these circumstances shaped their strategies for building a new government. We need to reconstruct how these politicians used such strategies to design their Constitution, provision by provision. Better answers to these questions can help us better understand how Americans have used the government they have inherited.

HOW HISTORIANS AND SOCIAL SCIENTISTS HAVE APPROACHED THE CONSTITUTION

I could not find satisfactory answers to these questions in the many published studies of the Constitution. The most prominent historians of the founding era, such as Bernard Bailyn, Gordon Wood, and Douglass Adair, chronicle the sweeping intellectual currents of American culture in the eighteenth century. By eloquently describing evolving ideas about republicanism and liberty, these beautifully narrated and inspiring intellectual histories underscore the breadth and flow of political thought in the founding period.[1] But these narratives do not aim to show how the delegates to the Constitutional Convention used these indefinite principles when they designed specific constitutional provisions, nor do they aim to explain systematically the political process of the Constitutional Convention.

Several historians give politics a much more prominent role in their narratives of the convention. Charles A. Beard memorably wrote that the Constitution was "an economic document drawn with superb skill by men whose property interests were immediately at stake; as such it appealed directly and unerringly to identical interests in the country at large."[2] Beard's bold explanation of the Constitution as the product of the delegates' material interests became a lightning rod for critics. Forrest McDonald, Robert E. Brown, and James Ferguson each discredited Beard's claim as simplistic.[3] McDonald's work provides a more

[1] Bernard Bailyn, *The Ideological Origins of the American Revolution* (Cambridge, MA: Belknap Press, 1967); Gordon S. Wood, *The Creation of the American Republic, 1776–1787* (Chapel Hill: University of North Carolina Press, 1969); Trevor Colbourn, ed., *Fame and the Founding Fathers: Essays by Douglass Adair* (New York: W. W. Norton for the Institute of Early American History and Culture at Williamsburg, 1974).

[2] Charles Beard, *An Economic Interpretation of the Constitution of the United States* (New York: Macmillan, 1913), p. 188. As Forrest McDonald pointed out, Beard (p. 73) was not accusing the delegates of writing a Constitution primarily to benefit themselves personally. See Forrest McDonald, *We the People: The Economic Origins of the Constitution* (Chicago: University of Chicago Press, 1958), p. 6.

[3] McDonald, *We the People*; Robert E. Brown, *Charles Beard and the Constitution: A Critical Analysis of "An Economic Interpretation of the Constitution"* (New York: W. W. Norton, 1965); E. James Ferguson, *The Power of the Purse: A History of Public Finance, 1776–1790* (Chapel Hill: University of North Carolina Press, 1961), pp. 251–86. According to a survey of 178 randomly selected members of the Economic History Association conducted by Robert Whaples, only a quarter of the economists and historians responding generally agreed with the statement that "The personal economic interests of delegates to the Constitutional Convention generally had a significant effect on their voting behavior." Forty-three percent of economists answering the survey agreed with the statement provisionally; 53 percent of the historians generally disagreed. Robert Whaples, "Where Is There Consensus among Economic Historians? The Results of a Survey on Forty Propositions," *Journal of Economic History* 55:1 (March 1995): 139–54.

politically nuanced account that emphasizes the way the delegates worked out arrangements that accommodated diverse interests, ideas, and personalities.[4] Jack Rakove provides exceptional insight into the politicians of the founding era and presents the best historian's account of the convention's politics.[5] Rakove views the convention as both an intellectual and a political process in which the delegates, representing diverse constituencies, balanced differences of ideas and interests as they hammered out constitutional compromises on specific provisions. McDonald, Rakove, Clinton Rossiter, and Lance Banning provide superb, indispensable historical narratives that weave the influence of politics into the story of constitutional design.[6] These historians provide a necessary starting point for the systematic political analysis of the Constitutional Convention.

These vivid histories could not decisively answer my questions about the Constitution, however. By privileging ideas, historians undervalue the role of politics.[7] Historians have produced no careful and systematic analysis of delegates' political interests to match the rich literature on republican ideas, even though historians such as Allan Nevins, Jackson Turner Main, and Peter Onuf provide excellent analyses of the political landscape of the states that the delegates represented.[8] Principle usually

[4] Forrest McDonald, *E Pluribus Unum: The Formation of the American Republic, 1776–1790*, 2nd ed. (Indianapolis, IN: Liberty Press, 1979); *Novus Ordo Seclorum: The Intellectual Origins of the Constitution* (Lawrence: University Press of Kansas, 1985); and *States' Rights and the Union: Imperium in Imperio, 1789–1876* (Lawrence: University Press of Kansas, 2000).

[5] Jack N. Rakove, *The Beginnings of National Politics: An Interpretive History of the Continental Congress* (New York: Alfred Knopf, 1979); "The Great Compromise: Ideas, Interests, and the Politics of the Constitution," *William and Mary Quarterly*, 3rd ser., 44:3 (July 1987): 424–57; *James Madison and the Creation of the American Republic* (Glenview, IL: Scott, Foresman/Little, Brown, 1990); and *Original Meanings: Politics and Ideas in the Making of the Constitution* (New York: Alfred A. Knopf, 1996).

[6] Clinton Rossiter, *1787: The Grand Convention* (New York: Macmillan, 1966); Lance Banning, *The Sacred Fire of Liberty: James Madison and the Founding of the Federal Republic* (Ithaca, NY: Cornell University Press, 1995).

[7] Historical studies' emphasis on intellectual history probably is compounded by a bias in Madison's convention notes. Madison's records may characterize the principles and logic of positions he supported more carefully than positions he opposed. Not surprisingly, ideas, which are so fully elaborated in the intellectual histories of this era, and which are so central to the theoretically minded Madison, seem to trump interests in explaining the most important convention dispute, on representation. This point also is suggested by Thornton Anderson in *Creating the Constitution: The Convention of 1787 and the First Congress* (University Park: Pennsylvania State University Press, 1993), p. 8n13.

[8] Allan Nevins, *The American States during and after the Revolution, 1775–1789* (New York: Macmillan, 1924); Jackson Turner Main, *Political Parties before the Constitution* (Chapel Hill: University of North Carolina Press, 1973) and *The Sovereign States, 1775–1783* (New York: New Viewpoints, 1973); Peter S. Onuf, *The Origins of the Federal*

speaks for itself in a way political interest seldom does – that is, politicians are more likely to frame issues in terms of principle than in terms of interest because principles legitimate and broaden support for their interests. Even Jack Rakove, who is unusually sensitive to the play of politics, considers the convention's conflict over representation chiefly as a philosophical conflict, distinct and separate from the interest-driven bargaining over the authority of the reconstituted government.[9] Historians occasionally cite specific social-science studies of the convention, but their narratives do not employ insights about political processes such as state building, policy making, political realignment, or legislative behavior.[10] A more systematic exploration of political interests, alignments, and processes reveals that political maneuvering permeated all of the convention's decisions.

Political scientists have not augmented historians' work with a thorough political analysis of the Constitution's design. Although many political scientists have claimed that the Constitution contributed to enduring political features of American government, they usually choose – more or less arbitrarily – certain "important" features of the Constitution to support a more general point about American politics.[11] Not surprisingly, political scientists have widely different views about the design of the Constitution. For William Riker, the Constitution represented a strategic victory for nationalists; for John P. Roche, the success of pragmatic political reformers; for Vincent Ostrom, a shrewdly crafted "compound republic" that promotes public control and economic efficiency; for Barry Weingast, "market-preserving federalism." Others characterize the founding in different but no less general terms – for

Republic: Jurisdictional Controversies in the United States, 1775–1787 (Philadelphia: University of Pennsylvania Press, 1983).

9 Rakove, *Original Meanings*, p. 15.

10 Rakove notes that historians generally interpret the convention in a familiar narrative that adds "little of interpretive value to our understanding of the framing of the Constitution. Certain stock themes are so essential to all accounts of the Convention as to defy authors to show a spark of originality" (*Original Meanings*, p. 13). On the other hand, Rakove characterizes the analysis of behavioral political science as "fine-milling techniques of roll-call analysis that are commonly used to explain decision-making in Congress, state legislatures, or, for that matter, any city council outside Cook County, Illinois" (p. 15).

11 William H. Riker, for example, trying to illustrate the art of political manipulation (and perhaps captivated by Gouverneur Morris's capacity for sound bites), oversimplifies the position of Madison's allies and opponents and misrepresents the underlying political logic of policy agency at the convention. Compare *The Art of Political Manipulation* (New Haven, CT: Yale University Press, 1986), pp. 34–51, with Chapters 5, 6, and 7 in this volume.

example, as a triumph for protocorporate elites or policy conservatism.[12] Political scientists most frequently have characterized the Constitution as a triumph for interest-group pluralism, using quotations from *Federalist* 10 and 51 to prove the point.[13]

A few social scientists have attempted to study voting behavior at the Constitutional Convention systematically.[14] Calvin Jillson's work, based

[12] William H. Riker, *The Strategy of Rhetoric: Campaigning for the American Constitution* (New Haven, CT: Yale University Press, 1996); John P. Roche, "The Founding Fathers: A Reform Caucus in Action," *American Political Science Review* 55:4 (December 1961): 799–816; Vincent Ostrom, *The Political Theory of a Compound Republic: A Reconstruction of the Logical Foundations of American Democracy as Presented in the Federalist* (Blacksburg: Virginia Polytechnic Institute, 1971); Barry R. Weingast, "The Economic Role of Political Institutions: Market-Preserving Federalism and Economic Development," *Journal of Law, Economics, and Organization* 7:1 (1995): 1–31; Kenneth M. Dolbeare and Linda Medcalf, "The Dark Side of the Constitution," in *The Case against the Constitution from the Antifederalists to the Present*, ed. John F. Manley and Kenneth M. Dolbeare (Armonk, NY: M. E. Sharpe, 1987), pp. 120–42; David Brian Robertson and Dennis R. Judd, *The Development of American Public Policy: The Structure of Policy Restraint* (Glenview, IL, and Boston: Scott, Foresman/Little, Brown, 1989).

[13] David B. Truman, *The Governmental Process: Political Interests and Public Opinion* (New York: Alfred A. Knopf, 1951), pp. 4–5; Paul F. Bourke, "The Pluralist Reading of James Madison's Tenth Federalist," *Perspectives in American History* 9 (1975): 271–98; John F. Manley, "Class and Pluralism in America: The Constitution Reconsidered," in Manley and Dolbeare, *The Case against the Constitution from the Antifederalists to the Present*, pp. 101–19. See also Emery G. Lee III, "Representation, Virtue, and Political Jealousy in the Brutus-Publius Dialogue," *Journal of Politics* 59:4 (November 1997): 1073–95.

[14] On the Confederation Congress, see Calvin C. Jillson and Rick K. Wilson, *Congressional Dynamics: Structure, Coordination, and Choice in the First American Congress, 1774–1789* (Stanford, CA: Stanford University Press, 1994); Keith L. Dougherty, *Collective Action under the Articles of Confederation* (Cambridge: Cambridge University Press, 2001). On the Constitutional Convention, see S. Sidney Ulmer, "Sub-group Formation in the Constitutional Convention," *Midwest Journal of Political Science* 10:3 (August 1966): 288–303; Gerald M. Pomper, "Conflict and Coalitions at the Constitutional Convention," in *The Study of Coalition Behavior: Theoretical Perspectives and Cases from Four Continents*, ed. Sven Groennings, E. W. Kelley, and Michael Lieserson (New York: Holt, Rinehart and Winston, 1970), pp. 209–25; Calvin C. Jillson and Cecil L. Eubanks, "The Political Structure of Constitution Making: The Federal Convention of 1787," *American Journal of Political Science* 28:3 (August 1984): 435–58; Robert A. McGuire and Robert L. Ohsfeldt, "An Economic Model of Voting Behavior over Specific Issues at the Constitutional Convention of 1787," *Journal of Economic History* 46:1 (March 1986): 79–111; Calvin C. Jillson, *Constitution Making: Conflict and Consensus in the Federal Convention of 1787* (New York: Agathon Press, 1988); Anderson, *Creating the Constitution*; Robert A. McGuire, *To Form a More Perfect Union: A New Economic Interpretation of the United States Constitution* (New York: Oxford University Press, 2003).

When employed without a careful interpretation of the political goals of the delegates, quantitative analysis can produce misleading findings. In his effort to quantify on an especially perceptive and systematic analysis of each vote at the convention, dovetails with Rakove's conclusions. Jillson showed that coalitions of states shifted as the convention dealt with different issues and argues that philosophical issues divided the delegates in debating "the general institutional structure for the new national government," whereas differences in narrow material interests divided them "when they voted on specific mechanisms for implementing various aspects of the constitutional design."[15]

Surprisingly, Jillson is the only political scientist identified with the field of American political development who has tried to analyze the politics of the Constitutional Convention so thoroughly. This is surprising because, according to two of the field's leaders, Karen Orren and Stephen Skowronek, "political development" refers to "a durable shift in governing authority." The Constitution was the most significant and durable shift in governing authority in American history.[16] But until recently, American political development scholars have rarely addressed the early American republic at all.[17] Rather, they draw on perfunctory descriptions

the impact of economic interests at the convention, for example, McGuire's *To Form a More Perfect Union* makes a heroic effort to determine individual delegates' votes and their meaning. Many of his interpretations are uncontroversial, but some are flawed. For example, McGuire incorrectly assumes that the proposal to join judges and the president in the exercise of the veto is an example of support for moderate amendments to the Confederation government, rather than support for a completely new and stronger national government (p. 56). As argued in Chapter 6, James Madison and James Wilson, two of the most determined supporters of a stronger, thoroughly reconstituted national government, introduced this proposal in the belief that the joint veto would strengthen resistance to legislative parochialism in favor of national interests. McGuire generally has great difficulty making sense of the positions of Madison and others in the Virginia delegation in terms of economic interest (pp. 90–1). McGuire concedes that he has stretched quantitative analysis when he admits that "It is plausible... that the lack of significant findings for a large number of the economic and other interests results from the relatively weak data set for the Philadelphia convention.... It may be that considerable error is introduced into the estimating procedure because the dependent variables (the votes) are themselves based on an inference of a delegate's actual vote on each issue" (pp. 92–3). Because Madison and his fellow Virginians set the initial agenda for the meetings, this interpretive limitation severely restricts the conclusions that can be drawn from his approach.

15 Jillson, *Constitution Making*, pp. ix–xi.

16 Karen Orren and Stephen Skowronek, *The Search for American Political Development* (Cambridge: Cambridge University Press, 2004), p. 123.

17 Richard R. John argues that American political development scholars have invested too little time in the study of the early American history; see "Governmental Institutions as Agents of Change: Rethinking American Political Development in the Early Republic, 1787–1835," *Studies in American Political Development* 11:2 (1997): 347–80. American political development scholars who have studied the early republic include Rogers Smith,

of the Constitution to analyze later eras in American political history. Stephen Skowronek in *Building a New American State* and Theda Skocpol in *Protecting Soldiers and Mothers* both begin their landmark books with brief sketches of the Constitution's complexity.[18] Skowronek's and Skocpol's sketches of the Constitution, in turn, depend almost exclusively on Samuel Huntington's argument that the Constitution implemented English political values of the seventeenth-century. Huntington held that Americans brought Tudor-era political principles to their colonies and, unlike the British, never transcended these ideas. Americans drew up their revolutionary state constitutions on these seventeenth-century precepts. The U.S. Constitution merely implemented the same constitutional notions on a national scale, creating a "Tudor polity." Huntington concluded that "American political institutions are unique, if only because they are so antique."[19]

But Huntington's glib portrayal of the Constitution is far too shallow to help us understand its design. From the very beginning, colonists had to adapt their mores and their governments to a situation profoundly different from that in Britain. American land was plentiful and labor was scarce, whereas in Britain land was scarce and labor plentiful. Acute labor

Civic Ideals: Conflicting Visions of Citizenship in US History (New Haven, CT: Yale University Press, 1997); Charles A. Kromkowski, *Recreating the American Republic: Rules of Apportionment, Constitutional Change, and American Political Development, 1700–1870* (Cambridge: Cambridge University Press, 2002); David J. Siemers, *Ratifying the Republic: Antifederalists and Federalists in Constitutional Time* (Stanford, CA: Stanford University Press, 2002) and *The Antifederalists: Men of Great Faith and Forbearance* (Lanham, MD: Rowman & Littlefield, 2003); Samuel Kernell, ed., *James Madison: The Theory and Practice of Republican Government* (Stanford, CA: Stanford University Press, 2003); Keith E. Whittington, *Constitutional Interpretation: Textual Meaning, Original Intent, and Judicial Review* (Lawrence: University Press of Kansas, 1999) and *Constitutional Construction: Divided Powers and Constitutional Meaning* (Cambridge, MA: Harvard University Press, 2001); Rogan Kersh, *Dreams of a More Perfect Union* (Ithaca, NY: Cornell University Press, 2001); James A. Morone, *Hellfire Nation: The Politics of Sin in American History* (New Haven, CT: Yale University Press, 2003), pp. 29–116; Bartholomew Sparrow, *Growing the Nation-State: U.S. Territorial Policy, 1783–1898* (unpublished manuscript, University of Texas at Austin, 2004) and "U.S. Government Lands and the Federal System," paper presented at the meeting of the Social Science History Association, St. Louis, October 2002.

18 Stephen Skowronek, *Building a New American State: The Expansion of National Administrative Capacities, 1877–1920* (Cambridge: Cambridge University Press, 1982), pp. 19–23; Theda Skocpol, *Protecting Soldiers and Mothers: The Political Origins of Social Policy in the United States* (Cambridge, MA: Belknap Press, 1992), pp. 67–72.

19 Samuel P. Huntington, "Political Modernization: America vs. Europe," *World Politics* 18:3 (April 1966): 378–414, and *Political Order in Changing Societies* (New Haven, CT: Yale University Press, 1968), pp. 93–133 (quotation from p. 98).

shortages undermined the feudal aspirations of early landholders in the Carolinas, the Hudson Valley, and elsewhere. For example, European status distinctions broke down under the pressure of American land and mobility. Americans gradually came to use prestigious titles such as "mister," "honorable," and "esquire" to express the status of those holding offices, instead of some natural status of the individuals themselves.[20] The presence of Native Americans forced settler communities to develop diplomatic skills and military capacity uncommon in England. The two most decisive factors in shaping American political development – extracting public revenues and mounting military operations – already distinguished the American colonies from Europe even before the American Revolution.[21]

Long before 1787, American politics was diverging steadily from British politics. Male freeholders were having an immediate, powerful impact on state policy that had no precedent in Tudor England; although there were severe restrictions on voting in the colonies, the lower houses of the colonial assemblies better represented public opinion than did the British Parliament. Blessed by abundant land and cursed by incessant conflict over its ownership, Americans constantly engaged in legal disputes. Courts strengthened; litigiousness blossomed in the American character. Judges turned away from British law when it did not suit the colonies' needs. American lawyers became singularly important quasi-public officials who mediated between private parties and the state.[22] As James Morone points out, religion uniquely framed Americans' approach to all these problems and all their solutions.[23] Presbyterians contested Quakers for political control in Pennsylvania, for example. "New Lights" challenged "Old Lights" for political control in Connecticut, while "up country" Presbyterians contested coastal Anglicans in South Carolina. The defense of religious liberty became a defining issue for such young politicians as James Madison.

[20] Jackson Turner Main, *Society and Economy in Colonial Connecticut* (Princeton, NJ: Princeton University Press, 1985), p. 371.

[21] See Roger H. Brown, *Redeeming the Republic: Federalists, Taxation, and the Origins of the Constitution* (Baltimore: Johns Hopkins University Press, 1993); John Shy, *A People Numerous and Armed: Reflections on the Military Struggle for American Independence* (New York: Oxford University Press, 1976), p. 233.

[22] William E. Nelson, *Americanization of the Common Law: The Impact of Legal Change on Massachusetts Society, 1760–1830* (Cambridge, MA: Harvard University Press, 1975), p. 10; Peter Charles Hoffer, *Law and People in Colonial America*, rev. ed. (Baltimore: Johns Hopkins University Press, 1998).

[23] Morone, *Hellfire Nation*, pp. 100–16.

Many delegates brought the most modern ideas about economic policy and republicanism to Philadelphia.[24] James Wilson professed admiration for the theory of British government but reminded fellow delegates that "we can't adopt it – we have no laws in favor of primogeniture – no distinction of families – the partition of Estates destroys the influence of the Few –."[25] George Mason, perhaps the delegate more inclined to Tudor ideas than any other, was defeated frequently, refused to sign the final product, and opposed its ratification in Virginia.[26] Like modern politicians who evoke revered, time-tested principles to legitimize actions that shatter the existing political order, the framers used widely accepted political axioms (including century-old arguments used against the British court) to justify the fundamental changes they were proposing. Immediate political exigencies, calculations, and compromises explain the Constitution much more fully than these seventeenth-century ideas. The hard lessons of Confederation experience, not a sentimental attachment to a distant English tradition, caused the delegates to consider national reconstitution a necessity.

I failed to find a comprehensive political narrative of the Constitution's design in any of these accounts. There exists no thorough political analysis of all the Constitution's provisions, centered on the delegates as politicians at work, moving through a sequence of contingent decisions toward a final product no one imagined in advance. The best historical and political science studies of the convention, by Rakove and Jillson, conclude that the delegates simply veered from material interests to philosophical principles as they voted on individual provisions, and the interests that mattered were unique to each specific choice the delegates made. But anyone familiar with the politics of large, complicated policy decisions will recognize that politicians in these situations tether their individual

[24] Madison's arguments in *The Federalist Papers* suggest that he thought the informed public in New York would not be attracted to a Constitution rooted in Tudor political ideas: "Is it not the glory of the people of America, that whilst they have paid a decent regard to the opinions of former times and other nations, they have not suffered a blind veneration for antiquity, for custom, or for names, to overrule the suggestions of their own good sense, the knowledge of their own situation, and the lessons of their own experience?" Alexander Hamilton, James Madison, and John Jay, *The Federalist*, ed. Jacob E. Cooke (Middletown, CT: Wesleyan University Press, 1961), no. 15, p. 88.

[25] *RFC* June 7, 1: 159; see also Edmund Randolph, June 1, 1: 66; Charles Pinkney, June 25, 1: 398.

[26] On two occasions at the Constitutional Convention, Mason sought to authorize the national government to pass sumptuary laws, which aimed to restrict public affectations of wealth and privilege.

decisions to deeply held political objectives and strategies. These strategies are flexible and hard to uncover in isolation, but they become more evident in close scrutiny of the *pattern* of choices that make up a complex political product like a constitution.

Existing studies arbitrarily select some "important" convention choices to analyze and ignore others. They downplay issues that may have mattered intensely to the delegates and shaped the outcome but that seem unimportant now because they were left out of the final Constitution. James Madison sought a national government power to veto state laws when he arrived at the convention, fought for it repeatedly during the meeting, and expressed deep regret about its failure afterward. Why? What does this tell us about Madison's political objectives and strategy, his intentions for national authority, national policy making, and the nation's political future? What does it tell us about the delegates who opposed his agenda? It is not sufficient to lay this glaring fact aside, concluding that Madison somehow did not really mean it. In convention narratives, the debate over the presidency fits oddly into the story, as if the delegates discussed the office in isolation from the compromise on representation and the constraints on national power. The story of the Constitutional Convention needs to be retold from a political point of view.

A POLITICAL APPROACH TO UNDERSTANDING THE CONSTITUTION'S DESIGN

The delegates who made the Constitution were first and foremost politicians, not philosophers, political scientists, or plundering speculators.[27]

[27] Many negative connotations burden the term "politician" in the early twenty-first century. I use the term "politician" neutrally and dispassionately to describe an individual who devotes a substantial amount of time and effort to an elective public office or other politically sensitive appointive position. All the delegates who substantially influenced the Constitution's design had political experience, and nearly all soon occupied an elective or appointive office in the reconstituted national government. My experience with American politicians today convinces me that they seem to be motivated by a similar mix of aspirations as the general population. Like politicians today – and, for that matter, our co-workers in organizations of all kinds – the convention delegates generally behaved in a way that reconciled their interests with their principles. As Anderson notes, there is a tendency to think that politicians begin with general principles and reason down to policy specifics, when more often they begin with outcomes and reason back or reconcile them with principles (*Creating the Constitution*, p. 71). Political self-interest rarely can be reduced to simple goals of reelection or officeholding, and often it cannot even be specified fully. To achieve any goals, politicians must gain offices with public authority and must manipulate competing claims on public authority to maximize the achievement of their goals.

These politicians had helped nurture a dozen infant state republics through a devastating war and the turbulence of economic depression. Circumstances forced them to learn the art of sustaining political support while conducting any government's most unpopular activities, such as collecting taxes. These republican politicians had mastered the skills of using policy to balance conflicting demands placed on government. A given set of economic policies could accommodate voters, pacify them, divide them, and selectively mobilize them. At the same time, economic policies could stabilize and grow state economies and secure the support of economic elites. These politicians fully understood that public policy makes politics, and the two are inseparable.[28] Those who seek public office must promise to use government in some beneficial way and deliver on these promises, while those who seek public policy depend on those who win and hold government office.

These politicians set out to change the path of American politics, to alter the nation's destiny. They ultimately succeeded by changing the process for selecting national policy makers, by expanding national government authority, and by building a new process for using that authority. They succeeded, first, because pressing political and economic problems made it an opportune moment to reconstitute the national government. The convention met in a political climate that provided some intense but vague and unfocused support for change. Second, they succeeded because the convention's leaders drew on their own diagnosis of the national situation to propose remedies for these problems. These remedies provided a malleable starting point for deliberating constitutional design. Third, they succeeded

[28] According to the *American Heritage Dictionary of the English Language*, "politics" is defined variously as "1. The art or science of political government; political science." "2. The policies, goals, or affairs of a government or of the groups or parties within it." "4. The methods or tactics involved in managing a state or a government." In this sense, the study of public policy is neither an analysis of general policy processes explicitly divorced from specific outcomes nor a narrowly applied technical specialty. The French word *politique* – used to express *both* the English concepts "politics" *and* "policy" – is a better word for the meaning of policy employed in this study. Scholars of American political development study policy in this broad, politically infused meaning. See, among many other works, Skocpol, *Protecting Soldiers and Mothers*; Karen Orren, *Belated Feudalism: Labor, the Law, and Liberal Development in the United States* (Cambridge: Cambridge University Press, 1992); Elizabeth Sanders, *Roots of Reform: Farmers, Workers, and the American State, 1877–1917* (Chicago: University of Chicago Press, 1999); Robert C. Lieberman, *Shifting the Color Line: Race and the American Welfare State* (Cambridge, MA: Harvard University Press, 1998); Suzanne Mettler, *Dividing Citizens: Gender and Federalism in New Deal Public Policy* (Ithaca, NY: Cornell University Press, 1998); Richard Franklin Bensel, *The Political Economy of American Industrialization, 1877–1900* (Cambridge: Cambridge University Press, 2001).

because most were willing to come to acceptable political compromises about that design, even though none anticipated the final Constitution or found it fully satisfactory.

At the convention, these delegates behaved like republican legislators because most of them *were* legislators. Even though the convention lacked the features of an established legislature today, the delegates employed familiar legislative scripts to develop the Constitution as they would a major change of law: they agreed to rules for debate and voting, used a Committee of the Whole to facilitate the initial consideration of the agenda, took hundreds of votes on substance and procedure, created special committees to deal with difficult issues, and relied on a Committee of Detail to develop a provisional draft.[29] Although they understood that a constitution had to be different from ordinary legislation, they conducted the *process* for crafting the Constitution much the way they had made public policy in Congress or in state legislatures.[30] The Constitutional Convention, then, can be studied with the analytical tools used to analyze other pathbreaking American policy developments, such as Reconstruction, the Sherman Anti-Trust Act of 1890, the Clayton Act of 1914, the National Industrial Recovery Act of 1933, the Social Security Act of 1935, the Civil Rights Act of 1964, the Clean Air Act of 1970, or other "super-statutes."[31] Like legislators today, some delegates attempted to manipulate the terms of the debates and the scope of conflict, and adjusted provisions to enlarge their political support. Through persuasion, bargaining, threats, and evasion, the delegates built coalitions, undermined others, and produced a series of interdependent, politically satisfactory decisions. The Constitutional Convention, of course, was no ordinary legislative process. The stakes were higher. The Constitution affected a virtually unlimited range

[29] In contrast to established legislatures today, the convention lacked, among other things, a formal calendar, formal leadership posts (other than the virtually silent convention president, George Washington), a staff (other than a recording secretary, William Jackson), and standing committees with jurisdiction over particular decisions.

[30] Edmund S. Morgan, *Inventing the People: The Rise of Popular Sovereignty in Early America* (New York: W. W. Norton, 1988), p. 256; *Federalist* 53, pp. 360–2.

[31] William N. Eskridge Jr. and John Ferejohn, "Super-Statutes," *Duke Law Journal* 50:5 (March 2001): 1215–76; Richard Rodriguez and Barry W. Weingast, "The Positive Political Theory of Legislative History: New Perspectives on the 1964 Civil Rights Act and Its Interpretation," *University of Pennsylvania Law Review* 151:4 (April 2003): 1417–1542. Although politics in the 1780s vastly differed from politics today, political *logic* then had much in common with political logic today. The political reasoning in *The Federalist Papers* sounds very modern, because its authors speak to timeless problems of republican polities.

FIGURE 1.1. Framework for Systematic Analysis of the Constitution

of politically significant issues, and the final product necessarily would be more general than a statute law.[32]

The Constitution's design resulted from a series of compromises about substantive issues, policy making procedures, and the control of policy makers. The goals of the Constitution are the collective goals of the thirty-nine individuals willing to sign the final product. The central analytical problem for this book is to describe that zone of acceptable compromise and to explain how the Constitution's provisions together satisfied the framers' goals.

Understanding the politics of the Constitution's design systematically requires three analytical steps (Figure 1.1). The study of the Constitution must begin with a methodical understanding of the political and economic circumstances that motivated American politicians to create path-breaking policy change in 1787. Second, it must provide a framework for interpreting the policy agendas that shaped the convention's politics. Third, it must start with a map that organizes all the Constitution's policy choices, independent of the debates or subsequent political developments, to make it possible to connect political circumstances and policy strategies systematically to constitutional outcomes. These steps are necessary for developing an analytical or institutional narrative of the Constitutional Convention.[33]

[32] As the Committee of Detail put it during the proceedings, the final product, unlike legislation, aimed "To insert essential principles only, lest the operations of government should be clogged by rendering those provisions permanent and unalterable, which ought to be accommodated to times and events," and "to use simple and precise language, and general propositions"; *RFC* 2: 137.

[33] Robert H. Bates, Avner Grief, Margaret Levi, Jean-Laurent Rosenthal, and Barry Weingast, *Analytic Narratives* (Princeton, NJ: Princeton University Press, 1998) and "The Analytic Narrative Project," *American Political Science Review* 94:2 (September 2000): 696–702; Douglass C. North and John V. C. Nye, "Cliometrics, the New Institutional Economics, and the Future of Economic History," paper presented at the meetings of the Economic History Association, St. Louis, 2002. Explicitly building on the idea of

Political and Economic Circumstances

Precisely what pressing policy problems were the delegates trying to solve? Political and economic circumstances drive demands for pathbreaking political change, create the opportunities for and constraints on specific kinds of change, and shape the experience of the leaders who bring about the change. Circumstances differed profoundly across the American Confederation. The convention delegates acknowledged at least three distinct regional economies whose interests were not wholly compatible. The southern economy, with extensive lands and a long growing season, was an export economy that benefited from free trade, western expansion, and slavery. The middle and northern regions grew a more diverse crop, on smaller farms. New England, with short growing seasons and poor soil, was developing a diversified economy with fishing, trade, and manufacturing. Unlike the plantation South, New England benefited from regulated trade and had little use for slavery. Other economic cleavages cut across these broad regional interests. Poorer backcountry areas resented wealthy creditors and coastal elites. Hemmed-in states with restricted lands resented Virginia and other states with expanses of land that reached far to the west. Massachusetts, New York, and Pennsylvania had port cities that could generate substantial public revenues from tariffs, sometimes at the expense of neighboring states. Other states, such as New Jersey, had suffered more economic damage from the Revolutionary War than others. Heavy public debts burdened South Carolina and Massachusetts more than many states.

State and local boundaries established political interests partially independent of these economic divisions. The states governed land, labor, capital, and commerce in the Confederation. From the perspective of the economic interests within any state, that state's economic authority provided them a valuable asset. For example, states could increase

an analytical narrative, North and Nye describe an "institutional narrative" as "a presentation of a historical case as a sequence of events which allow us to highlight the critical turning points that . . . show us how states came to deal with specific problems or changing circumstances" (p. 9). Both models aim to apply analytical tools, particularly the tools of microeconomic theory, to explain critical historical cases and placing these cases in a larger narrative. In this book, I use economic concepts and public choice concepts (such as fiscal illusion, public goods, and the dilemma of cooperation) and political science concepts (such as agenda setting, issue framing, and coalition building). I contend that "analytical narratives" or "institutional narratives" will provide limited advances in knowledge unless they self-consciously specify, rigorously and exhaustively, the dependent variables that constitute the turning points they seek to explain. The policy map offered here aims to provide this specification for the Constitution.

tariffs on certain products made in neighboring states, thus protecting the market for in-state manufacturers of the product. Influenced by differences in factor endowments, culture, and leadership, each state pursued a different mix of commercial, financial, and other economic policies. The economic depression of the 1780s accelerated state economic policy experimentation. Many states' policies benefited some domestic (that is, in-state) interests by exporting policy costs to neighboring states. Connecticut, New Jersey, Delaware, and Maryland, situated next to the larger states with more economic assets – Virginia's land, New York's port, or Pennsylvania's diverse economy – became key supporters of added national powers if these specific powers could offer protection against their advantaged neighbors.

Like leaders in any organization, state political leaders had developed a stake in protecting their institutions' existence and independence.[34] These leaders had helped develop basic policy-making institutions in their respective states and built governing coalitions tailored to each state's unique economic, cultural, and political circumstances. Delaware, for example, the most amorphous creation, was initially considered part of Pennsylvania. Delaware sent residents of other states to represent it in the Continental Congress even in the early 1780s. By 1787, though, Delaware government was more fully institutionalized, and Delaware residents both represented and governed the state.[35] The states managed diverse economic assets and enjoyed varied political advantages, including some not under their control, such as relative population size and growth potential. These state leaders naturally resisted the loss of control over taxes,

[34] Sociologist James D. Thompson argues that organizations are driven by the need to minimize uncertainty and dependence; see *Organizations in Action* (New York: McGraw-Hill, 1967). W. Richard Scott elaborates on this perspective in *Organizations: Rational, Natural and Open Systems*, 5th ed. (Upper Saddle River, NJ: Prentice-Hall, 2002). This compelling need to retain policy autonomy also provides additional insight into the state governments' motives and relationships in the Confederation period. Many scholars have elaborated the notion that politicians have sunk costs and opportunity costs in their institutional prerogatives. For Congress, see David Mayhew, *Congress: The Electoral Connection* (New Haven, CT: Yale University Press, 1974), and Morris P. Fiorina, *Congress: Keystone of the Washington Establishment* (New Haven, CT: Yale University Press, 1977). For bureaucracy, see Anthony Downs, *Inside Bureaucracy* (Boston: Little, Brown, 1957), and Gordon Tullock, *The Politics of Bureaucracy* (Washington, DC: Public Affairs Press, 1965). In international relations, see Robert Gilpin, *The Political Economy of International Relations* (Princeton, NJ: Princeton University Press, 1987).

[35] John A. Munroe, *Federalist Delaware, 1775–1815* (New Brunswick, NJ: Rutgers University Press, 1954).

commerce, and property, the most politically potent policy tools at their disposal.

A systematic analysis of these political and economic interests requires a thorough, inclusive study of economic histories and state histories.[36] Concepts drawn from political economy help identify political and economic relationships.[37] The concept of public goods, or goods often provided by government (such as national defense) when private suppliers provide little or none, is especially helpful for understanding conflicts over government economic policy in the 1780s.[38] Political scientist Keith Dougherty

[36] Ferguson, *The Power of the Purse*; Curtis P. Nettels, *The Emergence of a National Economy, 1775–1815* (New York: Holt, Rinehart, and Winston, 1962); Gary M. Walton and James F. Shepard, *The Economic Rise of Early America* (Cambridge: Cambridge University Press, 1979); Alice Hanson Jones, *Wealth of a Nation to Be: The American Colonies on the Eve of the Revolution* (New York: Columbia University Press, 1980); Robert A. Becker, *Revolution, Reform, and the Politics of American Taxation, 1763–1783* (Baton Rouge: Louisiana State University Press, 1980); John J. McCusker and Russell Menard, *The Economy of British America, 1607–1789* (Chapel Hill: University of North Carolina Press, 1985); Roger H. Brown, *Redeeming the Republic: Federalists, Taxation, and the Origins of the Constitution* (Baltimore: Johns Hopkins University Press, 1993); Cathy D. Matson, "The Revolution, the Constitution, and the New Nation," in *The Cambridge Economic History of the United States*, vol. 1: *The Colonial Era*, ed. Stanley L. Engerman and Robert E. Gallman, (Cambridge: Cambridge University Press, 1996); Margaret Ellen Newell, "The Birth of New England in the Atlantic Economy: From Its Beginning to 1770," in *Engines of Enterprise: An Economic History of New England*, ed. Peter Temin (Cambridge, MA: Harvard University Press, 2000), pp. 11–68. Richard Franklin Bensel details geographical conflicts of economic interest in American political development in his major studies, *Sectionalism and American Political Development* (Madison: University of Wisconsin Press, 1984), *Yankee Leviathan: The Origins of Central State Authority in America, 1859–1877* (Cambridge: Cambridge University Press, 1990), and *The Political Economy of American Industrialization, 1877–1900*.

[37] Edmund S. Phelps, *Political Economy: An Introductory Text* (New York: W. W. Norton, 1985); Dennis C. Mueller, ed., *Perspectives on Public Choice: A Handbook* (Cambridge: Cambridge University Press, 1997); Allan Drazen, *Political Economy in Macroeconomics* (Princeton, NJ: Princeton University Press, 2000); Torsten Persson and Guido Tabellini, *Political Economics: Explaining Economic Policy* (Cambridge, MA: MIT Press, 2000).

[38] Mancur Olson, *The Logic of Collective Action: Public Goods and the Theory of Groups* (Cambridge, MA: Harvard University Press, 1965); Duncan Snidal, "Public Goods, Property Rights, and Political Organizations," in *The Moral Dimensions of Public Policy Choice: Beyond the Market Paradigm*, ed. John Martin Gillroy and Maurice Wade (Pittsburgh: University of Pittsburgh Press, 1992), pp. 285–311. More formally, a public good is a good that can be shared by any member of a community without causing less to be available to any other member. Such a good is nonrivalrous in supply (that is, all members of the community receive the benefit) and nonexclusive in consumption (that is, one individual who benefits from the good cannot block others from consuming it without paying for it). A contemporary example is a radio broadcast. These characteristics create two kinds of problems: the free-rider problem (individuals who share the benefits of the good without bearing their share of the cost), and the failure to produce enough of the good to maximize the benefit to society as a whole.

uses the concept of public goods to analyze systematically the financial policies of the Continental Congress.[39] As elaborated in Chapter 2, the states provided most of the public goods in the Confederation period, but inevitably produced too few of these goods, stimulating demands for a better-funded, more-credible national authority. A related concept is the dilemma of cooperation, in which one individual, eschewing cooperation and acting instead for personal gain, leaves himself and every other party worse off than they would have been had they cooperated. The states, which governed the American economy with little or no interference from the Confederation government, were caught in a dilemma of cooperation. State politicians sought to control tax, currency, debt, property, and other policies necessary to manage their economics and politics. But state policy control was a double-edged sword. When neighboring states' political leaders made trade, currency, and other policies that harmed their constituents and their economies, state politicians urged national rules. At the same time, the national government's inability to fund its activities and develop commercial agreements with other nations also hurt their constituents. Their states' very policy independence, ironically, compelled the delegates to seek a national government more capable of providing specific public goods.

Policy Strategies for the Constitution

Circumstances created an opportunity for pathbreaking policy change as the delegates arrived in Philadelphia, but circumstances did not decide the Constitution's provisions. What did the delegates make of these circumstances? What solutions did they put forward to address these problems, and how did the delegates negotiate their way to common political ground? The delegates to the Constitutional Convention, like later policy makers confronting the task of constructing pathbreaking policies, had a mandate that was both urgent and ambiguous: making "the federal Constitution adequate to the exigencies of Government & the preservation of the Union."[40] The delegates had to define problems, interpret the political conditions, weigh policy alternatives, and forecast the likely consequences of each of their policy choices. The delegates framed the Constitution provision by provision over the course of three and a half months. None could have anticipated the twists and turns of the

[39] Dougherty, *Collective Action under the Articles of Confederation.*
[40] "Resolution of Congress," February 21, 1787, in *RFC* 3: 13–14.

convention's process, and none could have predicted the actual product of the convention when they began on May 25, 1787.

The delegates' policy strategies require systematic analysis because they provide the intellectual bridge that connects the Confederation's circumstances to specific constitutional provisions. Policy strategy refers to the set of related premises about goals, expectations, assumptions, political tactics, and other ideas that policy makers use when they pressure government to act in a specific way.[41] Individuals draw on experience, aspirations, and invention to forge strategies that are linked to circumstances but not determined by them. Policy strategy influences policy outcomes by shaping the policy agenda, the formulation of policy alternatives and structure of choice, and strategies of opposition.[42] Policy strategy is revealed in statements of support and opposition for specific policy provisions. Policy debate is full of explicit inferences about political necessity, impossibility, interests, tactics, and expectations about policy effects.[43]

The delegates' strategies matter so much because the framers did not and could not write into the Constitution "directly and unerringly" the interests of the nation's propertied elites. The most influential delegates – particularly James Madison – were rebuilding the American state to make it stable and powerful enough to pursue the nation's long-term interests.[44] Their government had to nurture the nation's prosperity long into the future. These state builders took it for granted that private property, free markets, and commercial expansion were essential for future prosperity,

[41] I elaborate on policy strategy in *Capital, Labor, and State: The Battle for American Labor Markets from the Civil War to the New Deal* (Lanham, MD: Rowman and Littlefield, 2000), pp. xiii–xvii, 13–27.

[42] John W. Kingdon, *Agendas, Alternatives, and Public Policies*, 2nd ed. (New York: HarperCollins, 1995); E. E. Schattschneider, *The Semisovereign People: A Realist's View of Democracy in America* (New York: Holt, Rinehart and Winston, 1960); Riker, *The Art of Political Manipulation* and *The Strategy of Rhetoric*.

[43] The tools of analytical philosophy are used to reconstruct policy strategy systematically to relate circumstances to policy outcomes. On conceptual analysis in politics and public policy, see Richard E. Flathman, ed., *Concepts in Social and Political Philosophy* (New York: Macmillan, 1973); William E. Connolly, *The Terms of Political Discourse* (Princeton, NJ: Princeton University Press, 1993); Deborah A. Stone, *Policy Paradox: The Art of Political Decision Making*, rev. ed. (New York: W. W. Norton, 2001). On the social construction of public policy, see Frank Fischer and John Forester, eds., *The Argumentative Turn in Policy Analysis and Planning* (Durham, NC: Duke University Press, 1993).

[44] Robert O. Keohane, *After Hegemony: Cooperation and Discord in the World Political Economy* (Princeton, NJ: Princeton University Press, 1984), p. 23.

and they appreciated that propertied elites were key agents for expanding markets and driving economic development. But many framers viewed the interests of these elites as too narrow, short-term, uninformed, and conflicted to provide much reliable guidance for redesigning the nation's basic political structure and recasting long-term policy.[45] The framers were trying to balance the government's basic needs (especially for revenue), their own ambitions for the nation's destiny, the clashing claims of different economic interests, and the demands of the more numerous citizens of modest means. Even when they were inclined to implement propertied elites' preferences, policy makers had to balance economic development against the demands of the nation's emerging democracy. Legislators needed a broader constituency to win elections to office. They had to show some responsiveness to the grievances of those with modest means. At the very least, elected policy makers had to make any program of market-driven economic development acceptable and legitimate for a majority of the constituents to whom their political fates were tethered.

In any case, it is impossible to enter the mind of an individual delegate to determine how he balanced principles and interests when he took a position on an issue of constitutional design. Jack Rakove observed that "[w]hat is elusive is the interplay between ideas and interests" in the Constitution's design.[46] A delegate's idealistic argument for strong national powers may have concealed a driving ambition to elevate his state or to seek the personal prestige and power of national office. Another delegate's defense of state prerogatives may have reflected sincere dedication to the principle of constituent representation and a deeply held belief in the superiority of the social, economic, and political order of his state. We can never know for certain. What is certain is that the delegates used ideas as rhetorical weapons to defend positions that closely matched their political interests. Political calculations shaped delegates' views of the stakes in most of the choices about the Constitution's design. Political calculations and negotiations, not just abstract

[45] Soon after the Constitution's adoption, when the new Congress convened in 1789, Representative James Madison observed that "I pay great respect to the opinions of mercantile gentlemen, and am willing to concede much to them, so far as their opinions are regulated by experience." But, he continued, "we know there is an essential difference between the interest of merchants and the interest of commerce; we know there may be distinctions also between the interest of commerce and of revenue, and that in some cases we must sacrifice the one to the other" (*DHFFC* May 9, 1789, 10: 562–3).

[46] Rakove, *Original Meanings*, p. 15.

ideas, settled the disputes these choices engendered. By expanding the concept of interest beyond personal pecuniary gain and selfish parochialism to include political interests, it is much easier to see how closely the delegates' ideas and interests aligned with one another in their policy strategies.

James Madison's policy strategy requires an especially careful analysis because Madison's ideas set the convention's agenda and shaped its politics. Madison's Virginia Plan sought to establish a national policymaking system independent of the state governments and armed with most of the authority to govern the national economy. The national government would assume full authority to manage economic development for the interest of the republic as a whole. Even after the defeat of provisions crucial to his agenda, Madison and his allies fought to inject this strategy into national government powers and institutions such as the presidency. Understanding the politics of the Constitution requires a careful understanding of the way Madison defined the nation's problems and the way his plan would mitigate them. Madison's writings in the years before 1787 and his reported comments during the convention provide the evidence for reconstructing Madison's political reasoning. Chapter 3 analyzes Madison's policy strategy for the Constitution.

By forcing the delegates to consider greater policy independence and authority for the national government, Madison's strategy provided a focal point that brought together the opponents of his scheme. The delegates who resisted Madison's proposals did so for different reasons. Many, like Connecticut's delegates, sought to avoid the unnecessary surrender of state prerogatives to the new national government. Connecticut's Roger Sherman and his colleagues became Madison's chief antagonists and relentless advocates for a rival constitutional strategy. The design of the U.S. Constitution reflects Madison's opponents' influence as much as Madison's. Chapter 4 deals with the policy interests and strategies of Madison's supporters and opponents.

Once Virginia's plan for reconstituting government was introduced on May 29, the delegates considered individual provisions piecemeal. The official journal recorded 569 votes by the time the convention adjourned on September 17. Although Madison brilliantly had supervised the convention's initial agenda, he found that incremental political decisions gradually chipped away at his coalition. Madison, his opponents, and other delegates adapted their strategies to changing opportunities and constraints as the meeting unfolded.

The design of the U.S. Constitution emerged from a dynamic, unpredictable sequence of path-dependent choices.[47] Each choice influenced and narrowed subsequent political calculations, options, choices, and outcomes. Many of the delegates' votes were so close that the shift of a few votes would have changed the convention's path and altered American government. For example, the delegates very nearly decided that there would be no authority to create federal courts other than the Supreme Court, that all new states would come into the Union with less representation than the original thirteen states, and that the Supreme Court would join the president in vetoing congressional legislation.[48] Because decisions were contingent on one another, the timing of decisions became critically important. Madison insisted on establishing convention support for proportional representation in both the House and the Senate before the convention considered national authority. But the longer the fight over representation dragged on, the more his opponents drew attention to the national government's authority, causing Madison to lose support for some of the key features of his initial plan. Several choices, therefore, became critical turning points that changed the political calculus of subsequent choices. The decisive victory for the Connecticut Compromise in mid-July caused Madison to support an independent presidency, Sherman to promote the powers of the Senate, and South Carolina's John Rutledge to advocate more limits on national powers. Once they were made, many choices became politically irreversible. When the delegates apportioned the number of representatives in the first House of Representatives on July 10, the number fixed for each state remained locked in despite repeated efforts to change the distribution of seats.

Although its written records provide the primary evidence for the convention's politics, these records are far from perfect. There exists no official record of the debates comparable with the modern *Congressional Record*. The delegates imposed a rule of secrecy on their debates, and they honored this rule. Although the official Journal of the convention is reasonably accurate, it provides only a list of the formal proceedings and a list of votes on each day of the convention, and so has limited utility

[47] On path dependence, see Stephen J. Gould, *The Panda's Thumb: More Reflections in Natural History* (New York: W. W. Norton, 1980); Douglass C. North, *Institutions, Institutional Change and Economic Performance* (Cambridge: Cambridge University Press, 1990); Paul Pierson, "Increasing Returns, Path Dependence, and the Study of Politics," *American Political Science Review* 94:2 (June 2000): 251–67.

[48] *RFC* June 5, 1: 119, 125; July 2, 1: 510; July 14, 2: 2–3; July 21, 2: 72, 80.

for exploring the policy strategies of the delegates. Several delegates took notes, but most of these notes are quite sketchy. Robert Yates took notes on the proceedings until his departure on July 5, but later Yates's notes were edited heavily for partisan purposes and cannot be relied upon as a fair record. James Madison's notes on the debates provide the most complete and reliable record of the proceedings.[49] However, because they evidently cover only a fraction of the actual floor discussion and provide virtually no record of the important informal discussions among the delegates off the convention floor, Madison's notes must be corroborated with other reliable records and actual decisions.[50]

Unlike most others who analyze the Constitution's design, I do not depend on *The Federalist Papers* and other evidence from the ratification debates to explain the delegates' intentions. I am explaining the design of the Constitution the delegates completed on September 17, 1787, not the Constitution's subsequent adoption by the states. The *Federalist* essays

[49] In his unpublished preface to the debates written late in life, Madison wrote "In pursuance of the task I had assumed I chose a seat in front of the presiding member with the other members, on my right & left hand. In this favorable position for hearing all that passed, I noted in terms legible & in abbreviations & marks intelligible to myself what was read from the Chair or spoken by the members; and losing not a moment unnecessarily between the adjournment & reassembling of the Convention I was enabled to write out my daily notes during the session or within a few finishing days after its close in the extent and form preserved in my own hand on my files.... In the labor and correctness of this I was not a little aided by practice, and by a familiarity with the style and the train of observation and reasoning which characterized the principal speakers. It happened, also, that I was not absent a single day, nor more than a casual fraction of an hour in any day, so that I could not have lost a single speech, unless a very short one." James Madison, "Preface to Debates in the Convention of 1787," *RFC* 3: 550. William Winslow Crosskey, in *Politics and the Constitution in the History of the United States* (Chicago: University of Chicago Press, 1953), argued that Madison had doctored his notes and falsely represented the content of the debates. James H. Hutson's thorough analysis shows that there is little evidence to support Crosskey's conclusions; see Hutson, ed., *Supplement to Max Farrand's "The Records of the Federal Convention of 1787"* (New Haven, CT: Yale University Press, 1987), pp. xx–xxiv. Later in life, Madison did make some minor edits in his original notes (Max Farrand, "Introduction," *RFC* 1: xviii–xix). In the quotations from Madison's notes in this book, Madison's later edits are indicated by angle brackets. My editorial changes are indicated by square brackets.

[50] Madison's notes exclude only one important speech – a speech by John Dickinson on May 30 – that is reported in another delegate's notes other than Yates (compare Madison's notes, *RFC* May 30, 1: 33–8, with McHenry's notes, *RFC* May 30, 1: 42). Madison's notes most likely emphasized the kinds of theoretical arguments that he himself wielded with such facility. Madison's own account of his speech on the veto is much more theoretical and abstract than Rufus King's report of Madison's speech. In King's account, Madison spells out the diversity of material interests in the United States (*RFC* June 4, 1: 100, 108).

justify the Constitution, but they do not explain accurately how the convention delegates designed the Constitution. First and foremost, they are polemical tracts written to urge New Yorkers to support ratification.[51] These essays must be used very sparingly, for they necessarily distort the politics of constitutional design by masking the political conflicts from which these provisions emerged.[52] The delegates agreed to compromises that few would have endorsed had they the power to design and adopt a constitution alone, regardless of the enthusiasm with which they defended the document afterward. Madison notably had a much more nationalized policy system in mind, and his private letters before the convention reveal much more about his true preferences than does his post hoc account of the Constitution in New York newspapers. After the convention, he criticized certain provisions of the Constitution in private correspondence even while his brilliant justification of its provisions were appearing in the *Federalist*.[53] Because the written record is so incomplete, it is important to use logic, social science, and the political context

[51] Roche, "The Founding Fathers: A Reform Caucus in Action"; Garry Wills, *Explaining America: The Federalist* (Garden City, NY: Doubleday, 1981); Samuel Kernell, "'The True Principles of Republican Government': Reassessing James Madison's Political Science," in *James Madison: The Theory and Practice of Republican Government*, ed. Samuel Kernell (Stanford, CA: Stanford University Press, 2003), pp. 92–125.

[52] *The Federalist Papers* evidently manipulated the Constitution's intent to ensure a positive reception. For example, its authors emphasized that the separation of judicial powers from the rest of the government had been copied from the constitutions of nine of the states, a claim that clearly exaggerated the comparison between these states and the proposed Constitution (no. 81, pp. 544–5). See William N. Eskridge Jr., "All about Words: Early Understandings of the 'Judicial Power' in Statutory Interpretation, 1776–1806," *Columbia Law Review* 101:5 (June 2001): 990–1106. Scholars who assume that *The Federalist Papers* provides an explanation of the delegates' reasoning sometimes underestimate the founders' political understanding of their own product. Robert A. Dahl concluded that Hamilton misunderstood the Electoral College in *Federalist* 68 because Hamilton expressed the view that the people would choose presidential electors, although relatively few voters actually did choose these electors; see *How Democratic Is the American Constitution?* (New Haven, CT: Yale University Press, 2001), p. 76. It is much more likely that Hamilton's assertion was politically motivated. The Electoral College, like other features of the Constitution, was designed to permit state officials to tailor many political choices to the necessities of state politics, a feature that allowed Hamilton to make this claim to New Yorkers. Hamilton himself had participated in the debate that allowed each state's legislature to determine how electors would be chosen (*RFC* September 6, 2: 525).

[53] James Madison to Thomas Jefferson, October 24, 1787, in *PJM* 10: 209–14; Charles F. Hobson, "The Negative on State Laws: James Madison, the Constitution and the Crisis of Republican Government," *William and Mary Quarterly* 36:2 (April 1979): 217; Richard K. Matthews, *If Men Were Angels: James Madison and the Heartless Empire of Reason* (Lawrence: University Press of Kansas, 1995), p. 15.

TABLE 1.1. *A Policy Map of the U.S. Constitution's Provisions Categorized by Policy Agency, Policy Authority, and Policy Process*

Policy agency	
Article I	
Section 2	House: Selection, eligibility, apportionment, term, vacancies
Section 3	Senate: Selection, eligibility, apportionment, term, vacancies
Section 4	Times, places, and manner of holding congressional elections
Section 5	Judgment of congressional election results and qualifications
Section 6	Compensation and other national offices
Article II	
Section 1	President and vice president: Selection, eligibility, term, vacancies
Section 4	Impeachment
Article III	
Section 1	Judges: Term, compensation
Article IV	
Section 3	New states; territories
Article V	Equal representation in Senate cannot be amended
Article VI	No religious test for office
Policy authority	
Preamble	Purposes
Article I	
Section 1	Allocation of legislative power
Section 8	Enumerated powers; "necessary and proper" clause
Section 9	Specific powers denied to Congress
Section 10	Specific powers denied to States
Article III	
Section 3	Treason
Article IV	
Section 1	Full faith and credit for state laws
Section 2	Privileges and immunities; runaway slaves
Section 3	Territorial law
Section 4	Protection against invasion and domestic violence
Article V	Slave trade protected until 1808
Article VI	National debts; supremacy clause; oath
Policy process	
Article I	
Section 2	House officers; impeachment
Section 3	Senate officers; impeachment
Section 4	Congressional meetings
Section 5	Quorum; attendance; rules; journal; adjournment
Section 6	Congressional privileges
Section 7	Revenue bills originate in the House; veto process
Article II	
Section 1	Executive power; oath
Section 2	Presidential powers
Section 3	State of union; special sessions; responsibilities

Article III	
Section 1	Supreme Court and inferior courts
Section 2	Judicial power; original and appellate jurisdiction; trials
Section 3	Treason
Article IV	
Section 4	Guarantee of republican government in the states
Article V	Amendment process
Article VII	Ratification

to identify unspoken and understated premises that fill gaps in convention argumentation. Identifying these key premises and their relationship depends on a comprehensive blueprint of constitutional decisions.

A Policy Map of the Constitution

A thorough understanding of the Constitution requires a comprehensive policy map of all of the Constitution's provisions, independent of the political controversies at the convention, in the ratification process, or in the subsequent history of American politics. I sorted the Constitution's provisions into three categories of policy choice: policy agency, policy authority, and policy process (Table 1.1). Chapters 5, 6, and 7, respectively, provide analytical narratives of the way the delegates developed constitutional provisions in each of these categories.

I used this map to guide my analysis of who the framers intended to govern the economy, for what purposes they intended it to be governed, and how they intended it to be governed. The map is essential for several reasons. First, a policy map forces us to observe and account for every choice the delegates made, not just an arbitrarily selected set of decisions. We must assume that any overt conflict over a constitutional provision had political significance for the delegates, no matter how seemingly minor or arcane.[54] It is our responsibility to identify and understand the

[54] Some of the passages in the Madison's notes present formidable challenges to interpretation. Here is an example of one of the most opaque sentences in the debates, and one that illustrates the political jockeying that pervaded the proceedings. After the delegates had begun to discuss the proposed Electoral College for selecting the president, "Mr Madison & Mr. Williamson moved to insert after 'Electors' the words 'who shall have balloted' so that the non voting electors not being counted might not increase the number necessary as a majority of the whole – to decide the choice without the agency of the Senate –" (*RFC* September 5, 2: 515). This nearly impenetrable sentence must be understood in the context of the deep, protracted political struggle between delegates like Madison who wanted to reduce the power of the Senate and those who sought to maximize its policy influence. The convention was considering whether the president would be elected

significance of such a conflict, not to choose which conflicts should or should not "count" in the narrative because of our arbitrary notions of their importance. Second, a policy map enlarges our vision of convention politics by forcing us to interpret an entire category of policy choices, instead of isolating each constitutional provision. By identifying a set of choices to be explained, this conceptual map forces us to relate all debates about agency, authority, and process to each other from the beginning of the convention to the end. The map makes it crucial to examine the relationship and the sequence among decisions within and across the categories of choice. Third, a policy map provides additional information about policy strategy by placing each choice in the context of related decisions. A better understanding of the political importance of a provision helps explain why the delegates viewed seemingly arcane choices about the definition of treason or the control of the militia as part of a broad struggle between competing models of American governance. Finally, a policy map forces us to interpret provisions that were defeated at the convention and to gain from those rejected proposals further insight into the delegates' intentions.

Policy agency refers to decisions about who governs, that is, about the persons who occupy policy-making positions and the control of policy-making offices. These decisions include the eligibility and rewards for different offices, the rules for selecting and removing officeholders, and the number and apportionment of officeholders. How many individuals are engaged formally in national policy making, and in what policy-making bodies? How are they chosen, and who do they represent? What are

by a majority of the votes of the presidential electors, but Madison wanted the president elected by a majority of those actually voting, not the potentially larger majority of all possible electors from all the states. Without a majority in the Electoral College, the Senate would elect the president, with each state casting an equal vote. Madison's motion aimed to increase the chances that the Electoral College instead of the Senate would choose the president, and to reduce the chance that electors from a given state would try to game the outcome of the presidential election by refusing to vote, therefore throwing the election into the Senate. Larger states would wield relatively more influence over presidential selection in the Electoral College, smaller states would have more influence in the Senate. The motion lost, four votes to seven, with states expecting larger than average electoral votes favoring the motion and smaller states against. Immediately after the motion's defeat, the convention moved to reduce political gaming by providing that the majority would be constituted by "the whole number of the Electors *appointed*" by the states (emphasis added), forcing states to appoint electors to influence the selection of the president. Later in the convention, the delegates provided that the House, not the Senate, would decide presidential elections in the event that no candidate had a majority of the Electoral College vote.

the rules for selecting or removing members, and who controls these processes?

Debates over representation at the convention were no mere philosophical disputes. If the Constitution had been merely an exercise in republican institution building disconnected from urgent political and economic problems, it would have failed politically. The delegates fought so hard over the selection of key legislators, the president, and other national policy makers because they perceived that the rules for selecting these officeholders had a direct policy impact on vital state and national policy interests. The delegates' disagreed about the states' relative influence over the choice of policy makers, and this disagreement deadlocked the convention in early July. States with large populations, such as Virginia and Pennsylvania, supported proportional representation in both houses of Congress because such representation would give these states much more influence over national policy outcomes than the power they currently exercised in the Confederation Congress. States with smaller populations insisted on equal state representation to protect a measure of the policy influence they enjoyed in the Confederation Congress. After the delegates compromised on proportional representation in the House of Representatives and equal state representation in the Senate, this dispute spilled over into other battles, most notably over the selection of the president. Chapter 5 deals with the design of policy agency.

Policy authority refers to decisions about the scope of public policy, that is, the legitimate right to make policy in a given field. What is governed? What is government allowed to do? What are the limits of public authority? These decisions involve the definition of legislative powers, the limits on those powers, and conditions under which the limits may be exceeded. The delegates generally agreed that the national government should have more authority to tax and to govern commerce, but they were divided over the scope of these powers and the need for even greater authority. As the distribution of seats in Congress became clearer in mid-July, delegates scrambled to set boundaries of national power in a way that permitted national policies to benefit their constituents while also making it difficult to enact policies that would harm their state. The delegates thus agreed to authorize national public goods that would benefit every state, such as commercial treaties, national revenue, and national defense. They also withdrew state powers to interfere with commerce. But the delegates left substantial economic authority in state hands, and did so to protect the political orders they had helped tailor to each state constituency. Chapter 6 examines the design of policy authority.

Policy process refers to decisions about how policy is made, that is, the rules for formulating, legitimating, and implementing public policy. The Constitution created policy-making roles for the House of Representatives, the Senate, the executive branch, and the courts. It guaranteed a republican government in every state and specified the processes of constitutional ratification and amendment. It forced separate institutions to share power, enabling different institutions to participate in formulating policy in ways that were unanticipated but not wholly unpredictable. After July 5 the delegates jockeyed to ensure a process that would make it difficult for the national government to make policies that could harm their state. Madison and his allies pressed to increase the power of the president in the process because the president was more likely to pursue purely national interests. The Connecticut delegates defended the policy influence of Congress in general and the Senate in particular because these institutions were more likely to protect the existing policy prerogatives of the states. The policy-making processes approved by the delegates, then, depended on the policy outcomes they expected these processes to produce. Chapter 7 analyzes the design of the policy process.

THE POLITICS THE CONSTITUTION MADE

The Constitution was both pathbreaking and path making. The politicians who wrote the Constitution sought a government that would produce better policies than the Confederation government. They tried to design a government more apt to protect national sovereignty and encourage market-driven economic development. Path-making policy projects like the Constitution always have emerged from intense, tortuous, and exhausting processes thoroughly permeated by politics. These grand policy initiatives usually have fallen short of their most ardent supporters' hopes, and when they do, supporters comfort themselves that their product is satisfactory, repairable, and the best that could be done under the circumstances. Today's policy makers would recognize instantly Benjamin Franklin's assessment of the political results of the Constitutional Convention.

> [W]hen you assemble a number of men to have the advantage of their joint wisdom, you inevitably assemble with those men, all their prejudices, their passions, their errors of opinion, their local interests, and their selfish views. From such an Assembly can a perfect production be expected? It therefore astonishes me, Sir, to find this system approaching so near to perfection as it does.... I consent, Sir, to this Constitution because I expect no better, and because I am not sure, that

it is not the best.... If every one of us in returning to our Constituents were to report the objections he has had to it, and endeavor to gain partizans in support of them, we might prevent its being generally received, and thereby lose all the salutary effects & great advantages resulting naturally in our favor among foreign Nations as well as among ourselves, from our real or apparent unanimity.[55]

Franklin and his colleagues understood that their Constitution would encourage and structure politics in the future.

Chapter 8 examines the Constitution's enduring effects on the path of American politics and policy. The Constitution's early years illustrate many of its enduring features: the use of the Constitution itself as a political weapon, the struggle between state and national policy authority, the struggle among separated national institutions to control public policy, and the difficulty and expense of using American government to solve public problems. The constitutional framework helps explain how American politics became so different from politics in comparable nations around the turn of the twentieth century.

In late May 1787, none of the delegates who later signed it could have predicted the Constitution's final design, much less its durability and impact on America's destiny. But the delegates did not set out on an unmarked path. Immediate crises and experiences set the direction for the convention. The Constitution principally aimed to solve immediate political and economic dilemmas that appeared to have put the Confederation on the brink of political disaster.

[55] *RFC* September 17, 2: 642–3.

2

The Policy Crisis of the 1780s

The thirteen colonies that declared themselves independent governments in 1776 soon faced severe political tests. Each new republic now had to assert control over its own territory, to police its commerce, property, and social life, and to make citizens pay taxes to fund these efforts. It was far from easy. The war brought havoc and enemy occupation to many parts of America. During the war, some state governments and their leaders, including Virginia's governor Thomas Jefferson, had to flee from enemy capture. When the war ended, economic depression caused even more havoc. Political conflict grew bitter, and resentments sometimes boiled over into violence.

State governments gradually grew stronger as they dealt with these formidable political challenges. Their leaders became more adept at using their newly enlarged authority to manage each state's politics and to balance democracy and development. Paradoxically, the growing political capacity of the states put national politics in severe jeopardy. Because the states differed in so many ways, state policy makers implemented public policies that exploited state economic advantages, often at the expense of creditors, merchants, citizens of other states, and the long-term economic interest of the nation as a whole. Their political power, then, put the states in a dilemma. Cooperation with other states, and more effective national powers, could in theory benefit their citizens. None of the states, though, could defer to other states, or let other states use national policy to their advantage, if by doing so they put themselves at a disadvantage relative to others. The national government under the Articles of Confederation seemed by 1787 as much a vehicle for fostering these interstate economic antagonisms as a solution to them. Conflicts about national finance, land, trade, currency, defense, and other issues made national cooperation nearly impossible and brought the Confederation Congress to the brink of political failure.

THE INDEPENDENT AMERICAN STATES

When the American colonies "totally dissolved" their "political connection" with Britain in 1776, each orphaned itself from British public policy. The British state had borne the substantial costs of making laws and enforcing security for the colonies. British government made the fundamental policy on property rights, commerce and trade, money, and taxes for the colonies. Some of this British policy infrastructure, such as common law, endured. The colonies lost the shield of the British military, the benefits of British administrative expenditures in the colonies, and the loss of commercial privileges within the British Empire's trading network. The king and his Parliament no longer set the path of American economic policy.

Each colony reinvented itself as an independent, self-governing republic and assumed full control over public policy.[1] Each state took responsibility for governing the key economic assets within its borders: land and natural resources, labor (farmers, slaves, merchants, and artisans), and capital (money and credit). Each state would determine its own tariff, currency, land, and debt policy. Before the national Articles of Confederation took effect in 1781, all the states had adopted written constitutions that established basic blueprints for exercising state policy authority. Although individual states found it challenging to exercise effective control over the territory they governed, all were making steady progress by 1787.[2]

The new states had long been accustomed to exercising many policy prerogatives. Particularly where religious dissenters dominated colonial

[1] Allan Nevins, *The American States during and after the Revolution, 1775–1789* (New York: Macmillan, 1924), pp. 117–70; Samuel H. Beer, *To Make a Nation: The Rediscovery of American Federalism* (Cambridge, MA: Belknap Press, 1993), pp. 200–6; Marc W. Kruman, *Between Authority and Liberty: State Constitution Making in Revolutionary America* (Chapel Hill: University of North Carolina Press, 1997), pp. 15–33, 111–16.

[2] It was not simple for Massachusetts, for example, to establish state government authority within its territory, even though it moved rapidly to do so. See Oscar Handlin and Mary Flug Handlin, *Commonwealth: A Study of the Role of Government in the American Economy: Massachusetts, 1774–1861* (Cambridge, MA: Belknap Press, 1969); Hendrick Hartog, "Losing the World of the Massachusetts Whig," in *Law in the American Revolution and the Revolution in American Law: A Collection of Review Essays on American Legal History*, ed. Hendrick Hartog (New York: New York University Press, 1981), pp. 143–66.

societies, as in New England, colonial legislatures zealously regulated, licensed, and taxed individual behavior. The British government left the colonies considerable autonomy in raising revenues, and each pursued a different tax policy suited to its resources and politics. In a nation rich in land but short of labor and hard money, disputes over property and debts flooded American courts with litigation and elevated the policy prominence of American courts, judges, and lawyers. Most of the states, especially the middle colonies, had learned to cope with chronic shortages of specie (that is, gold or silver coins) in the eighteenth century by establishing land banks to circulate paper money and bills of credit to keep up a continuous flow of credit. The states in effect governed commerce through import and export duties, bounties, inspection laws, embargoes, tonnage duties, and a variety of port regulations. For a century, New England governments had taken an especially active role in encouraging such enterprises as mills, glassworks, and saltworks with bounties, tax abatements and concessions, patents, monopoly rights, and road and bridge building.[3] New England states were mimicking many of the self-enriching mercantilist policies of Britain on a microscopic scale.

Independence and war forced the states to expand their policy powers. The new states, especially the states in the path of battle, had to develop substantial governing capacity quickly. Virginia, for example, assumed nearly dictatorial power late in the war. The states took control over hundreds of millions of acres of land previously owned by the British king and British nobility. Virginia, Maryland, South Carolina, and Pennsylvania acted as sovereign nation-states in seeking loans abroad. Both Virginia and New York refused to repeal laws that were in conflict with the peace treaty that Congress signed with England. After the war, Virginia ratified the peace treaty as a separate nation, and Maryland negotiated for recovery of its stock in the Bank of England. Nine states organized navies. Other states established their own systems of privateering and profited

[3] Robert A. Becker, *Revolution, Reform, and the Politics of American Taxation, 1763–1783* (Baton Rouge: Louisiana State University Press, 1980), pp. 13–14, 41; Charles Hoffer, *Law and People in Colonial America*, rev. ed. (Baltimore: Johns Hopkins University Press, 1998), pp. 80–2, 100–2; Roger H. Brown, *Redeeming the Republic: Federalists, Taxation, and the Origins of the Constitution* (Baltimore: Johns Hopkins University Press, 1993); E. James Ferguson, *The Power of the Purse: A History of Public Finance, 1776–1790* (Chapel Hill: University of North Carolina Press, 1961), pp. 4–5; Albert Anthony Giesecke, *American Commercial Legislation before 1789* (1910; New York: Burt Franklin, 1970); Margaret Ellen Newell, "The Birth of New England in the Atlantic Economy: From Its Beginning to 1770," in *Engines of Enterprise: An Economic History of New England*, ed. Peter Temin (Cambridge, MA: Harvard University Press, 2000), p. 41.

from preying on British commerce. States defined citizenship and administered naturalization. States codified and expanded laws affecting health and safety, alcohol, gambling, lewd conduct, and other vices.[4]

By developing their tax systems, the states were strengthening the most important tool for establishing government independence and power. European nation-states had consolidated their authority and autonomy by developing their ability to extract revenues from recalcitrant taxpayers.[5] Now American states, which often had to impose a heavier burden than the colonial governments that preceded them, rapidly grew skilled in the political arts of taxation. The states drew from a full toolbox of taxes: head or "poll" taxes on individuals, property taxes, excise taxes, professional taxes, import and export taxes. Because taxes inescapably forced state policy makers to place different burdens on different constituents, any substantial tax unleashed potentially explosive internal conflicts. Poll taxes lay heavier on the poor than the wealthy; taxes on land harmed owners of real property to the advantage of those controlling securities and nonagricultural forms of wealth; import taxes disproportionately hurt those who consumed imported goods and helped domestic producers of those goods.

[4] Ferguson, *The Power of the Purse*, pp. 61–2; Nevins, *The American States during and after the Revolution, 1775–1789*, pp. 652–6, 659–60; Giesecke, *American Commercial Legislation before 1789*, p. 123. On citizenship, see Rogers M. Smith, *Civic Ideals: Conflicting Visions of Citizenship in U.S. History* (New Haven, CT: Yale University Press, 1997), pp. 86–114. On alcohol, see W. J. Rorabaugh, *The Alcoholic Republic: An American Tradition* (New York: Oxford University Press, 1979), pp. 49–50. On the tradition of state public regulation of moral behavior in the early republic, see William J. Novak, *The People's Welfare: Law and Regulation in Nineteenth-Century America* (Chapel Hill: University of North Carolina Press, 1996), pp. 149–89. Maryland's lawmaking record from this period is online at State of Maryland, Archives of Maryland Online, Early State Records, Session Laws, http://www.mdarchives.state.md.us/megafile/msa/speccol/sc4800/sc4872/003180/html/m3180-0487.html accessed July 26, 2004. For example, chapter VI of Maryland's laws of the June 1778 session of the legislature stated that "Whereas true religion and good morals are the only solid foundation of public liberty and happiness," the general assembly sought to promote these values by providing "the most effectual measures for the suppressing of theatrical entertainments, horse-racing, gaming, and such other diversions as are productive of idleness, dissipation, and a general depravity of principles and manners" (pp. 486–91). A few U.S. Supreme Court decisions extensively have listed many of the Confederation-era laws of the states; for example, see the list of inspection laws in *Turner* v. *State of Maryland*, 107 U.S. 38 (1883).

[5] Carolyn Webber and Aaron Wildavsky, *A History of Taxation and Expenditure in the Western World* (New York: Simon and Schuster, 1986); Hendrick Spruyt, *The Sovereign State and Its Competitors: An Analysis of Systems Change* (Princeton, NJ: Princeton University Press, 1994).

As states adapted to these crosscutting conflicts, each state government learned through trial and error to tailor taxes to their unique constituents and circumstances. For example, New York reduced its need for unpopular property taxes by imposing duties on goods imported through its port at New York City, whereas Virginia taxed exports of tobacco to Europe. The states adjusted these taxes to the changing dictates of politics. The Virginia legislature enacted a tariff on distilled spirits, a proposal that appealed to both religious purists and western Virginia distillers. Virginia's legislators repealed the tax, however, when the wealthy landowners who consumed ample quantities of European spirits protested angrily. Economic policy in the former colonies steadily grew more diverse. Tax collection also expanded state power, forcing the states to become more adept at policing their own promulgations. Tax collection remained challenging and inconsistent, in part because of opposition to taxes manifested in tax withholding, attacks on state tax assessors and collectors, and rioting.[6]

Swept up in revolutionary zeal and struggling to establish their own legitimacy, the new state republics forged short chains between the public officials who wielded these prerogatives and the mass of white male voters. Voting rights were extended, and by 1790 60 to 70 percent of adult white males in the United States could vote.[7] Popularly elected state legislators, in turn, exercised nearly all of the state's policy authority. To ensure their fealty to voters, these legislators typically faced annual elections. Pennsylvania, Georgia, and Vermont created unicameral legislatures, in which one popularly elected legislative house largely made state law.[8] The other ten states created bicameral legislatures in which the

[6] Brown, *Redeeming the Republic*, pp. 32–40; Jackson Turner Main, *Political Parties before the Constitution* (Chapel Hill: University of North Carolina Press, 1973), pp. 53–9; Rorabaugh, *The Alcoholic Republic*, p. 50; Ferguson, *The Power of the Purse*, p. 30. Rorabaugh's description of the Virginia case provides an early example of a political alliance of convenience between moralists devoted to a policy goal and producers who gain economically from the same policy. See Bruce Yandle, "Bootleggers and Baptists: The Education of a Regulatory Economist," *Regulation* 7:3 (May–June 1983): 12–16.

[7] Sean Wilentz, "Property and Power: Suffrage Reform in the United States, 1787–1860," in *Voting and the Spirit of American Democracy: Essays on the History of Voting and Voting Rights in America*, ed. Donald W. Rogers (Urbana: University of Illinois Press, 1992), p. 35; Gordon S. Wood, *The Creation of the American Republic, 1776–1787* (Chapel Hill: University of North Carolina Press, 1969), pp. 166–7; Alexander Keyssar, *The Right to Vote: The Contested History of Democracy in the United States* (New York: Basic Books, 2000), p. 24.

[8] Pennsylvania created a "house of representatives of the freemen of the commonwealth or state of Pennsylvania"; Georgia, a house of assembly; Vermont, an "Assembly of the Representatives of the Freemen."

popularly elected house of representatives (the "lower" house) shared legislative power with a less numerous senate or council (an "upper" house). These senates, though, had limited influence over the agendas and enactments of the popularly elected lower houses. In many states, these upper legislative chambers could not initiate policy proposals or alter the spending plans laid out by the lower house.[9] Upper houses often responded to the same pressures as the lower houses in any case. Senates in South and North Carolina, New Jersey, New York, and Rhode Island refused to block popular laws inflating state currency in the mid-1780s.[10]

The new American state constitutions limited executive power, aiming primarily to protect the courts and the legislature from executive manipulation. State governors could not set legislative agendas or formulate programs, adjourn legislatures, or – with the exception of executives in Massachusetts, New York, and South Carolina – veto legislation. Only four states permitted the governor substantial power to appoint public officials. Pennsylvania's constitution of 1776 embodied revolutionary republican policy making in its most radical form, vesting the "supreme legislative power" in a single house of representatives elected annually and limited to four years of service. Any Pennsylvania law required assent by the legislature in two consecutive years, a provision that assured that new policies would be scrutinized by differently constituted legislatures.[11] Although it was the most democratic of the new state constitutions, the Pennsylvania constitution was "only an extension and exaggeration of what was taking place elsewhere in America."[12]

Not only did the state constitutions insist on popular influence in the policy process, but the states also created many new political offices and filled them with officials tied directly or indirectly to the voters. The number of seats in state legislatures nearly doubled. Political scientist Charles Kromkowski found that there were more than sixteen hundred state legislators alone in the thirteen states in 1786.[13] Because republican theory

9 Nevins, *The American States during and after the Revolution, 1775–1789*, pp. 139–40; Wood, *The Creation of the American Republic, 1776–1787*, p. 155; Kruman, *Between Authority and Liberty*.

10 Jackson Turner Main, *The Sovereign States, 1775–1783* (New York: New Viewpoints, 1973), pp. 195–200, 205.

11 Ibid., p. 192; Nevins, *The American States during and after the Revolution, 1775–1789*, p. 152; Wood, *The Creation of the American Republic, 1776–1787*, pp. 13–8, 148, 155, 352.

12 Wood, *The Creation of the American Republic, 1776–1787*, pp. 84–5, 450–1.

13 Charles A. Kromkowski, *Recreating the American Republic: Rules of Apportionment, Constitutional Change, and American Political Development, 1700–1870* (Cambridge:

insisted on separating policy authority to prevent tyranny, states established many other executive and judicial posts. By 1787 each state had institutionalized dozens of public offices – judges, governors, secretaries of states, attorneys general, treasurers, sheriffs, justices of the peace, tax collectors, and militia officers. Each officeholder had a stake in protecting the prerogatives of his office. Many had invested a substantial part of their lives establishing state autonomy and building state political capacity. George Clinton, for example, served as governor of New York from 1777 to 1795, and William Livingston as governor of New Jersey from 1776 to 1790. John and Edward Rutledge had sunk much time and effort into building South Carolina's polity, as had Patrick Henry and Thomas Jefferson in Virginia, George Read in Delaware, and Roger Sherman in Connecticut. Because most of America's leading politicians were experienced state legislators, governors, and judges, their time in office profoundly shaped their perspective on public policy.

Factional strife had long simmered in every colony, but now the states' new authority and new public offices inflamed factional rivalries. Many of these factional battles set the "have-nots" against the "haves," over taxes, debt, currency, and land. Other rivalries cut across class lines. Privileged churches fought to protect and expand their public support, while religious dissenters battled against religious establishment.[14] James Madison championed Baptists and others fighting for religious freedom in Virginia. In Massachusetts, South Carolina, and other states, rural, backcountry interests battled more cosmopolitan interests in cities, towns, and coastal areas. Eastern New Jersey opposed western New Jersey. Sometimes factions festered simply because alliances formed around those particular leaders who held office, such as Governor Clinton in New York, while shared resentment forged alliances among those who did not. Historian

Cambridge University Press, 2002), p. 231. According to Kromkowski, many of these legislative elections were not very competitive (p. 233). The issue of state officeholders' vested interest in their power was made explicit at the Constitutional Convention. The convention notes of William Paterson of New Jersey include this comment from Massachusetts delegate Elbridge Gerry: "About 2,000 Men in the smaller States, who compose the Executives, Legislatives, and Judiciaries; all interested in opposing the present [Virginia] Plan, because it tends to annihilate the State-Governments" (*RFC* July 7, 1: 555).

[14] Ten of the thirteen states had had established churches at one time, and in 1787 five states still had established churches. Massachusetts, Connecticut, and New Hampshire established Congregational worship, and South Carolina and Maryland still supported the Church of England as the established church. Pennsylvania, Rhode Island, and Delaware had never established a religion. Carl Zollman, *American Church Law* (St. Paul, MN: West Publishing, 1933), pp. 2–4.

Forrest McDonald counted thirty-four different factions in the thirteen states by 1787. Pennsylvania already had recognizable political parties.[15]

All the new state governments and their officials struggled to establish their legitimacy, extend their control, and balance competing interests. Compared with policy makers today, state politicians in the 1780s felt far more urgent pressure to legislate in response to constituents' immediate demands. They simultaneously were building state institutions, forging political coalitions, responding to crises, and laying the foundation for future development.

THE STATES' DIVERSE AND CONFLICTING INTERESTS

Across the new nation, these policy demands were diverse and, increasingly, in conflict. Without the unifying force of British government or revolutionary ardor, the states' different cultures, religious traditions, habits, political dynamics, and economic interests began to send them on divergent paths of economic and policy development. These differences had been pronounced long before the war.[16] The revolution created a fragile sense of common American national identity in the battle against Britain. Even then, many revolutionaries fought for the independence of Virginia, Maryland, New York, and other new republics rather than for an American nation.[17] The bonds of shared revolutionary passion faded rapidly in the 1780s.

The economic assets of the new American republics differed substantially, and these differences ensured that the states' interests would clash

[15] Forrest McDonald, *We the People: The Economic Origins of the Constitution* (Chicago: University of Chicago Press, 1958), pp. 21–37; Main, *Political Parties before the Constitution*; James A. Morone, *The Democratic Wish: Popular Participation and the Limits of American Government* (New York: Basic Books, 1990), pp. 46–7.

[16] For example, Josiah Quincy of Massachusetts, as a twenty-nine-year-old visitor to South Carolina in 1776, recorded many striking contrasts between that state and his home state, including criticisms of the state constitution and the observation that "The state of religion here is repugnant not only to the ordinances of Jesus Christ, but to every law of sound policy. The Sabbath is a day of visiting and mirth with the rich, and of license, pastime and frolic for the negroes." See further David M. Potter and Thomas G. Manning, *Nationalism and Sectionalism in America, 1775–1877* (New York: Henry Holt, 1949), quotation from p. 20.

[17] Mary R. Murrin, *To Save This State from Ruin: New Jersey and the Creation of the United States Constitution, 1776–1789* (Trenton: New Jersey Historical Commission, 1987), pp. 344–5; Merrill Jensen, *The Articles of Confederation: An Interpretation of the Social-Constitutional History of the American Revolution, 1774–1781* (Madison: University of Wisconsin Press, 1940), pp. 118–19, 161–2, 176; see Wood, *The Creation of the American Republic, 1776–1787*, p. 357.

as their economies developed. As many as half a dozen distinct regional identities existed in the new United States: northern New England, Long Island and the Hudson valley, the Delaware River basin, the Chesapeake Bay, the James and Pee Dee river basins in Virginia, and the settlements near Charleston, South Carolina. Because communication was difficult, most individuals rarely came into contact with people in other communities, much less those in other regions.[18]

Agriculture, the livelihood of nine of ten Americans, differed fundamentally from one end of the eastern seaboard to the other. Southern states enjoyed a vast expanse of fertile, accessible, tillable land, and the southern climate permitted a long growing season. Virginia, North and South Carolina, and Georgia specialized in the production of cash crops such as tobacco, rice, and indigo. In the 1770s these southern economies had remained the most colonial: they exported these few products to Great Britain in bulk and used the profits to import finished goods from Britain. Specialized southern farms came to depend on slaves because their size and the long growing season made slaves a profitable investment. Slaves made it possible to expand the scale of export farms, facilitating the growth of large plantations for the more-efficient production of specialized export crops. Large plantations with ten or more slaves had a considerable market advantage. Sharp price fluctuations for these commodities also favored the larger plantations that could use surplus crops to weather economic downturns. Slaves constituted about one-third of all of the private physical wealth in the South, compared with less than 5 percent in the middle states and virtually none in New England. Southern states, then, had a stake in policies that protected slavery and free, direct trade with Europe. These states had little interest in the economic diversification that was occurring in states to their north. These states also favored free and competitive trade and access to the Mississippi River as a trade route. They particularly were at cross purposes with northern traders who sought to protect American carriers and limit competition with them. The South's advantage in cash crops made it by far the wealthiest of the three regions. In 1774 the average wealth per person in the south was £137, in contrast to £46 in the middle colonies and £38 in New England.[19]

[18] Main, *The Sovereign States, 1775–1783*, pp. 1–16; Murrin, *To Save This State from Ruin*, p. 343.

[19] Gary M. Walton and James F. Shepard, *The Economic Rise of Early America* (Cambridge: Cambridge University Press, 1979); Gary M. Walton and Hugh Rockoff, *History of the American Economy*, 8th ed. (Fort Worth, TX: Dryden Press, 1998), pp. 94–7, 101; Alice Hanson Jones, *Wealth of a Nation to Be: The American Colonies on the Eve of*

The middle states – Maryland, Pennsylvania, Delaware, New Jersey, and New York – had fertile land but a less advantageous climate, too cold to produce food during several months of the year. The typical middle-state farm was a family operation, decidedly smaller than a southern plantation, dependent not on slaves but on a few indentured servants or itinerant workers if needed for additional help. Unable to cultivate a few cash crops on a large scale, farmers in the middle states diversified their crops, raising wheat and also corn, rye, oats, barley, some fruits and vegetables (such as potatoes), and livestock. These farms increasingly produced surplus for export, particularly bread and flour, but were not as dependent on European demand as the farms to the south.[20] In this region, New York and Philadelphia had become important ports. Nascent industries, such as iron manufacture, were growing. Thus, while free trade was less politically significant here than in the South, the middle states had a greater stake in the development of internal commerce, manufacturing, and investment.

New England had gone furthest to break with its colonial role and to develop a diversified market economy of its own. New England's soil, terrain, and climate were much less hospitable for agriculture than the other regions. The typical farm in Connecticut, Rhode Island, Massachusetts, and New Hampshire was small and produced corn, wheat, and other hardy foodstuffs for the household. Because New England could not produce enough food for its own needs and had to import food, New England farmers became accustomed to combining other enterprises with farming. New Englanders on the seacoast took advantage of the rich opportunities for whaling and fishing, particularly for cod. New England merchants (originally protected by British mercantile laws) became heavily involved in the "carrying trades," shipping goods among the colonies and between the colonies and their export partners.[21] Plantation colonies

the Revolution (New York: Columbia University Press, 1980), p. 31. Of the South's wealth per person, £55 consisted of land and £58 slaves, in contrast to £27 of land in New England and none for slaves; Ross M. Robertson and Gary M. Walton, *History of the American Economy*, 4th ed. (New York: Harcourt Brace Jovanovich, 1977), p. 101.

[20] Walton and Shepard, *The Economic Rise of Early America*, p. 81; Walton and Rockoff, *History of the American Economy*, pp. 97–9; Allan Kulikoff, *From British Peasants to Colonial American Farmers* (Chapel Hill: University of North Carolina Press, 2000), p. 211.

[21] Main, *The Sovereign States, 1775–1783*, p. 76; Joseph L. Davis, *Sectionalism in American Politics, 1774–1787* (Madison: University of Wisconsin Press, 1977), pp. 16–19; Walton and Rockoff, *History of the American Economy*, pp. 94–113, 147–50.

shipped commodities that needed minimal processing. New England, in contrast, produced and shipped products that fostered many additional enterprises, including processing grain and timber; building ships; making casks, barrels, and fishing equipment; providing capital and insurance, and maintaining storage and transport facilities necessary for cargo transport.[22] New England had little stake in slavery or the slave trade. British carriers brought most of the slaves to the North American colonies. The region had a much greater interest than the South in a diversified, independent economy and in trade measures that could protect its own commercial and embryonic manufacturing interests.

Population and land disparities cut across regional interests and created rivalries among the states in each of these three regions. The 1790 census would show that 18 percent of the U.S. population lived in Virginia, and that nearly half the population lived in four states (Virginia, Pennsylvania, North Carolina, and Massachusetts) that were scattered across the economic regions. By 1787 Americans believed that population growth would inevitably favor the South. Foreign immigrants and Americans in the northern states were migrating across the Ohio River into the western areas of established southern states, into Kentucky and Tennessee, and into southern territories in such areas as Natchez and west Florida.[23] *Most* states were "small," at least from the perspective of Virginians like Washington and Madison or the Pennsylvanian James Wilson, and had strong reasons to feel threatened by the power of their larger neighbors nearby.[24]

[22] Newell, "The Birth of New England in the Atlantic Economy," p. 46.

[23] Kromkowski, *Recreating the American Republic*, p. 179; U.S. Census Bureau, *Historical Statistics of the United States* (Washington, DC: Government Printing Office, 1975), part I, pp. 24–37; Drew McCoy, "James Madison and Visions of American Nationality in the Confederation Period: A Regional Perspective," in *Beyond Confederation: Origins of the Constitution and American National Identity*, ed. Richard Beeman, Stephen Botein, and Edward Carter III (Chapel Hill: University of North Carolina Press, 1987), pp. 230–2.

[24] Some of the framers themselves discounted the small- versus large-state distinction as misleading. Both may be understood as strategic efforts to redefine the problem on more-favorable terms. Madison noted that it was "Pretty well understood that the real difference of interests lay, not between the large & small but between N[orthern] & South[er]n States. The institution of slavery & its consequences formed the line of discrimination" (*RFC* July 14, 2: 10). Hamilton observed that "The only considerable distinction of interests, lay between the carrying and non-carrying States, which divide instead of uniting the largest States" (*RFC* June 29, 1: 466). The characterization of state divisions as small versus large benefited both sides. Representatives of the three large states appealed to the injustice of equal representation in the Confederation Congress. Some of the representatives of states other than Virginia, Pennsylvania, and Massachusetts could appeal to

Disparities in access to land also cut across regions' political interests. Massachusetts, Pennsylvania, and the four southern states enjoyed land in abundance. Connecticut, New Jersey, Delaware, and Maryland had much less territory and sought to share access to the lands of other states. After the Revolution, the states took possession of the Northwest Territory and millions of acres of other ungranted lands formerly owned by the king, as well as the lands of many loyalists. The states used these lands to encourage the spread of small communities, as rewards for military service, and as a source of revenue for wartime debts.[25] But the evaporation of British control also removed the one constraint that prevented land rivalries from erupting into heated conflict. Rival land speculators struggled to enlist governments as allies in boosting their claims.[26] Virginia claimed part of Pennsylvania. Maryland claimed land in Virginia. New York sought to absorb Vermont, but the New England states insisted that Vermont remain an independent entity aligned with New England. Virginia and other southern states at one time opposed the admission of Vermont to the Confederation because they feared that another small state would join with existing small states in challenging the land-rich states' western claims. By opposing the admission of Vermont, the southern states also cultivated a political alliance with New York and separated it from potential northern allies.[27] In 1754 settlers from Connecticut purchased the Wyoming Valley in northeastern Pennsylvania from Indians, despite Pennsylvania's claim to the land. The Connecticut legislature designated the area a part

the rest as a block with a shared interest threatened by potential collusion among these states. The shifting voting alignments of the convention belie the claim that either the ten small states or the three large states shared a common purpose across issues.

[25] Curtis P. Nettels, *The Emergence of a National Economy, 1775–1815* (New York: Holt, Rinehart, and Winston, 1962), pp. 138, 146; Nevins, *The American States during and after the Revolution, 1775–1789*, p. 598; Forrest McDonald, *Novus Ordo Seclorum: The Intellectual Origins of the Constitution* (Lawrence: University Press of Kansas, 1985), pp. 218–19.

[26] Charles Beard, *An Economic Interpretation of the Constitution of the United States* (New York: Macmillan, 1913); McDonald, *We the People*; Robert E. Brown, *Charles Beard and the Constitution: A Critical Analysis of "An Economic Interpretation of the Constitution"* (New York: W. W. Norton, 1965).

[27] Jensen, *The Articles of Confederation*, p. 117; Nevins, *The American States during and after the Revolution, 1775–1789*, pp. 578–83, 595. The unequal value of land complicated these resentments. While the South had many tracts of sparsely developed land with modest value, much of New England's land had been improved substantially. This disparity conflict complicated national tax policy during the Confederation because southerners sought national taxes based on land values, whereas New England's representatives insisted on national taxes based on simple acreage; Ferguson, *The Power of the Purse*, p. 165.

of Connecticut and named it Westmoreland County in 1776. Despite its location within Pennsylvania, Westmoreland County elected members annually to the Connecticut legislature, paid Connecticut taxes, and lived under Connecticut laws upheld by Connecticut courts. Armed clashes between Connecticut and Pennsylvania settlers broke out. A special national commission ruled in 1782 that Pennsylvania held jurisdiction over the area. The dispute dragged on until 1787, and disputes over private claims were not addressed until 1799.[28]

The issue of control over the vast western lands overshadowed these smaller and more-limited disputes during the first years of the Confederation. Virginia's claim to land as far west as the "south seas" and to the northwest seemed to give Virginia unlimited territory. Land speculators recognized their opportunity and "found it easy to stake out vast areas west of the Alleghenies through their influence upon or presence in the Virginia legislature."[29] The half dozen states without any claims to western lands viewed the abundant western lands of Virginia and other states with resentment and apprehension. The settlement and cultivation of these lands would vastly increase the wealth and population of states like Virginia, enhancing the land-rich states' relative economic and political power and permitting the state to pay its debts effortlessly. Massachusetts and other physically constrained states anticipated the emigration of thousands of their residents to the superior climate and soils of the trans-Allegheny west.

Those speculators with influence in the legislatures of Virginia and other "landed" states pressured for the states to retain control over their lands. Speculators in other states lobbied state and national legislators to nationalize lands over which they sought control. Regional leaders also resented the financial burden placed on their developed land and argued for congressional control of Virginia's western lands to redistribute the costs of national governance. Maryland completed the Confederation only when British troops were approaching the state and Virginia began to show more willingness to relinquish its land claims. Virginia agreed to cede its western lands to the Confederation government if that government met certain conditions intended to protect its interests. Virginia ceded its title to lands north of the Ohio River to the United States government in 1784, at a time when the lands were becoming a burden to the state. The

[28] Nevins, *The American States during and after the Revolution, 1775–1789*, pp. 583–90; Roger Sherman Boardman, *Roger Sherman: Signer and Statesman* (Philadelphia: University of Pennsylvania Press, 1938), p. 162.

[29] Jensen, *The Articles of Confederation*, p. 151.

cession of Virginia's lands only intensified the states' interest in controlling the Confederation's land policy.[30]

Other issues cleaved the political interests of states with each region. Access to a supply of slaves split the southern states. The upper South had slaves in abundance and tended to favor a ban on the importation of slaves. The lower South, which received three-quarters of slaves in the late colonial period, opposed such a ban.[31] In the North, thriving port cities advantaged two middle states – Pennsylvania and New York – at the expense of their regional neighbors. If, for example, New York imposed an import tax on goods bound for New Jersey, New York could in effect pass the costs of governing itself along to the citizens of the neighboring state. In the years 1784–7, New York was deriving more than half its revenue from its imposts. Citizens in Maryland, New Jersey, and Connecticut depended on the ports of New York and Philadelphia for many goods, and they faced tariff-driven price increases for goods brought in through those ports. Foreign imports shipped through New York cost New Jersey buyers alone £40,000 annually.[32] Merchants and manufacturers also had conflicting policy interests. Merchants generally opposed tariffs because they raised the cost of transport. But domestic manufacturers, a growing force since the Revolution, often supported tariffs when they raised the costs of foreign competitors' goods. The northern cities contained the nation's three private banks: Philadelphia's Bank of North America, the Massachusetts Bank in Boston, and the Bank of New York.[33] Differences in agriculture, manufacture, commerce, population, wealth and income, land, ports, and the need for slaves fostered interstate resentments over their states' relative ability to fund their own governments and the Confederation.

The economic and political vulnerabilities of smaller states closer to the geographical center of the Confederation – Rhode Island, Connecticut, New Jersey, and Delaware – gave them a special stake in an improved

[30] Nevins, *The American States during and after the Revolution, 1775–1789*, p. 592; Jensen, *The Articles of Confederation*, pp. 150–1, 225–38; Davis, *Sectionalism in American Politics, 1774–1787*, p. 37; Stanley Lebergott, *The Americans, an Economic Record* (New York: W. W. Norton, 1984), pp. 75–6.

[31] Walton and Shepard, *The Economic Rise of Early America*, p. 102; McDonald, *Novus Ordo Seclorum*, pp. 217–18.

[32] Thomas C. Cochran, *New York in the Confederation: An Economic Study* (Philadelphia: University of Pennsylvania Press, 1932), p. 167; Merrill Jensen, *The New Nation: A History of the United States during the Confederation, 1781–1789* (New York: Vintage Books, 1965), p. 338; Robertson and Walton, *History of the American Economy*, pp. 69–70, 75, 87; Brown, *Redeeming the Republic*, p. 148.

[33] Main, *The Sovereign States, 1775–1783*, p. 81.

national policy infrastructure even while it made them anxious to ensure their autonomy within it. New Jersey, for example, had no public lands to sell and no ports to produce tariff revenues. Because its farmers had to ship their products through out-of-state ports, tariffs collected in Philadelphia and New York drained profits away from New Jersey residents into adjoining states.[34] New Jersey farmers, like their counterparts in Connecticut, supported fundamental change in the national government to end what they considered New York's discrimination against their products.[35] The state assumed the obligation of paying interest on Continental securities held by New Jersey citizens. State officials grew indignant as New Jersey received requests for additional funds for the Confederation while neighboring states funded their governments with revenues extracted from New Jersey citizens.[36] At the Constitutional Convention, James Madison pointed to New Jersey's situation as symptomatic of the problems of small states.[37]

By the 1780s it was clear that the states' diverse economic resources gave each state increasingly distinct economic advantages, disadvantages, and interests. It was equally clear that their policy autonomy gave them the means and the motive to exploit their economic endowments to the nation's disadvantage. The American states, in short, confronted a "prisoners' dilemma."[38] Because the states controlled tax, tariff, currency, and

[34] Put in more formal terms, New Jersey farmers were vulnerable to rent seeking from adjoining states. "Rent" here is a term used in economics to describe income that exceeds the level needed to attract it to any alternative use, or the excess of income over opportunity cost.

[35] Nettels, *The Emergence of a National Economy, 1775–1815*, p. 93.

[36] Ferguson, *The Power of the Purse*, pp. 230–1; Richard P. McCormick, *New Jersey from Colony to State* (New Brunswick, NJ: Rutgers University Press, 1964), pp. 164–8.

[37] "N[ew] Jersey has been made one society out of two parts. Should a separation of the States take place, the fate of N[ew] Jersey w[oul]d be worst of all. She has no foreign commerce & can have but little. P[ennsylvani]a & N[ew] York will continue to levy taxes on her consumption" (*RFC* June 29, 1: 462).

[38] The name is taken from an imaginary situation in which two individuals are arrested for a theft in which both participated. The police keep each in isolation from the other and interrogate them separately. Each knows that there is enough evidence to convict them both on a minor charge that will result in a one-year sentence, and if both keep quiet, both will receive a one-year sentence. The police want a stiffer sentence, however. Each is told in interrogation that if she confesses to the crime, she will receive a short sentence (say, three months), although the other defendant will receive a very long sentence (for example, ten years). But each also knows that if *both* confess, each will receive a five-year sentence. Clearly, each prisoner is tempted to act opportunistically, to benefit herself at the expense of the other. If each prisoner acts in her self-interest alone, she will choose to confess, but if each confesses, both will be worse off (with five-year sentences) than if they did not confess (one-year sentences). In other words, each individual would make a rational choice to benefit herself, but in doing so, that choice would *collectively* make

land policy, and because they had different endowments of land, labor, capital, and other economic resources, each state had very strong incentives to resist policies that sacrificed their constituents' interests for the good of the nation as a whole. Each state could gain more in the short term from acting independently than by cooperating for the common good. As Alexander Hamilton put it in 1782, "Urge reforms or exertions and the answer constantly is what avails it for one state to . . . make them without the concert of the others?"[39] These incentives were made even stronger by the fact that state legislators, elected for short terms by relatively large electorates, had every reason to accede to their constituents' immediate demands, and no reason to compromise with the legislators in other states. No state was so economically dominant that it could unilaterally make economic sacrifices in order to benefit smaller neighbors to induce them to cooperate in a common economic policy. Nation-states in the contemporary international political economy face a similar dilemma.[40]

Although the Constitution's framers did not use the term "prisoners' dilemma," they understood that economic differences and cooperation problems were putting the Confederation's political economy under serious stress.[41] The national government was poorly equipped to rectify these problems. The Articles of Confederation had established a national government meant to protect state sovereignty and the protection of state comparative advantages. It did this all too well.

THE POLITICS OF THE ARTICLES OF CONFEDERATION

Emissaries from thirteen infant polities formed the Continental Congress that declared American independence. State delegates to Congress were

both prisoners worse off than if they cooperated with each other. The importance of the game is to set forth rigorously the problem of getting individuals, organizations, or nation-states to cooperate with one another when they have strong incentives not to do so. See Russell Hardin, *Collective Action* (Baltimore: Johns Hopkins University Press, 1982); Robert M. Axelrod, *The Evolution of Cooperation* (New York: Basic Books, 1984), pp. 3–24.

[39] Hamilton to Robert Morris, July 22, 1782, in *PRM* 6: 7–8. Madison later made a similar argument in the Virginia convention called to ratify the Constitution (ED June 11, 1788, 3: 250).

[40] Beth V. Yarborough and Robert M. Yarborough, "Cooperation in the Liberalization of International Trade: After Hegemony, What?" in *International Political Economy: A Reader*, ed. Kendall W. Stiles and Tsuneo Akaha (New York: HarperCollins, 1991), pp. 159, 164.

[41] At the Constitutional Convention of 1787, Charles Pinckney, referring to diverse state commercial interests, remarked that the states pursued "their interests with less scruple than individuals" (*RFC* August 29, 2: 449).

agents of their states. With unusual candor, Rhode Island had directed its delegates to consult with other delegates, "taking the greatest Care to secure to this Colony, in the strongest and most perfect Manner, its present established Form, and all the Powers of Government, so far as relates to its internal Police and Conduct of our own Affairs, civil and religious."[42] Only North Carolina actually required its delegates to accept the collective decisions of this first Congress. John Adams and other leaders described Congress as a "diplomatic assembly."[43]

The very name "Congress," a word that suggests conclaves of sovereign European nations in the seventeenth century, indicated the independent, equal status each colony enjoyed. From the start, congressional rules provided each state with one equal vote on legislation. No other voting formula would ensure that every colony would remain in the coalition. The rule continued into the second Continental Congress, and it became routine for states to be represented equally on important committees.[44]

When it declared in 1776 that the British Crown no longer made legitimate policy for the American colonies, the Second Continental Congress immediately confronted the urgent need for national public policy to replace it. The rebels needed a Continental military force, Continental emissaries to potential allies abroad, and revenues and supplies for both. When the first Continental Congress declared that the states should cooperate in refusing to trade with Britain, its action marked the first national public-policy initiative of the United States. As it moved toward declaring the colonies' independence in the spring of 1776, the Second Congress had been coordinating American military policy for a year, planned the defense of New York, and placed George Washington in command of the Continental military. Congress borrowed money, negotiated treaties, selected national military officers, and established a navy and marine corps. On May 10, 1776, Congress adopted a resolution urging states that had not yet reconstituted their governments as independent entities to do so. On June 12, 1776 – a day after it created the committee that drafted the

[42] *JCC* May 14, 1776, 4: 353.

[43] Nevins, *The American States during and after the Revolution, 1775–1789*, pp. 624, 660; Jack N. Rakove, *Original Meanings: Politics and Ideas in the Making of the Constitution* (New York: Alfred A. Knopf, 1996), p. 206.

[44] Nevins, *The American States during and after the Revolution, 1775–1789*, pp. 606–7; Jack N. Rakove, *The Beginnings of National Politics: An Interpretive History of the Continental Congress* (New York: Alfred Knopf, 1979), pp. 141–4; Benson Bobrick, *Angel in the Whirlwind: The Triumph of the American Revolution* (New York: Simon and Schuster, 1997), pp. 93–4, 104–5.

Declaration of Independence – Congress appointed a representative from each state to a committee charged with drafting a set of rules for establishing a permanent government for the confederation of the American states.

The committee, dominated by cautious republicans such as John Dickinson of Pennsylvania, initially proposed to increase the power of the Continental Congress substantially.[45] The final committee draft, heavily influenced by Dickinson, proposed a confederation government that would determine peace and war, negotiate foreign treaties, establish post offices, coin money, incur loans, and settle boundary disputes. Each of the thirteen states would continue to cast one vote in Congress. A simple majority (seven votes) would determine routine policy matters, and nine votes would be required for treaties and important economic policy decisions, such as spending and borrowing. The national government could not tax the states but could requisition funds from them. The larger and wealthier the state, the larger the requisition payment it would be obligated to pay to the Confederation government. A Council of State would provide executive continuity when Congress was in recess. This Dickinson draft of the Articles explicitly limited state sovereignty and established national policy supremacy: "Each Colony shall retain and enjoy as much of its present Laws, Rights and Customs, as it may think fit, and reserves to itself the sole and exclusive Regulation and Government of its internal police, in all matters that shall not interfere with the Articles of this Confederation." This provision placed the burden of proof on the states for retaining the exercise of policy authority.[46]

The Dickinson plan's steps toward centralized power forced state interests to the surface of the congressional debate. Delegates from the larger states insisted that representation in Congress be made proportional to population size – that is, states with larger populations would have more representatives in Congress than states with smaller populations. Smaller states defended the states' equal votes. Roger Sherman of Connecticut

[45] Merrill Jensen distinguishes between conservative and radical American leaders in *The Articles of Confederation* and labels Dickinson a conservative. But divisions in the Continental Congress occurred within a consensus on republican values and played out in different ways on different issues. Jack Rakove questions the validity and utility of Jensen's uncomplicated distinction between radicals and conservatives in the Continental Congress in *The Beginnings of National Politics*, pp. xiv–xvii, 171–2. Accordingly, I avoid the term "conservative" to label members of Congress who shared Dickinson's instincts.

[46] Jensen, *The Articles of Confederation*, pp. 127–39, 254–61; Ferguson, *The Power of the Purse*, pp. 111–12; Rakove, *The Beginnings of National Politics*, pp. 151–8.

explicitly viewed the delegates as state agents, argued that proportional representation would result in the dominance of three states, and urged that votes require a concurrent majority of *both* the states and individual members of Congress. Delegates from states with western lands feared that landless states (and the politically influential speculators in them) would command national power to confiscate their land assets. Slave-holding states objected to the apportionment of state financial obligations on the basis of population, demanding that these obligations be distributed on the basis of land values, placing a relatively greater financial burden on the North. North Carolina's Thomas Burke, warning colleagues against a strong central government, advocated greater protections for the sovereignty of the states.[47]

Torn by these bitter crosscutting rivalries, Congress prolonged debate on the Articles through late 1777 and finally changed Dickinson's plan to further protect the states' authority. After designating the Confederacy as "The United States of America," the final version of the Articles incorporated Burke's motion that "Each state retains its sovereignty, freedom, and independence, and every power, jurisdiction, and right, which is not by this Confederation expressly delegated to the United States" and bound the states to "a firm league of friendship with each other, for their common defense, the security of their liberties, and their mutual and general welfare." The Articles imposed few absolute limitations on state government, other than the republican principle that no state could grant a title of nobility and that states would not maintain standing military power in peacetime (Article VI). Only on issues of war and diplomacy did the Articles prohibit state action without the consent of Congress (Articles VI, IX). Each state, regardless of size, would continue to cast a single vote in Congress. State legislatures controlled the choice of delegates and their pay. The Articles provided that the state legislatures could choose delegates to Congress in whatever fashion they chose, send as few as two or as many as seven delegates, and recall them at any time. Once adopted, the Articles could not be changed or amended without the consent of every state.

The final Articles made it nearly impossible for Congress to act without extraordinarily widespread agreement among the varied states. The

[47] Jensen, *The Articles of Confederation*, pp. 138–41; Christopher Collier, *Roger Sherman's Connecticut: Yankee Politics and the American Revolution* (Middletown, CT: Wesleyan University Press, 1971), p. 157; Rakove, *The Beginnings of National Politics*, pp. 158–82; Kromkowski, *Recreating the American Republic*, pp. 158–95.

Articles required a supermajority of nine states to enact major defense and financial policies and required large majorities for establishing a quorum to undertake any business. These rules permitted a single state or a few states to use the rules to block action. In practice, the states' diverse interests ensured that coalitions would form and break apart in Congress repeatedly and from issue to issue. No stable coalitions emerged to help organize and resolve policy disputes in Congress. The agenda was haphazard and uncoordinated, so that it was difficult for a majority to steer a program through Congress. Delegate turnover undermined policy stability. The supermajority of nine required for any significant government action, accentuated with absenteeism rates that increased as time went on, made it increasingly difficult for Congress to legislate at all. When the common threat from Britain receded after 1781, national issues became even more divisive. The unanimity of common revolutionary cause gave way to a series of policy disputes that Congress proved incapable of resolving. The president of Congress chaired legislative sessions, corresponded with state governors and diplomats, and signed congressional resolutions and addresses, but had no power over the members or the way they were chosen. Not surprisingly, the position lacked appeal. Congress had fourteen presidents from 1774 through 1789.[48]

The final Articles conceded to the national government only those limited powers viewed widely as indispensable for protecting the collective independence of the states. The Confederation government could declare war, control a national military, negotiate peace, engage in international diplomacy, and regulate trade with the Indians. It had sole power to regulate the value of money, fix uniform standards of weights and measures, and establish post offices. The Articles "solemnly pledged" to redeem debts incurred by the national Congress (Article XII).

At the same time, the revised Articles protected each state's economic assets. On the bitterly divisive question of the control of land, Virginia delegate Richard Henry Lee successfully added a provision "that no State shall be deprived of territory for the benefit of the United States," marking a complete victory for the landed states. Congress could not exercise any

[48] Calvin C. Jillson and Rick K. Wilson, *Congressional Dynamics: Structure, Coordination, and Choice in the First American Congress, 1774–1789* (Stanford, CA: Stanford University Press, 1994), pp. 134–63; Keith L. Dougherty, *Collective Action under the Articles of Confederation* (Cambridge: Cambridge University Press, 2001); Richard B. Morris, *The Forging of the Union: 1781–1789* (New York: Harper and Row, 1987), pp. 92–4, 99–101.

exclusive power over the nation's interior.[49] Most important, Article IX confirmed state control over interstate trade, banning any commercial treaty that would compromise the states' power to impose "such imposts and duties on foreigners, as their own people are subjected to, or from prohibiting the exportation or importation of any species of goods or commodities whatsoever." These rules permitted a state with a large port, such as New York, to tax imports from abroad and exports to other states. States could impose import taxes unless these interfered with national agreements with France or Spain. Instead of establishing clear national policy guidelines for the states, the Articles encouraged the states to harmonize their legal relationships. Article IV guaranteed American citizens freedom of travel, trade, and commerce among the states and entitled them to "all privileges and immunities of free citizens in the several States." Criminals could not flee to another state to escape justice. States were obliged to give full faith and credit to the judicial proceedings and records of other states. Article IX established a convoluted process for resolving interstate disputes. Temporary commissions would judge any dispute, a provision that ensured that Congress would not develop the ongoing capacity to umpire interstate conflict.

Public finance exposed the basic ineffectiveness of the Confederation government. A steady revenue is an indispensable requirement for effective government, but the Articles denied the national government a reliable revenue stream. The Confederation Congress could borrow money, and could requisition funds from the states, but had no independent source of revenue, no power to tax, and no power to compel the states to pay their requisitions (Article XI). By allowing the states to choose how to raise the funds to pay their share of the Confederation's costs, the Articles allowed states to protect their own revenue sources and shift the fiscal burden onto a minority or onto residents of neighboring states. The final version of the Articles based each state's share of the nation's financial burden on the value of lands plus improvements, a formula particularly disadvantageous to New England. Congress approved this provision of the Articles on a five-to-four vote, with the New England states yielding to the rest, but resistance to this funding formula plagued government under the Articles. When Congress stopped issuing paper money in the fall of 1779, states were asked to assume the costs of conducting the Revolution, diminishing the Confederation's influence still further. With Congress nearly helpless

[49] Rakove, *The Beginnings of National Politics*, p. 159.

in 1780, the states at the military front used their authority directly to procure supplies for the Continental army.[50]

Even when the cumbersome national policy process produced a decision, such as a requisition for money, the Articles made the policy hard to implement. At its first opportunity to implement a decision, regarding desertion from the Continental army, Congress delegated enforcement to the states.[51] The final draft removed the Dickinson proposal to vest enforcement powers in a Council of State and provided for a weaker body, a Committee of the States.[52] Separate administrative departments did not exist until 1781. After the end of the revolution, the only surviving single-headed departments were War, Foreign Affairs, and the Post Office. A three-member commission received responsibility for financial affairs, and congressional investigating committees constantly questioned its decisions.[53] Fraud and corruption during the war, when exigency made public and private interest hard to sort out, diminished the legitimacy and respect for national administration. States could appoint the officials responsible for managing state requisition payments to Congress.[54] Superintendent of Finance Robert Morris organized a group of federal financial administrators, but these Confederation offices did not survive after he left his post in 1784.

As a confederation of independent nation-states, the Articles created a comparatively strong bond between sovereign polities, a league "as cohesive and strong as any similar sort of republican confederation in history."[55] But as a national government, the Articles granted relatively little authority to the central government, and it could not use that authority very effectively. In its letter urging the states to approve the Articles, Congress acknowledged that the final product reflected the difficulty of reconciling the interests of the different states. This letter made it plain that the Articles resulted not from philosophical speculation but political compromise among rival states, for it could not be expected "that any

[50] Ferguson, *The Power of the Purse*, pp. 46–7, 61.

[51] Jensen, *The Articles of Confederation*, pp. 171–9.

[52] Morris, *The Forging of the Union*, pp. 97–8. Rakove views the Committee of the States as a reversion toward the Dickinson draft of the Confederation; see *The Beginnings of National Politics*, p. 180. The committee did not meet until the summer of 1784, and proved exceptionally difficult to organize.

[53] Morris, *The Forging of the Union*, pp. 95–6.

[54] Ferguson, *The Power of the Purse*, pp. 27–8, 81–105, 141.

[55] Wood, *The Creation of the American Republic, 1776–1787*, p. 359.

plan, in the variety of provisions essential to our union, should exactly correspond with the maxims and political views of every particular State."[56] Congress's apologetic testimonial foreshadowed the deepening policy crisis of the 1780s.

FINANCE, TRADE, AND THE POLITICAL FAILURE OF THE CONFEDERATION

In the half dozen years that followed the British surrender at Yorktown in 1781, the state governments steadily gained strength and experience. The states developed more effective tax systems, printed money, governed credit and property, and managed commerce. They also developed more distrust and rivalry. Even before the war's end, some in the four southern colonies feared that other Americans would end hostilities with Britain on terms that would permit it to retain control over the south.[57] These rivalries converged in the Confederation government, which seemed to grow more helpless and irrelevant as state cooperation seemed increasingly impossible to engineer. Finance and commerce lie at the heart of policy divisions in the 1780s. Revenue and trade policies brought the nation to the brink of disunion, the national government to the brink of irrelevance, and a growing number of Americans to the conviction that specific changes in national policy making would result in indispensable benefits.

Economic depression in the 1780s intensified pressures on state legislatures to use their authority to protect the mass of their voting constituents. Propelled by the evaporation of wartime demand and by the closure of the British West Indies to American trade in 1783, per capita gross national product dropped from $804 (in 1980 dollars) in 1774 to $437 in 1790, a decline comparable with that during the Great Depression of 1929–33. Only at the beginning of the nineteenth century did the United States return to the levels of income and wealth of the 1770s. The South and New England were hit particularly hard. Farm prices fell, money became scarce, and pauperism and indebtedness rose. Bankers and creditors gained at the expense of a majority of citizens, stoking mass resentment. A perceived shortage of gold and silver coins drove down prices and put debtors, especially small farmers, under increasing pressure. Foreign producers required Americans to pay for imports in specie, further increasing

[56] *JCC* November 17, 1777, 9: 933.
[57] Davis, *Sectionalism in American Politics, 1774–1787*, pp. 25–6.

financial burdens. There were no mints in the country to produce additional specie. Congress failed to ensure a supply of money. The three private banks tended to withdraw notes from circulation during the depression. State government debts grew.[58]

Finance: The Foundation of Government Power

State legislators naturally drew on their arsenal of policy tools to relieve their constituents, paying little attention to the consequences of their policies beyond their jurisdictions. Most legislators had been reluctant to tax their hard-pressed constituents even with the British military on their doorstep. When the desperately indebted freeholders demanded government relief in response to the economic battering and the hounding creditors of the 1780s, state legislators responded rapidly. State governments revived the paper money emissions used by their colonial predecessors. Georgia, South Carolina, North Carolina, New Jersey, New York, Rhode Island, and Pennsylvania issued paper currency to help raise prices and aid the debt-ridden farmers. Paper money proponents were narrowly beaten back in four other states. To put this currency in the hands of debtors, states issued bills of credit to pay state debts and loaned money to citizens on the security of their land.

This paper money often depreciated rapidly, and, as it fell in value, many creditors refused to accept it in payment for debts. Some states, in response, simply used their policy authority to require creditors to accept the paper bills as they would accept gold or silver. New York's courts agreed with litigants who sought to enforce New York's paper issue of 1786 as legal tender. Other states enacted "stay" laws that suspended debt payments for a period of time. South Carolina in 1782 delayed debt repayments until 1786. Rhode Island issued an exceptionally large amount of currency and made it available at unusually low interest rates. A state law fined creditors who refused to accept the money in payment for debts (including state government debts). Another law provided for a special trial for offending creditors without a jury or right of appeal. When merchants refused to accept the money anyway and closed their stores, rioting erupted. Rhode Island then abrogated the debts. Although its policies were

[58] John J. McCusker and Russell Menard, *The Economy of British America, 1607–1789* (Chapel Hill: University of North Carolina Press, 1985), pp. 366–7, 373–6; Morris, *The Forging of the Union*, pp. 134, 136–7; Nettels, *The Emergence of a National Economy, 1775–1815*, p. 93; Main, *The Sovereign States, 1775–1783*, pp. 261–7.

widely reviled outside the state, Rhode Island was nearly debt-free when it joined the Union in 1790.[59]

Many of these state financial policies seemed to help voters in these states at the expense of Americans in other states. North Carolina merchants had to accept state-issued notes in payment for debts, but merchants found that these notes were not accepted as payments for debts outside the state or overseas. New Jersey's large issue of legal-tender bills of credit in 1786 depreciated rapidly in neighboring New York and Pennsylvania, where many New Jersey citizens were in debt to creditors and merchants. Massachusetts and Connecticut residents refused to ship produce and goods to Rhode Island.[60]

Massachusetts's contrary financial policy resulted in an even greater threat to creditors across the nation. Massachusetts after 1777 followed an unusually restrictive policy favored by creditors instead of debtors. Massachusetts rejected paper money, imposed the highest taxes of any of the states, developed a strict enforcement system, and collected much of its revenue in specie. These policies burdened citizens who were barely subsisting in the depression. Hostility to this policy mounted. When the state imposed heavy tax burdens to compensate for the depression, taxes went unpaid and many farmers were taken to court in foreclosure proceedings. Massachusetts's government seemed to lose control over parts of the state. In western Massachusetts, Daniel Shays, a veteran of the Revolutionary War, organized an army of debtors that forced local courts to suspend foreclosures. Shays's followers seized several towns and threatened to take the military garrison in Springfield. Massachusetts was not alone. In New Hampshire, paper money advocates descended on the legislature and held it captive until the militia came to its rescue.[61]

[59] Nettels, *The Emergence of a National Economy, 1775–1815*, pp. 75–81; Nevins, *The American States during and after the Revolution, 1775–1789*, p. 525; Main, *The Sovereign States, 1775–1783*, p. 235; Irwin H. Polishook, *Rhode Island and the Union, 1774–1795* (Evanston, IL: Northwestern University Press, 1969); Ferguson, *The Power of the Purse*, pp. 243–4; Brown, *Redeeming the Republic*, pp. 83–96.

[60] James Madison to Thomas Jefferson, August 12, 1786, in *PJM* 10: 231–2; Mary M. Schweitzer, "State-Issued Currency and the Ratification of the U.S. Constitution," *Journal of Economic History* 49:2 (June 1989): 311–22; Nettels, *The Emergence of a National Economy, 1775–1815*, p. 83; McDonald, *Novus Ordo Seclorum*, p. 156.

[61] Ferguson, *The Power of the Purse*, pp. 245–9; Main, *The Sovereign States, 1775–1783*, p. 235; Becker, *Revolution, Reform, and the Politics of American Taxation, 1763–1783*, pp. 121–8; David P. Szatmary, *Shays's Rebellion: The Making of an American Insurrection* (Amherst: University of Massachusetts Press, 1980); Brown, *Redeeming the Republic*, pp. 108–21; Leonard L. Richards, *Shays's Rebellion: The American Revolution's Final Battle* (Philadelphia: University of Pennsylvania Press, 2003); Nettels, *The Emergence of a National Economy, 1775–1815*, p. 86.

Without the fundamental government power to tax, the national government's finances fell hostage to the states' increasingly effective policy independence. State legislatures were very reluctant to transfer hard-won state revenues along to the Congress to fulfill their financial obligation to the federation. Each state government cited its previous sacrifices for the nation's independence.[62] Virginia claimed expenses for Revolutionary War expenditures that were not authorized by Congress and poorly documented. New York claimed the prolonged occupation of New York should exempt the state from requisitions.[63] None of the states came close to contributing the full quota of funds that the Congress requisitioned for the national treasury. During the Confederation period, states at best provided one dollar for every eight dollars requested by the Congress, and compliance dropped considerably from nearly 12 percent in mid-1784 to less than 2 percent from mid-1786 to mid-1787. Congress had run up an enormous debt during the Revolution, and the increasing failure of requisitions to fund the national government's expenses pressed it harder and harder. By midsummer of 1786, Congress was out of money. The Confederation government had stopped paying the principal on foreign debts and now defaulted on the interest. It could not fund its own immediate expenditures or provide for adequate defense.[64]

These efforts to give the national government the power to levy taxes failed. Congress in 1781 sent the states an amendment to the Articles of Confederation authorizing it to tax imports up to 5 percent. Although a dozen states ratified the amendment, Rhode Island's refusal to ratify prevented the required unanimity and the proposal died. Rhode Island leaders argued that the proposed impost "derogated from the Sovereignty and Independence of the State." Its congressional representative, David Howell, complained that Rhode Island was being asked to surrender its commercial advantage to states such as Virginia with an unfair claim to western lands. Rhode Island, Howell wrote, "is subjected from its maritime situations to greater losses and risks in war, without any claim of reimbursement" and therefore "if any revenue can be raised from trade ... the State is entitled to the exclusive benefit thereof, and that the amount annually passed to the credit, and be collected by officers of their own appointment."[65] Rhode Island's refusal caused Virginia to rescind its approval.

[62] Robert Morris to the President of Congress, August 28, 1781, in *PRM* 2: 124–35; Nevins, *The American States during and after the Revolution, 1775–1789*, p. 574.

[63] Ferguson, *The Power of the Purse*, pp. 206–9.

[64] Dougherty, *Collective Action under the Articles of Confederation*, pp. 43, 80–1; Ferguson, *The Power of the Purse*, pp. 220–1.

[65] David Howell to Robert Morris, c. July 31–August 2, 1782, in *PRM* 6: 113–14.

Virginia held that taxes levied on Virginians by any body other than the state legislature would injure Virginia's "Sovereignty and may prove destructive to the rights and liberty of the people."[66]

In 1783 Congress took up a new amendment permitting a tax on imports, as well as a new bill for Confederation requisitions. New England interests forcefully put the case that the Articles imposed an unfair burden on their region and protected the South. Representatives from New England also sought to make population, rather than land (as specified in the Articles), the basis for apportioning state obligations for federal finance. When this debate resulted in a requisition bill that based state obligations on population, it made the counting of slaves a sensitive political issue. The Congress compromised on a formula that counted slaves for tax purposes on a basis of three-fifths of the white population, a formula carried over into the representation in the House of Representatives under the Constitution.[67]

In April 1783 Congress also proposed a new amendment to the Articles to authorize a national impost. Bowing to the states' earlier objections, this new proposal permitted the states to retain some power to administer the taxes and limited the authorization to twenty-five years. Rhode Island approved this version of the national impost, but now New York refused, in part because the federal tax threatened to reduce state tariff collections from its great port. Upstate agricultural interests could expect little but increased land taxes if New York sacrificed its tariff income.[68] When the New York legislature took up the impost amendment in the spring of 1786, it struck the provision permitting Congress to control the collection of the impost and replaced it with New York's 1784 law providing entirely for state administration of import duties. New York now directly challenged national authority. The state proposed to retain effective control of how and how much it would contribute to the Continental treasury. A congressional committee declared the New York bill out of compliance with the impost and asked New York governor George Clinton to call

[66] Ferguson, *The Power of the Purse*, p. 153; Nettels, *The Emergence of a National Economy, 1775–1815*, p. 95; Davis, *Sectionalism in American Politics, 1774–1787*, pp. 37–9; Becker, *Revolution, Reform, and the Politics of American Taxation, 1763–1783*, p. 205; Janet A. Riesman, "Money, Credit, and Federalist Political Economy," in Beeman, Botein, and Carter, *Beyond Confederation*, p. 143.

[67] Davis, *Sectionalism in American Politics, 1774–1787*, p. 49.

[68] Cochran, *New York in the Confederation*, pp. 159, 168; Nettels, *The Emergence of a National Economy, 1775–1815*, p. 95; Davis, *Sectionalism in American Politics, 1774–1787*, p. 48.

a special session of the legislature to rectify it. Clinton declined. When Congress insisted, Clinton declined more forcefully, and the state legislature and public opinion began to rally to his defense.[69]

Gradually, Congress lost virtually all control over public finance. By the mid-1780s, states even began to assume control over payments of national government debts. By taking over control of the payments to constituent-debtors, the states further strengthened their financial authority and weakened the Confederation. By assuming payment of national obligations, states independently raised their own revenues without regard for interstate interests or national commerce. Most notably, New Jersey asserted its financial independence of the Confederation. The state's citizens held a large share of the public debt. New Jersey officials resented the fact that their voters were paying, in effect, a share of New York's Confederation obligations when they paid an impost on goods from New York. While New York was rejecting the impost amendment, New Jersey resolved to withhold its requisition payment to Congress until all the states had ratified the amendment. To all intents and purposes, New Jersey formally seceded from the congressional requisition system in 1786 and defied the Articles. It announced that it was assuming direct control over Confederation debt within its borders. After a congressional committee hastily conferred with New Jersey leaders, the state legislature rescinded the resolution, but it did not comply with the requisition.[70]

In mid-1786 the Continental Board of Treasury gave a thoroughly gloomy assessment of the national government's finances:

> If it be asked what expectations there are that the several States will raise by the ordinary mode of Requisition, the Sums required by the proposed Report, the Answer obviously is, That no reasonable hope of this nature can possibly exist.... almost the whole of the Specie required by the Requisition of the 27th. September last, which amounted to One Million of Dollars, is still unpaid; though the period of payment was fixed for the First of May last; together with a Specie Balance due on the Requisition of the 27th April, 1784, of about One Million of Dollars; so that the actual Sum which ought to be paid by the several States, into the Public Treasury before the First of January next, is at least 3,700,000 Dollars. In examining the measures which have been adopted by the several States for

[69] Cochran, *New York in the Confederation*, pp. 172–6; Davis, *Sectionalism in American Politics, 1774–1787*, p. 57; Linda Grant De Pauw, *The Eleventh Pillar: New York State and the Federal Constitution* (Ithaca, NY: Cornell University Press, 1966), pp. 34–43; Dougherty, *Collective Action under the Articles of Confederation*, pp. 70–2.

[70] Ferguson, *The Power of the Purse*, pp. 221, 231; Murrin, *To Save This State from Ruin*, pp. 65–6; Dougherty, *Collective Action under the Articles of Confederation*, pp. 72–3.

carrying into execution the last Requisition ... [only seven states] have passed Acts directing the payment of the full Sums in Specie ... Connecticut, New Jersey, Delaware, and North Carolina have passed no Acts ... in compliance [and] from the State of South Carolina ... no payment can be expected. ... In considering what Expedients may probably be adopted for making up the deficiency of the Specie Sums which are essentially necessary to Support our Existence in a National Character. Nothing occurs as a probable mode of relief, but a Sale in Europe of part of the Western Territory, which has been ceded to the United States. The more our Reflections are employed on this Subject, the more we are impressed with a Conviction, that nothing but an immediate and general Adoption of the Measures recommended by the Resolves of Congress of the 18th. April, 1783, can rescue us from Bankruptcy, or preserve the Union of the several States from Dissolution.[71]

Its 1787 requisition waived all stipulations on the states and permitted the states to service the public debt within their borders in any way they chose.[72] Congress had completely surrendered the control of public finance to the states.

Commerce: The Foundation of Economic Management

Establishing national direction of trade and commerce proved as discouraging as public finance. State legislatures seemed to have limitless power to embargo or slap fees on imports, exports, or vessels from other countries or states. During the war, Pennsylvania and other states embargoed the export of necessary foodstuffs to their neighbors.[73] Although the states eliminated duties on imports after they declared independence, they reestablished tariffs in the 1780s to gain needed revenues. State imposts were politically attractive. Imposts disguised taxes in the higher prices constituents paid for goods, relieving legislatures of some of the blame for the tax burden, and sometimes protected in-state producers by limiting competition.[74] The states steadily grew more accustomed to these economic tools and bolder in using them to build political support among their constituents.

[71] *JCC* June 27, 1786, 30: 359–66.

[72] Ferguson, *The Power of the Purse*, p. 227.

[73] Giesecke, *American Commercial Legislation before 1789*, pp. 124–5.

[74] The general principle that constituents underestimate the cost of indirect and hidden taxes, such as tariffs and value-added taxes, is termed "fiscal illusion"; see Wallace E. Oates, "On the Nature and Measurement of Fiscal Illusion: A Survey," in *Taxation and Fiscal Federalism: Essays in Honour of Russell Mathews*, ed. G. Brennan, B. S. Grewel, and P. Groenwegen (Sydney: Australia University Press, 1988), pp. 65–82.

By the end of the 1770s the thirteen states were pursuing different trade policies attuned to their economic interests and their political orders. In the South, duties remained low. But soon Virginia and the middle and northern states began to develop elaborate impost schedules structured to the state's economic advantage. Initially, these tariffs aimed to discriminate against Britain. In July 1785, for example, New York imposed double duties on all goods imported from Britain. Next, most of these northern and middle states established protective tariffs, as Pennsylvania put it frankly in 1785, "to encourage and protect the Manufactures of this State, by laying additional Duties on the Importation of certain Manufactures which interfere with them." New York, Pennsylvania, Massachusetts, and most of the New England states laid duties of 5 to 15 percent on hats, boots, shoes, and saddles from Europe.[75]

States began to regard their neighbors' trade laws as predatory. New York's 1785 tariff law imposed identical duties for British goods brought in from neighboring states as from England. The law raised port fees and tonnage duties for vessels from Connecticut and New Jersey, increasing the effective price of produce from these two states in New York, to the advantage of New York producers. Some of the states imposed tonnage duties on any ship owned outside the state, including ships from other states; these duties were intended for revenue and not protection. Although adverse effects of such laws were much the exception rather than the rule, these self-serving state commercial laws created an apparently growing and politically ominous precedent.[76]

The middle states of New Jersey, Connecticut, and Delaware, vulnerable to the superior commercial muscle of the ports of Philadelphia and New York, seized on the opportunities that their neighbors' growing mercantilism created. New Jersey in 1784 designated Perth Amboy and Burlington as free ports for twenty-five years. Delaware also created free ports in 1786. By the spring of 1787 New York added entrance and clearance fees for all vessels bound to or from Connecticut and New Jersey. When New Jersey complained to the Continental Congress about New York's action, Congress could do little more than advise the state

[75] Davis, *Sectionalism in American Politics, 1774–1787*, p. 85; Giesecke, *American Commercial Legislation before 1789*, pp. 127–35.

[76] Giesecke, *American Commercial Legislation before 1789*, pp. 135, 139. Madison later recalled that, at the Constitutional Convention, "New Jersey, placed between Phil[adelphi]a & N[ew] York, was likened to a Cask tapped at both ends: and N[orth] Carolina between Virg[ini]a. & S[outh] Carolina to a patient bleeding at both Arms." James Madison, "Preface to Debates in the Convention of 1787" (*RFC* 3: 542).

to retaliate.[77] Britain, seeking to exploit the commercial autonomy of the states, was planning to send consuls to approach individual states with trade agreements, thus bypassing the national government altogether. Collective action even for regional advantage became impossible. When New Hampshire, Massachusetts, and Rhode Island prohibited British vessels from unloading in their ports in 1785, Connecticut took advantage, discriminating against foreign imports brought in from other states and welcoming direct British trade through the ports of New Haven and New London.[78]

While commercial rivalry within regions grew more serious, national cooperation foundered on the increasingly intense rivalry between states in different regions of the country. When Britain cut off American trade with the West Indies in 1783, antagonism to Britain prompted support for national laws permitting Congress to prohibit imports and exports of foreign goods on foreign ships. In late 1784 Congress discussed an amendment to the Articles giving Congress permanent power to regulate trade between foreign nations and the United States and among the American states, and to set imposts on this trade. Even this proposal was laced with precautions to protect state sovereignty: any state could still prohibit the import or export of any kind of goods. States would collect all duties, and these collections would be kept as state funds.[79] But two years later only Massachusetts, New York, New Jersey, and Virginia had agreed to the plan, and these states made their acceptance conditional on acceptance by all of the other states. Delaware, Georgia, and South Carolina had ignored the request, and the rest of the states demanded amendments.[80]

Congress found national commercial reform increasingly divisive. Northern states, with ships and seamen, were ready to assert themselves in world trade. Northern interests supported a national commercial law that would favor American carriers and manufacturers. By the mid-1780s southern leaders suspected that New England sought to monopolize American trade at the South's expense. The South, with staple export

[77] Giesecke, *American Commercial Legislation before 1789*, pp. 126, 135; Nevins, *The American States during and after the Revolution, 1775–1789*, pp. 558–61; Nettels, *The Emergence of a National Economy, 1775–1815*, pp. 69, 72–3.

[78] Nevins, *The American States during and after the Revolution, 1775–1789*, p. 564; Jensen, *The New Nation*, p. 339; Davis, *Sectionalism in American Politics, 1774–1787*, pp. 73–5, 100–1.

[79] Jensen, *The New Nation*, pp. 403–4; Davis, *Sectionalism in American Politics, 1774–1787*, p. 90.

[80] Jensen, *The New Nation*, pp. 400–7.

crops as its comparative advantage, had no incentive to help strengthen New England's trade position if it meant higher transportation costs and lost British markets. Southerners wanted to ensure as much merchant competition, including competition between American and foreign merchants, as possible to reduce the costs of exporting their products and importing finished goods.[81]

Conflict over trade on the Mississippi hardened sectional economic rivalries and paralyzed Congress by mid-1786. Spain had closed the Mississippi to American trade in 1784. Spain's action posed a serious threat to the South. Southerners viewed the Mississippi basin as an indispensable trade artery to expand southern territory, population, and political influence into the developing West. As southern support for an open Mississippi grew, northerners became more willing to acquiesce to Spain's action. Northern merchants who depended on the Atlantic feared competition from western states with access to the Mississippi as a trade route and feared a drain of population to the West. Northern leaders began to view the Mississippi as "a key to western expansion and a future southern domination of the Union." Massachusetts instructed its delegates to defend America's claim to the free navigation of the Mississippi as late as 1785, but it reversed its position by the following year.[82]

When Secretary of Foreign Affairs John Jay proposed a commercial agreement in 1786 that conceded Spain's right to block the Mississippi for twenty-five years, intense and intractable regional animosity immobilized the national government. Northern merchants, who emphasized the importance of trade with Spain, supported the proposed Jay-Gardoqui agreement. Southerners viewed the willingness to concede the closure of the Mississippi as at best a blatant example of northern selfishness and at worst an indication of "a larger northern scheme to seize control of the nation." Virginia's James Monroe accused the northerners of a plot "to throw the weight of the population eastward and keep it there to appreciate the vacant lands in New York and Massachusetts."[83]

[81] Davis, *Sectionalism in American Politics, 1774–1787*, pp. 13, 76, 85–6, 92, 108.

[82] Davis, *Sectionalism in American Politics, 1774–1787*, pp. 16–21, 110–20; McCoy, "James Madison and Visions of American Nationality in the Confederation Period"; Jensen, *The Articles of Confederation*, p. 221.

[83] Nettels, *The Emergence of a National Economy, 1775–1815*, pp. 65–9; Davis, *Sectionalism in American Politics, 1774–1787*, pp. 27, 125; Rakove, *The Beginnings of National Politics*, pp. 349–50. See also John Campbell to James Madison, February 21, 1787, in *PJM* 9: 287.

The Confederation policy process collapsed under the burden of this interstate rivalry. When the seven northern states refused to remove the secrecy from the Spanish negotiations, southerners in Congress felt confirmed in their suspicion that the North was determined to maintain the favorable balance of power at their expense. Debate reached "an emotionally and politically debilitating deadlock" by the end of the summer of 1786. Obstruction and stalemate continued into 1787. Congress never approved the treaty.[84]

FROM CRISIS TO CURE

Five years after the British surrender at Yorktown, the American states had established effective authority to govern their diverse economies and guide them along varied paths. American politics now bore faint resemblance to British politics. States developed effective republican institutions with a stake in defending that authority and managing state politics and economic development. State politicians now had the will, the resources, the skill, the experience, and the constituencies to defend their economic policy prerogatives.[85] In stark contrast, the United States national government, designed around the protection of state prerogatives, had become virtually immobilized by them. Interstate policy antagonism made it impossible for Congress to govern by the late 1780s.[86] Congress could pursue no economic policy, and it had no financial capacity to pursue a coherent policy even if it had one.

In 1787 the United States faced a crisis of policy outcomes and a crisis of policy process. Contemporary rhetoric may have overstated the nation's problems and ignored hopeful signs of improvements. The economic advantage that states gained from the pursuit of their self-interest is doubtful (that is the nature of the "prisoners' dilemma").[87] But in late 1786 it was more than reasonable for Americans to view the economic union in North America as imperiled and the trends as ominous. In a letter to Thomas Jefferson, James Madison wrote that "[t]he difficulties

[84] Nevins, *The American States during and after the Revolution, 1775–1789*, pp. 566–8; Davis, *Sectionalism in American Politics, 1774–1787*, p. 125; Jillson and Wilson, *Congressional Dynamics*, pp. 267, 273.

[85] Wood, *The Creation of the American Republic, 1776–1787*, p. 361.

[86] Morris, *The Forging of the Union*, pp. 92–4, 99–101; Wood, *The Creation of the American Republic, 1776–1787*, p. 359; *PJM* 9: 275.

[87] McCusker and Menard, *The Economy of British America, 1607–1789*, pp. 340–1; Jensen, *The New Nation*, pp. 338–9.

which present themselves are on one side almost sufficient to dismay the most sanguine, whilst on the other side the most timid are compelled to encounter them by the mortal diseases of the existing constitution."[88] These circumstances were fueling political support across the nation for major enhancements in national policy authority. The nation faced a political crisis: individuals with different interests in different places were being driven by specific problems into a growing coalition of grievance against the status quo. Madison molded these complaints into a diagnosis and cure that set the initial agenda for reconstituting American government.

[88] Madison to Jefferson, March 19, 1787, in *PJM* 9: 318.

3

James Madison's Plan for the Constitutional Convention

The new nation's mounting problems deepened American leaders' anxiety for the nation's future. Support for far-reaching institutional change was growing in all parts of the nation by 1787. Many American political leaders discussed pathbreaking remedies for the nation's economic and political troubles. Nearly all the states endorsed a convention to grapple with these issues. James Madison, already an accomplished policy strategist, constitutional expert, and experienced legislator, seized this opportunity to plan a thorough reconstitution of American economic policy making.

Madison's plan to structure America's political future began with a thorough critique of the states' handling of economic policy. He warned that the state governments' economic policies were menacing not only America's future prosperity but also the potential of republican government itself. The states, he concluded, must no longer govern the American economy. Authority over economic policy must be transferred to a reconstituted national government. Madison proposed to restructure the national government and to empower national policy makers to pursue the economic interests of the nation as a whole, independent of the interests of individual states or coalitions of states. His proposals aimed to (1) make the national government the presumptive, sovereign economic policy maker for the nation; (2) create a national policy-making process that would motivate national officials to focus on the pursuit of national interests instead of state interests; and (3) enable national policy makers to monitor and veto any state policies at will. These proposals, in turn, depended on an early and decisive convention vote to eliminate equal state representation in Congress and replace it with representation adjusted to population size. By winning an early vote on the principle of proportional representation before taking up the details of constitutional design, Madison believed he could cement a coalition of large and southern states powerful enough to sweep his remaining agenda through the convention. The Virginia Plan, which embodied Madison's core ideas, set the convention's initial agenda.

GROWING SUPPORT FOR NATIONAL POLITICAL REFORM

From the moment the United States declared their independence, a small number of wealthy elites backed a strong national government. Affluent property owners, creditors, merchants, and manufacturers held most of the nation's wealth in the Confederation, and most of these wealthy citizens instinctively supported specie, cautious credit policies, and strict protection of property rights. Some envisioned a conservatively managed economy in which their own interests could prosper. In the 1780s George Washington sought more national power for defense, western expansion, and public works. Washington had a personal stake in the economic development of the Potomac River.[1] Some of these elites feared that the radical republicanism unleashed by the Revolution imperiled the economy. Less virtuous men, if not mobs, seemed in command of the state governments.[2] Governor William Livingston of New Jersey voiced the elites' disdain for the debt-ridden farmers who demanded paper money

[1] Glenn A. Phelps, *George Washington and American Constitutionalism* (Lawrence: University Press of Kansas, 1993), pp. 74–9.

[2] Alice Hanson Jones, *Wealth of a Nation to Be: The American Colonies on the Eve of the Revolution* (New York: Columbia University Press, 1980); E. James Ferguson, *The Power of the Purse: A History of Public Finance, 1776–1790* (Chapel Hill: University of North Carolina Press, 1961), pp. 114, 284–6; Gary M. Walton and Hugh Rockoff, *History of the American Economy*, 8th ed. (Fort Worth, TX: Dryden Press, 1998), p. 112; Roger H. Brown, *Redeeming the Republic: Federalists, Taxation, and the Origins of the Constitution* (Baltimore: Johns Hopkins University Press, 1993), p. 149. Alexander Hamilton was particularly concerned about mob rule: "Here we find the general disease which infects all our constitutions, an excess of popularity. . . . The inquiry constantly is what will *please* not what will *benefit* the people. In such a government, there can be nothing but temporary expedient, fickleness and folly" (Hamilton to Robert Morris, August 13, 1782, in *PRM* 6: 188). A more florid version surfaces in *Federalist* 21: "The tempestuous situation, from which Massachusetts has scarcely emerged, evinces that dangers of this kind are not merely speculative. Who can determine what might have been the issue of her late convulsions, if the mal-contents had been headed by a Caesar or by a Cromwell? Who can predict what effect a despotism established in Massachusetts, would have upon the liberties of New-Hampshire or Rhode-Island, of Connecticut or New-York?" Alexander Hamilton, James Madison, and John Jay, *The Federalist*, ed. Jacob E. Cooke (Middletown, CT: Wesleyan University Press, 1961), p. 31.

and debt relief: "[T]he money in question is only wanted... by those very same idle spendthrifts, dissipating drones of the community who have felt the sweets, during the legal tender of depreciated paper, of living upon the sweat of their neighbors' brows." During the convention, Alexander Hamilton was "more and more convinced that this is the critical opportunity for establishing the prosperity of this country on a solid foundation."[3] These elites believed that the nation would prosper only if economic power were entrusted to policy makers less directly responsive to the mass of American voters. By early 1787 public support for more-effective national economic policy had broadened and deepened well beyond these wealthy elites.

As economic conditions deteriorated in the 1780s, more creditors, merchants, and manufacturers grew anxious about the management of the nation's economy and became more supportive of change. Americans who owned state and Confederation securities worried that state policies and Confederation ineffectiveness would destroy the value of their assets. They insisted on conservative national currency policies and a steady revenue base for funding the Confederation government. Most of these creditors lived in the key commercial cities outside the South.[4] While financial problems were motivating creditors to press for stronger national financial control, merchants grew increasingly frustrated by the stalemate in U.S. commercial policy while trade declined. Urban merchants and manufacturers sought uniform regulations to facilitate interstate commerce. Self-serving state currency laws, transportation rules, and product quality regulations were beginning to threaten interstate trade. Just before the start of the Constitutional Convention, for example, the merchants of Providence, Rhode Island, wrote to their unofficial representative in

[3] William Livingston, January 9, 1786, in *The Papers of William Livingston*, ed. Carl E. Prince, 5 vols. (Trenton: New Jersey Historical Commission, 1979–88), 5: 217–18; Hamilton to George Washington, July 3, 1787, in *RFC* 3: 53.

[4] According to Ferguson, citizens in the South controlled little of the national total of $3,761,000 in Quartermaster and Commissary certificates by the mid-1780s. New York, New Jersey, and Pennsylvania controlled 83 percent of these certificates, and New York alone had more than 31 percent. "This sectional imbalance increased the disparity between general holdings of public securities in the south and the rest of the nation, since the south was also deficient in other forms of public debt.... [together,] three kinds of securities comprised the great bulk of the public debt after its consolidation [beginning in 1782], amounting to $25,400,000. The south held only $4,170,000, or 16 percent, of the total, whereas its proportion of the white population in 1790 was 38 percent." *The Power of the Purse*, p. 183. See also pp. 115, 242–3, 285; Merrill Jensen, *The New Nation: A History of the United States during the Confederation, 1781–1789* (New York: Vintage Books, 1965), pp. 344–5; Brown, *Redeeming the Republic*, pp. 171 –3.

Philadelphia urging a policy to nurture a national free market, so that all American goods

> may be Transported to any of the United States free of any further Duty or Excise, That all Goods Imported from any Foreign Nation that pays the National Impost at the first port of Entry may be Transported to any of the United States free of any further Duty or Impo[s]t. That the carrying Trade shou'd be Insured to the Ships and Vessels that belong to the subjects of the United States on reasonable terms. And we hope the Consideration of a General Currency throughout the United States will not be forgot by the Convention, As it is so nearly connected with Trade and Commerce.[5]

"Real estate brokers, retailers, and ambitious tradesmen joined in the attack against state sovereignty by arguing that banks and other urban institutions would boost commodities exchange, money transactions, invention, education, and a host of services."[6] Merchants in Boston, New York, and Philadelphia especially demanded more congressional power to battle British trade restrictions. John Jay argued that the lack of government credibility itself was harming the national economy.[7]

Support for basic change broadened even further in the mid-1780s, when economic disarray and state rivalry seemed to grow while the Confederation Congress virtually ground to a halt.[8] Shays's Rebellion, for example, converted propertied citizens in Massachusetts to support nationalist solutions. In 1786, when Rhode Island's economic policies and

[5] Rhode Island Committee to James Varnum, May 14, 1787, in *Supplement to Max Farrand's "The Records of the Federal Convention of 1787,"* ed. James H. Hutson (New Haven, CT: Yale University Press, 1987), p. 2.

[6] Cathy D. Matson, "The Revolution, the Constitution, and the New Nation," in *The Cambridge Economic History of the United States*, vol. 1: *The Colonial Era*, ed. Stanley L. Engerman and Robert E. Gallman (Cambridge: Cambridge University Press, 1996), p. 384.

[7] Madison to Jefferson, August 20, 1785, in *PJM* 8: 344; Forrest McDonald, *Novus Ordo Seclorum: The Intellectual Origins of the Constitution* (Lawrence: University Press of Kansas, 1985), p. 217. John Jay wrote to Thomas Jefferson in December 1786 that "Our country is fertile, abounding in useful Productions, and those Productions in Demand and bearing a good Price, yet Relaxation in Gover[nmen]t and Extravagance in Individuals, create much Public and private Distress, & much public and private want of good faith" (quoted in Brown, *Redeeming the Republic*, p. 258). Jay's comment acknowledges the problem of "credible commitment," that is, government's ability to assure economic actors that "political bodies will not violate contracts of parties or engage in conditions that will alter radically the wealth and income of parties"; see Douglass C. North, *Institutions, Institutional Change and Economic Performance* (Cambridge: Cambridge University Press, 1990), p. 59.

[8] Peter Gourevich, *Politics in Hard Times: Comparative Responses to International Economic Crises* (Ithaca, NY: Cornell University Press, 1988).

Shays's Rebellion created new anxieties about the states' political direction, newspapers published more pieces favorable to national government reconstitution. Influential Americans "in each region, occupation, and socioeconomic standing" were questioning state insularity by mid-1786.[9] Ultimately, citizens of more-modest means were as likely to rally to support the ratification of the Constitution as to oppose it.[10]

MOMENTUM FOR MARKET-DRIVEN ECONOMIC DEVELOPMENT

Who, then, supported constitutional change in the late 1780s – an alliance of patriotic Americans inclusive of all classes, or a small number of propertied Americans? "Consensus" historians in the nineteenth century argued that the nation's crisis stimulated very broad support for major changes in the national government. Charles Beard and other "Progressive" historians in the early twentieth century, in contrast, argued that only a relatively small minority of the wealthiest Americans supported a new Constitution and that it benefited its interests rather than the majority of Americans of modest means. The truth lies in between.

Support for constitutional revision united a loose coalition of Americans – perhaps a narrow majority, perhaps a large minority – who were committed to economic development driven by free markets and who sought stronger protections for property, contracts, currency, and national security. Historian Jackson Turner Main provides important clues about this loose coalition in his portrait of founding-era state politics. Main argues that economic conflicts generally pitted "cosmopolitans" against "localists" in all the states. Main terms "cosmopolitans" those citizens who were better educated, had more property, higher incomes, and lived closer to the seacoast than "localists." Cosmopolitans favored trade, market expansion, and the conservative economic policies that fostered it. Merchants, lawyers, doctors, large landowners, city dwellers, and farmers near cities all tended to be cosmopolitans. Eventually, support for ratification of the Constitution was especially strong in areas that were

[9] Ferguson, *The Power of the Purse*, p. 249; Brown, *Redeeming the Republic*, p. 173; Matson, "The Revolution, the Constitution, and the New Nation," pp. 382–3. Even Gunning Bedford Jr., Delaware's attorney general and an opponent of the Virginia Plan, exclaimed "what will be the consequence if nothing should be done! The condition of the U[nited] States requires that something should be immediately done." *RFC* July 5, 1: 531–2.

[10] Forrest McDonald, *We the People: The Economic Origins of the Constitution* (Chicago: University of Chicago Press, 1958).

more affluent and more exposed to commerce and cosmopolitan ideas, especially areas closer to the Atlantic coast.

In Massachusetts, a swing state where "cosmopolitans" and "localists" were closely divided, the cosmopolitan position gained ground in the mid-1780s. From March 1785 to June 1786, Massachusetts legislators cast four different votes on a bill that served as a litmus test for stronger, more-conservative national governance: a special fund to support the Confederation Congress, financed by poll and property taxes that would disproportionately burden rural citizens of moderate means. On the initial vote, the proposal lost soundly. Support for the fund increased gradually on each of the four votes on the issue, until finally the bill won by a vote of fifty-nine to forty-five, a reversal fueled "partly from a change in public opinion and partly from a power shift within the legislature."[11] This legislative change in a swing state like Massachusetts strongly suggests that some pivotal American voters in 1786–7 were shifting toward support for a stronger national governance of the American political economy.

These clues indicate that by 1787 there existed a sizable constituency open to a national government that could more effectively protect property rights, promote commerce, and nurture markets. This constituency had been growing. More Americans, particularly those of substantial means, felt more vulnerable, more threatened, and more uncertain about the economic future. The electorate's general political passivity and disengagement in mid-1780s probably made this swing appear even larger.[12] James Madison recalled much later that public opinion had advanced rapidly in the "desired direction" of effective, expanded national powers.[13] The constituency had become sufficiently large to embolden those politicians who had supported stronger, conservative economic policies early in the Confederation. The political situation in 1787 bears a resemblance to national elections in which a segment of voters, driven

[11] Jackson Turner Main, *Political Parties before the Constitution* (Chapel Hill: University of North Carolina Press, 1973), esp. pp. 97–9. On the geographical distribution of support for ratification, see Owen G. Libby, *The Geographical Distribution of the Vote of the Thirteen States on the Federal Constitution, 1787–8* (1894; Grand Forks: University of North Dakota Press, 1969).

[12] On low voter participation rates in the 1780s, see Jack N. Rakove, *The Beginnings of National Politics: An Interpretive History of the Continental Congress* (New York: Alfred Knopf, 1979), pp. 365–6; Charles A. Kromkowski, *Recreating the American Republic: Rules of Apportionment, Constitutional Change, and American Political Development, 1700–1870* (Cambridge: Cambridge University Press, 2002), p. 231.

[13] James Madison, "Preface to Debates in the Convention of 1787," in *RFC* 3: 545.

by personal anxiety and ominous economic developments, become more willing to consider strong measures to change the nation's policy direction. Such a shift occurred, for example, in the U.S. presidential election of 1980.

But this shift in support did not determine the Constitution's design, because it was too amorphous, fluid, and internally divided to provide much more than a warrant to make some kind of change. The states' economic assets, market development, and political cultures differed too greatly to determine exactly what authority the national government required. National guidance of economic development meant different things to different people. Western settlers wanted a national government with the power to open the Mississippi and stave off Indians. Slave owners wanted national rules committed to helping them recover escaped slaves. Leaders in the deep South wanted a national government empowered to prohibit taxes on exports and interference in the slave trade. Tobacco planters from the upper South, with more slaves than they needed, wanted a national government empowered to limit the slave trade. Delegates from Massachusetts and Pennsylvania supported a national government with the power to restrict competition from foreign vessels. New Jersey and Connecticut farmers wanted a national power to prevent New York from discriminating against their products.[14] United mainly by their antagonism to the states' recent policies, some Americans had diametrically opposed preferences for policy and institutional reform. Others had only the most general notion of the direction reform should take.

Proponents of constitutional change especially agreed on the principle that government reforms should promote commerce. In practice, however, they were deeply divided about the specific regulations they sought. Northern shipbuilders, fishermen, and manufacturers wanted national protective tariffs that could provide large, sheltered markets unencumbered by state barriers to trade. Northern merchants, though, opposed such tariffs and sought regulations that merely limited competition from merchants in other countries or regions (thus northern merchants did not oppose the Spanish blockade of trade on the Mississippi). Southerners favored free international trade and resisted protective duties. By the mid-1780s southern leaders suspected that New England sought to monopolize American trade at the South's expense. Making national commercial control palatable to the South also made it unacceptable

[14] Curtis P. Nettels, *The Emergence of a National Economy, 1775–1815* (New York: Holt, Rinehart, and Winston, 1962), p. 93; McDonald, *Novus Ordo Seclorum*, pp. 217, 224.

to the North.[15] The nation's climate of opinion, then, merely presented a window of opportunity to change the path of American politics. Politicians who had long supported stronger national powers now seized the moment.

THE ROAD TO PHILADELPHIA

Some American political leaders had advocated stronger national power from the start. When support for the union ebbed after the Revolution's end, nationalist political leaders kept the concept of union alive in newspapers, letters, and speeches.[16] The frustrations of Confederation finance had severely cramped General George Washington's military efforts. Washington stressed these problems in a circular letter to state governors in 1783.[17] Robert Morris, wealthy Philadelphia merchant and creditor, and political leader of the faction opposed to Pennsylvania's democratic constitution, agreed to serve as Congress's superintendent of finance in early 1781 when Confederation finances threatened the Revolution's success. During his two years in that post, Morris served as a surrogate prime minister and architect of much of the congressional policy agenda. Morris and his allies initiated plans for a federal impost, for a new federal funding program, and for a national bank chartered by

[15] Nettels, *The Emergence of a National Economy, 1775–1815*, pp. 71, 92–4; Jensen, *The New Nation*, pp. 344–5; Matson, "The Revolution, the Constitution, and the New Nation," p. 384; Joseph L. Davis, *Sectionalism in American Politics, 1774–1787* (Madison: University of Wisconsin Press, 1977), pp. 13, 76, 85–6, 92, 108. As Edmund Pendleton warned James Madison: "I think Congress want additional Powers, but can't suppress my fears of giving that of regulating Commerce. The subject, at all times delicate, is rendered more so by the heteogenious and diversified emploiments of the United States. To pass over all trivial matters, the tobacco States are distinguished from all the others, in having a valuable staple for export and few manufacturers to furnish them with the implements of husbandry, and necessarys for their Families which they must purchase from others. It is therefore evidently their Interest to open their Ports to all the world, to derive from Rivalship, the best price for their crops, and necessaries at the lowest rates. Whereas in manufacturing States, an high price for necessaries must be their Interest, and suggest the Policy of excluding the trade of all." Pendleton to Madison, December 19, 1786, in *The Letters and Papers of Edmund Pendleton, 1734–1803*, ed. David John Mays (Charlottesville: University Press of Virginia, 1967), 2: 491–4. William R. Davie, a delegate from North Carolina, summarized some of these divisions in a speech at the North Carolina ratifying convention, July 24, 1788 (*ED*, 4: 22–3).

[16] Rogan Kersh, *Dreams of a More Perfect Union* (Ithaca, NY: Cornell University Press, 2001), pp. 32–68.

[17] George Washington, "Circular to the States," June 8, 1783, in *The Writings of George Washington*, ed. John C. Fitzpatrick (Washington, DC: Government Printing Office, 1938), 26: 483–96.

Congress. He battled for state requisitions payments and against state assumption of national debts.[18] Morris's plans would have established and stabilized national revenues, squeezed the state role in financial policy, and increased capital available for investment. Morris abandoned these plans and left his post in frustration in 1783. His departure from the Confederation government increased the anxieties of economic elites just as the economic depression emboldened state legislatures to invent ways to relieve debtors. Even Morris's critics, such as Richard Henry Lee, Patrick Henry, and James Monroe, began to sympathize with the need to shore up the national government's revenues.[19]

In the mid-1780s, growing concerns about commerce accelerated the movement for more interstate cooperation. Massachusetts in 1785 called for a convention to enlarge Congress's ability to control foreign trade, as did the New York City Chamber of Commerce and citizens of Philadelphia. State governments made efforts to cooperate for their mutual commercial benefit. Delegates from Virginia and Maryland met at Mount Vernon to settle issues concerning common waterways such as the Chesapeake Bay. Virginia's legislature urged other states to form a national commission "to consider how far an uniform System in their Commercial regulations maybe necessary to their common Interests and their permanent Harmony."[20] Nine states agreed to send delegates to this commercial convention, which met at Annapolis in September 1786. Though only Delaware, New Jersey, New York, Pennsylvania, and Virginia actually sent delegations to Annapolis, James Madison and Alexander Hamilton participated in the meeting. The Annapolis Convention characterized the nation's situation as "delicate and critical" and recommended another meeting in Philadelphia the following May to "render the constitution of the Federal Government adequate to the exigencies of the Union."[21]

[18] The retention of national control over the debt was politically crucial. National control gave the Confederation government substantial leverage over finance and public revenue. State control further strengthened the states' economic role.

[19] Ferguson, *The Power of the Purse*, pp. 242–3; Ferguson, "The Nationalists of 1781–1783 and the Economic Interpretation of the Constitution," *Journal of American History* 56:2 (September 1969): 241–61; Rakove, *The Beginnings of National Politics*, pp. 297–329; Lance Banning, *The Sacred Fire of Liberty: James Madison and the Founding of the Federal Republic* (Ithaca, NY: Cornell University Press, 1995), p. 50.

[20] "Resolution Authorizing a Commission to Examine Trade Regulations," in *PJM* 8: 471; Davis, *Sectionalism in American Politics, 1774–1787*, pp. 74–5; Brown, *Redeeming the Republic*, p. 29.

[21] "Debates and Resolutions Related to the Regulation of Commerce...," in *PJM* 8: 406–9.

A confluence of widespread economic problems, supportive public opinion, and creative policy leadership had opened a policy window for pathbreaking reform in 1787.[22] In February, Boston and New York newspapers suggested one option: a separate New England confederacy.[23] Speculation about the nation's potential breakup alarmed nationalists like Rufus King, a Massachusetts delegate to the Constitutional Convention. He wrote a preconvention letter to fellow delegate Elbridge Gerry, noting that "Events are hurrying us to a Crisis, prudent and segacious men should be ready to seize the most favorable Circumstances to establish a more perfect & vigourous Government." King's letter added a hopeful note. "Madison is here. I presume he will be preparing himself for the Convention.... he professes great Expectations as to the good Effects of the Measure."[24]

JAMES MADISON AS POLICY STRATEGIST

James Madison was in a superb position to shape the convention's initial agenda.[25] Already an experienced politician though barely thirty-six years old, Madison was a knowledgeable and respected authority on American politics and public policy. He had helped write Virginia's

[22] John Kingdon argues that policy windows occur when three separate streams of public policy converge: policy problems, policy solutions, and politics (including swings in public opinion, national politics, and changes of leadership). John W. Kingdon, *Agendas, Alternatives, and Public Policies*, 2nd ed. (New York: HarperCollins, 1995), pp. 165–90. Adopting Kingdon's perspective, the three streams converged to make 1786–7 an opportune moment for pathbreaking political change. Economic problems, trade frustrations, and state policies increased anxiety over the direction of national policy. Political leaders, particularly Robert Morris, had floated a number of incremental solutions to address national policy shortcomings. Public opinion was more open to national reform than it had been previously, and innovative leaders such as Madison were now in a position to press for inventive proposals to cure the nation's policy ills.

[23] *PJM* 9: 292n7; Allan Nevins, *The American States during and after the Revolution, 1775–1789* (New York: Macmillan, 1924), p. 603; William Pierce to George Turner, May 19, 1787, in Hutson, *Supplement to Max Farrand's Records*, p. 10; Jack N. Rakove, *Original Meanings: Politics and Ideas in the Making of the Constitution* (New York: Alfred A. Knopf, 1996), p. 33.

[24] Rufus King to Elbridge Gerry, February 11, 1787, in *LDC* 24: 90–1.

[25] In Kingdon's view, effective policy entrepreneurs such as Madison construct policy agendas that couple together the separate streams of political problems, solutions, and interests. Mouw and MacKuen use the term "strategic agenda" to refer to the ways that legislators frame policy choices, observing that "skillful politicians alter the attractiveness of any proposal by modifying its mixture of policy considerations." Calvin Mouw and Michael MacKuen, "The Strategic Agenda in Legislative Politics," *American Political Science Review* 86:1 (March 1992): 102n1.

Constitution of 1776, served in the state's House of Delegates, and represented Virginia in the Continental Congress. In Congress, he served on many key committees and worked behind the scenes to broker coalitions supportive of extending Congress's powers. He played a major role in initiating the Annapolis Convention of 1786.[26]

Madison, a natural political strategist, had mastered the arts of republican politics and policy making.[27] He was proficient at manipulating agendas, locating points of policy compromise, and building coalitions. He understood how procedural motions could be used tactically to gain leverage in the legislative process. He instinctively appreciated that he could advance his agenda by breaking apart legislative proposals (or by combining them).[28] He creatively coupled problems and solutions to win allies for policy measures he favored. Just three months before the convention, for example, he used national security concerns to justify Confederation aid to Massachusetts for suppressing Shays's Rebellion. Madison conceded that although "there might be no particular evidence" of British interference, "there was sufficient ground for a general suspicion of readiness in [Great Britain] to take advantage of events in this Country, to warrant precautions ag[ain]st her."[29] He worked behind the scenes to cultivate allies in state legislatures and other political bodies where he had

[26] William Pierce, "Character Sketches of the Delegates to the Federal Convention," in *RFC* 3: 94–5; "Liste des Membres et Officiers du Congrés," in *RFC* 3: 237; Ralph Ketcham, *James Madison: A Biography* (Charlottesville: University Press of Virginia, 1971); Gordon S. Wood, "Interests and Disinterestness in the Making of the Constitution," in *Beyond Confederation: Origins of the Constitution and American National Identity*, ed. Richard Beeman, Stephen Botein, and Edward C. Carter II (Chapel Hill: University of North Carolina Press, 1987), pp. 69–109; Banning, *The Sacred Fire of Liberty*, p. 422 n47; Richard K. Matthews, *If Men Were Angels: James Madison and the Heartless Empire of Reason* (Lawrence: University Press of Kansas, 1995), pp. 1–3; Kromkowski, *Recreating the American Republic*, pp. 239–42; "The Annapolis Convention, September 1786," in *PJM* 9: 115–19.

[27] Madison's expectations about republican politicians sound strikingly modern. For example, he supported longer rather than shorter terms for national legislators. Incumbents would have to serve in a distant legislature, making the votes "much more susceptible of impressions from the presence of a Rival candidate." It should then be expected "that the members from the most distant States would travel backwards & forwards at least as often as the elections should be repeated" (*RFC* June 21, 1: 361).

[28] For example, as a member of Congress in 1783, Madison led the drive for more-effective enforcement of state requisitions. After two members of Congress balked at a motion that "permanent & adequate funds are necessary for restoring public credit, & funds should be collected under the authority of Congress," he broke the motion in two parts and tried to get agreement on the statement of need in the first phrase, leaving the enforcement as a separate question to be addressed afterward (*PJM* 6: 136–7, 142).

[29] "Notes on Debates," February 19, 1787, in *PJM* 9: 277–8.

no direct influence.[30] Madison was patient and tenacious in policy combat, displaying a doggedness that may have worn even on his allies.[31] And when his efforts produced results that fell short of his goals, he repeatedly accepted half a loaf rather than none, "much disposed to concur in any expedient not inconsistent with fundamental principles."[32]

Madison was not chiefly a political philosopher but rather a policy strategist, adept at using broad theoretical ideas to advance his goals.[33] It is difficult to read Madison's writings without appreciating his gift for abstraction and generalization, his tendency to develop theory and then apply its logic to sort through facts, his propensity to use lists of general reasons to justify his claims, and his willingness to use global abstractions to combat adversaries.[34] An opponent at the convention, William Paterson, may well have had Madison's style in mind when he noted that "A little practicable Virtue [is] preferable to Theory."[35]

[30] For example, at the Annapolis Convention, Madison approached Abraham Clark, then a leading figure in New Jersey's state legislature, to persuade the state to instruct its Congressional delegates to return to Virginia's coalition opposing Jay's proposed revision of the treaty with Spain. Mary R. Murrin, *To Save This State from Ruin: New Jersey and the Creation of the United States Constitution, 1776–1789* (Trenton: New Jersey Historical Commission, 1987), p. 59.

[31] For example, in the convention's final week, the delegates took up the provision for a bill to become law without the president's signature ("if any bill shall not be returned by the president within ten days . . . after it shall have been presented to him &c"). Madison "moved to insert between 'after' and 'it,' the words 'the day on which' – in order to prevent a question whether the day on which the bill be presented, ought to be counted or not as one of the ten days." Gouverneur Morris called the amendment "unnecessary" ("The law knows no fractions of days"). Madison's own notes record that, "A number of members being very impatient & calling for the question," the motion was defeated (*RFC* September 13, 2: 608).

[32] *RFC* June 28, 1: 446.

[33] Madison's role as a policy strategist rather than a political philosopher accounts for his ability to adjust his tactics to political circumstances. For example, at the convention, on the very day after a key vote on Congress unraveled his political strategy for the convention, Madison fell back to a defense of the presidency as a vehicle for his goals (see Chapter 5). Most famously, his assertions of states' rights during the presidential administration of John Adams seemed a huge, even inconsistent adjustment of his philosophy, unless one takes into account that policy outcomes rather than philosophical consistency were the key to understanding his approach to politics. Madison compounded the difficulty when he tried to rationalize these inconsistencies away.

[34] Madison was fond of mathematical references: "When the weight of a set of men depends merely on their personal characters; the greater the number, the greater the weight. When it depends on the degree of political authority lodged in them the smaller the number the greater the weight." Therefore authority brings about the "coolness," system, and wisdom required in the Senate (*RFC* June 7, 1: 151–2).

[35] *RFC* June 16, 1: 274; Paterson had used this phrase in 1777, notes John E. O'Connor in *William Paterson: Lawyer and Statesman* (New Brunswick, NJ: Rutgers University

Madison prepared more carefully for the convention than any other delegate because he fully understood that the meeting's initial agenda could determine its outcome. Drawing on his political experience, he clarified his basic ideas for reconstituting American national government in private memoranda, "Notes on Ancient and Modern Confederacies," written in 1786, and "Vices of the Political System of the United States," written in the months immediately prior to the Convention. He built support for his ideas in letters to friends and key potential allies.[36]

His notes, as well as his political record, reveal that Madison was a dedicated republican and advocate for religious freedom, for free markets, and for Virginia. Madison expressed unyielding dedication to republican values both in private letters and in his speeches at the convention.[37] When the delegates debated whether citizens should elect any legislators directly, Madison insisted that "an election of one branch at least of the Legislature by the people immediately" was "a clear principle of free Gov[ernmen]t." When the delegates debated property qualifications for voters, Madison emphasized that "[M]en cannot be justly bound by laws in making of which they have no part."[38] Madison crusaded for religious liberty and

Press, 1979), p. 139. After a long, closely reasoned argument by Madison on August 13, John Dickinson observed that "Experience must be our only guide. Reason may mislead us. It is not Reason that discovered the singular & admirable mechanism of the English Constitution" (*RFC* August 13, 2: 276–8). Abstract theoretical arguments on behalf of a policy proposal can be very vulnerable to opponents who emphasize the practical consequences of these proposals; on this point, see Jane J. Mansbridge, *Why We Lost the ERA* (Chicago: University of Chicago Press, 1986), pp. 141–2, 191.

36 "Notes on Ancient and Modern Confederacies," in *PJM* 9: 3–25; "Vices of the Political System of the United States," in *PJM* 9: 345–58; Rakove, *Original Meanings*, pp. 46–56; Madison to Thomas Jefferson, March 19, 1787, to Edmund Randolph, April 8, 1787, and to George Washington, April 16, 1787, in *PJM* 9: 317–22, 368–71, 382–7.

37 James Madison to George Washington, February 21, 1787, in *PJM* 9: 286; Banning, *The Sacred Fire of Liberty*, pp. 77–107.

38 *RFC* June 6, 1: 134; see also May 31, 1: 49–50; August 7, 2: 204 n17. At the convention, Madison consistently argued that legislative instability was a threat to republicanism. Citizens naturally would become impatient with the policy results of republican systems like those of the Confederation, he believed, and fundamental changes in policy-making rules were necessary to save republicanism from itself. He "conceived it to be of great importance that a stable & firm Gov[ernment] organized in the republican form should be held out to the people. If this be not done, and the people be left to judge of this species of Gov[ernmen]t by ye. operations of the defective systems under which they now live, it is much to be feared the time is not distant when, in universal disgust, they will renounce the blessing which they have purchased at so dear a rate, and be ready for any change that may be proposed to them" (*RFC* June 12, 1: 219). However, it is important to note that Madison showed considerable sympathy for limiting suffrage to freeholders (owners of real property) on August 7, a position clearer in the notes of Rufus King and John Francis Mercer than his own (*RFC* August 7, 2: 203–4, 208, 210).

the strict separation of church and state. He battled for religious liberty in Virginia's Declaration of Rights, in opposing religious establishment in Virginia, and in adding religious freedom to the U.S. Bill of Rights. No individual deserves more credit for ensuring the protection of freedom of conscience in America.[39]

Madison's economic views largely matched those of Adam Smith. Free markets should drive economic development. He took the superiority of free markets to be self-evident, and he plainly preferred a policy to permit "perfect freedom" of trade.[40] Although he was sensitive of the need to assuage "the most respectable people of America," he also opposed policies antithetical to economic liberalism because they harmed honest citizens of modest means. He opposed an emission of paper money in Virginia in late 1786, for example, on the grounds that it would be unjust not only to property holders and creditors but also to debtors, who would suffer because they would face difficulty in obtaining specie and speculators would profit unfairly at their expense. In the convention, his arguments for free-market economics were theoretical rather than elitist. He emphasized the need for enhanced national powers to assure economic growth rather than the privileges of the wealthy.[41]

The principle of free trade conveniently allowed him to equate Virginia's economic interest with the national economic interest.[42] With

[39] James Madison, "Memorial and Remonstrance against Religious Assessments," in *PJM* 8: 295–306; Gary Wills, *James Madison* (New York: Times Books, 2002), pp. 17–18; Vincent Phillip Munoz, "James Madison's Principle of Religious Liberty," *American Political Science Review* 97:1 (February 2003): 17–32. Munoz argues that Madison took a religion-blind position and sought to prohibit the state from taking cognizance of religion.

[40] Madison to James Monroe, August 7, 1785, in *PJM* 8: 334; see also Madison to George Washington, December 9, 1785, in *PJM* 8: 439; Drew R. McCoy, *The Elusive Republic: Political Economy in Jeffersonian America* (Chapel Hill: University of North Carolina Press, 1980), p. 121; Matthews, *If Men Were Angels*; Rakove, *Original Meanings*, p. 314; Samuel Fleischacker, "Adam Smith's Reception among the American Founders, 1776–1790," *William and Mary Quarterly*, 3rd ser., 59:4 (October 2002): 897–924. Fleischacker notes that Smith's *Wealth of Nations* could be found in many American libraries. Madison, Hamilton, Robert Morris, and Edmund Randolph explicitly had drawn attention to the book.

[41] "Notes on Debates," February 21, 1783, in *PJM* 6: 272; "Notes for Speech Opposing Paper Money," in *PJM* 9: 158–9.

[42] "The State of this Country in relation to the Countries of Europe it ought to be observed, will be continually changing, and regulations adapted to its commercial & general interests at present, may hereafter be directly opposed to them. The general policy of America is at present pointed at the encouragement of Agriculture, and the importation of the objects of consumption. The wid[er] therefore our ports be opened and the more extensive the privileges of all competitors in our Commerce, the more likely we shall be to buy at cheap & sell at profitable rat[es]. But in proportion as our lands become settled, and spare

a Virginian's perspective on America's comparative advantage, he wrote to the Marquis de Lafayette that "The commerce of the United States is advantageous to Europe in two respects, first by the unmanufactured produce which they export; secondly by the manufactured imports which they consume."[43] His preferences for commercial policy, then, reinforced his dedication to his state's interests. He had a strong record of using his political talents to Virginia's advantage, protecting his state's interests in political disputes over western lands, war debts, the admission of Vermont, and commerce. He had more trust, however, in the potential of national policy than that of most Virginia legislators.[44]

Madison had experienced little but frustration after years of political efforts to reform national finance and commercial regulation. Barely a month after taking his seat at the Confederation Congress in March 1780, the "confused and critical state" of national finance shocked the twenty-nine-year-old legislator.[45] Madison worked on three-member congressional committees that aimed to obtain the states' requisitions and to establish a national impost, on committees to discourage Pennsylvania and New Jersey from assuming the payment of federal obligations, and on a committee that recommended using "the force of the United States" against states that shirked their obligations. Madison generally supported Superintendent of Finance Robert Morris in his efforts to ensure the government's solvency in the early 1780s. Initially more reluctant to interfere with the states' commercial powers than their finances, he had opposed a special commercial convention in 1783. Interstate commercial rivalries

hands for manufactures & navigation multiply, it *may* [emphasis in original] become our policy to favor those objects by peculiar privileges, bestowed on our own Citizens; or at least to introduce regulations inconsistent with foreign engagements suited to the present state of things." Madison to Edmund Randolph, May 20, 1787, in *PJM* 7: 58–64; see also Banning, *The Sacred Fire of Liberty*, pp. 178–81; Ketcham, *James Madison*, p. 176; McDonald, *Novus Ordo Seclorum*, p. 204.

43 Madison to Marquis de Lafayette, March 20, 1785, in *PJM* 8: 252–3.

44 Madison to Thomas Jefferson, November 18, 1781, in *PJM* 3: 307–8; Madison to Edmund Randolph, January 22, 1782, in *PJM* 4: 38–9; Banning, *The Sacred Fire of Liberty*, pp. 17–19, 50–1, 178–81. The priority that Madison gave to Virginia's interests is indicated by his shifting position on the important issue of federal assumption of state debts. His support for the national assumption of state debts was firm in the 1780s, when that position worked to Virginia's advantage, but his position changed by 1790 when Virginia would no longer enjoy relative benefit from that action; Ferguson, *The Power of the Purse*, pp. 210–11; "Debates and Resolutions Related to the Regulation of Commerce by Congress," in *PJM* 8: 407.

45 "Our great danger at present arises from the dilatory proceedings of the States and the real difficulty of drawing forth those resources from which the new System is to operate upon"; Madison to John Page, May 2, 1780, in *PJM* 2: 21–2.

and the Mississippi controversy drove Madison to make national commercial authority a top priority by the mid-1780s. He tried to press the Virginia legislature to endorse stronger national commercial powers but failed. As late as August 1786, Madison was deeply skeptical about the potential success of the Annapolis Convention and had little optimism about a widely discussed "Plenipotentiary Convention for amending the Confederation" more thoroughly.[46]

Sensing a great opportunity for pathbreaking change in early 1787, Madison's ambition seemed restored. Despite past frustrations with national policy reform, Madison now boldly reversed course and developed a comprehensive plan for addressing faults of the Confederation thoroughly and systematically. The right proposal could focus the amorphous discontent with the Confederation into a formidable political force. Incremental reform proposals failed because they were incomplete and easily picked apart by parochialism. The forthcoming convention "will only be useful in proportion to its superiority to partial views and interests."[47] Madison wrote on the eve of the convention that "In general the members seem to accord in viewing our situation as peculiarly critical and in being averse to temporizing expedients. I wish they may as readily agree when particulars are brought forward."[48] At the convention, Madison emphasized that the delegates had an open-ended warrant to fix the nation's political problems.

> [I]f the opinions of the people were to be our guide, it w[oul]d be difficult to say what course we ought to take. No member of the Convention could say what the opinions of his Constituents were at this time; much less could he say what they would think if possessed of the information & lights possessed by the members here; & still less what would be their way of thinking 6 or 12 months hence. We ought to consider what was right & necessary in itself for the attainment of a proper Governm[en]t. A plan adjusted to this idea will recommend itself – The respectability of this convention will give weight to their recommendation of

[46] *JCC*, November 8, 1780, 28: 1033–5; February 3, 1781, 29: 112–13; May 2, 1781, 20: 469–71; "Notes on Debates," December 4, 1782, in *PJM* 5: 363; Madison to James Monroe, August 7, 1785, in *PJM* 8: 333–6; "Debates and Resolutions Related to the Regulation of Commerce by Congress," in *PJM* 8: 404–10, 413–15; Madison to James Monroe, December 30, 1785, in *PJM* 8: 431–2; "Notes on Debate on Commercial Regulations by Congress," in *PJM* 8: 431–2; Madison to Thomas Jefferson, January 22, 1786, in *PJM* 8: 472–82; Madison to Thomas Jefferson, August 12, 1786, in *PJM* 9: 96; "The Annapolis Convention," in *PJM* 9: 116; PRM 1: 20–1; Ferguson, *The Power of the Purse* and "The Nationalists of 1781–1783 and the Economic Interpretation of the Constitution"; Banning, *The Sacred Fire of Liberty*, pp. 13–42, 54–5, 72.

[47] Madison to Edmund Randolph, March 11, 1787, in *PJM* 9: 307.

[48] Madison to Edmund Pendleton, May 27, 1787, in *PJM* 10: 12.

it. Experience will be constantly urging the adoption of it[,] and all the most enlightened & respectable citizens will be its advocates. Should we fall short of the necessary & proper point, this influential class of citizens will be turned against the plan, and little support in opposition to them can be gained to it from the unreflecting multitude.[49]

Madison articulated an idealistic vision at the convention, reminding delegates that they had it in their power to alter the nation's political order forever. The delegates were "framing a system which we wish to last for ages," he told them; "it was more than probable we were now digesting a plan which in its operation [would] decide forever the fate of Republican Gov[ernmen]t."[50] Madison must have approached the Philadelphia meeting as his best chance to shape the most important political agenda of his lifetime.

To achieve such sweeping change, Madison had to begin with a comprehensive narrative about the root causes of the nation's many public problems. Madison's plan depended on explaining the situation persuasively. A far-reaching cure implied a far-reaching diagnosis of the policy failures of the Confederation. If he could frame a convincing definition of the problem that pulled together disparate symptoms and strongly implied a sweeping enhancement of national economic authority, it would make the solution he preferred obvious and compelling, and the delegates much more likely to support it.

MADISON'S DIAGNOSIS

Madison concluded that the states had too much authority over economic policy, and by abusing that power, they were damaging the nation. Selfish parochialism was the fundamental flaw in American policy in the 1780s, autonomous state legislation the instrument, and national harm the result. Madison's preconvention notes on the "Vices of the Political System of the United States" emphasized that state policy autonomy was subverting the national economic interest.[51] Madison ranked the failure of the Confederation requisition system as the foremost of these "Vices," and

[49] *RFC* June 12, 1: 215. Similarly, Gouverneur Morris "wished gentlemen to extend their views beyond the present moment of time; beyond the narrow limits of place from which they derive their political origin.... Much has been said about the sentiments of the people. They were unknown; They could not be known" (*RFC* July 5, 1: 529).

[50] *RFC* June 26, 1: 422–3.

[51] "Vices," in *PJM* 9: 348–57. Madison injected much of his analysis of the vices of the Confederation into his attack on the New Jersey Plan on June 19 (*RFC* 1: 315–22).

blamed it on "the number and independent authority of the States." The second vice involved "Encroachments by the States on federal authority." At the convention, he listed such examples of these state "encroachments" as unauthorized state treaties with Indians, interstate compacts, and state military activity. The third vice entailed state violations of treaties with foreign nations. "The files of Cong[res]s contain complaints already, from almost every nation with which treaties have been formed," Madison told the delegates.[52] The fourth vice, "Trespasses of the States on the rights of each other," described as "destructive of the general harmony" those state laws that interfere with national markets for credit and commodities.[53] "[M]ost of our political evils," he wrote to Jefferson, "may be traced up to our commercial ones, as most of our moral may to our political."[54] The fifth vice addressed the "lack of concert" in economic policy. The sixth vice criticized the inability of the states to engage the national government in protecting themselves against such economically inspired violence as Shays's Rebellion. The seventh vice disparaged the Confederation's inability to implement rules such as national requisitions.

These "Vices" all flowed logically from state legislators' incentives to serve their voters' immediate demands without regard for the nation's long-term interests. "Is it to be imagined that an ordinary citizen or even an assembly-man of R[hode] Island in estimating the policy of paper money, ever considered or cared in what light the measure would be viewed in France or Holland; or even in Mass[achuset]ts or Connect[icut]? It was a sufficient temptation to both that it was for their interest: it was a sufficient sanction to the latter that it was popular in the State; to the former that it was so in the neighbourhood." Rhode Island legislators printed paper money because they had the power to benefit themselves politically and were rewarded for using it, regardless of the problems they caused their neighbors. This problem was endemic and evident in

[52] *RFC* June 19, 1: 316–17. "Vices" did not allude to the state assumption of federal debts as an encroachment on national power, though an earlier congressional committee headed by Madison had noted that, to the extent that states assume the union's debts, "the federal constitution must be so far infringed"; *JCC* October 1, 1782, 23: 630.

[53] "The practice of many States in restricting the commercial intercourse with other States, and putting their productions and manufactures on the same footing with those of foreign nations, though not contrary to the federal articles, is certainly adverse to the spirit of the Union, and tends to beget retaliating regulations, than they are destructive of the general harmony" (*PJM* 9: 350). The historical record of confederacies, Madison believed, proved that the lack of a central trade policy was an endemic and fatal problem for them (*PJM* 9: 11, 17; *RFC* June 19, 1: 317).

[54] Madison to Thomas Jefferson, March 18, 1786, in *PJM* 8: 502.

all the states. Rhode Island merely exemplified the economic perversity of unconstrained policy decentralization. Worse, state legislators' narrow, short-term incentives jeopardized not only economic well-being but also republicanism and basic rights. State policy makers lacked means and motive to defend effectively the fundamental values of republicanism, individual liberty, or commercial liberalism. The inherent logic of state policy making was the root cause of the unjust and counterproductive laws that threatened the nation.[55]

Incremental reforms would not cure the nation's economic ills. The Confederation Congress could not change state politicians' incentives, and it lacked the economic powers to pursue national interests. The Confederation was merely a "treaty of amity of commerce and of alliance, between so many independent and Sovereign States." The architects of the Confederation originally had "a mistaken confidence that the justice, the good faith, the honor, the sound policy" of the state legislatures would make it unnecessary to protect the national interest. But, in practice, state legislators could not escape their parochial shackles and the dilemma of cooperation.

> It is no longer doubted that a unanimous and punctual obedience of 13 independent bodies, to the acts of the federal Government, ought not be calculated on.... How indeed could it be otherwise? In the first place, Every general act of the Union must necessarily bear unequally hard on some particular member or members of it. Secondly the partiality of the members to their own interests and rights, a partiality which will be fostered by the Courtiers of popularity, will naturally exaggerate the inequality where it exists, and even suspect it where it has no existence. Thirdly a distrust of the voluntary compliance of each other may prevent the compliance of any, although it should be the latent disposition of all.... If the laws of the States, were merely recommendatory to their citizens, or if they were to be rejudged by County authorities, what security, what probability would exist, that they would be carried into execution? Is the security or probability greater in favor of the acts of Cong[res]s which depending for their execution on the will of the state legislatures, w[hi]ch are tho' nominally authoritative, in fact recommendatory only.[56]

One could expect the states to encroach on the shrinking sphere of national power "in almost every case where any favorite object of a State shall present a temptation." It is important to note that Madison believed

[55] "Vices," in *PJM* 9: 353–6. At the convention, he described the multiplicity, mutability, injustice, and impotence of state laws as "a dreadful class of evils" that "indirectly affect the whole" nation (*RFC* June 19, 1: 318–19).

[56] "Vices," in *PJM* 9: 351–2.

the states were encroaching on the Confederation's *authority*, jurisdiction, and power, and not its physical territory.[57]

Because political incentives motivate political behavior, Madison believed that it was necessary to make far-reaching changes in American political incentives. Only a thorough reconstitution of the Confederation's policy-making incentives could cure its ills.[58] State policy makers pursued *state* economic interests because states had the power to manage the economy. Madison concluded that transferring economic policy authority to national policy makers should motivate them to pursue *national* economic interest.

MADISON'S CURE

Madison proposed to transfer economic policy authority to the national government and to disconnect national policy makers from the state governments. The national government needed a restructuring so thorough that national policy makers' ambitions would be driven by a material concern for *national* objectives and nothing else. In words similar to those he used in *Federalist* 10 in late November 1787, Madison noted in "Vices" that sovereign power must attend to the "public good and private rights" of the *entire* society (that is, the nation as a whole): "The great desideratum in Government is such a modification of *the Sovereignty* as will render it sufficiently neutral between the different interests and factions, to controul one part of the Society from invading the rights of another, and at the same time sufficiently controuled itself, from setting up an interest adverse to that of *the whole Society*."[59] Madison was asserting that there exists a national interest (an interest "of the whole Society")

[57] "Vices," in *PJM* 9: 348.

[58] Madison stated this basic premise most memorably in *Federalist* 51. A well-constituted government must give "those who administer each [government] department the necessary constitutional means and personal motives to resist encroachments of the others.... Ambition must be made to counteract ambition. The interest of the man must be connected to the constitutional rights of the place" (p. 349).

[59] *PJM* 9: 357 (emphasis added). In the preceding sentences, Madison states that "If an enlargement of the sphere is found to lessen the insecurity of private rights, it is not because the impulse of a common interest or passion is less predominant in this case with the majority; but because a common interest or passion is less apt to be felt and the requisite combinations less easy to be formed by a great than a small number. The Society becomes broken into a greater variety of interests, of pursuits, of passions, which check each other, whilst those who may feel a common sentiment have less opportunity of communication and concert" ("Vices," in *PJM* 9: 356–7). I am interpreting Madison here to use the terms common interest, sentiment, or passion as common to a majority, but not the entire polity. Compare Madison's *Federalist* 10, pp. 60–1.

and that it is theoretically possible to construct government so that its policy makers pursue that national interest.[60] His discussion of "Government" and "Sovereignty" (both singular) in the concluding paragraphs of "Vices" is not about individual states but about the nation. His discussion is characteristically theoretical and addresses national government and sovereignty in the context of national values and interests within a Republic, whether small or "extended."

What was this "national interest," in Madison's mind? It must be inferred from the core values he espoused. Madison advocated three principle values for statecraft: first, a government directed by the people's representatives; second, political and religious liberty; and third, economic prosperity driven by free markets. Madison, then, expressed America's national interest as a balance between democracy and market-driven economic development. The most famous passage in Adam Smith's *Wealth of Nations* speaks to the latter goal when it equates economic liberty with aggregate economic growth, and economic growth with the national interest. Each individual who pursues his own economic interest, wrote Smith, "necessarily labours to render the annual revenue of the society as great as he can" as if by an "invisible hand," even though he "generally, indeed, neither intends to promote the public interest, nor knows how much he is promoting it."[61] The state had the authority to manage a balance between these elements of the national interest that would advance the well-being of the nation as a whole. For that reason, it was imperative that the state's decisions not be corrupted by partial views.[62] Clearly, the United States

[60] The idea of a "true" polity-wide interest resurfaces in *Federalist* 51, where the possibility exists for the national interest to influence policy unimpeded by parochial concerns: "In the extended republic of the United States, and among the great variety of interests, parties, and sects which it embraces, a coalition of a majority of the whole society could seldom take place on any other principles than those of justice and the general good; whilst there being thus less danger to a minor from the will of a major party, there must be less pretext, also, to provide for the security of the former, by introducing into the government a will not dependent on the latter, or, in other words, a will independent of the society itself" (pp. 352–3). If Madison viewed sovereignty as indivisible, as was commonly supposed, then it is not surprising that he blurred the distinction between geographic scope and the scope of policy authority.

[61] Adam Smith, *The Wealth of Nations* (New York: Modern Library, 1937), p. 423.

[62] On the distinction between the national interest and the aggregate interests of individuals within it, see Stephen D. Krasner, *Defending the National Interest: Raw Materials Investments and U.S. Foreign Policy* (Princeton, NJ: Princeton University Press, 1978), pp. 42–5. There is no evidence that Madison drew the obvious implication that there could be multiple and conflicting visions of national interests, even though policy debates in Britain and in the states made the difference plain. This blind spot may have been theoretical self-deception as Madison focused on other issues. More likely it was

did not enjoy that kind of governance in 1787. The Confederation had tilted toward an unvarnished republicanism that ran roughshod over the sound money, solid property rights, and predictable contracts that were essential for market-driven economic growth.

The nation's interests required a liberal economic policy produced by an effective, national republican policy-making process. But how could one be sure that national republican policy making would produce economic policy truly beneficial to the nation as a whole? In his "Vices" notes, Madison elaborated on the "great desideratum in Government" with an analogy that indicates his solution to the problem: by expanding the scope of a republican government's *authority* (not just its physical reach), republican policy makers could pursue the nation's true interests.

> In absolute Monarchies, the prince is sufficiently neutral towards his subjects, but frequently sacrifices their happiness to his ambition or his avarice. In small Republics, the sovereign will is sufficiently controuled from such a Sacrifice of the entire Society, but is not sufficiently neutral towards the parts composing it. As a limited Monarchy tempers the evils of an absolute one; so an extensive Republic meliorates the administration of a small Republic.[63]

As a king's authority must be *limited* to achieve the public good, a republic's authority must be *expanded*, according to Madison. In a monarchy, constitutional limits on a king's policy authority keeps the national government attentive to the national interest (particularly the national economic interest). If a monarch's power is not restricted, unlimited economic authority will tempt the king to use this power to enrich or otherwise benefit himself. Rather glibly, Madison draws the conclusion that republics require precisely the opposite remedy: *more* national authority, not less. A republic requires expanded national authority – not merely expanded geographical scope – to motivate and empower national policy makers to pursue the national interest in the face of the powerful centrifugal force of parochial interest. He put it in a slightly different way to Washington:

tactical. To move economic policy forward, the United States needed a government more capable of pursuing *some* version of national interest. His opponents at the convention suspected that the government he had in mind was rigged to pursue national interests in a way very consistent with Virginia's interests. Clearly he was willing to settle for a more capable government than the Confederation, but by 1790, he had reason to regret that Alexander Hamilton envisioned a very different way to put the national government to use. See Chapter 8.

[63] *PJM* 9: 355–7. Compare Madison's *Federalist* 51, pp. 347–53. While this notion of "the great desideratum" of government is substantially reproduced in *Federalist* 10, he did not elaborate it with the analogy he used before the convention.

"The great desideratum which has not yet been found for Republican Governments, seems to be some disinterested & dispassionate umpire in disputes between different passions & interests in the State."[64]

If state policy authority gave policy makers the incentive to pursue parochial interests, then expanding national authority could give national government officials the incentive to pursue purely national interests.[65] Madison used this analogy to monarchy at the convention on June 6, when he spoke in favor of including some members of the national judiciary in the veto process. Judges should join the executive in vetoing legislation, he argued, to augment "that personal interest ag[ain]st betraying the national interest, which appertain to an hereditary magistrate."[66] Madison could have said that national ambition counteracts parochial ambition – an argument understandably absent in his later public letters advocating ratification to undecided New Yorkers.[67] In light of his private analysis of the economic problems of the United States prior to the

[64] Madison to George Washington, April 16, 1787, in *PJM* 9: 383–4. What did Madison mean by a "disinterested & dispassionate umpire"? One view is that Madison, an eighteenth-century patrician, hoped that diverse interests would neutralize each other in a new national government "and thereby allow liberally educated, rational men... to promote the public good in a disinterested manner"; see Wood, "Interests and Disinterestness in the Making of the Constitution," pp. 83–4, 92, and Matthews, *If Men Were Angels*, p. 85. It is not likely that a politician as thoughtful and experienced as Madison could find this simple answer satisfactory, however. He had more than enough firsthand evidence that "Enlightened statesmen will not always be at the helm" (*Federalist* 10, p. 60). His belief that angels would not govern men came from experience, not theology. See also Jennifer Nedelsky, *Private Property and the Limits of American Constitutionalism* (Chicago: University of Chicago Press, 1990), p. 157.

[65] Hamilton thought along similar lines. Hamilton's own notes for his day-long speech of June 18 conclude with these thoughts: "But this proves that the [national] government must be so constituted as to offer strong motives. In short, to interest all the *passions* of individuals. And turn them into that channel" (*RFC* June 18, 1: 311).

[66] *RFC* June 6, 1: 138.

[67] There is a hint that this logic was more evident at the convention than the records reveal. On June 2 Dickinson of Delaware argued that the state legislatures should have the power to request the removal of the national executive. A strong executive "could only exist in a limited monarchy. In the British Gov[ernment] itself the weight of the Executive arises from the attachments which the Crown draws to itself, *& not merely from the force of its prerogatives* [emphasis added]. In place of these attachments we must look out for something else. One source of stability is the double branch of the Legislature. The division of the Country into distinct States formed the other principal source of stability. This division ought therefore to be maintained, and considerable powers to be left with the States" (*RFC* 1: 86). In this passage, Dickinson is directly addressing James Wilson's arguments against state agency in the selection of the national executive and may be indirectly addressing Madison's theory that interest follows the prerogatives of office. Given that much of the convention activity, both on and off the floor, went unreported, and that the quotation is taken from Madison's own notes, this interpretation is plausible.

convention, it is striking that Madison in *The Federalist Papers* is so insistent about the need for national policy makers to counteract each other but is deafeningly silent about national power to counteract state officials.

To reconstitute national policy making incentives, Madison proposed three fundamental reforms. First, the national government needed unlimited control over economic policy. Second, the national government needed discretion to veto state policy at will. Third, national policy making had to be divorced from state influence as much as possible.

Madison presumed that the nation's interests required the national government to be sovereign in economic policy, "armed with a positive & compleat authority in all cases where uniform measures are necessary."[68] Early in the convention, Madison told the delegates that it was impractical to enumerate national powers and that he would "shrink from nothing which should be found essential to such a form of Gov[ernmen]t as would provide for the safety, liberty and happiness of the Community."[69] Madison clearly argued for the subordination of state to national authority at the convention. On June 28, after the introduction of the New Jersey Plan, Madison asserted that there existed a stark contrast between

> the two extremes before us . . . a perfect separation & a perfect incorporation, of the 13 States. In the first case they would be independent nations subject to no law, but the law of nations. In the last, they would be mere counties of one entire republic, subject to one common law. In the first case the smaller states would have every thing to fear from the larger. In the last they would have nothing to fear. The true policy of the small States therefore lies in promoting those principles & that form of Gov[ernmen]t which will most approximate the States to the condition of Counties.[70]

Madison believed that public opinion in smaller states would support his position. Four months earlier, Madison had told the Confederation Congress that "it would seem that the great body of the people particularly in Connecticut, are equally indisposed either to dissolve or divide the Confederacy or to submit to any antirepublican innovations."[71]

[68] Madison to Thomas Jefferson, March 19, 1787, to Edmund Randolph, April 8, 1787, and to George Washington, April 16, 1787, in *PJM* 9: 317–22, 368–71, 382–7.

[69] *RFC* May 31, 1: 53. As a member of Congress, Madison was willing to send frigates to states that were delinquent in paying their requisitions (Madison to Jefferson, October 3, 1785, in *PJM* 8: 373–6); but at the convention, he pulled back from the position of threatening force against uncooperative states (*RFC* June 8, 1: 164–5).

[70] *RFC* June 28, 1: 449.

[71] "Notes on Debates," February 21, 1787, in *PJM* 9: 292.

Nationally uniform measures were most urgent in finance and commerce. The national government should command all the basic tools of national economic development: commercial law, corporate law, at least some property rights (such as patents and copyrights), infrastructure development, the militia, and some role in higher education.[72] Commerce is indivisible, and only one government should bear responsibility for managing all the nation's commerce. The burden of proof should fall on the states for exercising any economic power that could possibly touch on interstate commerce. Up to the end, Madison attempted to include specific national powers to establish a national university and grant charters of incorporation.[73]

Thus Madison's idea of an "extended republic," at least before and during the convention, meant "extended" authority, not just extensive territory and a large population. When he was planning for the convention in the months before May 1787, Madison faulted the national government for its lack of power, not the size of its geographical responsibility. The Confederation government simply lacked the authority to pursue the nation's interests. In his first speech at the convention, when Madison launched into his discussion of the extended republic, he directed his speech at the narrowness of Roger Sherman's proposal to authorize a few new powers for the Confederation Congress. A government with a very broad authority would provide "more effectually for the security of private rights, and the steady dispensation of Justice... evils which had more perhaps than any thing else, produced this convention." The only practical way to protect the interest of the nation against the oppressive policies supported by mere majorities "is to enlarge the sphere, & thereby divide the community into so great a number of interests & parties, that in the [first] place a majority will not be likely at the same moment to have a common interest *separate from that of the whole or of the minority*; and in the [second] place, that in case they sh[oul]d have such an interest, they may not be apt to unite in the pursuit of it."[74] In secret deliberations,

[72] The economic problems of confederacies extended to "the want of uniformity in the laws concerning naturalization & literary property; of provision for national seminaries, for grants of incorporation for national purposes, for canals and other works of general utility, w[hi]ch may at present be defeated by the perverseness of particular States whose concurrence is necessary" ("Vices," in *PJM* 9: 350).

[73] *RFC* August 28, 2: 442; September 14, 2: 615; September 15, 2: 625; see also *RFC* August 23, 2: 332.

[74] *RFC* June 6, 1: 134–6 (emphasis added).

Madison argued that "enlarging the sphere" of power and territory not only prevents majority oppression but also permits the otherwise fragile national interest (the "common interest . . . of the whole") to root itself in the premises of policy choice.[75] In the polemical *Federalist* 10, written after the convention for an audience dubious about national power, Madison wrote of "extending the sphere" of government and defended "an extensive Republic," using "extensive" clearly to refer to a large population and territory.[76] But *Federalist* 10 does not reveal the premises for which Madison fought in Philadelphia.

Second, national policy makers needed the authority to veto state laws.[77] In his preconvention letter to Washington, he wrote that, over and above the expansion of national power, a national veto was a necessary condition for establishing national officials' material stake in the national interest.

> [A] negative *in all cases whatsoever* [emphasis in original] on the legislative acts of the States, as heretofore exercised by the Kingly prerogative, appears to me to be absolutely necessary, and to be the least possible encroachment on the State jurisdictions. Without this defensive power, every positive power that can be given on paper will be evaded & defeated. The States will continue to invade the national jurisdiction, to violate treaties and the law of nations & to harass each other with

[75] When Madison first discussed the concept of "enlarging the sphere" at the convention on June 6, he was addressing Sherman's claim of limited policy jurisdiction and the problem of faction in small states such as Rhode Island. He did not distinguish jurisdiction from the size of the territory governed in arguing for expanding the sphere. Hamilton's undated notes of this period take Madison's claim to be geographical, but he is unpersuaded by the claim, noting that "There is truth in both these principles but they do not conclude so strongly as he supposes" (*RFC* 1: 146–7). On May 31 King's notes indicate that Madison favored large districts for the first branch to decrease the chance of demagogues, but Madison's own notes do not indicate that he made this geographical argument, evidence that suggests that geographical scope was not as singularly important to Madison during the convention as it became afterward (*RFC* 1: 49–50, 56). On June 29 Madison clearly expressed his view that authority and geographical scope are related when he observed that "There was a gradation . . . from the smallest corporation with the most limited powers, to the largest empire with the most perfect sovereignty" (*RFC* 1: 463–4).

[76] In a sense, *Federalist* 9 and 10 may be read as elaborate rhetorical exercises in begging the question. In these numbers, Hamilton and Madison respectively argue for the value of a confederation of small republics, in effect suggesting that their opponents occupied an extreme position of disputing the need for any kind of national policy making. On the tendency of Federalists to argue in public that the states would continue to dominate under the new Constitution, see William H. Riker, *The Strategy of Rhetoric: Campaigning for the American Constitution* (New Haven, CT: Yale University Press, 1996), p. 41.

[77] Note that the very need for a national veto implies that the states would retain some substantial powers, and that these powers had the potential to undermine national interests.

rival and spiteful measures dictated by mistaken views of interest. Another happy effect of this prerogative would be its controul on the internal vicisitudes of State policy; and the aggressions of interested majorities on the rights of minorities and individuals.[78]

When delegates at the convention questioned the practicality of a national veto, Madison cited the historical example of the royal veto on colonial laws to prove that it could work. Immediately after the convention defeated proportional representation in the Senate, he pressed the delegates to adopt a national veto, explaining that its "utility is sufficiently displayed in the British System. Nothing could maintain the harmony & subordination of the various parts of the empire, but the prerogative by which the Crown, stifles in the birth every Act of every part tending to discord or encroachment."[79] Madison was no royalist. He was extending his key analogy between monarchies and republics, adapting the policy tools of monarchy to the practical needs of the American republic.

The national veto was indispensable because it required the constant national evaluation of state policy in terms of national purpose, forcing national policy makers to define and emphasize national goals continuously. Moreover, states anticipating a veto would more likely abstain from policy wrongdoing. A negative on state laws was "the mildest expedient that could be devised for preventing [state] mischiefs. The existence of such a check would prevent attempts to commit them," and the absence of such a provision "left the door open" for "pernicious machinations among ourselves."[80] His belief in the national veto explains why

[78] Madison to George Washington, April 16, 1787, in *PJM* 9: 383–4.

[79] *RFC* June 8, 1: 168; July 17, 2: 28. He used a similar comparison in a postconvention letter to Jefferson: "If the supremacy of the British Parliament is not necessary . . . for the harmony of that Empire; it is evident I think that without the royal negative or some equivalent controul, the unity of the system would be destroyed" (Madison to Jefferson, October 24, 1787, in *PJM* 10: 210). See also Charles F. Hobson, "The Negative on State Laws: James Madison, the Constitution and the Crisis of Republican Government," *William and Mary Quarterly* 36:2 (April 1979): 215–35. Near the end of his life, Madison continued to explain the national veto in this way, indicating that it "was suggested by the negative in the head of the British Empire, which prevented collisions between the parts & the whole, and between the parts themselves. It was supposed that the substitution, of an elective and responsible authority for an hereditary and irresponsible one, would avoid the appearance even of a departure from the principle of Republicanism ("Preface to Debates in the Convention of 1787," in *RFC* 3: 549).

[80] *RFC* June 8, 1: 164; June 19, 1: 319. To Thomas Jefferson, a former state governor and a politician sympathetic to state powers, Madison defended the national veto by writing that "The effects of this provision would be not only to guard the national rights and interests against invasion, but also to restrain the States from thwarting and molesting each other, and even from oppressing the minority within themselves by paper money

Madison fought so fiercely for it at the convention, and why he identified the absence of that veto as the central flaw of the Constitution in a letter to Jefferson after the convention. The imperative need for a national veto was indispensable, given Madison's assumptions, and was not merely driven by his alarm over state actions.

Third, Madison insisted that the state governments be denied any influence in selecting of national policy makers. It was essential to Madison to avoid "too great an agency of the State Governments in the General one."[81] Madison, like most of the delegates, viewed policy makers generally as the agents of those who put them in office (as James Wilson paraphrased the French philosopher Montesquieu, it was expected that "an officer is the officer of those who appoint him").[82] Madison insisted that the voters directly choose the members of the House of Representatives, the foundation of the national policy-making system. The House would elect the Senate from slates proposed by the states, and the national legislature would then choose the national executive and judiciary. States would have virtually no influence as states in Madison's idealized republican government. Keen to ensure that policy would be stable, he supported relatively long terms of office, including a three-year term for the House of Representatives and a seven-year term for the Senate.[83]

Madison described this method as a "policy of refining the popular appointments by successive filtrations," aimed at solving the fundamental dilemma of republican politics: balancing popular control of government with acceptable policy outcomes. Direct election to "one branch of the

and other unrighteous measures which favor the interests of the majority" (Madison to Jefferson, March 19, 1787, in *PJM* 9: 318). Rufus King recorded Madison's comments on the national veto in a cryptic way that somewhat clouds Madison's intentions. "I am of the opinion that ye Gen[era]l Gov[ernmen]t will not be able to compel the large and important State to rescind a popular law passed by their Legislature. If this power does not rest in the national Legisl[ature] there will be wanting a check to the centrifugal Force which constantly operates in the several States to force them off a common Centre, or a national point" (*RFC* June 8, 1: 171).

[81] *RFC* June 6, 1: 134; McDonald, *Novus Ordo Seclorum*, p. 206. It would have been impolitic to extend the argument to the states in *Federalist* 51, since these letters aimed to allay New Yorkers' fears that the Constitution would inhibit their state policy makers' pursuit of economic advantages that were in their interest. After the convention, and in public argument, he had to state the same point in a way that would persuade the New York constituency of the implausibility of the fear that national policy would threaten their interests. For New York readers, Madison necessarily emphasized the geographical dimension of the concept.

[82] As James Wilson characterized Montesquieu's thought, according to James McHenry (*RFC* September 6, 2: 530–1).

[83] *RFC* June 12, 1: 214, 218.

national Legislature" would ensure the "necessary sympathy" between the people and their rulers. But, as Madison noted later, "symptoms of a leveling spirit... have sufficiently appeared in certain quarters to give notice of the future danger" that the populace would demand the redistribution of property. "How is this danger to be guarded [against] on republican principles? How is the danger in all cases of interested coalitions to oppress the minority to be guarded [against]?" "Successive filtrations" in selecting policy makers – the House selecting the Senate, and both appointing the executive and the judiciary – could ensure a balance of responsiveness, stability, and national vision. It is possible that Madison hoped that this method of making appointments would naturally place government power in the hands of rational patricians and filter out others. An alternative possibility is that Madison, always concerned with political calculation and skeptical of humans' motives regardless of their station, may have convinced himself that this method would motivate politicians to pursue national interest in the process of pursuing their own self-interest. Such a scheme might produce social benefits in politics reminiscent of the economic benefits produced by Adam Smith's invisible hand. In any event, Madison urged the delegates to raise, on the foundation of direct election to the House of Representatives, "a great fabric" that would be "stable and durable."[84] At first, he viewed the Senate as the key to this process. The Senate could temper the House and, with the House, control the executive. Acknowledging that "A Government without a proper Executive & Judiciary would be the mere trunk of a body without arms or legs to act or move," Madison wanted the national executive and judiciary to reach into all the nation's jurisdictions.[85] At the same time, he wanted executive powers "confined and defined" because excessive executive power would create "the Evils of elective Monarchies." He thought the "best plan will be a single Executive of long

[84] *RFC* May 31, 1: 49–50; June 26, 1: 423. Compare *Federalist* 10, p. 62: "[T]he delegation of government... by a small number of citizens elected by the rest... [has the effect] to refine and enlarge the public views, by passing them through the medium of a chosen body of citizens, whose wisdom may best discern the true interest of their country, and whose patriotism and love of justice, will be least likely to sacrifice it to temporary or partial considerations." See also Emery G. Lee III, "Representation, Virtue, and Political Jealousy in the Brutus-Publius Dialogue," *Journal of Politics* 59:4 (November 1997): 1073–95. Madison was familiar with the writings of the Marquis de Condorcet, who had written about the inherent instability of legislatures. He understood that bicameralism could mitigate the problem; see Thomas H. Hammond and Gary J. Miller, "The Core of the Constitution," *American Political Science Review* 81:4 (December 1987): 1155–74.

[85] *RFC* June 5, 1: 124.

duration [with] a Council, with liberty to depart from their Opinion at his peril."[86]

For Madison, changing the rule of equal state representation in the Confederation Congress was of primary tactical importance, the indispensable first step along the path to realizing his plan. Proportional representation in both houses of Congress would further nationalize policy by reducing the influence of state governments as units of representation. It also would substantially increase the influence of Madison's Virginia by giving it the largest state delegation in the nation's most important economic policy-making body. Virginia, the largest state and a southern state, could bring order to national policy making as the broker of a coalition between the South (Georgia and the Carolinas) and the most populous states (Pennsylvania and Massachusetts).

Madison's political strategy for the meeting depended on establishing the "doctrine of proportional representation" before taking up other issues.[87] By proportional representation, he meant that the number of a state's representatives in the House of Representatives and the Senate should depend on its size. The larger the state, the more representatives and senators it would send to the legislature. As he wrote to Washington,

> I would propose as the ground-work that a change be made in the principle of representation.... I am ready to believe that such a change would not be attended with much difficulty. A majority of the States, and those of greatest influence, will regard it as favorable to them. To the Northern States it will be recommended by their present populousness; to the Southern, by their expected advantage in this respect. The lesser States must in every event yield to the predominant will. *But the consideration which particularly urges a change in the representation is that it will obviate the principal objections of the larger States to the necessary concessions of power* [emphasis added].[88]

Madison, then, intended to use proportional representation to forge a majority faction that would support a strong national government.

He aimed to forge a six-state coalition united in support of proportional representation in a reconstituted national legislature (Table 3.1). If his faction carried this point, it would sweep the rest of Madison's proposals into a final Constitution. Massachusetts, Pennsylvania, and Virginia

[86] *RFC* June 1, 1: 70–1. After the grand compromise on representation established equal state representation in the Senate, however, Madison became more wary of the Senate and more supportive of presidential power.

[87] At the convention, he referred to the "doctrine of proportional representation" on June 30; *RFC* 1: 481.

[88] Madison to George Washington, April 16, 1787, in *PJM* 9: 383.

TABLE 3.1. *Madison's Expected Convention Coalition*

States	Population in 1790	Percent of Thirteen States' Population	Population Rank	Slaves in 1790
In Expected Coalition				
Virginia	747,550	20.5	1	292,627
Pennsylvania	433,611	11.9	2	3,707
North Carolina	395,005	10.9	3	100,783
Massachusetts	378,556	10.4	4	0
South Carolina	249,073	6.8	7	107,094
Georgia	82,548	2.3	11	29,264
TOTAL	2,286,343	62.8		533,475
Outside Expected Coalition				
New York	340,241	9.4	5	21,193
Maryland	319,728	8.8	6	103,036
Connecticut	237,655	6.5	8	2,648
New Jersey	184,139	5.1	9	11,423
New Hampshire	141,899	3.9	10	157
Rhode Island[a]	69,112	1.9	12	958
Delaware	59,096	1.6	13	8,887
TOTAL	1,351,870	37.2		148,302

[a] Rhode Island did not send a delegation to the convention.
Source: U.S. Bureau of the Census, *Historical Statistics of the United States* (Washington, DC: Government Printing Office, 1975).

would gain from proportional representation in the short run because of their current population advantage. Georgia and the Carolinas would gain from proportional representation because their populations were expected to overtake those of the eastern states in the foreseeable future. He drew out the political consequences only slightly differently for Jefferson: "[I]f a majority of the larger States concur, the fewer and smaller States must finally bend to them. This point being gained, many of the objections now urged in the leading States ag[ain]st renunciations of power will vanish."[89] Madison's political strategy depended crucially on delaying debate

[89] Madison to Thomas Jefferson, March 19, 1787, in *PJM* 9: 318–19; see also Madison to Edmund Randolph, April 8, 1787, in *PJM* 9: 369–70; Madison to George Washington, April 16, 1787, in *PJM* 9: 383. Madison put the same point to Washington this way: "[T]he consideration which particularly urges a change in the representation is that it will obviate the principal objections of the larger States to the necessary concession of power." On July 5, in response to the proposed Connecticut compromise, Madison made this argument to the delegates in language that tested his ability to balance firmness with diplomacy: "He was not apprehensive that the people of the small States would

on the substance of economic policy, particularly the divisive issues of the impost, trade, and the public lands, until after the delegates had approved proportional representation. Note that Madison's plan for forging a coalition of large and southern states implied that the states would vote equally at the convention.

THE VIRGINIA PLAN

Energized by the prospect of reconstituting American government and better prepared than any other delegate, Madison arrived in Philadelphia nine days before the convention's scheduled start. He met with Pennsylvania delegates Robert Morris, Gouverneur Morris, and James Wilson to plan and build support. Madison had persuaded his fellow Virginian George Washington to attend, acutely aware that Washington's presence would increase Virginia's influence. When May 14, the scheduled date for the convention, passed without a quorum to open business, the Virginia delegates met for "two or three hours every day" to develop a common agenda and to build connections with other delegates. The seven Virginia delegates (including Madison, Washington, Governor Edmund Randolph, and George Mason) were persuaded to fall in behind Madison's approach.[90]

When a quorum of delegates finally assembled on May 25, Madison's careful preparations were in place. The convention chose Washington to preside over the meeting, as Madison had anticipated. Over the objections

obstinately refuse to accede to a Gov[ernment] founded on just principles, and promising them substantial protection. He could not suspect that Delaware would brave the consequences of seeking her fortunes apart from the other States, rather than submit to such a Gov[ernment].... As little could he suspect that the people of N[ew] Jersey notwithstanding the decided tone of the gentlemen from that State, would choose rather to stand on their own legs, and bid defiance to events, than to acquiesce under an establishment founded on principles the justice of which they could not dispute, and absolutely necessary to redeem them from the exactions levied on them by the commerce of the neighbouring States.... Harmony in the Convention was no doubt much to be desired. Satisfaction to all the States, in the first instance still more so. But if the principal States comprehending a majority of the people of the U.S. should concur in a just & judicious plan, he had the firmest hopes that all the other States would by degrees accede to it" (*RFC* July 5, 1: 528–9).

[90] Stuart Leibiger, *Founding Friendship: George Washington, James Madison, and the Creation of the American Republic* (Charlottesville: University Press of Virginia, 1999), pp. 58–70; George Mason to George Mason Jr., May 20, 1787, in *RFC* 3: 23; Rakove, *Original Meanings*, p. 59; Ketcham, *James Madison*, pp. 191–4. Washington was reluctant to go to the convention and received letters of encouragement from many correspondents; see Phelps, *George Washington and American Constitutionalism*, p. 93.

of the Pennsylvania delegates, the Virginians pressed for rules that gave each state an equal vote. Consistent with Madison's expectation of six supporting votes (three large states and the three southern states), the Virginia delegation gambled that smaller states could be prevailed upon "in the course of the deliberations, to give up their equality for the sake of an effective Government."[91] Madison may have calculated that unit voting and equal state votes at the convention would help discipline those delegates from large states should they waver on the need for the sweeping national authority he had in mind. The convention's rules committee (chaired by Virginia's George Wythe) reported and the delegates adopted a rule that the states vote as units, as in Congress, but that a simple majority would carry a vote.[92]

At the convention's first working session on May 29, Virginia's most prominent state official, Governor Edmund Randolph, set the agenda by offering fifteen resolutions for reconstituting national policy making. Madison did not write this Virginia Plan alone, but he was recognized as the plan's chief architect.[93] Randolph's presentation was structured in Madison's own characteristic style. Randolph listed familiar Confederation problems much like Madison's "Vices," attributing many problems to the states. Randolph's list aimed to build initial consensus on the problems and the impossibility of reaching satisfactory policy outcomes under the Confederation as constituted. After preparing the convention with this diagnosis, Virginia's proposed cures seemed reasonable on their face. The resolutions were arranged to make proportional representation the first order of business.

[91] Madison to John Tyler, c. 1833, in *RFC* 3: 525; *RFC* May 28, 1: 10–11n; Calvin C. Jillson, *Constitution Making: Conflict and Consensus in the Federal Convention of 1787* (New York: Agathon Press, 1988), pp. 45–8. Jillson characterizes the Virginia delegation as timid, forcing the unit voting rule on an unwilling Madison. It is equally reasonable to view it as a strategic calculation in which Madison joined willingly, believing that a concession on rules would prevent small states from withdrawing from the game; see Kromkowski, *Recreating the American Republic*, p. 265. This rule change did not alter Madison's vote count before the convention, but that vote count proved overoptimistic, and the small states more resilient than expected.

[92] *RFC* May 29, 1: 7–13, 15–17. To encourage frank discussion, these rules required secrecy. Votes were recorded by state and not by individual delegate. Early in the proceedings, Nathaniel Gorham of Massachusetts, as chair of the Committee of the Whole, ruled that a vote of five states for, four against, and one divided counted as an affirmative vote (*RFC* June 1, 1: 69).

[93] Ketcham, *James Madison*, pp. 194–5; Jack N. Rakove, *James Madison and the Creation of the American Republic* (Glenview, IL: Scott, Foresman/Little, Brown, 1990), p. 55.

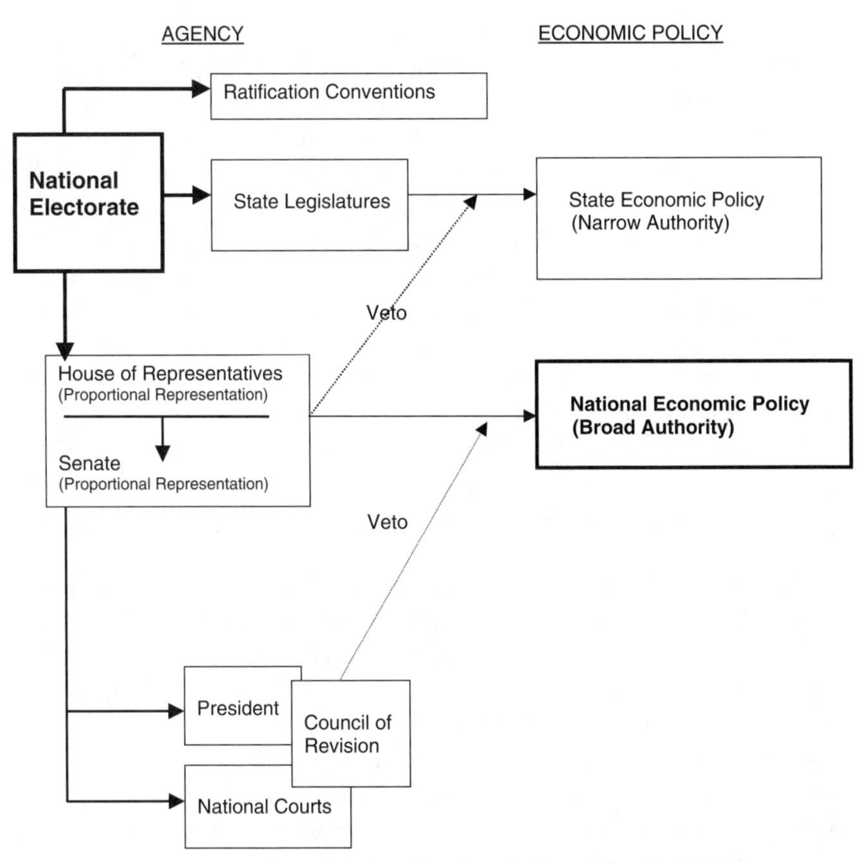

FIGURE 3.1. Agency and Economic Policy for Madison: The Virginia Plan

Virginia's first resolution aimed to put the delegates on record in support of the apparent consensus that the Articles of Confederation "ought to be so corrected & enlarged" to realize the "common defence, security of liberty and general welfare." The second resolution, and the first substantive proposal, suggested that the consensus logically implied proportional representation in the national legislature: "therefore that the rights of suffrage in the National Legislature ought to be proportioned to the Quotas of contribution, or to the number of free inhabitants." The Virginia Plan's remaining resolutions systematically proposed to dismantle nearly all of the states' independent influence in choosing national policy makers and to slash state economic policy authority (Figure 3.1).

The Continental Congress would be replaced by a bicameral legislature. By placing this proposal after the resolution on proportional representation in the legislature – singular – the delegates would record support of proportional representation in both chambers before they began to consider either one. The first branch would be popularly elected, with term limits and a recall provision. The second branch would be elected by the first branch, from slates chosen by the respective state legislatures. Like most of the several plans for reconstituting the national government circulating inside and outside the convention, the plan proposed to establish a national executive and judiciary separate from the legislature.The national legislature would select a national executive who would serve a single term and would enjoy the "general authority to execute the National laws." The executive, together with members of the national judiciary, would constitute a "council of revision" with veto power over acts of the national legislature. The new legislature, in addition to powers already granted under the Articles, would have expanded powers to make laws "in all cases to which the separate States are incompetent, or in which the harmony of the United States may be interrupted by" individual state laws. The national legislature could veto "all laws passed by the several States, contravening in the opinion of the national legislature the articles of Union" (subject to review by the Council of Revision). Each state was guaranteed a republican government, and the National Legislature could use the "force of the Union" against any state that failed to fulfill its "duty under the articles thereof."[94] State officials would swear an oath of support for the national government.

MADISON'S CHALLENGE

Independence had made the American states policy orphans, and now, in James Madison's view, the visible hand of national government was needed to ensure the pursuit of national interests and the survival of republicanism in America. Madison proposed to remove the state governments as agents of national policy making. The national government

[94] *RFC* May 29, 1: 18–23; Banning, *The Sacred Fire of Liberty*, p. 113. Shlomo Slonim sees a distinction between the national veto described in Madison's correspondence and the national veto in the Virginia Plan; see Slonim, "Securing States' Interests at the 1787 Constitutional Convention: A Reassessment," *Studies in American Political Development* 14:1 (Spring 2000): 1–19. It is doubtful that this distinction made a difference for Madison. Madison's national policy makers would be inspired to evaluate state policy initiatives in light of national interest under either formulation.

required the authority to govern the American economy, he believed, and his plan would give national economic policy makers the means and the motive to pursue national interests independent of the states. The Virginia Plan laid out the essential elements for realizing Madison's vision of the reconstituted republic.

Madison challenged the delegates to place the nation's future above the present autonomy of the states they represented. Madison's very ambition invited strong opposition. His bold challenge to the states' prerogatives soon focused opponents on the most controversial flashpoints of his plan. As the members connected Madison's plan to their interests, positions, aspirations, and constituents, the opposition solidified. Madison had made representation the central political battleground of the meeting. The issue of representation would bring the convention to the brink of failure. None of the delegates could have foreseen the Constitution that resulted from their efforts to save it.

4

The Political Landscape of the Constitutional Convention

Like Madison, the other delegates came to the Constitutional Convention to change the course of American politics. Virginia's bold agenda forced them to confront the prospect of a strong national government and to consider many specific choices about national policy authority, policy agency, and the policy process. Republican principles provided little or no help in making these constitutional decisions. All the delegates embraced republican ideals, but these ideals alone could not resolve the fundamental dilemma the delegates faced: reconstituting the Confederation government so it could produce better policy outcomes, without harming the vital interests of their constituents. Political interests, not republican values, determined the delegates' approach to the specific problems of reconstituting American government.

Madison's plan to restructure America's political future directly challenged the nation's political present. Virginia's resolutions threatened the existing distribution of political power by redistributing basic tools of political management to the national government and increasing the agency of larger states in determining how these tools would be used. As representatives of existing polities, each delegate evaluated Madison's proposed changes in light of the present and future consequences for the welfare of his state and the nation.

As Madison expected, the delegations from the large and southern states initially lined up behind Virginia's plan. The plan's ambitious scope, however, helped unify delegates from states outside his coalition and provided opportunities to delay fundamental choices and chip away at key provisions. Madison's skilled adversaries, notably Connecticut's Roger Sherman, exploited the political weaknesses of his plan to defend the state policy prerogatives that were Madison's main target.

THE IMPRECISION OF REPUBLICAN IDEALS

Nearly all of the fifty-five individuals who participated in the Constitutional Convention were experienced politicians. As state legislators, judges, and administrators, most of these delegates had helped guide their respective colonies to political independence, formed republican governments in the vacuum of British authority, or nurtured their states through military invasion and economic hardship. Elder statesmen such as Benjamin Franklin of Pennsylvania, Roger Sherman of Connecticut, John Dickinson of Delaware, and George Mason of Virginia had years of experience in British colonial assemblies or administration long before the Revolution.[1] Fully half of the convention delegates were younger men, born in the 1740s and early 1750s. The men in this younger cohort had honed their political skills by helping develop new governments for the American states and the Confederation.[2] Nearly all the delegates had served in colonial or state legislatures. A quarter of them had held prominent offices of statewide power, such as governor, state attorney general, speaker of the lower house, or judge of the supreme court. Forty-one of the fifty-five delegates had served in the Continental Congress. Several served on Washington's military staff, where they gained experience in national administration. Together, the delegates represented most of the major political factions in the twelve participating states.[3]

[1] A few of the most prominent American politicians were missing from the convention, including John Adams, Thomas Jefferson, and John Jay. Influential supporters of state and local policy autonomy – Erastus Wolcott of Connecticut, Abraham Clark of New Jersey, Samuel Chase of Maryland, and Patrick Henry of Virginia (who "smelled a rat"), among others – declined to serve as delegates and refused to be associated with the convention. See Peter S. Onuf, *The Origins of the Federal Republic: Jurisdictional Controversies in the United States, 1775–1787* (Philadelphia: University of Pennsylvania Press, 1983), pp. 95–6, 60–1, 142, 95–6, 205–7.

[2] Stanley Elkins and Eric McKitrick, "The Founding Fathers: Young Men of the Revolution," *Political Science Quarterly* 76:2 (June 1961): 181–216.

[3] Forrest McDonald, *We the People: The Economic Origins of the Constitution* (Chicago: University of Chicago Press, 1958), *E Pluribus Unum: The Formation of the American Republic, 1776–1790*, 2nd ed. (Indianapolis, IN: Liberty Press, 1979), pp. 258–70, and *Novus Ordo Seclorum: The Intellectual Origins of the Constitution* (Lawrence: University Press of Kansas, 1985), pp. 185–224; Clinton Rossiter, *1787: The Grand Convention* (New York: Macmillan, 1966), pp. 79–156; James H. Charleton and Robert G. Ferris, eds., *Framers of the Constitution* (Washington, DC: Smithsonian Institution Press, 1986); U.S.

These delegates included some of the most accomplished and gifted republican politicians in the world. They had built republican polities by establishing new governing institutions, breathing life into new public offices, and fashioning unfocused, diverse factions into robust political coalitions.[4] No one had done more to build the South Carolina polity than John Rutledge, the New Jersey polity than William Livingston, or the Connecticut polity than Roger Sherman. Twelve states sent delegates to Philadelphia as spokesmen for their state's interests. Their state colleagues charged these representatives with the responsibility of making the union "adequate to the exigencies of Government and, the preservation of the Union."[5] Rhode Island, where a strong legislative majority still supported paper money and generally opposed stronger national powers, sent no delegates.

Whether they were dedicated republicans like Madison or ambivalent ones like John Dickinson, all the delegates believed that any reconstituted national government also must be founded on republican principles. Connecticut explicitly had instructed its delegates to consider any reforms "agreeable to the general principles of Republican Government."[6] Randolph assured the delegates that republican principles set the foundation for Virginia's agenda. Although Dickinson personally preferred limited monarchy, he conceded that the "spirit of the times – the state of our affairs, forbade the experiment, if it were desireable." Madison and Hamilton warned the convention's choices would "decide forever the fate" of republican government.[7] The delegates never

Congress, *Biographical Directory of the United States Congress, 1774–1989* (Washington, DC: Government Printing Office, 1989); Patrick T. Conley and John P. Kaminski, eds., *The Constitution and the States: The Role of the Original Thirteen in the Framing and Adoption of the Federal Constitution* (Madison, WI: Madison House, 1988); Thornton Anderson, *Creating the Constitution: The Convention of 1787 and the First Congress* (University Park: Pennsylvania State University Press, 1993).

4 Skowronek developed the idea of "making" politics in *The Politics Presidents Make: Leadership from John Adams to Bill Clinton* (Cambridge, MA: Belknap Press, 1997). Skowronek, in turn, drew on James MacGregor Burns's distinction between those he termed "transactional" leaders, who forge political coalitions, and "transformational" leaders, who aspire to bring together interests that "are presently or potentially united in pursuit of 'higher' goals, the realization of which is tested by the achievement of significant change that represents the collective or pooled interests of leaders and followers." See Burns, *Leadership* (New York: Harper and Row, 1978), pp. 425–6.

5 With only one exception, the state legislatures chose the delegates to send to Philadelphia. In South Carolina, the governor designated the state's delegates.

6 *RFC* 3: 585.

7 *RFC* May 29, 1: 19; June 2, 1: 87; June 26, 1: 423–4. Gouverneur Morris later observed that Hamilton disdained republican government, but whatever his true position on republicanism, he recognized the political necessity of producing a republican Constitution.

questioned the desirability of guaranteeing republican government for every state.[8]

Republican principles, however, were far too ambiguous to determine *how* the delegates should reconstitute policy agency, authority, and process in the national government. None of the delegates disagreed with George Mason's observation that "The people of America, like all other people, are unsettled in their minds, and their principles fixed to no object, except that a republican government is the best, and that the legislature ought to consist of two branches."[9] Republican principles stipulated only two very broad principles for government design. First, republicanism required that key policy makers should be the agents of the people. In republican theory, public policy is legitimate only when made by institutions representative of the citizens.[10] As John Adams had put it, the people's representative assembly should "think, feel, reason, and act like them."[11] Similarly, George Mason told the convention that "you sh[ould] draw the Representatives immediately from the people. [I]t sh[ould] be so much so, that even the Diseases of the people sh[ould] be represented."[12] Second, republicanism stipulated that institutions with different policy responsibilities must be kept separate. Government power could be abused if a single leader or public body unilaterally could make laws, enforce them, interpret them, and punish those who disagreed. In writings that influenced the American republicans profoundly, the Baron

Morris to Robert Walsh, February 5, 1811, in *RFC* 3: 418. On the tension between republican, liberal, and other values, see James A. Morone, *The Democratic Wish: Popular Participation and the Limits of American Government* (New York: Basic Books, 1990), and Rogers Smith, *Civic Ideals: Conflicting Visions of Citizenship in US History* (New Haven, CT: Yale University Press, 1997).

[8] *RFC* June 11, 1: 194; July 18, 2: 48–9. Early in the convention, Paterson asked the delegates to delay consideration of Virginia's resolution on guaranteeing all states a republican government, probably because the proposal implied that the national government would use force to implement the guarantee (*RFC* June 5, 1: 121). Gouverneur Morris and Jonathan Dayton, citing Rhode Island's policy results, objected to an *unqualified* guarantee of republican government to the states (*RFC* July 18, 2: 47–8; August 30, 2: 467).

[9] *RFC* June 20, 1: 346.

[10] Gordon S. Wood, *The Creation of the American Republic, 1776–1787* (Chapel Hill: University of North Carolina Press, 1969), p. 55; Bernard Bailyn, *The Ideological Origins of the American Revolution* (Cambridge, MA: Belknap Press, 1967), pp. 280–6. The Continental Congress in 1776 had called on the colonies to form their own governments with "all the powers of government exerted, under the authority of the people of the colonies" (*JCC* May 15, 1776, 4: 358).

[11] Jack N. Rakove, *Original Meanings: Politics and Ideas in the Making of the Constitution* (New York: Alfred A. Knopf, 1996), p. 203.

[12] *RFC* June 6, 1: 138.

de Montesquieu argued that policy making ought to be placed in separate hands from policy enforcement.[13] All the states put these principles into practice when they established their revolutionary governments. All vested ultimate power in their citizens, and all formally separated their legislatures, executives, and courts.[14] Most of the several plans for Confederation reform circulating in 1787 proposed to separate the national executive and judiciary from the legislature. The delegates widely accepted the general principle of separated powers balancing and checking one another.[15]

[13] Charles-Louis de Secondat, Baron de Montesquieu, *The Spirit of the Laws* (New York: Hafner Press, 1948), book 9, pp. 150–60. Montesquieu wrote that "the legislature is the general will of the state – the executive is the execution of that general will." He added that "[i]n every government there are three sorts of power: the legislative; the executive in respect to things dependent on the law of nations; and the executive in regard to matters that depend on the civil law... [by this third power, the prince or magistrate] punishes criminals, or determines the disputes that arise between individuals. The latter we shall call the judiciary power, and the other simply the executive power of the state" (or, in current terms, the power of policy implementation). See also Wood, *The Creation of the American Republic*, pp. 150–61, 446–53; Rakove, *Original Meanings*, pp. 245–56; Marc W. Kruman, *Between Authority and Liberty: State Constitution Making in Revolutionary America* (Chapel Hill: University of North Carolina Press, 1997), pp. 109–30. The delegates invoked Montesquieu's writings selectively during the convention (see *RFC* June 7, 1: 71; June 18, 1: 308; June 23, 1: 391; June 30, 1: 485, 495; July 11, 1: 579–80; July 17, 2: 34; September 6, 2: 534). Madison and his allies usually enlisted Montesquieu to defend their position. Later, in the battle to ratify the Constitution, both sides tried to use the French author as an ally. In *Federalist* 47, Madison invoked "the celebrated Montesquieu" as "The oracle who is always consulted and cited on" the subject of separation of powers, and said that the U.S. Constitution was consistent with his maxims. Alexander Hamilton, James Madison, and John Jay, *The Federalist*, ed. Jacob E. Cooke (Middletown, CT: Wesleyan University Press, 1961), pp. 324–7 (see also pp. 52–6, 292, 295, 523). Luther Martin and other opponents of the Constitution later used Montesquieu's authority to strengthen their arguments; see Martin's November, 1787 tract, "Genuine Information," in *RFC* 3: 197.

[14] M. J. C. Vile, *Constitutionalism and the Separation of Powers* (Oxford: Clarendon Press, 1967), p. 128; Wood, *The Creation of the American Republic, 1776–1787*, pp. 150–61. The Maryland, Virginia, North Carolina, and Georgia constitutions explicitly incorporated the separation of powers, and the rest separated powers implicitly. For example, according to Virginia's 1776 constitution, "The legislative, executive, and judiciary departments, shall be separate and distinct, so that neither exercise the Powers properly belonging to the other; nor shall any person exercise the powers of more than one of them at the same time, except that the Justices of the County Courts shall be eligible to either House of Assembly." In *The Founders' Constitution*, ed. Philip B. Kurland and Ralph Lerner (Chicago: University of Chicago Press, 1987), 1: 7–9.

[15] Roger H. Brown, *Redeeming the Republic: Federalists, Taxation, and the Origins of the Constitution* (Baltimore: Johns Hopkins University Press, 1993), pp. 171–83; Vile, *Constitutionalism and the Separation of Powers*, pp. 153–4; Gerhard Casper, *Separating Power: Essays on the Founding Period* (Cambridge, MA: Harvard University Press, 1997), pp. 7–8.

These broad, open-ended republican principles did little to answer the delegates' central dilemma: reconstituting national government so it could promote the national interest without harming interests they considered vital. In practice, republican government in Rhode Island and other states was producing unacceptable policies.[16] As the convention reached an impasse over congressional representation, Georgia delegate Abraham Baldwin put the predicament this way: "It appears to be agreed that the government we should adopt ought to be energetic and formidable, yet I would guard against the danger of becoming too formidable."[17] Broad principles did not specify precisely *how* powers should be separated, checked, and balanced.[18] Each of these state republics had implemented these principles in a different way, and none offered an obvious model for how policy authority should be separated. Pennsylvania's constitution reflected little concern about the arbitrary exercise of *legislative* authority, and so it invested substantial power in its single-house legislature, and relatively little power in its state president.[19] New York's constitution makers, torn between the fear of executive despotism and the fear of direct popular control of policy outcomes, established a strong Senate and an independent governor to check the lower house. New York also provided a council of revision (including the governor and supreme court justices) that could veto legislation. Only Massachusetts, however, authorized its governor to veto the legislature's bills.[20] None of the states' republican experiments had produced entirely satisfactory policy outcomes.

[16] Elbridge Gerry, summarizing the disappointment of many delegates with the current practice of republicanism, said at the convention's outset that he had "been too republican heretofore: he was still however republican, but had been taught by experience the danger of the levilling spirit" (*RFC* May 31, 1: 48).

[17] *RFC* June 29, 1: 475.

[18] Vile, *Constitutionalism and the Separation of Powers*, p. 154; Casper, *Separating Power*, p. 8.

[19] Kruman points out that a number of checks were designed into the Pennsylvania constitution to prevent rash lawmaking. The state constitution required that two-thirds of the members be present to establish a quorum. All proceedings were publicized, and any two members could demand a roll call, a provision that made it easy to slow down policy making. Except for emergency legislation, no bill could become law until put before the citizens and until after another legislative election. In addition, the appointment of government officials mainly rested in the hands of the executive council and president, a provision, which in Kruman's view made the Pennsylvania constitution adhere "more closely to the doctrine of separation of powers than the fundamental law of any other state." Kruman, *Between Authority and Liberty*, pp. 149–50.

[20] Wood, *The Creation of the American Republic*, pp. 150–61, 446–53; Rakove, *Original Meanings*, p. 433; Kruman, *Between Authority and Liberty*, pp. 123–6. South Carolina initially gave its governor veto power in its 1776 constitution, but changed the constitution after Governor John Rutledge actually used it.

Republican values could not help resolve whether Madison's daring plan would do more harm than good. The delegates had to go beyond republican principles and draw on their state experiences, foreign events, and historical examples to settle disputes about the design of Congress, the executive, and the courts. The Committee of Detail in early August inadvertently articulated the uncertainty of republican sentiments when it reported that "the departments shall be distinct . . . and independent of each other, except in specified cases."[21] Substantive political interests, not republicanism, divided the convention, dragged out its deliberations, and ultimately accounted for most of the Constitution's specific provisions.

POLITICS AND CONSTITUTIONAL DESIGN

The rough-and-tumble of actual republican politics influenced the delegates' specific decisions much more directly than the broad principles of republicanism to which they all subscribed. The state constitutions had unleashed intense and vibrant republican politics across the nation, and the delegates had thrived in this intensely political environment. Political coalitions – "parties" and "factions" – pervaded the delegates' political world. Only such coalitions could actually build the legislative majorities required to determine the outcomes of republican policy making. The most influential delegates at the Constitutional Convention were its most able and effective politicians. Delegates like Robert Morris of Pennsylvania, George Read of Delaware, John Langdon of New Hampshire, and Edmund Randolph of Virginia, for example, themselves led factions in their states.[22] All took it for granted that the same robust republican politics would permeate the national policy-making process they were building. National economic policy, therefore, would and should be the product of the political arts, especially the enduring art of assembling a winning political coalition through shrewd framing of issues; structuring choices; timing political action; and using persuasion, rhetoric, pressure, threats, and political deals. National economic policy ultimately would result from compromises about acceptable collective choices, rarely from optimal decisions. The record of the Constitutional Convention proves

[21] *RFC* 2: 138. In *Separating Power*, Gerhard Casper writes, "What was strikingly absent [in the Constitutional Convention], however, was anything that one might view as a coherent and generally shared idea of separation of powers" (p. 18).

[22] McDonald, *We the People*, pp. 21–37.

that the delegates were willing and often dexterous practitioners of these political arts.

To improve national economic development, the delegates had to reconstitute national policy making so that its inevitable politics would produce beneficial economic policy outcomes and inhibit bad ones. The delegates fully appreciated how difficult it would be to accomplish this goal. They expected that the reconstituted national government would attract the kinds of clever, even devious politicians who opposed them in the states and the Confederation Congress. Such politicians would try to use national power to make the kinds of economic policies that appalled the delegates and prompted the Constitutional Convention in the first place. The architects of these policies were particularly skilled in building coalitions of the disaffected and resentful, including the masses of voters with little property to lose. Factions of policy hunters permeated state legislatures, and they would pervade a revamped Congress, too. From start to finish, delegates warned that one specific constitutional provision or another would advantage such politicians and instigate their political "cabals" and "intrigues." For example,

- Oliver Ellsworth worried that if presidential terms were too short, the president would shrink from performing necessary but unpopular duties, and because "There will be *outs* as well as *ins*," the president's "administration therefore will be attacked and misrepresented."[23]
- "In all public bodies there are two parties," observed Gouverneur Morris. "The Executive will necessarily be more connected with one than with the other. There will be a personal interest therefore in one of the parties to oppose as well as in the other to support him. Much had been said of the intrigues that will be practiced by the Executive to get into office. Nothing had been said on the other side of the intrigues to get him out of office. Some leader of party will always covet his seat, will perplex his administration, will cabal with the Legislature, till he succeeds in supplanting him."[24]
- Judges should not be involved in legislative business, said Charles Pinckney, because "it will involve them in parties, and give a previous tincture to their opinions."[25]
- When John Dickinson proposed that state legislatures play a role in removing the president, Madison and James Wilson warned that "it

[23] *RFC* July 19, 2: 59 (emphasis in original).
[24] *RFC* July 24, 2: 104.
[25] *RFC* August 15, 2: 298.

would open a door for intrigues ag[ain]st him in States where his administration tho' just might be unpopular, and might tempt him to pay court to particular States whose leading partizans he might fear, or wish to engage as his partizans."[26]

- Wilson thought that, if the Senate had the power to elect the president, the senators would "contrive so to scatter" the states' electoral votes by conspiring to press for "various and improbable candidates" to ensure that the election would be thrown into the Senate.[27]
- Rufus King argued that "State Creditors" are "an active and formidable party" that would oppose the Constitution if it did not transfer state debts to the national government and thought Madison's proposal for national corporate charters would cause the States to be "divided into parties."[28]
- Nathaniel Gorham asserted that the "absolute prohibition of paper money would rouse the most desperate opposition from its partizans."[29]

The delegates expected that coalitions demanding unsound economic policies would emerge naturally in the new government. Only the constitutional rules for choosing policy makers, defining their authority, and organizing the policy process could stand between these ambitious politicians and the pursuit of bad economic policies (if, indeed, anything could stand in the way of such coalitions).

Normal republican politics, then, posed the most serious problem for reconstituting national government. The delegates had to make republicanism safe for the nation's economy. They had a strong desire to protect the unique equilibrium of economic and political interests in each state. They also had to produce a document that could be ratified by the states, although, beyond fidelity to republicanism, the delegates did not agree on what was politically feasible and what was not.[30]

[26] *RFC* June 2, 1: 86.

[27] *RFC* September 6, 2: 523.

[28] *RFC* August 18, 2: 327; September 14, 2: 616.

[29] *RFC* August 28, 2: 439.

[30] The records of the debate do not support a claim that political expediency alone determined much of the design of the Constitution. It is true that delegates invoked the need to draft a document that would be politically acceptable to the states. Debates about several provisions involved assertions that the provision in question would be unacceptable to certain states, regions, or the people generally. Elbridge Gerry was fond of alluding to what the voters of Massachusetts and New England would accept. But it also was asserted that the political climate was receptive to solutions in general, and that the reception to specific proposals could not be predicted. A wide variety of influential delegates, such

The problem of restructuring national politics colored every choice at the convention with immediate political implications. The prospect of future politics pervaded the debates. Many a delegate must have sat silently in the convention imagining other participants as future partners or rivals in the struggle for the control of specific national policies. These perceptions almost certainly increased as weeks of debate magnified the political stakes in every choice. Madison's effort to nationalize economic authority, reduce state policy authority, and redistribute agency in Congress threatened to change every state's political order fundamentally. Each state's political leaders, however, viewed these changes in a different way.

Policy Authority

State political leaders had learned that the tools of economic management – especially taxes, trade, and currency – were at least as valuable for managing politics as for managing the economy.[31] A shrewdly constructed set of tax, trade, debt, and other policies could benefit one's core constituency, forging an alliance of key economic elites even as it earned the loyalty of a sizable bloc of voters. At the same time, a carefully fashioned political program could divide one's opponents and neutralize potential

as Hugh Williamson, expressed hope that "the expressions of individuals would not be taken for the sense of their colleagues, much less of their States which was not and could not be known" (*RFC* July 5, 1: 532). John Dickinson equated feasibility with existing state institutions and practices (see *RFC* August 13, 2: 278). Clearly, political feasibility did not deter the delegates from considering an extensive reconstitution of the national government, despite some early reservations about the convention's warrant (*RFC* May 30, 1: 34–5).

Policy debates abound with claims that a given proposal is or is not politically expedient. Such assertions are partly tactical. They aim to strengthen political argument. Often, however, such assertions are supported by little or no hard evidence, other than the speaker's presumed political expertise and reputation for fairness. Some delegates invoked a broad political warrant when it suited their interests and then invoked the constraints of feasibility on a different issue. Randolph, for example, urged the delegates to consider both the intensity and the brevity of their window of policy opportunity to make major changes (*RFC* June 16, 1: 255–6). On a specific point he wanted to win, however, he invoked the need to take into account the "permanent temper of the people" and the need for "necessary confidence" (*RFC* June 2, 1: 88). Even Madison, who argued that the citizens expected a good document from the convention, could invoke the tactical need to allay suspicions "within & without doors" (RFC August 11, 2: 261–2).

[31] David A. Lake observes the enduring tendency of politics to trump economic theory when he notes that "the law of comparative advantage is one of the basic tenets of economics. Yet in perhaps no other area is the gap between economic theory and political practice so large." In *Protection and Free Trade: International Sources of U.S. Commercial Strategy, 1887–1939* (Ithaca, NY: Cornell University Press, 1988), p. 19.

political enemies.[32] No one was in a better position to understand the conflicts among American propertied interests than the politicians who had to broker and balance conflicting policy demands. Through trial and error, state political leaders had learned to use these policy tools to balance competing political and economic interests in their states.

Leaders in each state took a different approach to managing war debts, for example, using their policy discretion in a way they believed politically expedient for their situation. Public officials in Massachusetts imposed substantial taxes to eliminate its war debts as rapidly as possible. These measures aimed to foster economic stability and growth, but by bearing down hard on farmers of moderate means, they created the political backlash that fueled Shays's Rebellion. Connecticut's lawmakers also increased taxes to pay off the war debt, but the Connecticut legislature heeded the popular backlash against this policy earlier than Massachusetts. Connecticut cushioned the tax increase by lengthening the process of debt redemption, paying only a small portion of the principal each year and easing the annual tax burden. Virginia devalued its paper currency, imposed a tariff on imports, and suspended tax collection from 1781 to 1786. Only in 1787 did Madison's state begin to impose a relatively heavy load of direct taxes to retire the debts. Initially, South Carolina's leaders attempted to retire debts quickly, but this conservative policy sparked riots and swelled political opposition. South Carolina's leaders then appeased the citizens by printing more currency, delaying the due date for private debts, and permitting the payment of debts in kind.[33]

Political leaders in each state, then, relied on their economic authority to build governing coalitions that balanced the competing demands of prosperity, political stability, popularity, the pressures of diverse interests, and their personal agendas. Many of the delegates had become

[32] Though usually connected to wealthy Americans, these delegates were not simply the agents of the wealthy. Generally, they invested more time and effort into public affairs than in the direct pursuit of material gain. A quarter of the delegates had supported debtor relief measures in their legislatures, and only three (all from Delaware) consistently had voted against debtor relief legislation in their state legislatures. Thirteen members were themselves heavily in debt, some to the point of bankruptcy. Thirty owned public securities, though of these, five of the largest securities holders left the convention or refused to sign the Constitution. Biographies of the delegates to the Constitutional Convention suggest they were motivated by the same mix of goals that motivate American politicians today: policy achievement, power, recognition, glory, gratitude. For thumbnail biographies, see especially McDonald, *We the People*, pp. 25, 37, 86–92; Rossiter, *1787: The Grand Convention*, pp. 79–156.

[33] Edwin J. Perkins, *American Public Finance and Financial Services, 1700–1815* (Columbus: Ohio State University Press, 1994), pp. 137–72.

sufficiently skilled at using these policy tools to advance their careers, protect their homes, help their allies, and make their communities more safe and prosperous. The delegates did not deny that the national government needed some specific additional powers to protect and benefit their constituents, particularly those creditors, property owners, merchants, and others roused to demand more-effective national action by some of the states' populist measures. Nationalized economic powers could benefit both these state constituents and the nation at large. An effective national revenue would relieve states of the burden of laying taxes to fund the national government, and would provide more-dependable funds for national public goods such as a military. Effective national power over currency could reduce the spillover effects of irresponsible currency emissions. Effective national power to regulate interstate commerce could reduce neighboring states' ability to extract resources from their own. In theory, effective national power to conclude commercial treaties could be used to help exporters, importers, and carriers.

But Virginia's far-reaching proposal to nationalize economic authority was vulnerable to a pair of political objections. First, by threatening the states' control of all economic policy prerogatives, Virginia's plan potentially jeopardized every one of these carefully constructed state political regimes. Each and every state stood to lose politically indispensable tools if the national government assumed all power to regulate commerce and could veto any state law. South Carolina and Georgia could lose the authority to import slaves, and national regulation of slavery could supersede the states' control of slaves throughout the South. New York could lose its power to tax imports, while New Jersey and Connecticut could lose their power to retaliate against New York when it taxed imports into their states. Connecticut could lose its authority to impose a tithe to support religion. States with public lands could lose major economic and political assets. Any given mix of national poll or property taxes could steal away a state's tax base, making it more difficult for a state to ask its citizens to pay more of the same kind of tax while forcing legislatures to turn to much more politically divisive revenue or spending options.

Second, national economic power could be used to advantage some states at others' expense even more effectively than unbridled state economic power. New England stood to gain more from a commercial treaty than the South. The South stood to gain more from a treaty opening the Mississippi to commerce. New York stood to lose if the national government acquired the right to tax imports. South Carolina stood to gain more than any other state if the national government assumed responsibility for state war debts. Georgia, at the national frontier, stood to benefit more from a national military than most states. Maryland would benefit from national authority to erect lighthouses and clear harbors. Specific provisions in commercial treaties could benefit one product, industry, state, or region and harm others.

As the delegates balanced these considerations, their thinking about national interests evolved during the convention. They were forced to consider the long-term power and wealth of the nation and their state, and the partial, short-term interests of the landed elites, merchants, manufacturers, creditors, debtors, and the larger mass of freeholding voters who made up their constituency.[34] In effect, they each viewed national interests in a different way, consistent with the interests of their varied constituencies, their own interests, their experiences, and their principles. The delegates sought to nationalize somewhat different sets of specific public goods. Massachusetts's Elbridge Gerry opposed a general national veto but had "no objection to authorize a negative to paper money and similar measures," and he sought a constitutional guarantee for creditors holding public securities. Many delegates, including Connecticut's Roger Sherman and Oliver Ellsworth, supported a national ban on fiat currency. John Rutledge and Sherman sought to nationalize the state debts. John Dickinson and Jonathan Dayton wanted national authority to suppress all domestic violence without a request from the state. George Mason wanted to authorize the national government to prevent the increase of slavery, to regulate the militia, and to regulate consumption. Dickinson, Langdon, Pierce Butler, and South Carolina's two Pinckneys (General Charles Cotesworth Pinckney and Charles Pinckney) also wanted national authority over the state militias.[35] One of the delegates most opposed to national power, Maryland's Luther Martin, insisted on national assumption of control over public lands. Martin, Dickinson, and New

[34] Compare Robert O. Keohane's comments about political leaders' choices in international relations: "The key tradeoffs for the United States in the 1980s, as for mercantilist statesmen in the seventeenth century . . . are not between power and wealth but between the long-term power/wealth interests of the state and the partial interests of individual merchants, workers, or manufacturers on the one hand or short-term interests of society on the other." *After Hegemony: Cooperation and Discord in the World Political Economy* (Princeton, NJ: Princeton University Press, 1984), p. 23.

[35] To distinguish the two Pinckneys in this book, I use the distinctions Madison used in his convention notes. "General Pinckney" refers to Charles Cotesworth Pinckney (1746–1825), who had reached the rank of brigadier general by the end of his Revolutionary War service; the Federalist Party nominated this Pinckney as its presidential candidate in 1804. The younger Charles Pinckney (1757–1824), a second cousin to General Pinckney, became a Democratic-Republican U.S. senator from South Carolina.

Jersey's William Paterson, among others, sought to stop the importation of slaves.[36]

While Virginia's broad plan to nationalize economic power took advantage of the delegates' general consensus on the need for more national authority, it also made it easier for Madison's opponents to question what government would do with that power. A grant of economic authority so encompassing could easily be characterized as a threat to any state's vital political interests. Each delegate could evaluate the balance between the benefits and risks of any specific national power for his own state and the nation. Madison, who fully appreciated the political sensitivity of such issues, understood that states would not surrender policy prerogatives to the national government unless a substantial number felt that they could sufficiently control national policy outcomes. For this reason, Madison believed that the convention had to change policy agency before it tackled policy authority.

Policy Agency

The delegates believed that the surest way to control what government did with its power was to control the selection and dependence of policy makers.[37] Most delegates assumed that policy makers' self-interest would cause them to serve the interests of those who chose them and kept them in office. Experience seemed to show that elected officials serve the interests of their voters, and appointees serve the interests of those who controlled their tenure in office. Thus, control of what policy makers did depended on who controlled their selection. History proved that no formal constraints on authority or process could contain indefinitely the power of a political leader who did not depend on other political actors.

[36] *RFC* June 8, 1: 165; July 9, 1: 561; August 16, 2: 309; August 18, 2: 326–7, 331–2; August 20, 2: 344; August 21, 2: 363–4; August 22, 2: 370, 372; August 28, 2: 439; August 30, 2: 464, 467. On South Carolina and state debts, see James Haw, *John & Edward Rutledge of South Carolina* (Athens: University of Georgia Press, 1997), pp. 211–12. Haw reports that South Carolina initially had responded to the Articles of Confederation by supporting a "confederated union of the States, upon a principle of equality, delegating only as much of our sovereignty as may be absolutely necessary for the general safety" (p. 106).

[37] Roger Sherman later wrote that "the greatest security against abuse [of government power] is, that the interest of those in whom the powers of government are vested is the same as that of the people they govern, and that they are dependent on the suffrage of the people for their appointment to, and continuance in office. This is a much greater security than a declaration of rights, or restraining clauses upon paper." December 8, 1787, in *Supplement to Max Farrand's "The Records of the Federal Convention of 1787,"* ed. James H. Hutson (New Haven, CT: Yale University Press, 1987), p. 286.

The rules for selecting, rewarding, and removing officeholders therefore would powerfully shape economic policy outcomes, because these rules would determine the interests to which national policy makers would respond and the purposes for which they would use national power. The state legislatures' recent economic policies, attributed to the direct dependence of state legislators on freeholders of modest means, seemed to validate this premise. Madison, Elbridge Gerry of Massachusetts, and Gouverneur Morris of Pennsylvania regularly warned that policy makers would tailor public policy to satisfy those on whom they depended. Even the most senior delegates reinforced these unsentimental expectations of their fellow politicians. It was grandfatherly Benjamin Franklin who, in the first week, warned ominously that

> there are two passions which have a powerful influence on the affairs of men. These are ambition and avarice; the love of power, and the love of money. Separately each of these has great force in prompting men to action; but when united in view of the same object, they have in many minds the most violent effects. [P]lace before the eyes of such men a post of *honour* that shall at the same time be a place of *profit*, and they will move heaven and earth to obtain it. The vast number of such places it is that renders the British Government so tempestuous.... And of what kind are the men that will strive for this profitable pre-eminence, through all the bustle of cabal, the heat of contention, the infinite mutual abuse of parties, tearing to pieces the best of characters? It will not be the wise and moderate, the lovers of peace and good order, the men fittest for the trust. It will be the bold and the violent, the men of strong passions and indefatigable activity in their selfish pursuits. These will thrust themselves into your Government and be your rulers.[38]

The delegates' exposure to the worst of human nature in war and politics made them very receptive to such arguments. To his peers, even Madison sometimes seemed too sanguine about political motivations. When Madison proposed to ban members of Congress from holding other offices, a Madison ally, Rufus King of Massachusetts, objected that "the idea of preventing intrigue and solicitation of offices was chimerical."[39]

The convention's most explosive and time-consuming debates involved the rules for apportioning seats in the reconstituted national legislature, because state interests depended on relative state political power in the premier policy-making body in the republican system.[40] Many delegates

[38] *RFC* June 2, 1: 82 (emphasis in original).

[39] *RFC* June 23, 1: 387.

[40] Jack N. Rakove views the conflict over representation as a philosophical conflict distinct from the political bargaining over the authority of the reconstituted government; see his "The Great Compromise: Ideas, Interests, and the Politics of the Constitution,"

were attentive and experienced vote counters who grasped instinctively that apportioning seats according to population would redistribute power away from medium and small states to Virginia, Pennsylvania, and Massachusetts. Counting slaves in the apportionment formula would shift power to the slave states, but ignoring slaves would shift power away from them. Adding new states in the West on an equal basis with the Atlantic states would shift power away from the coast. An extra seat for South Carolina or for New Hampshire could make a substantial policy difference, not just for those states but also for their regions and the economies they represented.

Virginia's proposal to base representation entirely on population had two political vulnerabilities. First, it gave the states outside of Madison's coalition a clear reason to coalesce around the defense of equal state representation, despite other differences that separated them. Second, because proportional representation obviously made it possible for southern and large states to coalesce, the obvious way to undermine Madison's coalition was to emphasize policy authority and, by doing so, to emphasize the substantive policy differences that divided Madison's supporters.

The Policy Process

The delegates knew that they were handing over more national power to politicians and that politics would animate the policy-making process. The delegates' disagreements about the process of making public policy – such as the size of majorities needed for legislation, internal controls over government spending, and the power to veto legislative bills – derived from their contests over the political use of policy authority and the politics of policy agency. As the delegates resolved questions about who would govern different policy institutions, it became critically important to defend the autonomy, prerogatives, and resources of those institutions most responsive to their interests. Because the policy process translated agency into outcomes, the delegates aimed to secure the influence of those policy-making institutions that were the most reliable agents of favored interests and invest them with authority to influence policy outcomes decisively.

William and Mary Quarterly, 3rd ser., 44:3 (July 1987): 424–57. But it is clear that the delegates were considering the material consequences of these choices as they debated them. It is equally plausible that, like Madison, the delegates were using philosophical arguments about liberty and fairness as rhetorical weapons to support positions that were fundamentally based on the economic and political interests of their states.

The design of the national policy-making process, then, was driven heavily by expectations about likely policy outcomes, policy agency, and policy authority. For example, when the delegates rejected Madison's proposal to require the Supreme Court to join the president in exercising the veto, Gouverneur Morris expressed regret because the proposal would signal markets that the new government would provide a strong barrier against Congress.[41] The president's policy influence, as well as his selection, became controversial because Madison and his allies began to see the president as their best hope for promoting national policy interests after the compromise on representation in Congress.

The very ambition of Madison's plan armed potential opponents with opportunities to undermine his strategy. Madison's plan could only succeed if he maintained a cohesive coalition of large and southern states long enough to win a swift, early victory for proportional representation, and then sweep other provisions of the Virginia Plan into effect. Tactically, it was imperative for Madison that the convention change the basis of representation before addressing any other issue and then focus on general principles rather than specific differences in material interests that potentially cleaved his coalition.[42]

MADISON'S COALITION

At the beginning, Madison had grounds to believe that if the convention could make quick, decisive choices about proportional representation, the basic elements of the Virginia Plan had a reasonable chance of success. As Madison likely hoped, most of the leading nationalists from other states, particularly from Pennsylvania, deferred to Virginia's leadership and its plan.

In *designing* the Constitution's provisions, fourteen delegates from five states exercised the most influence: Madison, George Mason, and Edmund Randolph of Virginia; Benjamin Franklin, James Wilson, Gouverneur Morris of Pennsylvania; Elbridge Gerry, Rufus King, and Nathaniel Gorham of Massachusetts; John Rutledge, General Charles Cotesworth Pinckney, and Charles Pinckney of South Carolina; and Roger Sherman and Oliver Ellsworth of Connecticut. Several other delegates also exercised notable influence in some of the key design choices: William Samuel Johnson of Connecticut, William Paterson of New Jersey, George Read and John Dickinson of Delaware, Luther Martin and Daniel Carroll

[41] *RFC* August 15, 2: 299.

[42] Calvin C. Jillson, *Constitution Making: Conflict and Consensus in the Federal Convention of 1787* (New York: Agathon Press, 1988), p. 47.

of Maryland, Hugh Williamson of North Carolina, and Pierce Butler of South Carolina.[43]

Throughout the proceedings, Wilson, Morris, and King were stalwart Madison allies who pressed for independent national agency and the elimination of state influence over the selection of national policy makers. Gorham and Charles Pinckney generally supported Madison's positions. Two nationally recognized leaders, Robert Morris of Pennsylvania and George Washington of Virginia, though virtually silent during the proceedings, also supported Madison (it is hard to tell how much influence each exercised away from the formal debates). Four of the five most influential delegations – Virginia, Pennsylvania, Massachusetts, and South Carolina – were part of Madison's expected coalition of large and southern states.

But Madison's potential allies formed a fragile coalition.[44] Even Madison's closest allies did not always agree with him. James Wilson, Madison's most dependable ally in the debates, preferred a system even more directly dependent on voters than Madison. Wilson initially hoped that the national electorate would directly elect both the House and the president, so that they would be independent of one another as well as independent of the state legislatures.[45] Another Madison ally,

[43] My classification draws on but differs from that of Clinton Rossiter in *1787: The Grand Convention*, pp. 247–53. Rossiter sorted the delegates into several categories ranked by importance: "Principal" (Washington, Madison, James Wilson, and Gouverneur Morris), "Influential" (Gorham, King, Gerry, Sherman, Ellsworth, Franklin, Randolph, Mason, Rutledge, and both Pinckneys), "Very Useful" (William Samuel Johnson, Paterson, Read, Dickinson, Luther Martin, Hugh Williamson, and Pierce Butler), useful (Livingston, David Brearley, Bedford, Daniel Carroll, William R. Davie, Richard Dobbs Spaight, Baldwin, Langdon), "Visible" (but with little evident influence, such as Caleb Strong of Massachusetts), "Ciphers" with no evident impact (Jared Ingersoll of Pennsylvania), "Dropouts" who left early (Lansing and Yates, who left in mid-July), and two talented, experienced "Disappointments" (Alexander Hamilton of New York, who attended irregularly, and Robert Morris of Pennsylvania, who did not contribute to the debates). Washington and Robert Morris undoubtedly made their preferences generally known, and we have no evidence for assessing their influence off the floor. Rossiter's classification, while reasonable, undervalues the influence of Madison's adversaries, notably Roger Sherman, who deserves to be included as "Principal." Ralph Ketcham includes five delegates as influential that I excluded because of my focus on constitutional design, rather than on participation. These five are Washington, Hamilton, William Paterson, William Samuel Johnson, and Luther Martin; Ketcham, *James Madison: A Biography* (Charlottesville: University Press of Virginia, 1971), p. 194. Of the delegates I list as influential, Wilson, Morris, Randolph, Madison, Ellsworth, Sherman, King, Rutledge, and both Pinckneys had extensive legal training.

[44] David J. Siemers, *Ratifying the Republic: Antifederalists and Federalists in Constitutional Time* (Stanford, CA: Stanford University Press, 2002), p. 20.

[45] *RFC* May 31, 1: 49; June 1, 1: 69.

Gouverneur Morris, preferred to place more distance between policy makers and voters. Still another supporter of national policy independence, Alexander Hamilton of New York, attended irregularly and, at a crucial moment, made a speech so uncompromising in its nationalism that it likely strengthened the opposition. Although the Pennsylvania delegation proved a staunch ally of Virginia, slavery strained the Virginia-Pennsylvania alliance.[46] Political diversity within the large states divided these delegations internally. In the Virginia delegation, Randolph's and Mason's support wavered as the convention whittled away at the Virginia Plan. The maverick Elbridge Gerry frequently broke with his Massachusetts colleagues. Gerry, Randolph, and Mason refused to sign the final document.

The states south of Virginia supported Madison's plan because they supported proportional representation in Congress. More weight in the national legislature would increase their control over national policies affecting slavery and other vital issues. South Carolina, which sent a particularly able and forceful delegation to Philadelphia, epitomized this attitude. John Rutledge and his brother Edward had built a political regime in which the coastal elite they represented governed South Carolina, with strategic policy concessions to voters in the backcountry away from the Carolina coast.[47] As Madison anticipated, Rutledge and his South Carolina delegates provided reliable votes for proportional representation. But the delegation frequently voted to protect state agency in choosing national officials, and it became one of the fiercest defenders of state control of economic assets, particularly slaves.[48] North Carolina's delegation was volatile and lacked effective members other than Hugh Williamson. Georgia's Abraham Baldwin arrived June 11 and remained at the convention, but his fellow Georgians attended irregularly and the delegation split on important votes.

Madison's expected coalition could hold together only by suppressing many intrinsic political cleavages. The divisions embedded in his

[46] S. Sidney Ulmer, "Sub-group Formation in the Constitutional Convention," *Midwest Journal of Political Science* 10:3 (August 1966): 288–303; see also Anderson, *Creating the Constitution.*

[47] Richard Barry, *The Rutledges of South Carolina* (New York: Duell, Sloan, and Pierce, 1942); Haw, *John & Edward Rutledge of South Carolina.*

[48] The South Carolina delegates supported a national government that could limit the backcountry demands for easy money. They also supported the backcountry's interest in the continued importation of slaves. Haw, *John & Edward Rutledge of South Carolina*, pp. 25–31, 79–81, 118, 144–5, 157–62, 182–97, 200.

coalition made a swift victory on proportional representation even more imperative. Madison's opponents, though at a disadvantage, quickly began to exploit the political vulnerabilities of his faction.

MADISON'S OPPONENTS

Madison's plan to nationalize economic authority and redistribute representation in Congress especially threatened the interests of the economically vulnerable middle and northern states. These states had the greatest stake in enabling the national government to be responsible for specific public goods such as providing national defense, blocking other states' from restricting commerce, and enforcing other states' financial obligations to the Confederation. For example, New Jersey's leaders had long expressed the need for a more effective and better-funded national government and particularly for the nationalization of western lands and tariffs. As early as 1778, New Jersey's state legislature suggested that Congress take sole authority to regulate foreign trade and to dispose of western lands, and it gave its delegates to the Annapolis Convention in 1786 the broadest mandate to overhaul the national policy-making system. Delaware, New Jersey, and Connecticut (like Pennsylvania and the Carolinas) quickly ratified the proposed 1783 amendment to the Articles establishing a 5 percent national tariff and additional duties on specific items. Madison himself played on the states' vulnerability at the Constitutional Convention.[49] But because these states had relatively few economic

[49] John E. O'Connor, *William Paterson: Lawyer and Statesman* (New Brunswick, NJ: Rutgers University Press, 1979), p. 32. *RFC* August 28, 2: 441. Nathaniel Gorham noted that, "[s]hould a separation of the States take place, the fate of N[ew] Jersey w[oul]d be worst of all. She has no foreign commerce & can have but little. P[ennsylvani]a & N[ew] York will continue to levy taxes on her consumption" (June 29, 1: 462). Connecticut's delegates to the Continental Congress, Samuel Huntington and Benjamin Huntington, had expressed similar concerns to their governor four years earlier: "Massachusetts . . . and Rhode Island are Collecting Duties on Trade in their own way and applying the Monies so Raised to the Payment of their own Quotas. The Burthen of this being sustained by the Consumer must be Eventually Borne by the Industrious Inhabitants of our State in Proportion to the Goods we Purchase from them whilst we have our whole Quota to Pay without an Equal Advantage of a Tax upon Commerce. This Naturally suggests to us the Necessity of Promoting Trade in our own State and withdrawing it from those States whose Policy is as much as Possible to lay their Burthens on us. This also is a Striking Proof of the Equitable Nature of a General Impost and of the Injustice that will take Place in Consequence of the Local and Illiberal Measures that will be Adopted by the Several States in their Separate Proceedings tending to Disaffection, Animosity and Disunion" (Connecticut Delegates to Governor Jonathan Trumbull Sr., September 2, 1783, in *LDC* 20: 615–16).

assets and because the larger states could harm them, it was even more important for them to defend their remaining economic prerogatives forcefully. New Jersey's support for increased national power was conditional: it sought to guarantee that larger states would not institutionalize their existing commercial and financial advantage over New Jersey into permanent policy advantages.

Madison initially may have been encouraged by the weaknesses of his potential opponents. Because New Hampshire's delegates did not arrive until July 23, and Rhode Island never sent an official delegation, Madison's six-state coalition theoretically could outvote the five remaining states during the convention's first two months.[50] The uneven attendance of New Jersey's delegates made that state's influence episodic. New York, unlike neighboring middle states, had in its port a lucrative economic asset. Two of the three New York delegates, Robert Yates and John Lansing, strongly opposed Madison. Both walked away from the convention early in July, before New Hampshire's delegates arrived, and their departure left New York without enough delegates to cast official votes during the final nine weeks of deliberations. Maryland's delegates deeply disagreed with one another, and its delegation cast more divided votes on contested issues than any other.[51]

Delegations outside Madison's expected coalition tended to be more divided and disengaged than those within it. Table 4.1 compares state absences and divisions on all 205 contested votes at the Constitutional Convention. Virginia cast aye or no votes on all but one of these issues. Madison's expected coalition of six large and southern states cast 95 percent of possible aye or no votes on these substantive questions. In contrast, the six states that attended and were outside his coalition cast only 75 percent of possible aye or no votes on these substantive questions.

Despite their political disadvantages, Madison's opponents were capable politicians adept at defending their interests. Delegates outside

[50] On June 10 Madison wrote to James Monroe that eleven states were represented and "the Convention is now as full as we expect it to be unless a report should be true that Rh[ode] Island had it in contemplation to make one of the party. If her deputies should bring with them the complexion of the State, their company will not add much to our pleasure, or to the progress of the business." In Hutson, *Supplement to Max Farrand's Records*, p. 67.

[51] On the divisions in the Maryland delegation, see James McHenry's notes, on receiving the Committee of Detail report, in *RFC* August 6, 2: 190–1. Of the fifty-five delegates attending the convention, Lansing and Yates of New York, Mason of Virginia, Gerry of Massachusetts, and John Francis Mercer and Luther Martin of Maryland all would oppose the Constitution's ratification in their states.

TABLE 4.1. *Divided Votes and Absences on 205 Contested Votes at the Constitutional Convention*

	Number of Divided Votes	Number of Absences	Total	As Percent of Contested Votes
Virginia[a]	1	0	1	0
South Carolina[a]	2	0	2	1
Connecticut	5	0	5	2
Delaware	5	6	11	5
Pennsylvania[a]	10	2	12	6
Georgia[a]	9	4	13	6
North Carolina[a]	7	7	14	7
Massachusetts[a]	10	8	18	9
Maryland	16	3	19	9
New Jersey	1	21	22	11
New Hampshire	7	86	93	45
New York	7	145	152	74

[a] State in Madison's expected coalition of three large and three southern states.

Madison's coalition recognized his strategy with little difficulty. Virginia's bold plan for national policy independence and proportional representation in the legislature raised understandable suspicions among these political realists. Delaware's Gunning Bedford portrayed Madison's basic political strategy explicitly and darkly:

If political Societies possess ambition avarice, and all the other passions which render them formidable to each other, ought we not to view them in this light here? Will not the same motives operate in America as elsewhere? If any gentleman doubts it let him look at the votes. Have they not been dictated by interest, by ambition? Are not the large States evidently seeking to aggrandize themselves at the expense of the small? They think no doubt that they have right on their side, but interest had blinded their eyes. Look at Georgia. Though a small State at present, she is actuated by the prospect of soon being a great one. [South] Carolina is actuated both by present interest & future prospects. She hopes too to see the other States cut down to her own dimensions. [North] Carolina has the same motives of present & future interest. Virg[inia] follows. Mary[land] is not on that side of the Question. Pen[nsylvania] has a direct and future interest. Mass[achusetts] has a decided and palpable interest in the part she takes. Can it be expected that the small States will act from pure disinterestedness.[52]

[52] *RFC* June 30, 1: 491.

The Connecticut and Delaware delegations were the most adroit and effective opponents of Madison's political strategy.[53] Delaware's leaders had prepared in advance for an attack on equal representation in Congress. George Read, the state's leading politician, personally had maneuvered its General Assembly to issue formal instructions prohibiting its delegates from changing Delaware's equal vote in the Continental Congress. This sophisticated tactic was intended to "relieve the commissioners or the state from disagreeable argumentation, as well as prevent the downfall of the State, which [otherwise] would at once become a cypher in the union."[54] Delaware's delegates injected these restrictions into the debate on the opening day of the convention.[55] Delaware's John Dickinson wielded great influence on behalf of the vulnerable states. One of the delegates best known nationally, Dickinson had written the initial draft of the Articles of Confederation, chaired the Annapolis Convention, and served as chief state executive in both Pennsylvania and Delaware. Dickinson's health, however, made it impossible for him to sustain his participation

[53] In *Creating the Constitution*, Thornton Anderson describes several of these delegates as "state federalists," in contrast to state sovereignty proponents, such as Luther Martin, and nationalists such as Madison, Wilson, and G. Morris (pp. 207–14). For Anderson, "state federalists" occupied a middle ground on state powers, between the other two groups. Anderson names fifteen delegates in this group, including Sherman, William Samuel Johnson, and Oliver Ellsworth from Connecticut; Dickinson from Delaware; Williamson, William R. Davie, and Richard Dobbs Spaight from North Carolina; Rutledge, General Charles Cotesworth Pinckney, and Pierce Butler from South Carolina; William L. Pierce and Abraham Baldwin from Georgia; and the three nonsigners, Mason, Randolph, and Gerry (p. 62). Like Ulmer before him, Anderson conducts a factor analysis that reveals the Connecticut delegation as taking somewhat iconoclastic positions relative to the rest of the delegations.

[54] John A. Munroe, *Federalist Delaware, 1775–1815* (New Brunswick, NJ: Rutgers University Press, 1954), pp. 105–8, and *History of Delaware* (Newark: University of Delaware Press, 1979), p. 79; Rakove, *Original Meanings*, p. 60, 378n7. Read's stated motive in January 1787 was to secure the "claims of the smaller and bounded states to a proportional share" of the "ungranted lands in most of the larger States" (George Read to John Dickinson, January 17, 1787, in *RFC* 3: 575–6n6). See also McDonald, *Novus Ordo Seclorum*, p. 229. Four days before the convention formally began, Read expressed wariness about the plan for a new national legislature with proportional representation in each of its two chambers. Noting that Delaware's weight in policy making would be reduced to one of eighty members in the lower house, Read advised fellow deputies from smaller states to watch closely "the movements and propositions from the larger States, who will probably combine to swallow up the smaller ones by addition, division, or impoverishment." George Read to John Dickinson, May 21, 1787, in *RFC* 3: 25–6; see also Jacob Broom to Thomas Collins, May 23, 1787, in Hutson, *Supplement to Max Farrand's Records*, pp. 16–17. Delaware's instructions had long precedent; in the 1770s, the Delaware legislature similarly had instructed its congressional delegates to protect its voting equality with other states.

[55] *RFC* May 25, 1: 4.

through critical phases of the convention.[56] It was Connecticut that sent Madison's most formidable opponents to Philadelphia.

ROGER SHERMAN'S COUNTERAGENDA

Connecticut's Roger Sherman emerged as the most tenacious opponent of Madison's plan for an autonomous national government with broad authority. Sherman, thirty years older than Madison, was the more accomplished politician. He represented a state accustomed to autonomy and as self-contented as any in the union.[57] He had invested many years in building the Connecticut polity and the Confederation governments. Sherman had served on the congressional committees that drafted the Declaration of Independence and (with Dickinson) the Articles of Confederation. Sherman and Robert Morris were the only convention delegates who signed the Declaration of Independence, the Articles of Confederation, and the U.S. Constitution.[58] In the mid-1780s Sherman simultaneously was serving as mayor of New Haven, as a state senator, as a state superior court judge, and as a Connecticut delegate to the Confederation Congress. His talented younger colleague, Oliver Ellsworth, and the respected William Samuel Johnson gave the relatively cohesive Connecticut delegation substantial influence in challenging many of the specifics of Madison's plan.[59] Connecticut's credentials enhanced the state's influence.

[56] Dickinson participated energetically in debates in the convention's first two weeks, but then spoke only on June 11, June 18, and June 21. He did not speak again until July 25. By that time, the convention had adopted the compromise on representation and was about to adjourn while the Committee of Detail crafted the existing resolutions into a draft Constitution. See James H. Hutson, "John Dickinson at the Federal Constitutional Convention," *William and Mary Quarterly*, 3rd ser., 40:2 (April 1983): 256–82.

[57] Connecticut seemed exceptionally simple, republican, and self-satisfied to domestic and foreign observers, as in this French report: "Les gens de cet Etat ont, en général, un charactère national qu'on ne trouve guères dans les autres parties de continent. Ils se raprochent pus de la simplicité républicaine; ils sont tous à leur aise sans connoître l'opulence. L'économie rurale et l'industrie domestiques sont poussées très loin dans le Connecticut; le peuple y est heureux" (French Ministry of Foreign Affairs document, "Liste des Membres et Officiers du Congrés," 1788, in *RFC* 3: 233–4).

[58] In Jonathan Trumbull's famous painting of the Declaration of Independence (completed in the 1790s), Sherman stands in a foreground, with John Adams to his right and Thomas Jefferson and Benjamin Franklin to his left.

[59] The Connecticut delegation generally was united; Christopher Collier, "Sovereignty Finessed: Roger Sherman, Oliver Ellsworth, and the Ratification of the Constitution in Connecticut," in Conley and Kaminski, *The Constitution and the States*, p. 98. Sherman and Ellsworth rarely expressed differences. Ellsworth was willing to provide marginally more power to the national government than was Sherman. Ellsworth, for example, wanted a specific national standard for militia discipline (*RFC* August 23, 2: 385), whereas Sherman opposed excessive national standards for the militia.

Unlike rules for New York or any other state, any one of the three delegates could cast a vote on behalf of Connecticut at the convention, a provision that virtually ensured that the state would weigh in on every vote.[60]

Other politicians considered Sherman politically shrewd and as "cunning as the devil."[61] Just before the convention, he was engineering congressional compromises that settled Connecticut's claims to western land on terms favorable to the state. William Grayson wrote to Madison that this arrangement was "nothing but a state juggle contrived by old Roger Sherman."[62] His mastery of public finance enhanced his influence. He thoroughly understood that taxes were an instrument of statecraft. He had long advocated indirect taxes such as tariffs, using what would become known as the "fiscal illusion" to ensure a steady stream of government revenue with minimal public opposition. In 1784 Sherman commented that the only practical way to raise public revenue was through an impost because "the consumer pays it insensibly and without murmuring."[63] Nathaniel Macon of North Carolina, who became acquainted with Sherman in the early 1790s in the new U.S. Congress, recalled an occasion when he rose to join a debate on the Senate floor. Sherman held him back. "My young friend," Sherman reportedly said, "withhold your strength, we are now in the majority – it is possible to say too much. It is the business of the minority to make speeches." On another occasion, Sherman pointed out that "minorities talk; majorities vote."[64]

Sherman became the most active adversary of Madison's convention strategy. Sherman spoke, made motions, or seconded motions 160 times

[60] Rossiter, *1787: The Grand Convention*, pp. 154–5. Georgia, New Hampshire, and South Carolina required two delegates to vote on their behalf at the convention. Virginia, New Jersey, North Carolina, Delaware, and Massachusetts required at least three delegates to cast a vote, and Pennsylvania required four.

[61] Ibid., p. 91. William Pierce, a delegate from Georgia, recorded his impressions of Sherman, which appear to include observations based on others' comments: "He is an able politician, and extremely artful in accomplishing any particular object; – it is remarked that he seldom fails.... He has been several years a Member of Congress, and discharged the duties of his Office with honor and credit to himself, and advantage to the State he represented" (*RFC* 3: 89).

[62] Roger Sherman Boardman, *Roger Sherman: Signer and Statesman* (Philadelphia: University of Pennsylvania Press, 1938), p. 160; Christopher Collier, *Roger Sherman's Connecticut: Yankee Politics and the American Revolution* (Middletown, CT: Wesleyan University Press, 1971), pp. 146–8. Grayson to James Madison, May 28, 1786, in *PJM* 9: 61.

[63] Christopher Collier, *Connecticut in the Continental Congress* (Chester, CT: Pequot Press, 1973), p. 61.

[64] Collier, *Roger Sherman's Connecticut*, p. 316.

during the convention, despite a six-day absence in July. Madison himself spoke or entered motions 177 times.[65] Sherman explicitly contradicted and opposed Madison 39 times, more often than any other delegate. He questioned the necessity of Madison's proposals and the outcomes they would produce. He urged the delegates to focus on the authority of the national government instead of representation in it, and to sanction only those extensions of national authority they thought necessary. By doing so, Sherman directly attacked Madison's central tactic for winning approval for his plan. He, Ellsworth, and Johnson also stood for a blunt pragmatism aimed at helping the convention compromise bitter policy divisions. On May 30, when Sherman questioned whether so great a change in the national government could be ratified, he made it legitimate to talk openly about the political feasibility of any constitutional provision.[66] Sherman worked to build majority coalitions for his positions. He advocated compromises on representation in Congress (Connecticut would help draft the New Jersey Plan, only to vote against it), on the continuation of the slave trade, on the origination of money bills in the House, and on the selection of the president. In the final substantive hours of deliberation, Sherman sandbagged the delegates by insisting on provisions that constitutional amendments could not change equal representation in the Senate or the states' control of their police powers (the former provision was included in the Constitution, but the latter was not).[67]

Sherman believed that the convention ought to enhance only a narrow set of specific national powers, while protecting broad state authority over the routine management of states' economic and social life. Sherman readily agreed with Madison and others that the Confederation required additional powers, "particularly that of raising money" and the management of commerce and currency. Connecticut had a vital interest in the national management of these public goods.[68] Beyond the nationalization

[65] Sherman did not speak from July 19 through July 26; on July 26 the convention adjourned until August 6, and thereafter Sherman spoke on every day but one. Boardman reports that Sherman was in New Haven on July 26; *Roger Sherman*, p. 241.

[66] *RFC* May 30, 1: 34–5.

[67] David Brian Robertson, "Madison's Opponents and Constitutional Design," *American Political Science Review* 99: 2 (2005): 225–43.

[68] *RFC* May 30, 1: 34; Collier, *Roger Sherman's Connecticut*, pp. 230–3. Connecticut's delegates to the Continental Congress, including Sherman, had written a draft of the Articles of Confederation in March 1776 that limited national power "precisely in those areas – the regulation of commerce and settlement of western lands – where the exercise of congressional power might bring the union into conflict with the specific interests of

of selected public goods, however, Sherman's views about reconstituting the national government diametrically opposed those of Madison. In Sherman's view, national economic authority should be expanded as little as possible, and states should retain control of as much authority to manage their economic assets as possible. Sherman argued, for example, that Congress be given the power to crush paper money, but states should retain even the power to embargo goods.[69]

Sherman's counteragenda is evident in his own plan, along with his recorded statements at the convention and from the New Jersey Plan (Figure 4.1). Sherman's plan centered on protecting state policy authority, and he questioned Madison's most ambitious proposals to extend national authority, including the national veto. Connecticut's position on authority unified the smaller states, along with the New York delegates jealous of their state's tariff prerogatives; this position also held an attraction to southern delegates bent on protecting slavery and the plantation economy. Sherman wanted Congress to depend on the states, and other national officers to depend on Congress. After the convention formally approved the compromise on representation (or "Connecticut Compromise") on July 16, Sherman championed the prerogatives of the Senate. For example, he opposed appointment of the president and a national treasurer by joint ballot rather than separate votes of each house, reasoning that a joint ballot would water down the independent role of the Senate

particular colonies"; Jack N. Rakove, *The Beginnings of National Politics: An Interpretive History of the Continental Congress* (New York: Alfred Knopf, 1979), pp. 146–7.

[69] RFC August 28, 2: 439–41; Collier, *Connecticut in the Continental Congress*, pp. 10, 47, 61, 68, 71–3; Rossiter, *1787: The Grand Convention*, p. 91. At the convention, Sherman wrote some propositions for a constitutional plan between July 2 and July 17. Sherman's plan proposed to add to the Confederation government the power to regulate international and interstate commerce, to impose tariffs, and to make laws "in all cases which concern the common interests of the United States: but not to interfere with the government of the individual states, in matters of internal police which respect the government of such states only, and wherein the general welfare of the United States is not affected." National laws would be executed by state courts and state executives, "as far as may be consistent with the common interests of the Union." There would be a supreme court (but no mention is made of a national executive). States would be prohibited from issuing currency or interfering with contractual obligations. The system of requisitions would continue, with the three-fifths compromise explicitly included for calculating state obligations, and state legislatures in arrears would "be authorised to order the same to be levied and collected of the inhabitants of such state, and to make such rules and orders as may be necessary for that purpose." Congress could enlist the people to help state and local officials execute U.S. law. Defendants had the right to a jury trial in the state where the offense was committed (*RFC* 3: 615–16).

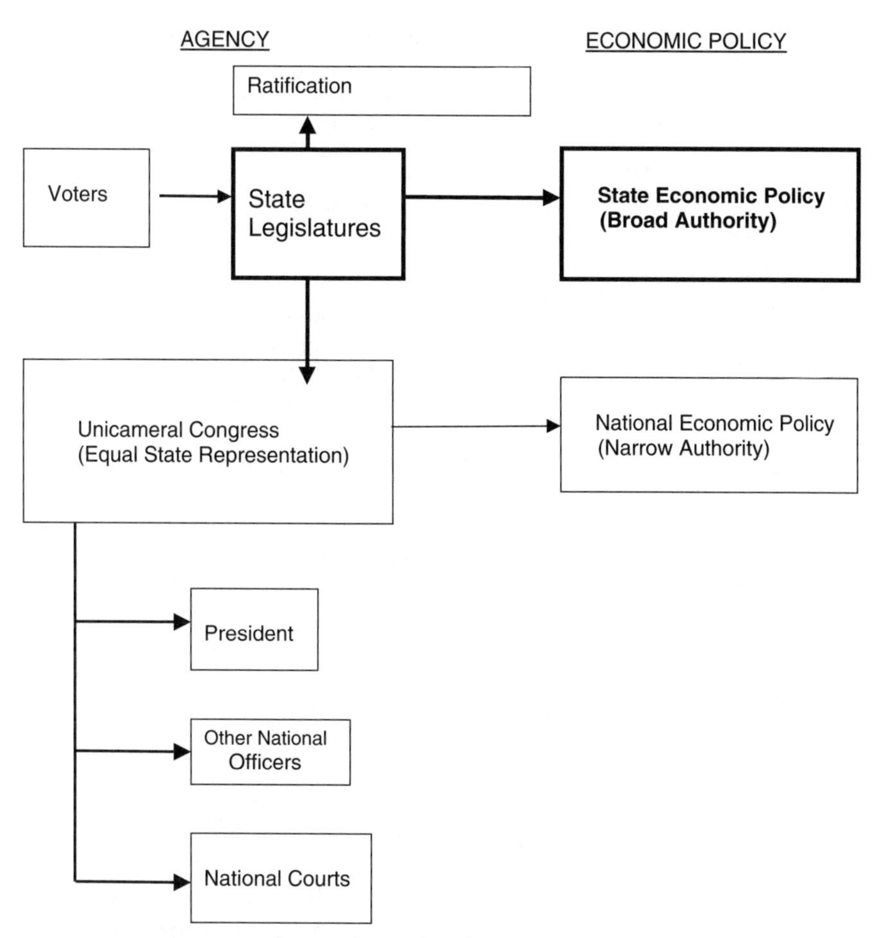

FIGURE 4.1. Agency and Economic Policy for Sherman: The New Jersey Plan

in exercising a veto over the selection of these officeholders.[70] Sherman vigorously pursued his agenda from May 30, the day he arrived at the convention.

THE HISTORY OF THE CONVENTION

On May 29, the day after the delegates had approved the rules and named Washington the president of the convention, Randolph laid out the Virginia Plan. On September 17 – after three and a half

[70] *RFC* August 17, 2: 314; August 24, 2: 403.

TABLE 4.2. *Chronology of Agendas and Key Events at the Constitutional Convention*

Date	Agenda	Key Event
May 29	Initial Virginia Plan	
June 15		New Jersey counteragenda proposed
June 19		New Jersey counteragenda rejected
June 20	Amended Virginia Plan	
July 2		Committee on representation established
July 5		Proposed compromise on apportionment of representatives
July 16		Agreement to compromise on apportionment of representatives
August 6	Committee of Detail draft	
August 24		Proposed compromise on commerce and slave imports
August 29		Agreement to compromise on commerce and slave imports
September 1	Committee on Postponed Matters report	
September 6		Agreement to compromise on presidency
September 10	Committee on Style draft	
September 15		Final vote on the Constitution
September 17		Signature and adjournment

months – thirty-nine of the delegates signed the final Constitution and the meeting adjourned.[71] The convention as a whole met for eighty-five working sessions during this period.[72] Table 4.2 outlines the agendas that structured the convention's deliberations, and the most significant dates during the proceedings.

The convention initially responded to Virginia's agenda, resolution by resolution. The convention approved an amended version of Virginia's resolutions on June 12. New Jersey's William Paterson introduced a formal alternative to the Virginia Plan on June 15.[73] Drawn up by delegates

[71] George Read signed the Constitution on behalf of John Dickinson.

[72] The convention did not meet on Sundays, adjourned for nine days beginning July 27, and adjourned for other shorter periods.

[73] Dickinson, undoubtedly drawing on his experience as an initial draftsman of the Articles of Confederation and as chair of the Annapolis Convention, used the occasion to scold Madison: "You see the consequence of pushing things too far. Some of the members

from New Jersey, Connecticut, New York, and Delaware (and Martin of Maryland), the New Jersey Plan aimed to protect the states' direct, equal control of national policy makers and limit the convention agenda to a specified set of urgent collective action problems beyond the capacity of the Confederation Congress. The convention rejected the New Jersey Plan four days later. The convention's agenda next focused on the amended Virginia resolutions, but agreement broke down over the issue of representation in Congress. Debates turned bitter by the end of June.

On July 5 a special committee reported a compromise plan for proportional representation in the House of Representatives and equal state representation in the Senate. The convention approved the compromise on July 16 after several days of heated debate (textbooks today describe this as the "Great Compromise" or "Connecticut Compromise"). The convention returned to the amended Virginia resolutions, and on July 26 it turned its work over to a Committee of Detail to flesh out a more complete document. The Committee of Detail draft structured the proceedings for more than a month. A major dispute concerning national authority over trade split southern and northern delegates. The delegates sent the dispute to another special committee, and it reported a compromise that the delegates approved on August 29. The convention designated yet another committee to report a plan for selecting the president, and that Committee on Postponed Matters report structured the agenda in early September. A Committee of Style produced a nearly complete version of the Constitution, and this draft structured debate in the convention's final week.

THE POLITICS OF CONSTITUTION MAKING

Madison did everything in his power to set the convention on a path of nationalizing economic management and establishing proportional representation in the national legislature. Initially, a formidable coalition of southern and large states seemed to fall in line with his plans. But Madison's ambitions endangered existing political arrangements, especially in the economically vulnerable middle and northern states. The very boldness of Madison's plan enabled shrewd politicians such as Roger Sherman to challenge Madison's priorities, exploit his coalition's weaknesses,

from the small States . . . are friends to a good National Government; But we would sooner submit to a foreign power than submit to be deprived of an equality of suffrage, in both branches of the legislature, and thereby be thrown under the domination of the large States" (*RFC* June 15, 1: 242).

and unify otherwise diverse opponents. Ultimately, Madison's opponents forced the convention to create a governmental plan that compromised both Madison's and Sherman's vision of national policy making.

Although Madison and Sherman supported rival models for agency in the reconstituted national policy-making system, it is crucial to emphasize that both supported models of government that were less complicated than those in the final Constitution. Madison wanted to build agency through voters' input into the foundation of the policy-making system, the House of Representatives, and make other national officials, indirectly, the agents of this electorate (see Figure 3.1). Sherman preferred to make Congress the agent of the state governments, and to make other national policy makers the agents of the Congress. No delegate proposed a plan in which agency was so separated and open to rivalry as in the final Constitution. As Madison, Sherman, and their allies made the risks of their rivals' policy regime clearer, delegates increasingly made decisions aimed at deterring unacceptable outcomes. The convention compromised on agency, drifted toward Sherman's position on authority, and established auxiliary precautions in the policy process to deter outcomes unacceptable to interests they represented. Of these issues, it was policy agency that brought the convention to the verge of collapse.

5

Who Governs?

Constituting Policy Agency

No issue tore at the Constitutional Convention more than the problem of choosing and controlling those who would govern. Virginia's plan directly challenged the equal state representation already established in the Confederation Congress. Madison and his allies insisted that the states' relative size, not their equal status as states, should determine their relative influence in national policy making. He also sought to eradicate as much state government influence over policy makers as possible. Madison's bold challenge to their existing political defenses galvanized the delegates from the vulnerable middle and northern states. Their delegates united to defend their states' influence in national policy decisions.

The issue of proportional representation in Congress dominated the convention's first month and a half. Sherman and his allies stopped the momentum of Madison's plan, cast his central premises in doubt, refocused the terms of the debate on material interests, and chipped away at his support. Once the delegates accepted the political compromise providing equal state representation in the Senate and proportional representation in the House of Representatives in mid-July, the struggle over policy agency shifted to other agency choices. Madison battled vigorously to give the president the independence to pursue future national interests, and fought to limit the powers of the Senate, now seen as the agent of state governments. Ultimately, the selection of the president was settled by another political compromise on presidential election and power. The delegates gave the president the power to select judges, ambassadors, and top administrators, but only on the condition that the state governments' agent, the Senate, consent to these appointments.

The convention's compromises on policy agency ensured more political complexity and rivalry than Madison, Sherman, or any other delegate initially intended. The unplanned complexity and separation of policy agency have motivated the House of Representatives, the Senate, the president, and the Supreme Court to pursue different, often conflicting, policy agendas.

POLICY AGENCY AND THE CONSTITUTIONAL CONVENTION

The delegates fought to ensure that national policy makers would be agents responsive to the interests of their constituents. Chapter 4 explained why they believed that control over policy agency was the most reliable way to control a government's public policy choices. The convention accordingly devoted much more time to the development of rules about the selection and dependence of policy makers than other types of decisions, such as substantive policy authority and the national policy process. Many hours of heated debate, and about half of the contested votes at the convention, turned on policy agency. These votes included choices about whether the states would elect senators, whether each state would get equal representation in the Senate, how slaves would be counted in proportioning representation, how frequently censuses would be taken, whether new states would enjoy representation under the same terms as the original thirteen states, whether the states or the national government would provide congressional salaries, whether property qualifications would be required for officeholders or votes, and whether Congress would elect the president and appoint judges.

Madison gambled that the early settlement of the issue of proportioning representation in Congress would open the door to extensive national authority to govern the economy. The delegates from the economically vulnerable states outside his coalition, however, fully appreciated that strong and equal state representation in Congress provided them political leverage that offset their economic disadvantages. Roger Sherman, John Dickinson, and other delegates from these states fought to retain equal state representation in Congress, to ensure state government influence over Congress, and to guarantee as much congressional control over the appointment of other new national policy makers as possible.

OPPOSITION TO THE VIRGINIA PLAN

After Governor Edmund Randolph presented Virginia's resolutions on May 29, the delegates accepted the Virginia Plan as its starting point. They approved the principle that "a national government be established with a supreme Legislative Executive & Judiciary" on May 30, the first day of substantive convention business. The vote may have encouraged Madison temporarily. His expected coalition of large and southern states carried the resolution, and Delaware joined them. Only Connecticut voted against it.[1] The convention never reversed its endorsement of a basic overhaul of the national government.

As soon as the delegates took up Edmund Randolph's second motion proposing that votes in the national legislature "be proportioned to the quotas of contribution [that is, to each state's relative contribution to national revenues], or to the number of free inhabitants," Delaware's John Dickinson counterattacked. Dickinson urged the convention to determine the additional national powers needed before it dealt with representation. Dickinson aimed to shift the convention's agenda and draw the delegates into a debate on material interests. The more these diverse interests were injected into subsequent convention debates, the more difficulties Madison encountered in moving forward Virginia's agenda. When the delegates postponed Randolph's second resolution, Madison at once tried to pressure the delegates into a quick, decisive commitment to the principle of proportional representation in Congress. He moved "that the equality of suffrage established by the articles of Confederation ought not to prevail in the national Legislature, and that an equitable ratio of representation ought to be substituted." He sought an immediate vote (to take "the sense of the members on this point and saving the Delaware deputies from embarrassment"), because his strategy for the convention depended on a speedy commitment to proportional representation. But the delegates seemed to bridle. James McHenry of Maryland explicitly noted that Madison's proposal "gave the large states absolute control over the lesser ones." Delaware's George Read reminded the convention of the limits of his state's credentials, persuading the delegates to delay the proposal indefinitely.[2] This postponement of the apportionment issue was a clear setback for Madison.

Madison's opposition began to crystallize during the first week. Sherman and Dickinson defended state government agency in Congress when the convention took up Randolph's proposal for direct popular election of the House of Representatives. Sherman argued that state legislatures ought to select these national policy makers, observing that voters

[1] *RFC* May 30, 1: 33–5. New York divided on this vote, and New Jersey, Maryland, and Georgia did not vote at all.

[2] *RFC* May 30, 1: 34–7, 40–2.

could not be fully trusted with direct influence over public policy. James Wilson took Sherman's bait, answering with a direct attack on state officials: "[T]he opposition of the States to federal measures had proce[e]ded much more from the officers of the States, than from the people at large."[3] A few days later, Wilson made a strong case for the most democratic interpretation of republicanism. Seeking a vigorous government with authority flowing "immediately from the legitimate source of all authority," the people, Wilson argued that "the Gov[ernmen]t ought to possess not only 1st. the *force* but 2ndly. the *mind or sense* of the people at large. The Legislature ought to be the most exact transcript of the whole Society. Representation is made necessary only because it is impossible for the people to act collectively." When Wilson warned that state officers, who "were to be losers of power," were the chief obstacles to popular control of Congress, Sherman pounced, painting the Wilson and Madison position as radical.[4] Meanwhile, fissures in Madison's coalition became more apparent. Although the delegates approved of popular election of the lower house, South Carolina deserted Madison on this vote. Support for state agency firmed up further when the convention turned to the selection of the Senate. Several delegates frankly believed the Senate should be a bastion of privilege. Dickinson, for example, sought a Senate "as near as may be to the House of Lords in England." Only Massachusetts and South Carolina joined Virginia to support election of the Senate by the House of Representatives. Sherman proposed that the state legislatures each select one senator, as in the existing Confederation Congress.[5]

The opposition gained ground as the convention took up the selection of the president and courts. Sherman insisted that the national executive be "absolutely dependent" on the national legislature.[6] Although Wilson tried to bypass Congress entirely, proposing that voters choose electors who would in turn elect the executive, the convention approved Randolph's proposal that Congress choose the executive. To increase the president's dependence on the state governments, Dickinson on June 2 proposed that a majority of the state legislatures be given the power to remove the president. In the course of explaining his proposal, Dickinson broached the idea of an eventual compromise: proportional

[3] *RFC* May 31, 1: 49.

[4] *RFC* June 6, 1: 132–3.

[5] *RFC* May 31, 1: 48–52; June 6, 1: 136. New Jersey also voted against popular election of U.S. representatives on May 31; Delaware and Connecticut were divided. Dickinson made his comment a few days later (June 6, 1: 136).

[6] *RFC* June 1, 1: 65, 68.

representation in the House of Representatives and equal state representation in the Senate. Madison took up Wilson's attack on state government power over national policy makers. South Carolina's John Rutledge, himself a state judge, defended the states' judicial powers. He unsuccessfully proposed to limit the national judiciary to a single Supreme Court, eliminating all lesser national courts that might crowd the states' judicial prerogatives.[7]

Sherman used every opportunity to quarrel with the elimination of the state legislatures' policy influence and to shift the burden of proof to Madison and his allies. Special state ratifying conventions were unnecessary, he argued, because the state legislatures could ratify changes in the Confederation structure, as the Articles provided.[8] When Sherman insisted that "the objects of the Union . . . were few," Madison responded with his first extended speech, applying his analysis of factions to discuss specific economic rivalries in the states. His response included the first mention of slavery ("the mere distinction of colour . . . a ground of the most oppressive dominion ever exercised by man over man").[9] Madison's response to Sherman validated the open discussion of slavery and other material interests, even though Madison's own strategy depended on establishing agreement on abstract principles before considering such substantive issues.

The more the convention dwelled on specific material interests, the more the vulnerable middle states jelled in opposition to proportional representation in Congress. Madison found it hard to combat the claim that large states would coalesce around policies that would benefit their interests at the expense of smaller states.[10] William Paterson felt that proportional representation struck "at the existence of the lesser States." Delaware's Gunning Bedford turned Madison's analysis against him, asserting that proportional representation "was meant . . . to strip the small States of their equal right of suffrage," reducing Delaware to one vote in ninety and giving Virginia and Pennsylvania one-third of the seats in

[7] *RFC* June 2, 1: 80–1, 85–7, 91; June 5, 1: 125. Dickinson expanded the scope of conflict in discussing this provision by stating that he "had no idea of abolishing the State Governments as some gentlemen seemed inclined to do" (June 2, 1: 85). By characterizing the proposal as an attack on state governments, Dickinson began to define the opposition to Madison in terms of the defense of state governments as governments, a premise that invited the defense of smaller states against larger ones.

[8] *RFC* June 5, 1: 122.

[9] *RFC* June 6, 1: 133–6.

[10] Bedford, *RFC* June 8, 1: 172, June 30, 1: 490; Ellsworth, June 28, 1: 469.

Congress. "Is there no difference of interests, no rivalship of commerce, of manufactures?" asked Bedford. "Will not these large States crush the small ones whenever they stand in the way of their ambitions or interested views?... It seems as if [Pennsylvania and Virginia] by the conduct of their deputies wished to provide a system in which they would have an enormous & monstrous influence." When the convention defeated Madison's proposed national veto of state laws by a seven-to-three vote, with only Massachusetts and Pennsylvania joining Virginia, the accusations about large states' political cooperation gained credibility. New Jersey delegates Paterson and David Brearley exploited this situation the following day. Brearley, chief justice of the New Jersey Supreme Court, predicted that three states, Virginia, Pennsylvania, and Massachusetts, would "carry every thing before them" in Congress.[11]

Madison's allies, in turn, made the crucial concession that the state governments had a legitimate interest in defending their autonomy in the national policy system. Pierce Butler of South Carolina and Randolph already had suggested the need to retain some state prerogatives and geographical balance in the policy process.[12] When Dickinson asserted that "The preservation of the States in a certain degree of agency is indispensible," George Mason admitted that, if the national government needed rules to protect them from the states, it followed that the states needed rules to protect them from the national government. Madison's opponents used Mason's argument against him with increasing effectiveness.[13]

A COUNTERAGENDA EMERGES

When the delegates convened on Monday morning, June 11, Sherman tried to seize the agenda by proposing that suffrage in the first house be proportional to free inhabitants, and that states be equally represented in the Senate. "[E]ach State ought to be able to protect itself," Sherman said, using Mason's concession against the Virginia Plan. He warned that without such protection, "a few large States will rule the rest." Madison won a

[11] *RFC* June 8, 1: 167–8; June 9, 1: 177–9. As early as 1777, concern about the political dominance of the three largest states had surfaced in congressional debates about the Articles of Confederation. North Carolina's Thomas Burke suggested that Pennsylvania, Massachusetts, and Virginia would combine to subvert the liberties of the smaller states. See Jack N. Rakove, *The Beginnings of National Politics: An Interpretive History of the Continental Congress* (New York: Alfred Knopf, 1979), p. 169.

[12] *RFC* May 31, 1: 53; June 1, 1: 51.

[13] *RFC* June 7, 1: 152–6.

Pyrrhic victory when the convention rejected equal state representation in the Senate and adopted the principle that the ratio of representation in the Senate would be the same as in the House. On these key votes, Madison's coalition of six large and southern states turned back a now-cohesive block of vulnerable middle states – Connecticut, New York, New Jersey, Delaware, and Maryland – six votes to five. Instead of drifting to his plan, Madison's potential opponents had united against him. They settled the issue of counting slaves by defining the "equitable ratio of representation" in the House as all whites and three-fifths of slaves, the formula already established for Confederation requisitions. Over the following days, the delegates from the vulnerable middle states battled proposals to reduce state policy influence, challenging a requirement that state officials take an oath to uphold the national government, that the national government fund congressional salaries instead of the states, that members of Congress be prohibited from holding state offices, and that the people ratify the Constitution instead of the state legislatures. Slavery, an issue first injected by Madison himself, began to split his southern from his northern allies.[14]

By June 13 the delegates had finished their initial work on the Virginia Plan. They had left the plan almost completely intact, providing for proportional representation in the House of Representatives and establishing that representation in the Senate "ought to be according to the rule established" for the House. The appointment of the Senate by the state legislatures was the only major concession to state influence in national policy making. Two days later, the states outside of Madison's coalition introduced their alternative, the New Jersey Plan.

Although its authors defended it vigorously, the delegates rejected the New Jersey Plan on June 19 and moved forward to consider the Virginia Plan in full convention. Seven states voted against the New Jersey Plan and only three, New York, New Jersey, and Delaware, voted for it. Maryland divided. By voting against the New Jersey Plan they themselves had helped write, Connecticut's delegates strengthened the pivotal role of their

[14] *RFC* June 11, 1: 196, 201–4; June 12, 1: 214, 217. The convention voted, nine states to two, in favor of using population as a basis for determining representation in the House, counting "in proportion to the whole number of white & other free Citizens & inhabitants of every age sex & condition including those bound to servitude for a term of years and three fifths of all other persons not comprehended in the foregoing description, except Indians not paying taxes, in each State" (June 11, 2: 201). The delegates explicitly were using the 1783 rule for apportioning quotas of revenue on the states. Only New Jersey and Delaware cast votes against this motion.

state.[15] The New Jersey Plan, however, had further damaged Madison's strategy by forging the connection between state control of national offices, state economic interests, and the expected economic policy of the new government. Debates turned bitter. The resolve of some of Madison's allies weakened. Madison's opponents held fast to the defense of state agency until they won equal representation in the Senate.

MADISON'S DEFEAT ON THE SENATE

Madison's coalition wore down as the struggle over policy agency wore on. Proponents of proportional representation in the Senate found it difficult to show how the Senate could remain relatively small while still providing all the states representation in proportion to their population.[16] Madison's allies antagonized the Virginia Plan's opponents when Wilson blamed the smaller states for the Confederation's crisis, and Hamilton disparaged the proceedings as a "contest for power, not for liberty." Charles Pinckney accused them of blackmail ("Give N[ew] Jersey an equal vote, and she will dismiss her scruples, and concur in the Nat[ional] system," he claimed).[17] The more Wilson and Madison denied that Virginia, Pennsylvania, and Massachusetts would collaborate to dominate other states, the more their evident cooperation at the convention belied their argument.[18] South Carolina's delegates supported state agency in a Congress

[15] *RFC* June 19, 1: 322. Clinton Rossiter speculated that Connecticut had received private assurances that a compromise would be worked out; see *1787: The Grand Convention* (New York: Macmillan, 1966), p. 177. An alternative view is that Connecticut's representatives supported the development of the plan to unify Madison's opposition around a counteragenda to stake out a bargaining position. Connecticut's vote against the plan signaled the conciliatory spirit its delegates articulated throughout the convention, and established Connecticut as a swing delegation whose vote could be won with acceptable concessions.

[16] Daniel Wirls, "Madison's Dilemma: Revisiting the Relationship between the Senate and the 'Great Compromise' at the Constitutional Convention," in *James Madison: The Theory and Practice of Republican Government*, ed. Samuel Kernell (Stanford, CA: Stanford University Press, 2003), pp. 156–83; Daniel Wirls and Stephen Wirls, *The Invention of the United States Senate* (Baltimore: Johns Hopkins University Press, 2004), chap. 4.

[17] James Wilson and Charles Pinckney, *RFC* June 16, 1: 254–5; Alexander Hamilton, *RFC* June 18, 1: 282–93, and June 29, 1: 464.

[18] *RFC* June 19, 1: 321; June 28, 1: 447–8. According to Forrest McDonald, "Indeed, when delegates from Virginia, Pennsylvania, and Massachusetts demanded that their states have a voice in the national councils commensurate with their population, it was clear that their claims to being more national-minded were spurious and that they were taking a position that would increase the influence of their own states, not the power of the nation." Forrest McDonald, *Novus Ordo Seclorum: The Intellectual Origins of the Constitution* (Lawrence: University Press of Kansas, 1985), p. 219.

with proportional representation, and joined Connecticut against Virginia to support state legislatures' power to choose U.S. representatives and provide compensation for national legislators.[19] Nathaniel Gorham of Massachusetts and George Mason of Virginia began to waver, openly suggesting that the delegates look for a compromise on representation. Mutual wariness increased as substantive economic issues, such as the western lands, trade, and slavery, became indivisibly intertwined with representation. For the first time, a procedural vote on June 25 caused all the northern states to align against all the southern states. Charles Pinckney pointedly discussed the divergent interests of northern and southern states, particularly South Carolina.[20]

Madison's opponents became more aggressive, challenging every element of the Randolph plan that threatened state policy prerogatives or influence, including the very word "national" itself. Three states, New York, New Jersey, and Delaware, voted against even a bicameral national legislature. Connecticut's delegates voted more strategically, supporting a bicameral legislature while urging "the necessity of maintaining the existence & agency of the States." Connecticut's representatives relentlessly emphasized the need to arm the states for political self-defense by providing them agency in national policy-making institutions. Benjamin Franklin now conceded the logic of that argument.[21] Sherman strategically positioned himself as a pragmatic proponent of state prerogatives. He would agree to a bicameral legislature with proportional representation in one house "provided each State had an equal voice in the other" house, a provision necessary to "secure the rights of the lesser States." Without such a bicameral compromise, "three or four of the large States would rule the others as they please." Ingeniously, Sherman used revered republican principles to defend states' rights: "Each State like each individual had its peculiar habits usages and manners, which constituted its happiness. It would not therefore give to others a power

[19] *RFC* June 21, 1: 358–60; June 22, 1: 374: June 23, 1: 385; June 26, 1: 420. Only Pennsylvania joined Virginia to vote against the selection of the Senate by the state legislatures, and only the three large states voted against a proposal to make U.S. senators eligible for state offices (June 25, 1: 408; June 26, 1: 429).

[20] *RFC* June 25, 1: 401–3, 407–8, 417; June 26, 1: 421; June 29, 1: 466. As George Read put it, give to the small states equal shares of the common lands which "the great states have appropriated to themselves . . . and then if you please, proportion the representation, and we shall not be jealous of one another" (June 25, 1: 412; see also McDonald, *Novus Ordo Seclorum*, p. 219).

[21] Ellsworth, *RFC* June 20, 1: 335, and June 25, 1: 406–7; William Samuel Johnson, June 29, 1: 461; Franklin, June 30, 1: 488.

over this happiness, any more than an individual would do, when he could avoid it."[22]

Madison's six-state coalition held together to approve proportional representation in the House of Representatives on a six-to-four vote on June 29. As Sherman had done on June 11, Ellsworth at once moved to establish equal representation of the states in the Senate. He noted that large states "will like individuals find out and avail themselves of the advantage to be gained by" proportional representation, and evoked the image of the large states cooperating to control valuable resources like ports and the appointment of national policy makers.[23] He reiterated Sherman's warning that four states would govern nine and reminded the delegates that the New Hampshire delegation, expected to arrive shortly, would likely vote with Connecticut.[24]

Hostility and mistrust peaked on Saturday, June 30. Madison uncharacteristically attacked Connecticut's delegates for hypocrisy in supporting the Confederation while they refused to comply with its requisitions. Increasingly arguing from material interests instead of abstract principles, Madison suggested that "if any defensive power were necessary, it ought to be mutually given to" slave and nonslave states. Ultimatums followed. Massachusetts's Rufus King rejected the idea of a government with equal state representation. Jonathan Dayton and Luther Martin refused to accede to a government with proportional representation. Dayton called the amended Randolph resolutions "an amphibious monster." Delaware's Gunning Bedford implied that small states would seek foreign allies if the Confederation refused to protect them against the large states. According

[22] *RFC* June 20, 1: 343.

[23] *RFC* June 29, 1: 468–9. On July 17, the day after the final vote on the compromise on representation, Charles Pinckney provided evidence that large states could work together for their own interest when he condemned congressional selection of the president: "The most populous States by combining in favor of the same individual will be able to carry their points. The Nat[iona]l Legislature being most immediately interested in the laws made by themselves, will be most attentive to the choice of a fit man to carry them properly into execution" (July 17, 2: 30).

[24] *RFC* June 29, 1: 468–9; June 30, 1: 484–5, 503. According to King, Ellsworth emphasized the southern-northern difference and the risk that the union would be cut asunder at Delaware (June 29, 1: 478). King conceded that he expected the New Hampshire delegates "very shortly if . . . at all" (June 30, 1: 481). New Hampshire had elected delegates on January 17, and elected delegates a second time on June 27; in neither case did the legislature provide funding or a letter of credit for the delegates, however (Rossiter, *1787: The Grand Convention*, p. 81).

to New York's Abraham Yates, Bedford bluntly declared to the large-state delegates that "*I do not, gentlemen, trust you.*"[25]

As soon as the delegates convened on Monday, July 2, they voted on Ellsworth's motion for equal state representation in the Senate. The convention deadlocked, five states to five. The three large states and the Carolinas voted against the proposal, while the five states that helped author the New Jersey Plan voted for it. Georgia divided. Luther Martin later reported that Maryland's Daniel of St. Thomas Jenifer, a supporter of Madison's perspective, was absent when this critical vote was taken. If Jenifer had been present, his vote would have divided Maryland's delegation and changed the outcome to a five to four vote in Madison's favor.[26] Madison's convention strategy had fallen short by a single delegate's absence.

Although Charles Pinckney moved to take up an alternative plan for proportional representation in the Senate, his colleague General Pinckney instead called for a committee "to devise & report some compromise." Sherman, declaring that "we are at a full stop," argued that only a committee could iron out the delegates' differences. Wilson protested that such a committee "would decide according to that very rule of voting which was opposed on one side." Despite Madison's and Wilson's opposition, though, nine states voted to form the committee. Even a majority of the Virginia delegation abandoned Madison on this vote. The membership of this decisive "grand committee" was stacked against Madison's agenda. In addition to Sherman and Rutledge, it included Robert Yates, Luther Martin, and Gunning Bedford, three of the most uncompromising defenders of state agency at the convention. The conciliatory Gerry, Franklin, and Mason represented the three large states instead of Madison or his allies King, Wilson, or Morris.[27]

The committee's compromise proposal provided for proportional representation in the House of Representatives (based on the whole number of free citizens and three-fifths of slaves) and equal state representation in the Senate. The committee did not specify each state's allocation of seats in the House of Representatives but rather allocated one representative for each 40,000 inhabitants. According to Madison, southern and

[25] *RFC* June 30, 1: 485–6, 490–2, 500.

[26] *RFC* July 2, 1: 510; for Martin's comment, see 3: 188. After Jenifer arrived, Rufus King asked that the vote be reconsidered, but his request was refused.

[27] *RFC* July 2, 1: 511–16.

large-state representatives on the committee agreed to the compromise only on the further condition that the House of Representatives initiate all spending and revenue measures (or "money" bills) and that the Senate be prohibited from changing these measures.[28]

After the grand committee announced its proposed compromise, Gouverneur Morris moved to specify the number of seats each state would receive in the first House of Representatives. The stakes for apportioning House seats were high. The first Congress would make many of the "principle acts of government."[29] It would create new administrative offices and courts, fill these positions with their initial leaders, locate the national capital, set tariffs, and set about to settle government debts. The convention set up a new, five-member committee to propose specific numbers of House seats for each state. The committee consisted entirely of delegates from Madison's expected coalition, including Gouverneur Morris, Nathaniel Gorham, and Rufus King of Massachusetts, Edmund Randolph of Virginia, and John Rutledge of South Carolina. The convention put off debate on the House control of money bills and on equal state representation in the Senate, pending the report of this committee on the allocation of House seats. Ominously for Madison, North Carolina joined Connecticut, New Jersey, Delaware, and New York (with Massachusetts and Georgia divided) to give his opponents an outright and decisive majority on delaying the debate on the Senate.[30]

The five-member committee report on July 9 proved that Sherman and Ellsworth had been right: proportional representation could give four states the majority they needed to push legislation through the House. The committee recommended a House with fifty-six seats. Virginia would have nine seats, Pennsylvania eight, Massachusetts seven, New York and the Carolinas five seats each, Connecticut and Maryland four each, New Jersey three, New Hampshire and Georgia two, and Rhode Island and Delaware one each. The three largest states (represented by four of the five members of the committee) received 43 percent of the proposed House seats. Any one of three pivotal states – New York, North Carolina, and South Carolina – could join the three large states to make a four-state coalition in control of a clear majority of twenty-nine of the chamber's fifty-six votes.[31]

[28] *RFC* July 5, 1: 526–7. See Gerry's recollection of the agreement in Gerry to the Vice President of the Convention of Massachusetts, January 21, 1788, in *RFC* 3: 265.

[29] Gerry, *RFC* August 21, 2: 357.

[30] *RFC* July 5, 1: 533–4; July 6, 1: 540–2; July 7, 1: 551.

[31] *RFC* July 9, 1: 559.

Sherman challenged the report on House seats immediately, contending that it "did not appear to correspond with any rule of numbers, or of any requisition hitherto adopted by Cong[ress]." Sherman moved to create a new, larger committee with a member from each state. Although South Carolina and New York voted against the creation of this second committee, the delegates approved it overwhelmingly. Sherman, Madison, Morris, and Rutledge served on this eleven-member committee. On July 10, this larger committee proposed a House with sixty-five seats, exactly five times the number of states that would be represented. Virginia would have ten seats in the House, or 15 percent of its members. Massachusetts and Pennsylvania would have eight seats in the House (12 percent of its members). Connecticut, South Carolina, and North Carolina would each have five seats, or precisely one-thirteenth of the members, perfectly maintaining the relative weight in the national legislature they currently enjoyed in Confederation Congress. In this new plan, smaller states gained seats relative to larger ones. Four states could no longer form a majority in the House, substantially reducing the potential power that New York or either Carolina might exercise over legislation. Paterson's notes indicate a clear understanding that this distribution of seats in the lower house meant that none of the three regions could muster the thirty-three delegates needed for a majority. New England had eighteen votes in this scheme, the middle states had twenty-five votes, and the South had twenty-three votes.[32] The slave states (the South plus Maryland) had twenty-eight votes.

The reality of these numbers changed the convention's dynamics. Delegates feverishly calculated relative state and regional advantage. As soon as hard numbers were attached to each state's House delegation, the delegates contested not only the number of seats for their state and region but also the frequency of the censuses on which reapportionment would be based.[33] The July 10 report particularly appalled delegates from New York and the Carolinas. Two New York delegates, Yates and Lansing, walked away from the convention after July 10 and never came back. North Carolina's Hugh Williamson called for the reduction of seats for some states because "the South[ern] interest must be

[32] *RFC* July 10, 1: 566, 573.

[33] The census, then as now, was important politically. Because some states were growing more rapidly than others, it became possible for more rapidly growing states to gain relative strength in the House of Representatives with every new census. Thus, the frequency of the census could change the balance of power among rivalrous sections, and between slave and free states. See *RFC* July 12, 1: 592, 594–7.

extremely endangered by the present arrangement." South Carolina's delegates began to fight ferociously to add all their slaves to the population counted in establishing House seats, to reduce the seats apportioned to the northern states, and to increase the seats held by the South.[34] Despite repeated efforts during the rest of the convention to add a seat here or subtract a seat there, though, this allocation became fixed in the Constitution.[35]

As the distribution of House seats grew clearer, substantive economic rivalries over western expansion and slavery became more urgent. Western development split Madison's allies as well as his opponents. Gouverneur Morris, Elbridge Gerry, and John Rutledge sought to stop any future western states from ever gaining enough seats to outvote the coastal states they represented. Gerry warned that western legislators "will oppress commerce, and drain our wealth into the Western Country." The committee of five that recommended a fifty-six-seat House aimed explicitly to put the government in the hands of the Atlantic states so that they could "take care of their own interest, by dealing out the right of Representation in safe proportions to the Western States." Madison and fellow Virginians actively promoted western expansion and opposed any discrimination against the representation of prospective western states. On this issue, Sherman agreed with Madison. The champion of Connecticut's Ohio lands, Sherman reminded the delegates that "our children & our grand Children" were "as likely to be citizens of new Western States, as of old states." A vote to limit the number of representatives from the western states narrowly lost, four states to five. New Jersey joined the four southern states in the majority, while Pennsylvania divided.[36]

With the slavery debate becoming more open and the Carolinas' leverage in the House less certain, many southern delegates calculated that they could not count on controlling national policy to protect their slaveholdings. South Carolina demanded that the number of its U.S. representatives be determined by its full population, including all slaves, not three-fifths

[34] *RFC* July 10, 1: 566–8; July 11, 1: 580.

[35] *RFC* August 21, 2: 356–7; September 8, 2: 553–4; September 14, 2: 612; September 15, 2: 623–4.

[36] *RFC* July 5, 1: 536; July 9, 1: 560; July 11, 1: 578, 585–6; July 14, 2: 2–3. South Carolina's constitution, for example, had provided for the overrepresentation of eastern, Tidewater interests and the underrepresentation of western, upcountry residents; E. James Ferguson, *The Power of the Purse: A History of Public Finance, 1776–1790* (Chapel Hill: University of North Carolina Press, 1961), p. 23.

of the slaves as the delegates had agreed in June.[37] Madison's northern allies, Wilson, Morris, and King, assailed not only the three-fifths rule but any recognition of slaves in determining the distribution of U.S. representatives. William Davie of North Carolina, charging that the northerners sought "to deprive the Southern States of any share of Representation for their blacks," implied that the lack of any accommodation would drive the South out of the convention. Gouverneur Morris stated frankly that

> the South[er]n Gentleman will not be satisfied unless they see the way open to their gaining a majority in the public Councils. The consequence of such a transfer of power from the maritime to the interior & landed interest will he foresees be such an oppression of commerce, that he shall be obliged to vote for ye. vicious principle of equality in the 2nd. branch in order to provide some defence for the N[orthern] States ag[ain]st it. But to come now more to the point, either this distinction is fictitious or real: if fictitious let it be dismissed & let us proceed with due confidence. If it be real, instead of attempting to blend incompatible things, let us at once take a friendly leave of each other. There can be no end of demands for security if every particular interest is to be entitled to it. The Eastern States may claim it for their fishery, and for other objects, as the South[er]n States claim it for their peculiar objects. In this struggle between the two ends of the Union, what part ought the Middle States in point of policy to take: to join their Eastern brethren according to his ideas. If the South[er]n States get the power into their hands, and be joined as they will be with the interior Country they will inevitably bring on a war with Spain for the Mississippi.[38]

James Wilson finessed this dispute with a tactical evasion that, in effect, finally established the three-fifths compromise in the Constitution.[39]

Defections from the southern flank of Madison's coalition doomed his convention strategy. On July 14 Charles Pinckney made a last-ditch

[37] *RFC* July 11, 1: 580. The South gained a small point when the delegates agreed to conduct a census every decade. A relatively frequent census was expected to benefit the rapidly growing southern states more than the alternative proposal for a census every twenty years (July 12, 1: 596).

[38] *RFC* July 13, 1: 604.

[39] *RFC* July 13, 1: 605–6. Wilson's tactical evasion, on July 12, took two steps. First, he proposed that representation be pegged to taxation. Second, he proposed that taxation be based on the three-fifths compromise of 1783, thus linking representation to the three-fifths formula without stating explicitly the inferior status of slaves. This tactic was approved, six states to two. Connecticut, Pennsylvania, Maryland, Virginia, North Carolina, and Georgia supported Wilson's maneuver. New Jersey and Delaware opposed it, as they had opposed the three-fifths compromise on June 11. Massachusetts and South Carolina divided their votes (*RFC* July 12, 1: 597). See Howard A. Ohline, "Republicanism and Slavery: Origins of the Three-Fifths Clause in the United States Constitution," *William and Mary Quarterly*, 3rd ser., 28:4 (October 1971): 563–84.

proposal to rescue proportional representation in the Senate.[40] By this point, explicit discussions about trade, slavery, and the West had made conflicting comparative advantages obvious to every delegate. The convention's slow pace grew aggravating. Caleb Strong of Massachusetts added his voice to those seeking conciliation. With Gorham absent, the Massachusetts delegation joined Connecticut, New Jersey, Delaware, North Carolina, and Georgia to defeat Pinckney's eleventh-hour proposal. Massachusetts's vote mortified Rufus King.[41]

The following Monday, July 16, the convention formally approved Connecticut's compromise on representation on a five-to-four vote, with Massachusetts divided. The first column of Table 5.1 indicates the apportionment of seats in the House of Representatives established on July 10, and the following columns indicate the way each state voted. The vote clearly turned on opposition to Madison's plan and was not simply a defeat of the "large" states by the "small" ones. Of the four smallest of the thirteen states, only one voted against the compromise. Georgia, a small state, voted with Madison's coalition as a southern state. Madison lost North Carolina, and enough of Massachusetts's delegates to neutralize its vote. The backbone of support for this compromise consisted of vulnerable middle states – Connecticut, Maryland, Delaware, and New Jersey, joined by North Carolina.

This compromise dealt a fatal blow to Madison's political agenda. Delegates from the larger states met the following morning to discuss the vote. According to a frustrated Madison, their opinions "differed so much as to the importance of that point" and to the risks of the convention's failure if they opposed it that they could not agree on how to proceed. The meeting's result, Madison noted, probably "satisfied the smaller States that they had nothing to apprehend from a Union of the larger, in any plan whatever ag[ain]st the equality of votes in the 2d. branch."[42] Delegates

[40] *RFC* July 14, 2: 5. Pinckney's eleventh-hour alternative proposed to give Virginia five senators; Massachusetts and Pennsylvania four senators each; Connecticut, New York, Maryland, and both Carolinas three senators each (thus offering them the same relative weight they enjoyed in the Confederation Congress); New Hampshire, New Jersey, and Georgia two senators each; and Delaware and Rhode Island one senator each. On June 8 Pinckney and Rutledge had introduced the idea of "three classes" of states, with the largest states receiving three senators, the average-sized states two, and the smallest states one (June 8, 1: 169).

[41] *RFC* July 14, 2: 12. New York was not likely to vote for the Virginia Plan and might have joined the vote for the compromise, but at this point it lacked a quorum because Governor Clinton's allies had abandoned the convention.

[42] *RFC* July 16, 2: 19–20.

TABLE 5.1. *The Vote on the Connecticut Compromise, July 16*

	Estimated House Seats July 10[a]	In Favor	Against	Divided	Absent
Virginia[b]	10		X		
Pennsylvania[b]	8		X		
Massachusetts[b]	8			X	
New York	6				X
Maryland	6	X			
North Carolina[b]	5	X			
South Carolina[b]	5		X		
Connecticut	5	X			
New Jersey	4	X			
New Hampshire	3				X
Georgia[b]	3		X		
Delaware	1	X			

[a] Number of seats in the House of Representatives assigned to each state under the Great Compromise, as approved July 9 and adjusted July 10; total of sixty-five House seats allocated (*RFC* July 16, 2: 15).
[b] States in Madison's expected coalition of three large and three southern states. Rhode Island sent no delegates to the convention.

from the large and southern states had to pursue other approaches to defend their interests.

WAR OF ATTRITION OVER POLICY AGENCY

The struggle to control national policy makers now shifted to a series of battles over the selection of the president, executive officials, and judges. Although the convention had beaten back his ambitions for the Constitution, the resilient Madison fought hard to inject his vision into the choices that remained. Madison and his allies immediately began to battle to make Congress less dependent on the states, and the executive and courts less dependent on Congress. For them, a Congress so dependent on the states could not be trusted to serve the national interest.[43] Now that Sherman and his allies had ensured a Senate that would serve as the state governments' agent in the national policy process, they fought equally hard to put the selection of national policy makers in the hands of Congress and especially the Senate. Defending the idea that Congress should elect the president, Sherman expressed confidence "that the sense

[43] *RFC* July 24, 2: 104.

of the Nation would be better expressed by the Legislature, than by the people at large," who would "generally vote for some man in their own State." The Senate should appoint judges because "Judges ought to be diffused, which would be more likely to be attended to by the [Senate] than by the Executive."[44]

After the delegates approved the compromise on representation and spent ten more days on the unfinished portions of the Virginia Plan, the convention turned over its work to a Committee of Detail on July 26. The Committee of Detail's August 6 draft marked the high point of state agency in the Constitutional Convention's work. The five-member Committee of Detail included Oliver Ellsworth, John Rutledge, Madison's ally James Wilson, the conciliatory Nathaniel Gorham, and the temporizing Edmund Randolph. Its report wove the various approved resolutions into a coherent draft and recommended additional specifics. The committee's final draft provided that the state legislatures directly choose U.S. senators and determine the voter qualifications, districts, and times of elections to the U.S. House of Representatives.[45] The August 6 draft made national legislators dependent on the state legislatures for their pay and allowed them to serve concurrently in state offices. Congress – especially the Senate, the states' national policy agent – would exercise remarkable control over other policy makers. Congress would appoint the president for a single seven-year term, and he could not serve a second term. The committee draft did not specify whether both houses would vote separately for the president as they did for laws, but if they did vote separately, the Senate would be able to veto any presidential candidate. The president of the Senate would succeed the president, on his removal, death, resignation, or disability. The Senate alone appointed Supreme Court judges and ambassadors, and, like the Confederation Congress, made treaties and controlled the process of settling disputes among the states. The president could appoint only less important executive officers. State and national officeholders would swear an oath to support the Constitution. Daniel Carroll of Maryland, sympathetic to Madison's views, complained that the "dependence of both houses on the State Legislatures is compleat.... The States can now say: if you do not comply with our wishes, we will starve you: if you do we will reward you."[46]

44 *RFC* July 17, 1: 29; July 18, 2: 41.

45 *RFC* August 6, 2: 177–86. The Committee of Detail provided that each state's rules for regulating the electorate for the lower house in its state legislature also would be used to determine the electorate eligible to vote for members of the U.S. House of Representatives.

46 *RFC* August 14, 2: 292.

The convention spent five more frustrating weeks hammering out their differences and transforming the Committee of Detail report into a final document. The delegations clashed over every rule that pitted one state's vital interests against another. This battle over policy agency mainly turned on the selection, removal, and appointment powers of the president, but it also surfaced in choices about congressional elections and vacancies, qualifications, pay, and representation of new states, about the selection of judges, and about the ratification of the Constitution.

Congress

The delegates jockeyed for advantage in designing Congress until the convention's final day, when they agreed to increase the size of the House by limiting House districts to thirty thousand constituents.[47] Subtle provisions steered the House toward the representation of state constituencies; House districts would be contained entirely within one and only one state, and each state would have at least one U.S. Representative. Several agency issues, such as staggering Senate terms to allow the election of only one-third of the senators in any one election, setting a minimum age for holding office, requiring attendance, providing for vacancies, and permitting expulsions, sparked little debate because they had no clear impact on state interests.[48] But several issues of congressional agency – the representation of new states, suffrage in House elections, member qualifications, and pay – became politically controversial because these choices potentially affected national policy outcomes and vital state interests.

The delegates' quarrels about adding new states reveal the extent to which political interests were driving the Constitution's design. The opposing coalitions completely reversed positions on this issue: Madison's allies demanded the protection of states' prerogatives, whereas his opponents insisted on eliminating the influence of existing states in creating new

[47] On the convention's final day, Gorham moved to reduce the size of House constituencies from forty thousand to thirty thousand (a change that would not affect the sixty-five seats established for the first Congress). Gorham indicated that the change would reduce opposition to the plan. George Washington spoke on behalf of this change, and it received unanimous agreement (*RFC* September 17, 2: 644).

[48] *RFC* August 8, 2: 223; August 9, 2: 231; August 10, 2: 254. The delegates early on had agreed to a minimum age of thirty for U.S. senators and twenty-five for House members (June 12, 1: 217–18; June 23, 1: 375). Wilson objected to giving state governors power to fill Senate vacancies, but his motion to strike this provision was defeated.

states. Pennsylvania's Gouverneur Morris, who previously had criticized state obstructionism but represented a state with a large land domain, moved that no new state could be created within the limits of an existing state unless that state's legislature approved. Luther Martin, the convention's most zealous states' rights advocate on other issues but keenly interested in the national control of western lands, argued forcefully against any state's right to obstruct the creation of new states, because that right would alarm the "limited States" (that is, states with relatively little land within their borders). Wilson objected to a rule that would "divide a State against its own consent." Martin pointed out the inconsistency in his opponents' position: "In the beginning, when the rights of the small States were in question, they were phantoms, ideal beings. Now when the Great States were to be affected, political Societies were of a sacred nature." Despite Martin's objections, Madison's coalition carried the vote. The six large and southern states voted together against the remaining five middle and New England states to require state legislatures to concur in creating new states within their boundaries.[49]

National rules for suffrage in House elections, notably proposals to limit voting rights to freeholders and long-term state residents, touched on a politically sensitive state prerogative. The Committee of Detail declined to recommend any such rules and simply recommended that the qualifications of voters be the same as qualifications set by each state for voting for the lower house of the state legislature. On the floor, Gouverneur Morris moved to establish minimum national property qualifications for anyone voting in House elections. "The right of suffrage was a tender point," responded Ellsworth, "strongly guarded by most of the <State> Constitutions.... The States are the best Judges of the circumstances and temper of their own people." Mason pointed out that "Eight or nine States have extended the right of suffrage beyond the freeholders" and asked "What will the people there say, if they should be disfranchised." Rutledge "thought the idea... would create division" and turn any citizens potentially disenfranchised in national elections into opponents of the Constitution. Defining property in a way that protected suffrage for merchants and manufacturers also raised difficulties. In the end, only Delaware voted for property qualifications for House elections.[50] Rather than uniformly exclude women, the poor, minorities, and children from the electorate, the delegates left such decisions to the states.

[49] *RFC* August 30, 2: 461–6.
[50] *RFC* 2: 139–40; August 7, 2: 201–6.

The delegates authorized the national regulation of House and Senate elections because they expected the states to manipulate these rules to control election outcomes. When Charles Pinckney and Rutledge moved to prohibit Congress from regulating state rules about the time and place of congressional elections, Gorham, King, and Gouverneur Morris objected. Madison warned that "It was impossible to foresee all the abuses that might be made of the discretionary power.... Whenever the State Legislatures had a favorite measure to carry, they would take care so to mould their regulations as to favor the candidates they wished to succeed." Sherman, who had dealt with such problems in Congress, signaled a willingness to accept congressional regulation of these elections, though he personally had "sufficient confidence in the State Legislatures." Congress was authorized to establish such national election rules, except for state legislative appointments of senators.[51]

Would those with little property or nonresidents be prohibited from serving in Congress? Many delegates wanted to limit Congress to the property-owning class. The convention instructed the Committee of Detail to limit eligibility for the national legislature to those with property. Gouverneur Morris worried that these rules could be drawn up "to exclude particular persons from office as long as they pleased." Instead of setting qualifications, the committee simply delegated to Congress itself the discretion to establish qualifications for its members. Charles Pinkney, who thought that the president should hold at least $100,000 worth of property and other officers at least half that, offered a motion to set some specific minimum property holding for national officials, "to make them independent & respectable." Rutledge pointed out that the committee could not agree on what property holdings to require, and Ellsworth argued that different economic circumstances in different states made it impossible to set fixed property standards. The delegates defeated Pinckney's motion, while they explicitly voted to retain property as a potential qualification for members of Congress.[52] Despite the delegates' sympathy for property qualifications in principle, delegating the issue to

[51] *RFC* August 9, 2: 239–42. Madison specified some of the choices states could make: "Whether the electors should vote by ballot or vivâ voce, should assemble at this place or that place; should be divided into districts or all meet at one place, sh[oul]d all vote for all the representatives; or all in a district vote for a number allotted to the district; these & many other points would depend on the Legislatures" (August 9, 2: 240–1). For Sherman's experiences with state elections, see *JCC* March 23, 1784, 26: 156–7.

[52] *RFC* July 26, 2: 121–3; August 10, 2: 248–50. In the final Committee of Style draft of the Constitution, however, the phrase alluding to property as an appropriate qualification for Congress disappeared without comment (*RFC* 2: 592).

the states made it easier to evade state differences than to confront them. The delegates found it less difficult to exclude outsiders. Rutledge moved to require seven years of residency in the state, limiting representation to long-term state residents. Mason and Ellsworth concurred with the principle of requiring some period of years of state residency, to prevent "Rich men of neighbouring States, [who] may employ with success the means of corruption in some particular district and thereby get into the public Councils after having failed in their own State." The convention finally required that representatives and senators be inhabitants of a state, though they defeated any specific length of residency. Worried about foreign influence in selecting U.S. representatives, they set the requirements for national citizenship to seven years for representatives and nine years for senators.[53]

The delegates considered control of legislators' compensation a potentially powerful tool for controlling their behavior. Even some of the Connecticut delegates had doubts about whether the states, instead of the national government, should pay their members of Congress. Mason observed that state payment would make "both Houses . . . the instruments of the politics of the States whatever they may be." Ellsworth conceded that state payment created "too much dependence on the States." Madison used the discussion as another occasion to complain about state agency. Only Luther Martin and Pierce Butler defended state payment of compensation to members of Congress. The delegates voted to restore national payment of members of Congress, nine states to two (Massachusetts and South Carolina opposed it). The delegates unanimously added Charles Pinckney's proposal to prohibit legislators or any other national officials from being forced to pass a religious test as a qualification for office (although Sherman thought the provision unnecessary).[54]

The President

After the apportionment of the Senate, selecting the president became the convention's most exasperating issue. Sherman, who sought to make the president completely dependent on Congress, expressed satisfaction with

[53] *RFC* August 8, 2: 218–19; August 10, 2: 251; August 13, 2: 268–72.

[54] *RFC* August 14, 2: 290–2; August 30, 2: 468. Several states required public officials to uphold the Christian religion. Delaware, Pennsylvania, and Vermont required officials to acknowledge that the Old and New Testaments were given by divine inspiration. Delaware further required that office holders profess to "faith in God the Father, and in Jesus Christ his only Son, and in the Holy Ghost, one God, blessed for ever more." Carl Zollman, *American Church Law* (St. Paul, MN: West Publishing, 1933).

the Committee of Detail's report. When Mason pointed out the possibility that one house could check the other's choice of president, Sherman replied that he looked forward to that possibility.[55] As soon as the convention adopted the compromise on representation, Madison treated the president as the chief advocate for national interests independent of the states. The president must have "free agency with regard to the Legislature," Madison insisted. Unlike Congress, the president would "be considered as a national officer, acting for and equally sympathising with every part of the U[nited] States." Congress therefore could not select the president and make him its agent. The president could not control the Congress's "strong propensity to a variety of pernicious measures" if the election process depended on Congress.[56] Worried about the president's dependence on Congress, Morris anticipated that "He will be the tool of a faction, of some leading demagogue in the Legislature."[57]

Through invention, compromise, and "tedious and reiterated" discussion, the convention moved toward a middle ground between Madison and Sherman. When the delegates rejected James Wilson's proposal for direct popular election of the president during the convention's first week, Wilson suggested that voters select special presidential electors, who in turn would cast ballots for president.[58] This politically intriguing

[55] *RFC* August 7, 2: 196–7.

[56] *RFC* July 17, 1: 34; July 19, 1: 56; July 21, 2: 80–1; July 25, 2: 109–11; Madison to Jefferson, October 24, 1787, in *PJM* 10: 208–9. Madison listed several "insuperable objections" to congressional selection of the president: "Besides the general influence of that mode on the independence of the Executive, 1. the election of the Chief Magistrate would agitate & divide the legislature so much that the public interest would materially suffer by it. Public bodies are always apt to be thrown into contentions, but into more violent ones by such occasions than by any others. 2. the candidate would intrigue with the Legislature, would derive his appointment from the predominant faction, and be apt to render his administration subservient to its views. 3. The Ministers of foreign powers would have and make use of, the opportunity to mix their intrigues & influence with the Election.... No pains, nor perhaps expence, will be spared, to gain from the Legislature an appointm[en]t, favorable to their wishes.... [Nor could state legislatures select the president.] The [state] Legislatures can & will act with some kind of regular plan, and will promote the appointm[en]t of a man who will not oppose himself to a favorite object. Should a majority of the Legislatures at the time of election have the same object, or different objects of the same kind, the Nat[iona]l Executive, would be rendered subservient to them" (*RFC* July 25, 2: 109).

[57] *RFC* July 19, 2: 53.

[58] Maryland used electors to choose its Senate. *RFC* June 2, 1: 80–1; Shlomo Slonim, "The Electoral College at Philadelphia: The Evolution of an Ad Hoc Congress for the Selection of the President," *Journal of American History* 73:1 (June 1986): 35–58; Marc W. Kruman, *Between Authority and Liberty: State Constitution Making in Revolutionary America* (Chapel Hill: University of North Carolina Press, 1997), p. 139. The Holy Roman Empire provided the most familiar example of the use of electors.

option begged the question of who would choose the electors. After the compromise on representation, Gouverneur Morris again proposed that the people should directly elect the president because appointment by Congress would result in "usurpation & tyranny." When the convention rejected this motion, Luther Martin moved that the state legislatures appoint electors to choose the president. Although Martin's proposal also lost, his suggestion indicated both sides could agree on the principle of using electors. Two days later, Rufus King proposed presidential selection by electors chosen by the people, and Ellsworth proposed electors chosen by the legislatures. The convention divided the question, agreed to use electors on a six to three vote, and then agreed, eight to two (with only Virginia and South Carolina opposed) that the state legislatures would choose the electors.[59]

But the apportionment of electors to each state raised the same problems as the apportionment of seats in Congress. Paterson and Ellsworth proposed a relatively flat distribution that would give at least one elector to every small state and no more than three electors to the largest. Instead, the delegates approved a North Carolina proposal more favorable to the large states, an apportionment of presidential electors similar to the apportionment of House seats.[60] Ellsworth disputed the idea of giving larger states extra weight in selecting the president. He claimed that "Citizens of the largest States would invariably prefer the Candidate within the State," giving the larger states too great an advantage in electing their favorite sons to the presidency. Vexed, the delegates temporarily gave the selection of the president back to Congress.[61]

When the House gained more influence in selecting the president, however, Sherman began to back away from direct congressional selection of the president. On August 24 the convention tentatively endorsed selection of the president by a joint, rather than separate, ballot of the House and Senate – a formula that worked in favor of the larger states and garnered the support of most of Madison's expected coalition.[62] Immediately, New Jersey's Dayton made a motion to equalize the state votes in choosing

[59] *RFC* July 17, 2: 31–2; July 19, 2: 56–8.

[60] *RFC* July 19, 2: 56–7; July 20, 2: 64. Connecticut voted with the large and remaining southern states in favor of the North Carolina proposal, while Georgia joined New Jersey, Delaware, and Maryland in opposition. No one disputed a motion requiring that electors not be members of Congress or officers of the United States (July 20, 2: 69), or that electors be paid out of the national treasury (July 21, 2: 73).

[61] *RFC* July 25, 2: 111; July 26, 2: 119–20.

[62] *RFC* August 24, 2: 403.

the president, but Madison's coalition (joined by New Hampshire) defeated this proposal. The delegates again rejected electors. The convention had reached another impasse, this time on the selection of the president. Sherman again proposed a committee to deal with the problem, along with other postponed matters. This eleven-member Committee on Postponed Matters brought together many of the convention's key protagonists, including Madison, Sherman, Gouverneur Morris, and John Dickinson.[63]

This committee reported a sort of "grand compromise" on the presidency that paralleled the compromise on representation in July. The committee proposed presidential electors chosen by the state legislatures. The number of electors allocated to each state would equal the sum of its seats in the U.S. Senate and U.S. House of Representatives. This formula mimicked a joint ballot by Congress and modestly leveled the influence of each state. The presidential electors would vote for two candidates, one of whom could not be an inhabitant of their state (a scheme that aimed to blunt the criticism that large states would choose favorite sons and dominate the presidency). The electors would physically cast their presidential ballots in their home states, to preclude them from conspiring to select a president. Congress could determine the time electors would be chosen and the time they would cast their ballots. A candidate who won an outright majority in this "electoral college" would be president, and the runner-up would be vice president. If two candidates tied, each with a majority, the Senate would appoint the president. If no candidate won a majority, the Senate would choose the president from a list of the five candidates receiving the most votes. Morris pointed out that this proposal largely severed the connection between Congress and the president, as well as the connections among electors from different states, and so reduced opportunities for intrigue, faction, and cabal.[64] This plan greatly

[63] *RFC* August 31, 2: 481. Among the many variations proposed for selecting the president, Wilson had suggested drawing electors from the legislature by lot (July 24, 2: 103). Ellsworth suggested that the legislature could appoint the executive initially, but he could be reelected by electors appointed by the state legislatures; Gerry proposed that state executives and their councils appoint the national executive (July 25, 2: 108–9).

[64] *RFC* September 4, 2: 497–500. Rhode Island and Delaware, with one House seat and three electoral votes, would each cast 1.5 percent of the votes in the first House of Representatives, but would cast more than 3 percent of the electoral vote for the first president. New Hampshire and Georgia gained 1 percent, and New Jersey .5 percent. Virginia cast 15 percent of the votes in the House but only 13 percent of the electoral votes. Massachusetts and Pennsylvania lost slightly more than 1 percent of their vote, New York about .5 percent. On July 25, Williamson, Madison, Morris, and Dickinson had floated the idea that voters could vote for two candidates, one required to be outside

reduced the conflicts over presidential selection, and most of its proposals were incorporated in the final Constitution.[65]

The role of the Senate in this arrangement instantly caused trouble. Mason, Rutledge, and Wilson warned that the Constitution now threw "a dangerous power" to the Senate. Wilson moved to replace "Senate" with "Legislature," a change to a joint ballot that would increase the influence of the large states. Wilson's motion lost seven states to three, with only Virginia, Pennsylvania, and South Carolina in favor. Madison, aiming to minimize the likelihood of a Senate vote, proposed that the person having one-third of the votes, instead of a majority, be elected president, but his proposal lost by a large margin.[66] Mason tried to limit the pool of candidates to three instead of five (a proposal favorable to large states, with more electoral votes and more likely to have favorite sons among the finalists). Sherman opposed Mason's suggestion, preferring seven or thirteen candidates instead. Although the delegates defeated

their state (July 25, 2: 113–15). The delegates also approved other safeguards for the separation of electors' interests from other policy makers and each other. The convention approved a provision to disqualify federal officeholders from serving as electors (as the state could do in Maryland) and rejected proposals to permit the electors to convene together (July 20, 1: 69; September 6, 2: 521, 526).

[65] Issues of presidential agency that garnered little opposition included the provisions that the president "receive a fixt compensation for the devotion of his time to the public service, to be paid out of the Nat[iona]l Treasury" (*RFC* July 26, 2: 120–1), that the president be at least thirty-five years old (August 22, 2: 367; September 7, 2: 536), and that the president be a natural-born citizen. This citizenship proviso seemed to eliminate aspirations to the presidency that might have been entertained by three of Madison's allies – Hamilton, Robert Morris, and Wilson. However, the committee on postponed matters added a clause requiring merely that the president be either a natural-born citizen or a fourteen-year resident of the United States, and the delegates approved it unanimously (September 4, 2: 497; September 7, 2: 536). The Committee of Style dropped even the fourteen-year requirement in favor of a requirement that the president be a natural-born citizen or a citizen at the time of the Constitution's adoption (*RFC* 2: 598).

[66] *RFC* September 5, 2: 512–14; September 6, 2: 522. When Sherman commented that the small states might have an advantage in the Senate, but the large states would have an advantage in choosing the candidates, Madison speculated at length about the political calculations this arrangement would set in motion. He "considered it as a primary object to render an eventual resort to any part of the Legislature improbable. He was apprehensive that the proposed alteration would turn the attention of the large States too much to the appointment of candidates, instead of aiming at an effectual appointment of the officer, as the large States would predominate in the Legislature which would have the final choice out of the Candidates. Whereas if the Senate in which the small States predominate should have the final choice, the concerted effort of the large States would be to make the appointment in the first instance conclusive" (September 5, 2: 513). It is at this point that Madison and Williamson unsuccessfully moved to insert after "Electors" the words "who shall have balloted" to increased the likelihood of a decision by the electoral college; see Chapter 1, n. 53.

Mason's proposal, the following day Williamson and Sherman each implicitly acknowledged the problem by proposing substitutes. Williamson suggested that the entire Congress elect the president if no candidate received a majority. Sherman proposed that the House settle a contested presidential election by voting as blocks of states rather than as individual members, with each state casting a single vote for president. This shrewd solution, reminiscent of the Confederation Congress, equalized the states' influence. Only Delaware voted against Sherman's solution.[67]

The Senate's role in removing and replacing the president fueled similar mistrust. Steeped in British political history, the delegates easily agreed on the need to arrange for removing a president. They had no trouble giving the House of Representatives the power to impeach him. The difficulty turned on who would have the power to try an impeached president, remove him from office, and select his successor. A Congress that could both appoint and remove the president could exercise a dangerous dominance over the executive branch. The Committee of Detail recommended that the Supreme Court try impeachments with a two-thirds majority required for conviction (and punishment limited to removal and disqualification from office). Morris, though, warned that the provision would entangle the court in political intrigues. But Morris also suggested that the chief justice succeed the president rather than the president of the Senate, while Madison, who also sought to reduce the Senate's influence, suggested a presidential council to fill the office.[68] Once the invention of the electoral college removed the Senate from influencing the choice of the president, the delegates could finally accept the Senate as the forum for impeachment trials. The office of vice president was invented, in part, to provide a presidential successor who would not be chosen by Congress, thus reducing Congress's incentive to impeach the president.[69]

[67] *RFC* September 5, 2: 515; September 6, 2: 527. An experienced legislator such as Sherman almost certainly understood the way this final arrangement could strengthen the representation of state interests in the House. This presidential election mechanism potentially would compel each state's House delegation to hammer out a consensus on vital state interests and the best candidate for those interests at the start of every other Congress. The delegates approved Madison's proposal to ensure that this vote would require the presence of two-thirds of the states, but, in another small victory for state interests, rejected his proposal to require a quorum of a majority of the House (September 6, 2: 528).

[68] *RFC* July 18, 2: 42; July 20, 2: 69; August 27, 2: 427.

[69] *RFC* September 4, 2: 498–500. The convention allowed Congress to designate officers that would succeed the president and vice president in case of death, resignation, or disability (September 7, 2: 535). Morris added the requirement that senators sitting in

Judges, Ambassadors, and Administrators

After the July 16 compromise on representation, Madison pressed to give the president the power to appoint judges, ambassadors, and national administrators because he sought to remove their selection from Congress and to strengthen the president. Madison soon moved that the president appoint national judges unless disagreed to by two-thirds of the Senate. Sherman, of course, wanted the Senate to select judges. Ellsworth, supporting Sherman, cautioned that the executive "will be more open to caresses and intrigues than the Senate" and "nomination under such circumstances will be equivalent to an appointment." The southern and smaller middle states joined to turn back Madison's motion.[70] In early September, Madison, Sherman, and the rest of the Committee on Postponed Matters recommended the president appoint Supreme Court judges, with Senate confirmation by a simple majority. Although James Wilson still objected to any role for the Senate at all, the delegates agreed to the committee proposal without dissent.[71]

impeachment trials take an oath (September 8, 2: 552–3). When Madison tried again to eliminate the Senate from impeachment, only Pennsylvania and Virginia voted for the motion (September 8, 2: 551). Rutledge and Morris moved that "that persons impeached be suspended from their office until they be tried and acquitted," but Madison successfully persuaded the delegates that "the President is too dependent already on the Legislature.... This intermediate suspension, will put him in the power of one branch only. They can at any moment, in order to make way for the functions of another who will be more favorable to their views, vote a temporary removal of the existing magistrate" (September 14, 2: 612).

[70] *RFC* July 18, 2: 41, 43–4; July 21, 2: 80–3.

[71] *RFC* September 6, 2: 523; September 7, 2: 538–9. Sherman remained uncharacteristically silent on the important issue of judicial appointment when the convention approved presidential appointment on September 7. Given his role on the committee and the unanimous vote, Sherman simply may not have felt the need to address this issue. But Sherman might have had two additional reasons to acquiesce to this conditional presidential appointment of judges. First, Sherman had achieved substantial success on presidential agency by softening electoral vote inequality, by ensuring the states an equal role in the case of an electoral tie, and by making the Senate the trial court for impeachment. He could afford to be conciliatory on the selection of judges. Indeed, it is not unreasonable to speculate that Madison, Sherman, and their colleagues on the committee arrived at a grand package of interrelated compromises on presidential, judicial, and administrative appointment (and on treaty approval). Second, Sherman might have been more willing to accede to an independent judiciary than an independent president. Courts were a much more retrospective vehicle for the national interest than a powerful chief executive. His plan of early July proposed a separate national judiciary but not a separate national executive. At the end of the convention, and responding to Madison's final admonition to consider the commerce power indivisible, Sherman invoked a supremacy clause as serving the purpose, by permitting the control of state interferences in trade "<when> such

The convention also came around to the idea of entrusting the appointment of ambassadors and national administrators to the president. Sherman had objected to the Committee of Detail's recommendation of a broad presidential appointment power. The delegates defeated an ingenious motion by Dickinson to allow Congress to establish offices and then authorize the state legislatures and governors to fill them. As with judges, the Committee on Postponed Matters included presidential appointment of these officers with the advice and consent of the Senate. The convention accepted this arrangement with little debate.[72] But controversy swirled around the appointment of offices responsible for "the purse and the sword." The delegates approved congressional power to appoint a national treasurer, but this provision disappeared in the Committee of Style draft of September 12.[73] The convention drew the line at national control of the state militias. The militias were an important state police power, and militia appointments were important political rewards for state citizens. When Madison moved to nationalize the appointment of general officers, Sherman objected that this was "absolutely inadmissible," while Gerry "warned the Convention ag[ain]st pushing the experiment too far." The delegates defeated Madison's motion, and even Virginia abandoned him on the vote.[74]

Ratification

While Madison considered it "essential" to bypass the state legislatures and entrust the ratification of the Constitution to special ratifying

interferences happen" (September 15, 2: 625). Sherman showed a preference for national review of state actions, but a more passive review than implied by Madison's national veto of state laws. It is plausible that the politically shrewd Sherman would support an independent judiciary as a passive check on the policy system in which he himself had helped guarantee the states substantial national agency and policy autonomy.

[72] *RFC* August 24, 2: 405–6; August 25, 2: 418–19; September 4, 2: 498–9; September 7, 2: 539. On September 15 Morris moved to permit Congress to delegate the appointment of such inferior offices as they thought proper, in the president, courts, or heads of departments. The delegates at first defeated the proposal but then accepted it after being urged that some such provision was indispensable (*RFC* 2: 627–8). The issue of the control over the creation of executive branch offices is discussed further in Chapter 7.

[73] *RFC* August 17, 2: 314–15; September 12, 2: 594–6. Compare the earlier draft of the Committee of Style, in 2: 569–70. After the delegates eliminated the position of treasurer, they added a requirement that "a regular Statement and Account of the Receipts and Expenditures of all public Money shall be published from time to time" (September 14, 2: 618–9).

[74] *RFC* August 23, 2: 388–9.

conventions, Sherman disagreed. Most delegates discussed the issue in frank terms of political expediency. King, for example, thought that it would be easier to secure ratification in a simple convention than in a bicameral state legislature. On June 12 Madison's coalition of six states carried the proposition for state ratification by conventions. When Ellsworth and Paterson moved for ratification by the state legislatures in late July, Randolph warned that "local demagogues who will be degraded" by the Constitution "will spare no efforts to impede that progress in the popular mind which will be necessary to the adoption of the plan." Again, Madison's coalition of southern and large states, joined by the newly arrived delegates from New Hampshire, defeated Ellsworth's motion.[75]

Political expediency explains why Gouverneur Morris subsequently moved to strike the word "conventions" so that states could "pursue their own modes of ratification." King countered that "Conventions alone, which will avoid all the obstacles from the complicated formation of the Legislatures, will succeed, and if not positively required by the plan, its enemies will oppose that mode." Madison calculated that "Legislatures would be more disinclined than conventions composed in part at least of other men; and if disinclined, they could devise modes apparently promoting, but really thwarting the ratification." Luther Martin, who would soon walk away from the convention, all but proved Madison's observation by insisting on ratification by the state legislatures. Morris's motion to strike out "Conventions" lost, four states to six, with Delaware and New Jersey joining New Hampshire, Massachusetts, Virginia, and South Carolina in opposition. Had Delaware and New Jersey stuck with Sherman's position, ratification might have bogged down indefinitely in state legislatures. The delegates came to an agreement on ratification by nine states only after they rejected Martin's proposal for ratification by all thirteen states and Sherman's and Dayton's motion for ratification by ten.[76]

THE CONSTITUTION, POLICY AGENCY, AND POLITICAL STRATEGY

Five months after Madison laid out his convention plans in a letter to Virginia's governor, and a week after thirty-nine delegates signed the Constitution, Roger Sherman and Oliver Ellsworth declared victory in a letter to Connecticut's governor. "The congress is differently organized," they

[75] *RFC* June 5, 1: 122–3; June 12, 1: 214; July 23, 2: 88–93.
[76] *RFC* August 31, 2: 475–81.

wrote, "yet the whole number of members, and this state's proportion of suffrage, remain the same as before." Indeed, Connecticut was entitled to one-thirteenth of the seats in the new U.S. House of Representatives and the U.S. Senate, and one-thirteenth of the votes in the Electoral College. Moreover, the Senate would be a bulwark for the interests of economically vulnerable states like Connecticut. "The equal representation of the states in the senate, and the voice of that branch in the appointment to offices, will secure the rights of the lesser, as well as of the greater states."[77] The Connecticut delegates glossed over the complicated structure of policy agency they had done so much to help create.

James Madison had set before the Constitutional Convention a clear, simple plan to change agency in national policy making (see Figure 3.1). Voters would send their agents to make national policy by electing representatives. "Successive filtrations" would fill the rest of the national offices: the House would pick the Senate, and the Congress would choose the president, judges, and other officers. Roger Sherman and other delegates had an equally clear, simple plan to protect the existing political influence of the vulnerable states (see Figure 4.1). Sherman's policy makers would serve as agents of the state legislatures, not the voters. National policy makers would respond to the state governments' perceived interests and pursue national interests accordingly. In comparison, Madison's national policy makers would be freed from such parochial concerns to pursue a much broader vision of the nation's future interests.

The delegates refused to choose between these models. Instead, they negotiated individual provisions until they had blended together a complicated mixture of agency that ensured policy influence to agents of their diverse constituencies. Politics, not theory, determined this hybrid design. Policy agency emerged gradually through a protracted sequence of difficult, specific decisions that no one could have predicted in advance. Specific choices on any given day depended on the partially finished framework the delegates provisionally had approved up to that moment. Later debates turned in part on counterbalancing earlier decisions.

As the weeks went on, the delegates grew more defensive, determined to make sure that the constituents they championed could check the policy agents of potential antagonists. Madison's coalition quickly won a House of Representatives in which large states enjoyed power proportional to their population. Connecticut and other vulnerable states masterfully

[77] Sherman and Ellsworth to the Governor of Connecticut, September 26, 1787, in *RFC* 3: 99–100.

responded by securing a Senate dependent on state governments acting as equals. In response to the Senate, Madison and his allies pressed for a president as independent of Congress as possible. By the time the delegates arrived at decisions about the appointment of judges, ambassadors, and top administrators, near stalemate produced a selection process that blended nomination by the president and assent by the Senate. Madison and his allies lost the major political battle, over the control of apportionment and selection to Congress, but they won battles for proportional representation in one House and significant independence for the president and his appointees. Sherman and his allies won equal representation in an influential Senate and disproportional influence in presidential selection.

These political compromises about "who governs" tethered different institutions to different constituencies and gave each institution more independence than any delegate had expected or favored. In the end, the delegates placed defensive powers in the hands of different players by putting agents of national, regional, and state interests in command of different policy-making institutions (Figure 5.1). U.S. representatives were the direct agents of the voters, U.S. senators the agents of the state legislatures, the president an agent of both the people and the states, and judges and administrators the conditional agents of the president. The delegates' compromises had created a government in which different policy makers had distinct, clashing policy incentives because they had to balance political obligations to regional, state, and national political interests in different ways.

This complicated system of policy agency created distinctive political strategies for using different parts of the national policy-making machinery. Beholden to different constituents, national policy makers in different institutions naturally would focus on different time horizons and define national interests in distinct and sometimes clashing ways. For Congress as a whole, "national interest" involved the combined interests of representatives from a large majority of the nation's geographical areas. Individual U.S. representatives would speak for relatively short-term, regional economic interests, and the House of Representatives would conceive of national interests in terms of the interests of a majority of these small regions. The Senate in effect defined national interests as an aggregation of a majority of state interests.

The president, as the agent of a national electorate, best represented Madison's original vision. Compared with Congress, the president had the national constituency that allowed him to pursue a broader vision of

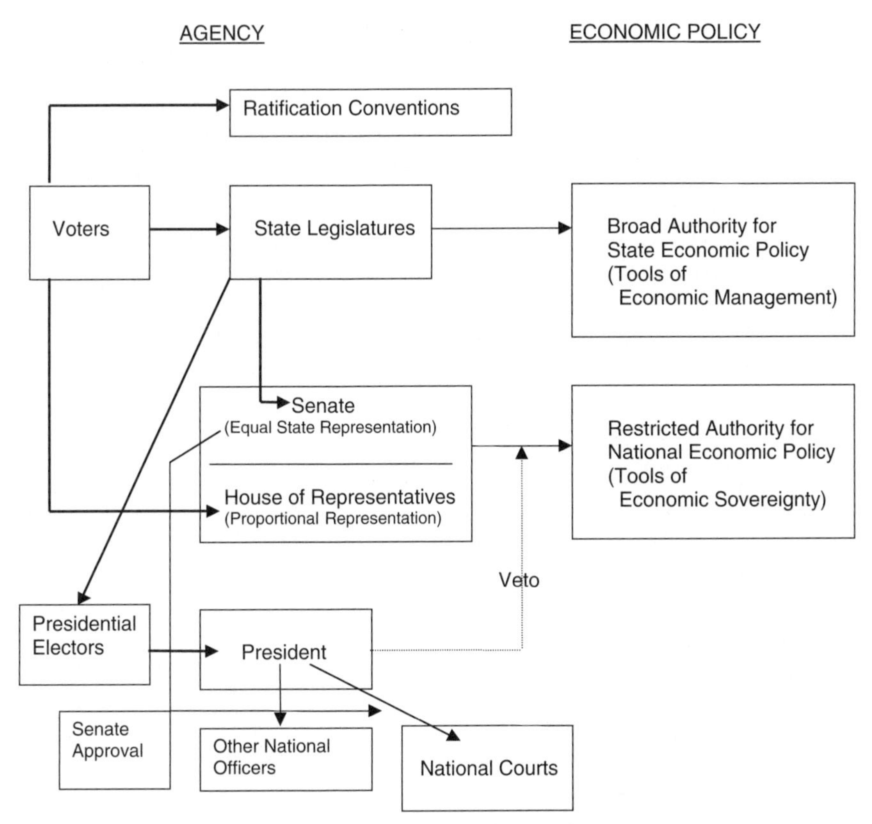

FIGURE 5.1. Agency and Economic Policy in the Final U.S. Constitution

national interests, and to do so further into the future. Presidents would have incentives to define national interests more proactively, more coherently, and for a longer time horizon than Congress. The national judiciary would be the agent of the president, but with the acquiescence of the Senate. Compared with Congress and like the president, national judges would have considerable discretion to define national interest, and in theory their indefinite terms would give them the longest time horizon of any national policy maker. But because judges could only react to existing disputes instead of laying out new legislative initiatives, they would have the incentive to apply previously established definitions of national interest to an individual case. If the president would serve as a "leading" indicator of new definitions of the national interests, then the courts would tend to serve as a "lagging" indicator of older, established definitions of national interests.

Policy agency was the most bitterly contested issue at the convention. The incremental choices about agency, and the delegates' growing defensive-mindedness toward the government they were creating, made many of them increasingly wary of the new government's authority. As policy agency grew more complex, it became harder to predict the kinds of policies the new government could and would produce. Mounting risks triggered rising caution. The delegates became less and less inclined to grant the new government the sweeping economic powers Madison urged, and more and more inclined to build up the countervailing power of the policy-making institutions they favored.

6

What Can Be Governed?

Constituting Policy Authority

The compromises on policy agency wrecked the foundation of Madison's plan for far-reaching national powers. As the selection of policy makers grew more complicated, the delegates grew more wary of national authority. Madison's opponents had battled to limit the government's reach and to protect the states' authority to manage their internal affairs. This inclination grew as the drive for proportional representation faltered. Key delegates, concerned about slavery, trade, and other vital interests, came around to Connecticut's argument that the national and state governments should share sovereignty.

The Constitutional Convention began to mark out this dual sovereignty with a crucial political deal that enabled the national government to supervise trade with other nations while allowing the states to manage slavery. The delegates reinforced shared sovereignty further by allowing the states substantial authority to manage property, commerce, economic development, the military, individual behavior, and rights. They could not avoid giving the national government the power to levy taxes, but they designed taxing authority to make it hard to use national taxes to help or harm particular constituencies. Other provisions gave the national government tools that could facilitate market-driven economic development without threatening individual states. The Constitution, though, left undefined many boundary issues between state and national authority. It delegated disputes about these boundary issues, along with contentious problems such as public lands, debts, and the location of the capital, to the politics of the new national policy-making process.

Policy authority in the Constitution was thus the unanticipated byproduct of a series of politically expedient compromises aimed at expanding national power while minimizing threats to the delegates' constituencies. The Constitution's distribution of national and state authority developed piecemeal from expedient political accommodations over individual issues. With pragmatic imprecision, the delegates steadily built an incomplete national policy workshop and furnished it with a limited range of policy tools. Fully expecting future politicians to use these tools in pursuit of their own political agendas, they nationalized only a limited set of enumerated public goods and established strong political defenses for the states' existing authority. In effect, they created a national government able to nurture markets without managing them, at least without widespread political consensus. These provisions ensured that state officials retained most of the tools of internal management, while the states surrendered to the national government the tools of economic sovereignty such as tariffs, import restriction, and currency manipulation. Without the tools of economic management, the national government could manage the nation's competitive position in the international economy but could not manage the effects of economic change on its citizens. Without the tools of economic sovereignty, states could not conceal, shift, or delay powerful and immediate market reactions to state policy efforts.

THE STRUGGLE OVER POWER AND SOVEREIGNTY

Madison boldly challenged the delegates to vest the national government with potentially sweeping powers. Key tools for managing the economy should be nationalized, not shared with the states, and the authority to use these tools had to remain open-ended. The national government should exercise sole authority to tax, to regulate commerce, to set military standards, to manage debts, and to supervise currency. When delegates worried about the Virginia Plan's broad warrant for national power, Madison assured them that he, too, "had brought with him into the Convention a strong bias in favor of an enumeration and definition of the powers necessary to be exercised by the national Legislature; but had also brought doubts concerning its practicability." His doubts had deepened, he declared, and now he would embrace anything essential for a government that "would provide for the safety, liberty and happiness of the Community..., all the necessary means for attaining it must, however reluctantly, be submitted to."[1] The delegates, he reasoned, must take it

[1] *RFC* May 31, 1: 53.

for granted that the U.S. national government should "have powers far beyond those exercised by the British Parliament when the States were part of the British Empire."[2] He argued that a national veto of state laws would establish the national government's economic sovereignty just as the king's veto had established British sovereignty.[3]

To win their battle for broad national authority, Madison and his allies relied on the conventional wisdom that sovereignty was indivisible. Authorities from British legal scholar Sir William Blackstone to American revolutionary Samuel Adams believed that government sovereignty could not be divided and shared among governments within the same geographical area.[4] Gouverneur Morris, James Wilson, Alexander Hamilton, and Rufus King joined Madison in insisting that sovereignty could not be divided and must be vested in the national government. On the day after the introduction of the Virginia Plan, Morris insisted that two supreme governments could not exist. As citizens surrendered their sovereignty when they entered civil society, Wilson observed, so too states must part with their sovereignty. Clarifying his controversial reference to abolishing the states, Hamilton stated that "no boundary could be drawn between the National & State Legislatures; that the former must therefore have indefinite authority. If it were limited at all, the rivalship of the States would gradually subvert it." Wilson admitted that the states needed to be

[2] *RFC* June 29: 1: 464.

[3] The colonists had considerable, and often unhappy, experiences with the royal veto. Most of the colonies were required to send all their laws to London for review by the king's Privy Council acting as the king's agent. The charters of Connecticut, Maryland, and Rhode Island exempted these states; Jack P. Greene, *Peripheries and Center: Constitutional Development in the Extended Politics of the British Empire and the United States, 1607–1788* (Athens: University of Georgia Press, 1986), p. 38. Of 8,563 laws sent to London by the colonies on the North American continent, the Privy Council disallowed 463. Andrew C. McLaughlin, *A Constitutional History of the United States* (New York: D. Appleton-Century, 1936), chap. 2, n. 1, at http://www.constitution.org/cmt/mclaughlin/chus.htm, accessed May 29, 2004.

[4] Blackstone wrote that there must be a "supreme, irresistible, absolute, uncontrolled authority, in which the *jura fummi imperii*, or the rights of sovereignty, reside"; Sir William Blackstone, *Commentaries on the Law of England* (Oxford: Clarendon Press, 1765–9), p. 49. Samuel Adams held that "imperia in imperio justly deemed a solecism in politics." After the convention, some of the Constitution's opponents also argued that sovereignty could not be divided; they did so to show that the document offered no protection for state autonomy. Gordon S. Wood, *The Creation of the American Republic, 1776–1787* (Chapel Hill: University of North Carolina Press, 1969), pp. 527–8; Jack N. Rakove, *Original Meanings: Politics and Ideas in the Making of the Constitution* (New York: Alfred A. Knopf, 1996), pp. 182–4, 188–9; Forrest McDonald, *Novus Ordo Seclorum: The Intellectual Origins of the Constitution* (Lawrence: University Press of Kansas, 1985), p. 277.

retained, but only because "All large Governments must be subdivided into lesser jurisdictions." Rufus King doubted that the states could be considered sovereign even under the Confederation.[5]

Roger Sherman, John Dickinson, and other delegates from the vulnerable states just as doggedly refused to accept Madison's argument that the national government had to absorb all the states' politically important economic policy tools. Whereas Madison presumed that the national government should control economic power, Sherman believed that states should retain economic power unless national control was necessary. He defended states' authority to tax, to regulate intrastate commerce, to manage militias, and even to conduct embargoes. Sherman admitted that Congress lacked sufficient power. But Sherman had studied the writings of the international law scholar Emmerich de Vattel, who had argued that a weak state could come under the protection of a more powerful state without surrendering its sovereignty.[6] Subtly, Sherman advanced the states' claim to a distinct sphere of authority by interpreting Virginia's plan as an affirmation "that the General & particular jurisdictions ought in no case to be concurrent." John Dickinson urged the delegates to begin by defining the powers needed to make the national government adequate for the confederated states.[7] Madison denied that it was practicable to enumerate the national powers needed, but now Sherman proved that it could be done.

> The objects of the Union, he thought were few. 1. defence ag[ain]st foreign danger. 2. ag[ain]st internal disputes & a resort to force. 3. Treaties with foreign nations 4 regulating foreign commerce, & drawing revenue from it. These & perhaps a few lesser objects alone rendered a Confederation of the States necessary. All other matters civil & criminal would be much better in the hands of the States.... He was for giving the General Gov[ernmen]t power to legislate and execute within a defined province.[8]

[5] *RFC* May 30, 1: 43–4; June 9, 1: 180; June 19, 1: 322–4. Wilson asked "What danger is there that the whole will unnecessarily sacrifice a part? But reverse the case, and leave the whole at the mercy of each part, and will not the general interest be continually sacrificed to local interests?" (June 8, 1: 167; see also 1: 172).

[6] Christopher Collier, *Roger Sherman's Connecticut: Yankee Politics and the American Revolution* (Middletown, CT: Wesleyan University Press, 1971), p. 74; Douglas G. Smith, "An Analysis of Two Federal Structures: The Articles of Confederation and the Constitution," *San Diego Law Review* 34 (Winter 1997): 249–342. Of the dozen state constitutions that were in effect, four states – Massachusetts, Connecticut, New York, and South Carolina – declared their state to be sovereign.

[7] *RFC* May 30, 1: 34–5, 42.

[8] *RFC* June 6, 1: 133.

In this view, the act of enumerating national powers would limit the scope of national authority. Rufus King thought that Sherman supported "a sort of collateral Government which shall secure the States in particular difficulties such as foreign war, or a war between two or more States."[9]

More than any other delegate, Sherman challenged the conventional wisdom that sovereignty could not be divided, and he pressed the counterargument that the state and national governments "should have separate and distinct jurisdictions."[10] National sovereignty could be limited to those public goods that the state governments could not provide for themselves effectively, the policy tools needed to manage the nation's international and interstate relations. States should retain full control of "police" powers needed to manage everyday life. For the legal scholar Blackstone, these police powers involved anything that threatened the "good order and economy" of the land and included the "due regulation and domestic order of the kingdom: whereby the individuals of the state, like members of a well-governed family, are bound to conform their general behaviour to the rules of propriety, good neighbourhood, and good manners; and to be decent, industrious, and inoffensive in their respective stations." Police powers thus provided an extraordinarily broad warrant for governing economic and personal life, from the health and safety conditions of enterprise to the intimacies of marriage and family.[11] In a plan he drafted during the convention, Sherman proposed to prohibit the national government from interfering "with the government of the individual states, in matters of internal police which respect the government of such states only, and wherein the general welfare of the United States is not affected."[12] He fought to limit national authority and to protect state police powers to the bitter end.

[9] *RFC* June 6, 1: 142–3.

[10] *RFC* June 7, 1: 150.

[11] Blackstone, *Commentaries on the Law of England*, pp. 162–76. New Jersey's Third Provincial Congress had formed a government in 1776 "to regulate the internal police of this colony"; John E. O'Connor, *William Paterson: Lawyer and Statesman* (New Brunswick, NJ: Rutgers University Press, 1979), p. 82. In June 1776 Pennsylvania's delegates in Congress received instructions from the Pennsylvania Assembly to concur in forming treaties with foreign nations, and reserved "to the people of this Colony the sole and exclusive right of regulating the internal government and police of the same"; Charles Page Smith, *James Wilson: Founding Father, 1742–1798* (Chapel Hill: University of North Carolina Press, 1956). For a nineteenth-century view of police powers, see Thomas M. Cooley, *A Treatise on the Constitutional Limitations Which Rest upon the Legislative Power of the States of the American Union*, 7th ed. (Boston: Little, Brown, 1903).

[12] *RFC* 3: 615–16.

DIVIDING SOVEREIGNTY

At first, broad national powers seemed to have strong convention support. The delegates quickly and overwhelmingly approved the Virginia Plan's broad warrant for national authority, nine states to none. Sherman stood alone in opposition, dividing Connecticut's vote. Without dissent, the delegates also approved the national veto and the use of force against delinquent states. With proportional representation still a real possibility, southern delegates did not yet express concerns about a threat to slavery. Although South Carolina voted with Madison, its delegates registered a preference for enumerating powers, and Pierce Butler expressed concern that "we were running to an extreme in taking away the powers of the States."[13] When Madison's allies tried to push national authority still further, wary delegates refused to go along.

On June 8 Charles Pinckney moved to broaden national authority by giving Congress "authority to negative all laws which they [should] judge to be improper." The "States must be kept in due subordination to the nation," Pinckney asserted. Madison seconded the motion, contending that "An indefinite power to negative legislative acts of the States" was "absolutely necessary to a perfect system." Delaware's Gunning Bedford countered by coupling broad authority with proportional representation, asking his colleagues whether "these large States" would not "crush the small ones whenever they stand in the way of their ambitions or interested views." Bedford also questioned whether the national veto was practicable. Ominously for Madison, his anticipated southern allies began to desert him. North Carolina's Hugh Williamson defended the need to protect the states' internal police powers relating to their separate "internal policy," and South Carolina's Pierce Butler vehemently opposed the proposal. Massachusetts's Elbridge Gerry warned that the veto would enable some states to use national policy to benefit themselves at others' expense. Bedford suggested that a Congress dominated by large states would allow Pennsylvania and Virginia to subsidize their constituents while they could gang up to defeat subsidies to a smaller state. Pinckney's proposal lost, supported only by the three large states. This vote seemed to confirm Bedford's dark political interpretation of the large states' intentions. Georgia and the Carolinas voted against it, as did George Mason and Governor Edmund Randolph in the Virginia delegation itself. Sherman,

[13] *RFC* May 31, 1: 53–4.

recognizing an opportunity to undermine Madison's position fundamentally, made the case for enumerating powers by observing that "the cases in which the negative ought to be exercised, might be defined."[14]

Madison's opponents pressed their opening. The following day, New Jersey's William Paterson took the initiative, arguing that "a confederacy supposes sovereignty in the members composing it."[15] A week later, the New Jersey Plan laid out a counteragenda of limited and enumerated national powers. It began by listing the public goods that the states needed to surrender to make "the federal Constitution adequate to the exigencies of Government" and national preservation. The plan included only powers that Sherman and Dickinson had indicated were necessary. It provided that national laws would "be the supreme law" and binding on the states, a much more passive form of national authority than a national veto, one that invited the national courts, rather than Congress, to set limits on state policy discretion.[16] The New Jersey Plan became a rallying point for the defense of state sovereignty against the Virginia Plan's effort to, in John Lansing's words, absorb "all power" other than "little local matters."[17]

The narrow margin of the New Jersey Plan's defeat seemed to encourage supporters of enumerated national powers. Sherman drew on the emotionally powerful and widely shared narrative of republicanism itself to defend the states.[18] Ellsworth's pithy phrase, "We were partly national; partly federal," turned dual sovereignty into a simple and

[14] *RFC* June 8, 1: 164–8, 171–2.

[15] *RFC* June 9, 1: 178.

[16] *RFC* June 15, 1: 242–5; 3: 611–15; James H. Hutson, ed., *Supplement to Max Farrand's "The Records of the Federal Convention of 1787"* (New Haven, CT: Yale University Press, 1987), pp. 85–6. The New Jersey Plan specified that "in addition to the powers vested in the U. States in Congress, by the present existing articles of Confederation, they be authorized to pass acts for raising a revenue, by levying a duty or duties on all goods or merchandizes of foreign growth or manufacture, imported into any part of the U. States, by Stamps on paper, vellum or parchment, and by a postage on all letters or packages passing through the general post-Office, to be applied to such federal purposes as they shall deem proper & expedient; to make rules & regulations for the collection thereof; and the same from time to time, to alter & amend in such manner as they shall think proper: to pass Acts for the regulation of trade & commerce as well with foreign nations as with each other . . ." (*RFC* 1: 243).

[17] *RFC* June 16, 1: 249.

[18] *RFC* June 20, 1: 341–3. Ellsworth elaborated later, stating that "What he wanted was domestic happiness. The Nat[iona]l Gov[ernmen]t could not descend to the local objects on which this depended.... He turned his eyes therefore for the preservation of his rights to the State Gov[ernment]s. From these alone he could derive the greatest happiness he expects in this life" (June 30, 1: 492).

compelling idea.[19] Sherman put Madison on the defensive by complaining that Madison "had animadverted on the delinquency of the States, when his object required him to prove that the Constitution of Cong[ress] was faulty. Cong[ress] is not to blame for the faults of the States. Their measures have been right, and the only thing wanting has been, a further power in Cong[ress] to render them effectual."[20]

The victory for equal state representation in the Senate on July 16 decisively shifted the convention against broad national powers because it made slavery and other state interests less secure. With national policy less controllable, South Carolina's delegates immediately asked that a committee enumerate those national government powers minimally necessary for the reconstituted government. Virginia (led by Randolph and Mason) and Georgia supported South Carolina.[21] Sherman grasped this opportunity and moved for his proposal to limit national authority to the common interests of the Union and explicitly to block national interference in "matters of internal police."[22] Madison's position lost further ground when the delegates again defeated the national veto, despite Madison's warning that the power was indispensable for countering state

[19] *RFC* June 29, 1: 468. William R. Davie of North Carolina echoed Ellsworth's formulation the following day (June 30, 1: 488). Gouverneur Morris's challenge to Ellsworth's "partly national, partly federal" formulation ("in what quality was it to protect the aggregate interest of the whole... particular States ought to be injured for the sake of a majority of the people, in case their conduct should deserve it") suggests that it had struck a chord in the convention (July 7, 1: 551–2). On the eve of his defeat on the representation compromise, Madison refused to concede "the Govern[ment] would... be partly federal, partly national" in effect" (July 14, 2: 8–9). Madison's *Federalist* 39, however, may be read as an elaboration on Ellsworth's comment; it concludes that the Constitution is "neither wholly *national* or wholly *federal*"; Alexander Hamilton, James Madison, and John Jay, *The Federalist*, ed. Jacob E. Cooke (Middletown, CT: Wesleyan University Press, 1961), pp. 251–7.

[20] *RFC* June 30, 1: 487; Hutson, *Supplement to Max Farrand's Records*, p. 131.

[21] *RFC* July 16, 2: 17. The following day, Gouverneur Morris warned that the compromise on representation would undermine the support for needed national authority (July 17, 2: 25).

[22] *RFC* July 17, 2: 25. Bedford, though, moved to enlarge national authority beyond Randolph's formulation, authorizing the government "'to legislate in all cases for the general interests of the Union, and also in those to which the States are separately incompetent, <or in which the harmony of the U[nited] States may be interrupted by the exercise of individual Legislation>." This formulation passed over the opposition of Connecticut, Virginia, South Carolina, and Georgia (July 17, 2: 26). This motion may be viewed as an effort to sharpen the definition of public goods that the national government would provide; alternatively, it may have reflected a more expansive definition of national public goods. Because Delaware was relatively less able than Connecticut to provide its own public goods, delegates such as John Dickinson had a more expansive notion of the appropriate scope for national authority than did Roger Sherman.

parochialism. Sherman portrayed the national veto as unnecessary, because state courts "would not consider as valid any law contravening the Authority of the Union, and which the [Congress] would wish to be negatived." As soon as the delegates rejected the national veto, Maryland's Luther Martin moved that national laws "shall be the supreme law of the respective States," as provided in the New Jersey Plan, and that "the Judiciaries of the several States shall be bound thereby in their decisions." The supremacy clause, approved without dissent, established a much less proactive and far-reaching brake on state policy than the national veto Madison envisioned.[23]

Three of the five members of the Committee of Detail – Ellsworth, Rutledge, and Randolph – now favored enumerated national powers and the protection of state policy prerogatives. The Committee of Detail jettisoned the broad language of the Virginia Plan, specified a list of appropriate national powers, listed several explicitly prohibited state powers, stipulated the supremacy of national law, and authorized the national government to make all laws "necessary and proper for carrying into execution" these enumerated powers.[24] The final Constitution largely included the Committee of Detail's enumeration. The committee's draft effectively underwrote the states' power to manage their own economic affairs and

[23] *RFC* July 17, 2: 25–9. Charles Pinckney gave Madison a final chance to defend the national veto on August 23, when he moved to authorize the national veto with the agreement of two-thirds of the House and Senate. Now that equality had been established in the Senate, Pinckney argued, "The objection drawn from the predominance of the large <States> had been removed by the equality established in the Senate." James Wilson "considered this as the key-stone wanted to compleat the wide arch of Government we are raising." Madison and Morris, more dubious about its prospects now, sought to keep it alive by referring it to committee. Sherman and Williamson argued that it was unnecessary because of the supremacy of national law. Rutledge attacked the national veto vehemently, asking "Will any State ever agree to be bound hand & foot in this manner. It is worse than making mere corporations of them whose bye laws would not be subject to this shackle." On a key vote, the proposal was defeated narrowly, five votes to six, with Massachusetts, Connecticut, and New Jersey joining the three southernmost states against (August 23, 2: 390–2).

[24] *RFC* August 6, 2: 182. John C. Hueston, "Altering the Course of the Constitutional Convention: The Role of the Committee of Detail in Establishing the Balance of State and Federal Powers," *Yale Law Journal* 100 (December 1990): 765–83. The word "necessary" had been used five times in the Articles of Confederation to set limits on congressional power. The Committee of Detail Report banned states from entering into treaties, alliances, or confederations and granting titles of nobility; "nor keep troops or ships of war in time of peace; nor enter into any agreement or compact with another State, or with any foreign power; nor engage in any war, unless it shall be actually invaded by enemies, or the danger of invasion be so imminent, as not to admit of delay, until the Legislature of the United States can be consulted" (*RFC* August 6, 2: 187).

limited the national government's responsibilities to international and interstate economic problems. National commercial power extended only to commerce "with foreign Nations & amongst the several States" and states would continue to govern commerce within their boundaries. It also imported the "full faith and credit" and the "privileges and immunities" clauses from the Articles of Confederation, avoiding active national management of interstate cooperation.[25] For Rufus King, the Committee of Detail report ended all hope that equal representation in the Senate had made the convention ready "to strengthen the Gen[era]l Gov[ernmen]t and to mark a full confidence in it."[26]

The issue of treason finally compelled the delegates to stipulate explicitly that the national government and the states would divide sovereignty. Connecticut's William Samuel Johnson observed that treason was "an offence ag[ain]st the Sovereignty which can be but one in the same community." Madison instantly seized on Johnson's admission to attack the concept of dual sovereignty. He warned that the Committee of Detail had left "the individual States . . . in possession of a concurrent power . . . which might involve double punishm[en]t." Sherman, though, saw no problem

[25] *RFC* August 6, 2: 181, 187–8. Article IV of the Confederation provided that "The better to secure and perpetuate mutual friendship and intercourse among the people of the different States in this Union, the free inhabitants of each of these States, paupers, vagabonds, and fugitives from justice excepted, shall be entitled to all privileges and immunities of free citizens in the several States. . . . If any person guilty of, or charged with, treason, felony, or other high misdemeanor in any State, shall flee from justice, and be found in any of the United States, he shall, upon demand of the Governor or executive power of the State from which he fled, be delivered up and removed to the State having jurisdiction of his offense. Full faith and credit shall be given in each of these States to the records, acts, and judicial proceedings of the courts and magistrates of every other State." The Committee of Detail largely adopted this language in their report. The committee dropped language in the Articles ensuring free travel and commerce, which were ensured by the prohibitions on state authority. The Committee of Detail later provided for congressional power to "prescribe the manner in which such acts, Records, & proceedings shall be proved, and the effect which Judgments obtained in one State shall have in another" (September 1, 2: 484). Morris moved to expand this power (by substituting "thereof" for the words after "the effect"), generating opposition from Randolph and Johnson for intruding on the states' authority. Morris's modification nevertheless passed, six votes to three, with Virginia, Maryland, and Georgia opposed. The privileges and immunities clause is understood to prevent states from legally favoring their citizens over citizens from other states. When the convention discussed the "full faith and credit" clause, Madison wanted to delegate it to a committee so that *Congress* "might be authorized to provide for the *execution* of Judgments in other States," a change justified "by the nature of the Union." Morris got at the idea in a different way, proposing that the "Legislature shall by general laws, determine the proof and effect of such acts, records, and proceedings" (August 29, 2: 448).

[26] *RFC* August 8, 2: 220; Rakove, *Original Meanings*, p. 178.

in recognizing treason against either level of government. "[R]esistance ag[ain]st the laws of the U[nited] States as distinguished from resistance ag[ain]st the laws of a particular State, forms the line," explained Sherman. Ellsworth added that "the U.S. are sovereign on one side of the line dividing the jurisdictions – the States on the other – each ought to have power to defend their respective Sovereignties." George Mason acknowledged dual sovereignty by agreeing that national authority was "a qualified sovereignty only" and that "the individual States will retain a part of the Sovereignty." Rufus King tried to force the issue by moving to give the national government the "sole" power to punish treason. A coalition of three vulnerable states (Connecticut, New Jersey, and Maryland) and three southern states (Virginia, North Carolina, and Georgia) voted King's motion down. Madison and Morris again warned of double punishment. Instead of limiting state authority by removing the possibility of treason against the states, the delegates further narrowed the scope of national power by restricting the definition of treason against the nation and its government.[27]

Although treason forced the delegates to accept dual sovereignty, they permitted a broad, ambiguous, and politically charged boundary to separate national and state authority. A special committee (of which Sherman was a member) recommended that the new Congress be authorized to discharge any debts that states incurred "for the common defence and general welfare." Because this language drew from the Articles of Confederation, Sherman thought this "general welfare" clause restricted national power, interpreting it to mean "neither more nor less than the confederation as it relates to this subject." The next day, the Committee of Detail proposed to add to the enumeration of powers the highly qualified power to "provide, as may become necessary, from time to time, for the well managing and securing the common property" and "general interests and welfare" of the United States "in such manner as shall not interfere with the Governments of individual States in matters which respect only their internal

[27] *RFC* August 20, 2: 345–50. A week earlier, Madison had used a discussion of dual citizenship to attack the concept of dual sovereignty; *RFC* August 13, 2: 270–1. The Committee of Detail originally had defined treason against the United States as "levying war against the United States, or any of them; and in adhering to the enemies of the United States, or any of them." It added safeguards against the abuse of the power over treason by providing that "No person shall be convicted of treason, unless on the testimony of two witnesses. No attainder of treason shall work corruption of bloods nor forfeiture, except during the life of the person attainted" (August 20, 2: 345). The final Constitution included the safeguards, but the delegates expanded the definition of treason to giving "Aid and Comfort" to the enemies of the United States.

Police, or for which their individual authorities may be competent." The "general welfare" wording was added to the Constitution's preamble and placed at the beginning of the enumerated powers, but the protection for state police powers was dropped.[28] Sherman could not restore it. On the

[28] *RFC* August 20, 2: 328; August 21, 2: 355–6; August 22, 2: 366–7. The Virginia Plan had also invoked the Articles in its first resolution, "that the articles of Confederation ought to be so corrected & enlarged as to accomplish the objects proposed by their institution; namely. 'common defence, security of liberty and general welfare'" (May 29, 1: 20). The "general welfare" provision recommended on August 22 was dropped temporarily, but later restored by the Committee on Postponed Matters and adopted without dissent in September (September 4, 2: 497, 499). The restoration of the "general welfare" clause connected two elastic clauses in the final Constitution's specification of national authority in Article I, Section 8. Authorization for Congress "to pay the debts and provide for the common defence & general welfare" became part of the first clause in Congress's enumerated powers. Authorization to make "all Laws which shall be necessary and proper for carrying into execution" all of the aforesaid powers was already part of the final clause in the list of enumerated powers. At the convention, Madison and his allies subsequently acted in a way consistent with a view that the "general welfare" provision provided a broad warrant for national authority. When McHenry asked about specific authorization for national action to improve harbors, Morris responded that the national government could undertake such actions under the warrant of "providing for the common defence and general welfare" (September 6, 2: 529–30). Madison and his allies Morris, Hamilton, King, and Johnson served on the Committee of Style, which incorporated this wording into the warrant of the Constitution's preamble: "WE, the People of the United States, in order to form a more perfect union, to establish justice, insure domestic tranquility, provide for the common defence, promote the general welfare, and secure the blessings of liberty to ourselves and our posterity..." (2: 590). On September 15 Morris said that the phrasing of the Constitution would authorize national management of the harbor improvements coveted by the Marylanders, although Madison disagreed with Morris (September 15, 2: 625). Because Madison's denial preceded his final claim that commerce was indivisible, Madison may have been making one last plea for authorization for unified control over commerce.

The convention sent to the Committee on Style the following phrasing: "The Legislature shall have the power to lay and collect taxes, duties, imposts and excises, to pay the debts and provide for the common defence and general welfare of the United States." The Committee on Style changed the punctuation as follows: "To lay and collect taxes, duties, imposts and excises; to pay the debts and provide for the common defense and general welfare of the United States" (compare 2: 569 and 2: 594). Luther Martin later claimed that he noticed the final wording in Section 8 and complained that "the grammatical construction is a general grant of power" (*Observations*, June 3, 1788, in Hutson, *Supplement to Max Farrand's Records*, p. 292). In 1798 Representative Albert Gallatin, a close ally of Jefferson and Madison, claimed that he "was well informed" that "those words had originally been inserted in the Constitution as a limitation to the power of laying taxes"; without naming names, Gallatin claimed that a member of the Committee on Style had tried to place the phrase in a separate paragraph, "but the trick was discovered" by a Connecticut delegate who could only be Roger Sherman, and "the words restored as they stand" (Gallatin in the House of Representatives, June 19, 1798, in *RFC* 3: 379). In a letter to Andrew Stevenson in 1830, Madison rejected the notion that "common defense & general welfare" were elastic clauses meant to convey expansive national authority (November 17, 1830, in *RFC* 3: 485–6).

convention's final day of substantive debate, he unsuccessfully tried to add a provision that the Constitution could not be amended to allow the national government to interfere with a state's police powers without its consent.[29]

The delegates recognized dual sovereignty, but they made the boundary between the state and national governments a matter of political negotiation. The delegates had rejected Madison's ambition for broad national economic authority, replacing it step by step with confined, enumerated national powers. The burden of proof for exercising national authority shifted from the states to the national government. The national government would exercise the authority necessary for national sovereignty, while the states would retain authority to manage their economies. The delegates institutionalized this arrangement by using it to settle the convention's most intractable clash of economic interests: southern slavery against northern commerce.

BARGAINING ON SLAVERY AND TRADE

The issue of slavery fueled bitter antagonism among the delegates. Outspoken opponents called the slave trade an injustice to humanity. Gouverneur Morris described slavery as a "nefarious institution . . . the curse of heaven on the States where it prevailed." George Mason anticipated divine vengeance, because slaves "bring the judgment of heaven on a Country. . . . By an inevitable chain of causes & effects providence punishes national sins, by national calamities." The slave trade was "inadmissible on every principle of honor & safety," said John Dickinson, who believed that slavery "ought to be left to the National Gov[ernmen]t not to the States particularly interested." Luther Martin thought that slaves "weakened one part of the Union which the other parts were bound to protect."[30]

These harsh comments about "one of" the South's "favorite prerogatives" provoked many southerners into a fierce defense of state authority. Georgia's Abraham Baldwin "had conceived national objects alone to be before the Convention, not such as like the present were of a local nature." South Carolina was adamant in defense of slavery. To slavery's critics, John Rutledge answered that "Religion & humanity had nothing to do with this question – Interest alone is the governing principle

[29] *RFC* September 15, 2: 630.
[30] *RFC* August 8, 2: 221; August 21, 2: 364; August 22, 2: 370, 372.

with Nations.... If the Northern States consult their interest, they will not oppose the increase of Slaves which will increase the commodities of which they will become the carriers."[31] The people of the Carolinas and Georgia, according to Rutledge, "will never be such fools as to give up so important an interest."[32]

Sherman and Ellsworth joined in defending the South's prerogatives, using the controversy to defend the states' police powers more generally. "[A]s the States were now possessed of the right to import slaves, as the public good did not require it to be taken from them, & as it was expedient to have as few objections as possible to the proposed scheme of Government," Sherman "thought it best to leave the matter as we find it." Ellsworth remarked that "The morality or wisdom of slavery are considerations belonging to the States themselves – What enriches a part enriches the whole, and the States are the best judges of their particular interest." Ellsworth warned against meddling, suggesting that "As population increases; poor laborers will be so plenty as to render slaves useless."[33] Historian Forrest McDonald has argued that Sherman and Rutledge made a political deal, in which Connecticut would support South Carolina's right to import slaves in return for South Carolina's support for provisions underwriting Connecticut's land claims. Richard Barry inventively describes a dinner at the Indian Queen Tavern on June 30 at which Rutledge and Sherman supposedly worked out such an arrangement. There is no evidence of such an explicit deal between the two delegates. But there is a much simpler way to explain their cooperation. Although South Carolina's delegation was willing to go along with Madison's initial plan, it was from the start the southern delegation most conscious of protecting state prerogatives. Once Madison's plan lost political momentum and faced increasingly certain defeat, Rutledge became as strong a proponent of enumerated powers as Sherman and, in part, for the same reason: the protection of the stability of his state's political order, which, in the case of South Carolina, involved the political dominance by a minority of coastal elites. Sherman and Rutledge had a common interest in protecting state police powers against an intrusive national government.

[31] *RFC* August 21, 2: 364. General Pinckney also appealed to northern economic interests in slavery, claiming that "S[outh] Carolina & Georgia cannot do without slaves.... The more slaves, the more produce to employ the carrying trade; The more consumption also, and the more of this, the more of revenue for the common treasury" (August 22, 2: 371).

[32] *RFC* July 13, 1: 605; August 22, 2: 372–3.

[33] *RFC* August 21, 2: 364; August 22, 2: 369, 371–5.

In Rutledge's case, the state police power most at risk was the regulation of slavery.[34]

Once the slave issue expanded to touch the vital interests of northern merchants and shippers, other northern delegates grew more willing to look the other way and to delegate authority over slavery to the southern states. Shrewdly, southern delegates tied slavery to the reconstituted government's power to make commercial treaties with foreign governments. Many of the northern delegates, particularly those in Massachusetts, cared most about national power to encourage American shipping and protect American access to fishing and foreign ports. The southerners began to argue that restrictive commercial treaties would harm southern interests, and therefore should be made very difficult to enact.[35] Fearing commercial treaties that would benefit these "carrying" states at their expense, Edmund Randolph sought to require extraordinarily large majorities in Congress to enact any commercial treaty.[36] Randolph and Rutledge wrote the South's position into the Committee of Detail report. The final committee report struck back at the North by requiring a two-thirds vote in the Senate and House to pass any "navigation act" (a pejorative term that evoked the oppressive British laws once imposed upon the colonies). It also protected the South by prohibiting any limitation on the slave trade and by banning national taxes on imported slaves and exported goods. The Committee of Detail report sparked considerable northern opposition. Rufus King and Gouverneur Morris objected forcefully to these concessions.[37]

As soon as the southern defense of slavery directly threatened commercial treaties, Massachusetts's Rufus King urged the convention to look

[34] Forrest McDonald, *E Pluribus Unum: The Formation of the American Republic, 1776–1790* (Boston: Houghton Mifflin, 1965), pp. 291–3; Richard Barry, *The Rutledges of South Carolina* (New York: Duell, Sloan, and Pierce, 1942), pp. 329–35; James Haw, *John & Edward Rutledge of South Carolina* (Athens: University of Georgia Press, 1997), pp. 329–30n28. McDonald infers this bargain; rather than providing hard evidence, he claimed that "it is the only way I know to reconcile the known facts about the hard-nose trading that went on behind the scenes at the convention" (p. 14).

[35] Charles Pinckney observed, "If that commercial policy is pursued which I conceive to be the true one, the merchants of this Country will not or ought not for a considerable time to have much weight in the political scale" (*RFC* June 25, 1: 401–2); General Pinkney pointed out that "it was the true interest of the S[outhern] States to have no regulation of commerce" (August 29, 2: 450).

[36] *RFC* July 10, 1: 567–8; July 23, 2: 95.

[37] *RFC* 2: 142–3, 168–9, 183; August 7, 2: 210–11; August 8, 2: 220, 222. Paterson first used the phrase "navigation act" in his notes objecting to the Virginia Plan (June 16, 1; 273).

at slavery "in a political light only."[38] The wealthy southern states, observed King, "would not league themselves with the North[ern] unless some respect were paid to their superior wealth. If the latter expect those preferential distinctions in Commerce & other advantages which they will derive from the connection they must not expect to receive them without allowing some advantages in return." Gerry thought that slavery could be left to the states as long as the Constitution gave it no sanction. Morris suggested that "These things may form a bargain among the Northern & Southern States." General Pinckney and John Rutledge expressed a willingness to establish another grand committee to work out an agreement. Randolph, George Read, and James Wilson agreed. Nine states voted to establish a grand committee on three divisive issues: navigation, slave imports, and export taxes. Madison, largely silent during this debate, served on the committee.[39] This committee, in effect, served as a grand committee on dealing with the most fundamental problems of policy authority, as the grand committee on representation had dealt with policy agency.

The committee members worked out a simple political arrangement, or, as Madison put it, "An understanding on the two subjects of *navigation* and *slavery*." The southern states would be allowed the authority to import African slaves until 1800 and the national government could not levy a prohibitory tax on imported slaves. In return, no extraordinary majority would be required for commercial laws or treaties, thus facilitating the exercise of national economic sovereignty toward other nations. Sherman, who had been unpersuaded by Madison's earlier claim that their diverse material interests would prevent a coalition of large states, now argued that the diversity of commercial interests "was . . . itself a security" against coalitions that would exploit minority regions.[40] This compromise ensured that the national government could provide commercial treaties beneficial to the national economy as a whole. At the

[38] *RFC* August 22, 2: 373. King already had accommodated himself to the three-fifths compromise on the representation of slaves; see July 9, 1: 562.

[39] *RFC* August 22, 2: 372–5. The committee included Madison, King, Hugh Williamson, and Charles Pinckney, as well as John Langdon, William Samuel Johnson, William Livingston, George Clymer, John Dickinson, Luther Martin, and Abraham Baldwin. Sherman wanted to take the committee plan as reported because "it was better to let the S[outhern] States import slaves than to part with them, if they made that a sine qua non."

[40] *RFC* August 24, 2: 400; August 29, 2: 449n, 450.

same time, this bargain limited national interference in a state's authority to pursue even a reprehensible policy, under the guise of exercising authority over its domestic economic assets. The convention accepted the compromise, fine-tuning specific provisions for additional advantages at the margins.[41] Later, the convention further protected property rights in slaves by guaranteeing that escaped slaves would be returned to their owners, establishing the most specific guarantee for property rights in the Constitution. The delegates were embarrassed to include slavery protections in the Constitution, and they bent over backward to avoid giving the public the impression that they condoned slavery.[42]

[41] North Carolina's delegates characterized this outcome as a political agreement to their governor immediately after the convention: "A navigation Act or the power to regulate Commerce in the Hands of the National Government by which American Ships and Seamen may be fully employed is the desirable weight that is thrown into the Northern Scale. This is what the Southern States have given in Exchange for the advantages we Mentioned" (North Carolina Delegates to Governor Caswell, September 18, 1787, in *RFC* 3: 83–4). General Pinckney moved to extend the deadline on slave import prohibitions to 1808, and despite Madison's objection that this would dishonor the "National character" as well as the Constitution, the delegates approved the extension seven states to four, with New England, the three southernmost states, and Maryland in the majority. Charles Pinckney tried to reinstitute an extraordinary majority for commercial regulation, but his South Carolina colleagues General Pinckney and Rutledge, acknowledging New England's concession on slave imports, thought "that no fetters should be imposed on the power of making commercial regulations." Although three of the southern states voted to take up Pinckney's motion, only Maryland voted with them, and the political deal was sealed (August 29, 2: 449–53). Note that the 1808 date for terminating the slave trade must have been perceived as allowing another census to take place and, given the expected growth of the South, for the South to gain relative power in Congress. It also bought additional time to satisfy the lower South's demand for slaves.

[42] *RFC* August 28, 2: 443; August 29, 2: 453–4. Paterson observed that the authors of the Articles had been ashamed to include the word slave (July 9, 1: 561). Randolph moved to remove the "servitude" from the draft and replace it with the word "'service'...the former being thought to express the condition of slaves, & the latter the obligations of free persons" (September 13, 2: 607). The delegates also carefully worded clauses on direct taxes "to exclude the appearance of counting the Negroes in the Representation," said Morris (September 13, 2: 607–8). The delegates resisted a South Carolina proposal to specify more clearly the return of fugitive slaves; Sherman "saw no more propriey in the public seizing and surrendering a slave or servant, than a horse" (*RFC* August 28, 2: 443). The term "slavery" itself does not appear in the original Constitution because, as Madison put it, "it was wrong to admit in the Constitution the idea that there could be property in men" (August 25, 2: 417). The word "legally" ("no person legally held to service in one state") in the escaped-slave clause was dropped on the final day of substantive debate "in compliance with the wish of some who thought the term <legal> equivocal, and favoring the idea that slavery was legal in a moral view," wrote Madison (September 15, 2: 628).

PROTECTING STATE AUTHORITY

The slavery battle taught the convention that it could most easily overcome political deadlock simply by delegating policy authority to the states. Allowing each state to govern its internal economy proved politically expedient as the delegates dealt with key tools of routine internal management: property, internal commerce, economic development, the military, and individual rights.

Property

Most of the delegates probably shared Pierce Butler's belief that the "great object of Govern[men]t" was the protection of property. Certainly many sought assurances that the reconstituted government would protect specific kinds of property in their states, such as slavery in the South and shipping in the North. Yet controversy surfaced nearly every time the delegates discussed specific property regulations, just as it had when they debated property qualifications for voters and officeholders. Rutledge and others became convinced that the distinctions, distribution, and governance of property differed too greatly across the states to allow consensus on national rules. The Committee of Detail report said nothing about protecting property rights. The word "property" appears in the Constitution only in Article IV, Section 3, guaranteeing that the U.S. Congress can regulate land held by the national government.[43] Although the delegates considered property protection an essential task of government, the Constitution delegated the protection of property to the states.

Commerce

To the end, Madison fought for national control of all internal commerce, within the states as well as between them, "convinced that the regulation of Commerce was in its nature indivisible and ought to be wholly under one authority."[44] For example, Madison moved that states should be denied the power to lay embargoes. Sherman countered that "the States ought to retain this power in order to prevent suffering & injury to their poor." Mason agreed, and the convention defeated Madison's

[43] *RFC* July 6, 1: 542; August 29, 2: 450. Provision for protecting property rights later was included in the Fifth Amendment to the Constitution.

[44] *RFC* September 15, 2: 625.

motion. Madison next moved to eliminate Congress's power to allow states to levy duties on imports, but Sherman urged the delegates to trust Congress with this power, and, again, Madison's effort to limit state prerogatives was defeated.[45] There is no doubt that the convention rejected a broad interpretation of the word "commerce" that included intrastate commerce.[46]

At the same time, the convention deliberately left the distribution of commercial authority ambiguous. When Maryland's delegates sought explicit language permitting states to impose duties on ships to fund harbors and lighthouses, Morris answered that no such provision was needed because the Constitution already allowed states to use their authority in this way. Madison, though, disagreed with Morris, commenting that the Constitution "seemed to exclude this power." Sherman was unconcerned about the ambiguity, trusting future politicians to resolve any doubts as needed. "The power of the U[nited] States to regulate trade being supreme can controul interferences of the State regulations <when> such interferences happen; so that there is no danger to be apprehended from a concurrent jurisdiction."[47] The delegates explicitly prohibited this power to the states without Congress's approval, an action that indicates that delegates assumed the states kept the power to regulate their internal commerce. The delegates then drew a very ambiguous distinction between state and national commercial powers and consciously left it to future politicians to negotiate precise boundaries.[48]

Economic Development

The delegates explicitly refused to authorize the national government to use key policy tools necessary for managing economic development. This decision reflected a jealousy for state policy prerogatives rather than a commitment to limited government. Even while he was recording Randolph's presentation of the Virginia Plan, Gunning Bedford noted that Congress should not have the power to build large-scale public-works projects, promote agriculture, or otherwise actively develop their

[45] *RFC* August 28, 2: 440–3.

[46] Randy E. Barnett, "The Original Meaning of the Commerce Clause," *University of Chicago Law Review* 68:1 (Winter 2001): 101–7.

[47] *RFC* September 15, 2: 625.

[48] In the case of *Gibbons* v. *Ogden* (9 Wheat 1, 1824), the U.S. Supreme Court argued that Congress possessed potentially extensive power to regulate commerce, but that states could exercise these dormant powers until Congress acts.

economies. Bedford thought that states should be left free to develop their economies, because "A state has the right to avail herself of all natural advantages."[49] Madison, bent on establishing far-reaching national authority to manage the economy, proposed in mid-August to add specific national powers to charter corporations, to create a national university, and to "encourage by premiums & provisions, the advancement of useful knowledge and discoveries." These proposals disappeared after referral to committee. Gerry's proposal to add post roads to the authority to establish post offices barely won approval. Morris sought a secretary of domestic affairs who would "attend to matters of general police, the State of Agriculture and manufactures, the opening of roads and navigations, and the facilitating communications thro' the U[nited] States," but these ideas went nowhere.[50]

On September 14 Benjamin Franklin proposed to add to the power to build post roads "a power to provide for cutting canals where deemed necessary." Building canals, though, required much more capital investment than roads. Sherman objected. This public good should not be nationalized because "The expence in such cases will fall on the U[nited] States, and the benefit accrue to the places where the canals may be cut." Madison moved to expand Franklin's proposal to include the power to "grant charters of incorporation where the interest of the U.S. might require & the legislative provisions of individual States may be incompetent." He aimed, he said, to make it possible to remove the natural obstacles to free economic intercourse among the states. Wilson agreed that the power was necessary "to prevent a State from obstructing the general welfare." Rufus King, however, called the power to charter corporations unnecessary and potentially divisive.[51] Franklin's motion was defeated, supported only by Virginia, Pennsylvania, and Georgia; Madison's additional motion fell with Franklin's. Madison's proposal to authorize a national university also failed, opposed by New Hampshire, Massachusetts, Delaware, New Jersey, Maryland, and Georgia, and with Connecticut divided by Sherman's opposition.[52]

[49] Bedford, May 29, 1787, in Hutson, *Supplement to Max Farrand's Records*, p. 27.

[50] *RFC* August 18, 2: 325; August 16, 2: 308; August 20, 2: 342–3.

[51] When Mason expressed concern that the national government would use the power to create monopolies, Wilson thought that the authority to create "mercantile monopolies" already was subsumed under the commerce power. Gerry, listing his objections to the Constitution, pointed out that "Under the power over commerce, monopolies may be established" (*RFC* September 15, 2: 632–3).

[52] *RFC* September 14, 2: 615–16.

The Military

The delegates accepted the need for additional national military capacity. Of the seventeen clauses enumerating congressional powers in the final Constitution, eight involve national security and defense. The states had serious misgivings about these new military powers, however.[53] A fully nationalized military would eliminate a vital state police power; for example, South Carolina's militia played an important role as a slave patrol. National military power also could threaten any state that deviated from national policy makers' agendas. The Constitution's limits on national military authority, then, derived as much from the defense of state prerogatives as the threat of a standing army. The Committee of Detail incorporated most of the specific provisions for defense and foreign affairs already included in the Articles of Confederation. Few of these provisions invited more than desultory debate over national authority.[54]

[53] Defense against foreign invasion and internal sedition was a fundamental reason for the union of the states, "the great objects of the federal system," said Rufus King (*RFC* August 8, 2: 220). On the support for military powers in the Constitution, see Max Edling, *A Revolution in Favor of Government: Origins of the U.S. Constitution and the Making of the American State* (New York: Oxford University Press, 2003), pp. 73–128. The Virginia Plan proposed to "correct and enlarge" national authority to accomplish the "common defence" and "security of liberty" that had been the Articles' stated goal. Virginia's resolutions called for the power "to call forth the force of the Union ag[ain]st any member of the Union failing to fulfill its duty under the articles," and proposed to guarantee every state a "Republican Government," a clause intended to authorize national military intervention against "dangerous commotions, insurrections and rebellions (*RFC* May 29, 1: 20–2; July 18, 2: 47). Some delegates expressed concern that the guarantee of republican government endorsed Rhode Island's policies. Wilson successfully "moved as a better expression of the idea, 'that a Republican <form of Governm[en]t shall> be guarantied to each State & that each State shall be protected ag[ain]st foreign & domestic violence'" (July 18, 2: 47–9). On South Carolina's slave patrols, see John Shy, *A People Numerous and Armed: Reflections on the Military Struggle for American Independence* (New York: Oxford University Press, 1976), p. 29.

[54] The Committee of Detail's report granted Congress the authority to make war, raise armies, build and equip fleets, and "call forth the aid of the militia, in order to execute the laws of the Union, enforce treaties, suppress insurrections, and repel invasions." It also provided more explicit authority to govern piracy, capturing, and counterfeiting. The committee's August 6 report prohibited states from "granting letters of marque and reprisals" and making foreign alliances and treaties, and, without Congress's consent, "keep troops or ships of war in time of peace," or "enter into any agreement or compact with . . . any foreign power; nor engage in any war, unless it shall be actually invaded by enemies," or face "imminent danger" (*RFC* 2: 182–7). Subsequently, the delegates discussed national authority to punish piracy and counterfeiting, and dabbled with the language on two occasions (August 17, 2: 315–16; September 14, 2: 614–15). The clauses on the power to declare war and to provide and maintain a navy were rephrased and adopted. Only Gerry and Martin expressed a concern about a standing army on

Provisions for regulating the militias and for suppressing internal rebellion naturally became lightning rods for the defense of state prerogatives. Determined to avoid a permanent national military, the delegates necessarily sought a measure of national authority over the state militias as an alternative. Mason proposed to extend national military authority "to make laws for the regulation and discipline of the Militia of the several States reserving to the States the appointment of the Officers," and General Pinckney argued against the "incurable evil" of divided military authority. Madison, of course, argued that military power was indivisible and that without national direction the states would not "have the due confidence in the concurrent exertions of each other." Ellsworth thought the idea impractical and "The whole authority over the Militia ought by no means to be taken away from the States whose consequence would pine away to nothing after such a sacrifice of power." Ellsworth proposed that national rules apply only when the militia was nationalized for an emergency. Sherman seconded Ellsworth, denying that the power was indivisible and arguing explicitly for the protection of this state authority: "States might want their Militia for defence ag[ain]st invasions and insurrections, and for enforcing obedience to their laws." A committee crafted finely balanced compromise language, allowing the states to implement national military standards. Congress would "make laws for organizing arming and disciplining the Militia, and for governing such part of them as may be employed in the service of the U[nited] S[tates] reserving to the States respectively, the appointment of the officers, and the authority of training the Militia according to the discipline prescribed by the U[nited] States."[55]

this occasion (August 18, 2: 329–33). The limitations on state compacts and military and diplomatic activity were approved without dissent (August 28, 2: 442–3). Madison put forward propositions on August 18 to be added to the enumerated powers, including the powers to regulate affairs with the Indians and to provide for "national forts, magazines, and other necessary buildings"; a power to grant letters of marque and reprisal also was proposed that day (2: 325–6). On the recommendation of the Committee on Postponed Matters, the convention without debate added authority to grant letters of marque and reprisal. The convention limited military appropriations to two years and showed concern for interfering with the states by requiring the consent of the state legislature for any purchase of land for military installations (September 5, 2: 508–10). The *process* for controlling military authority sparked considerable debate; see Chapter 7.

55 *RFC* August 18, 2: 326, 330–3; August 21, 2: 356. Sherman and Ellsworth, still concerned about the "vast extent" of the word "discipline," proposed to let Congress set general plans "but leave the execution of it to the State Gov[ernmen]ts." This motion lost, with Connecticut voting in favor and ten states opposed (August 23, 2: 385–7). At the end of the convention, Mason, now largely alienated from the enterprise, proposed to amend

The Committee of Detail authorized the national government to send the military to help states battle domestic insurrections when the state's legislature asked for assistance. Charles Pinckney moved to strike out this provision for state consent, permitting the national government to put down internal rebellion at will. Martin, Mercer, and Gerry expressed horror at this intrusion on the states' rights. Gerry colorfully warned against "letting loose the myrmidons of the U[nited] States on a State without its own consent." Two weeks later, the convention provided that a governor could apply for national intervention when the legislature could not meet.[56] The delegates, then, inserted protections for state authority over internal peace keeping, a fundamental prerogative for a sovereign government.

Individual Behavior

The delegates had little stomach for the national regulation of individual conduct. Twice, George Mason moved to authorize Congress to enact sumptuary laws, which regulated individual extravagance. Mason urged his colleague to give "proper direction" to the natural human "love of distinction." Ellsworth contended that taxes were the best remedy for overconsumption, while Gerry thought that "the law of necessity is the best sumptuary law." Mason's motion was defeated, winning only the support of Delaware, Maryland, and Georgia. Late in the proceedings, Mason asked the convention to create a committee to encourage frugality, economy, and American manufactures. Five of the most senior delegates – Franklin, Mason, Johnson, Livingston, and Dickinson – were assigned to this committee. It never gave a report.[57]

Rights

Nor did the convention feel it necessary to protect individuals with an inclusive bill of rights. From the beginning, George Mason urged national guarantees of citizen rights, and he was demanding a bill of rights

the clause on providing for national discipline of the militia by adding "And that the liberties of the people may be better secured against the danger of standing armies in time of peace." Madison supported this motion, perhaps as a gesture to Mason, but Morris and Pinckney opposed it as a slap at the military. It was defeated nine to two, with the support of only the Virginia and Georgia delegations (September 14, 2: 616–17).

[56] *RFC* August 17, 2: 317–18; August 30, 2: 466–7.

[57] *RFC* August 20, 2: 344; September 13, 2: 606–7.

as the meeting ended. Charles Pinckney proposed to include several specific guarantees of civil rights and liberties, including the right of habeas corpus, freedom of the press, subordination of the military to civil authorities, a ban on the quartering of soldiers, and a ban on religious tests for oaths of office. The delegates were not inherently hostile to ensuring such rights, and the Constitution included several. Without dissent, the convention banned bills of attainder, and with little debate it prohibited the suspension of habeas corpus. Treason could not be extended to a guilty party's heirs. It proscribed ex post facto laws on a vote of seven to three, despite arguments from Morris, Wilson, Ellsworth, and Johnson that the language was unnecessary. It provided for jury trials for offenses committed out of any state.[58]

But the delegates generally accepted Sherman's arguments that explicit guarantees could not be needed in a government with such restricted authority. "The State Declarations of Rights are not repealed by this Constitution," he reassured the delegates, "and being in force are sufficient...." In the convention's final week, Gerry and Mason proposed a committee to work up a bill of rights. The convention unanimously rejected the idea. When a last-minute effort sought an explicit guarantee of freedom of the press, Sherman again said that it was unnecessary because "The power of Congress does not extend to the Press."[59]

NEUTRALIZING TAXES

Protecting the states' tax base from the national government's taxing authority was not so simple. All the delegates recognized the national government's urgent need for more-reliable revenues. Potentially sizable sums might be needed to defend the nation, service its debts, and meet the obligations of sovereignty. Sherman acknowledged that the "national debt & the want of power somewhere to draw forth the National resources,

[58] RFC May 31, 1: 49; August 6, 2: 187; August 20, 2: 342; August 22, 2: 375–6; August 28, 2: 438; September 12, 2: 587–8. Habeas corpus is an individual's right not to be held in custody unlawfully. An ex post facto law is a law passed after an act occurs and that makes the act illegal (or changes its legal status in some other way). A bill of attainder is a legislative act that punishes an individual without a trial in court. Ellsworth argued that "there was no lawyer, no civilian who would not say that ex post facto laws were void of themselves. It cannot then be necessary to prohibit them." Wilson "was against inserting anything in the Constitution as to ex post facto laws. It will bring reflexions on the Constitution – and proclaim that we are ignorant of the first principles of Legislation, or are constituting a Government which will be so" (August 22, 2: 376).

[59] *RFC* September 12, 2: 587–8; September 14, 2: 617–18.

are the great matters that press." Madison believed that the power to tax should be unconditional because a "compleat power of taxation" was "the highest prerogative of supremacy."[60] This general consensus on the need to improve the flow of national revenue created a serious political dilemma, however.

No national power looked more menacing to the states than national power to levy taxes. First, taxes provided state political leaders with the most supple, far-reaching tool for managing both their economies and their politics. The Confederation's requisition system had fostered the states' tax proficiency by allowing the states to meet their national obligations through any means the state governments considered expedient. Second, a national tax might be levied on the same sources from which the states drew their own revenues, forcing the states to extract revenues in more politically difficult ways. New York jealously guarded its tariff prerogative, and undoubtedly the threat of surrendering the tariff to the national government contributed to two New York delegates' early exit from the convention. Third, the national government might use taxes to manage the *national* economy and politics, with potentially disastrous consequences for any state out of favor with incumbent national leaders. The national government arbitrarily could extract resources from a given state or region and redistribute benefits to states with more immediate political importance.[61]

The convention dealt with this political dilemma by creating ample national taxing authority while making it hard to use national taxes to help particular constituents or hurt others. Until the acceptance of the compromise on representation, delegates such as John Rutledge tried to deal with the political threat of national taxation by basing representation on revenues paid to the national government instead of population. This rule would ensure that any states' policy influence would be tied closely to its contribution to national revenue.[62] After the compromise on

[60] *RFC* June 20, 1: 341; June 28, 1: 447. On the support for fiscal authority among supporters of the Constitution, see Edling, *A Revolution in Favor of Government*, pp. 149–205.

[61] Robert A. Becker, *Revolution, Reform, and the Politics of American Taxation, 1763–1783* (Baton Rouge: Louisiana State University Press, 1980), pp. 149–53.

[62] Rutledge was particularly keen to link representation in Congress to each state's share of national revenues (*RFC* June 11, 1: 196–200). On July 5, Rutledge again moved "that the suffrages of the several States be regulated and proportioned to according to the sums to be paid toward the general revenue by the inhabitants of each State respectively." This motion was defeated nine to one, with only South Carolina voting for it (1: 534). With the compromise on representation becoming more inevitable, Rufus King asserted that taxation and representation "ought to go together" (July 9, 1: 562; see also

representation on July 16, delegates sought to limit and set conditions on the national power to tax. Sherman again took the lead, proposing that the Constitution specify a national power to levy indirect taxes (tariffs) but not direct taxes (such as sales, excise, and property taxes) that were so important to the states. When Gouverneur Morris responded that this distinction would eventually force the national government to return to the Confederation's requisition system, Sherman agreed that some alternative provision had to be made to prevent this possibility.[63] The final Committee of Detail report established "the power to lay and collect taxes, duties, imposts and excises" as the leading enumerated power of Congress. The Committee of Detail, though, tried to make it impossible to use *direct* taxes for economic management by requiring that such taxes be levied on a per capita basis – that is, counting all "white and other free citizens and inhabitants" and three-fifths of the slaves. This provision aimed to make taxes too inflexible to harm state interests; it would be almost impossible to apply this to real property, for example. The report also banned state taxes on imports. The final Constitution included these provisions.[64]

It proved harder to constrain the use of *indirect* taxes, notably national tariffs. Tariffs were expected to provide "the only sure source of revenue... to be given up to the Union" and the lion's share of national funds.[65] Yet tariff rates for particular goods could substantially harm or help regions that produced those goods. To blunt the political impact of this powerful policy tool, Randolph and Rutledge had included language providing that indirect taxes be "common to all" in early drafts of the Committee of Detail report, but the language was dropped in the final

3: 255). Morris tried reversing the relationship, moving that "direct taxation shall be in proportion to representation" in the House of Representatives; Wilson, Gerry, Mason, and General Pinckney endorsed this position (July 12, 1: 592; July 13, 1: 600–1). Morris hoped that the Committee of Detail would strike the provision tying direct taxation to representation altogether, arguing that the provision has been intended only as a tactic to bridge temporarily the issue of counting slaves in legislative apportionment. It was no longer necessary, Morris said (July 24, 2: 106). The provision remained, however. Article I, Section 2 of the Constitution provides that "Representatives and direct Taxes shall be apportioned among the several States which may be included within this Union, according to their respective Numbers."

[63] *RFC* July 17, 2: 26. Later, Madison's opponents split on Martin's motion to restore some state discretion over taxes by partially restoring the Confederation requisition system. Martin made a motion that, whenever the national government needed revenues over and above tariff collections, each state would be given a requisition quota to fill as it chose. Maryland divided on this vote, New Jersey voted in favor of it, and Connecticut and Delaware voted against it (August 21, 2: 359).

[64] *RFC* July 17, 2: 26; Committee of Detail report, in 2: 142–5, 168, 182–3.

[65] *RFC* July 26, 2: 126; August 18, 2: 327.

report. The committee's final draft alarmed Maryland's delegates, who feared that Maryland "would have this resource taken from her, without the expences of her own government being lessened" so that "what would be raised from her commerce and by indirect taxation would far exceed the proportion she would be called upon to pay under the present confederation."[66] The convention delegated the problem to a committee, and Sherman, reporting for the committee, recommended language that "all duties, imposts & excises, laid by the Legislature shall be uniform throughout the U.S." and that no "regulation of commerce or revenue give 'preference to the ports of one State <over> those of another.'" Madison thought the provision would impede the national management of commerce and sought to remove it. The delegates, though, accepted these protections against geographical favoritism with little dissent.[67]

To circumvent another sensitive regional dispute, the delegates eliminated both the states' and the national government's authority to tax exports. National power to tax exports agitated the South. If the national government taxed exports, even a uniform application would extract a disproportionate share of revenues from the southern export economies. State export taxes were politically valuable tools for the exporting states because they allowed them to shift some of the cost of government to consumers beyond their borders. The Committee of Detail report banned Congress from taxing exports. Ellsworth thought that national export taxes would "engender incurable jealousies," and Gerry felt that they "might ruin the Country" because a national export tax "might be exercised partially, raising one and depressing another part of it." Morris, however, fulminated that this ban on export taxes was "radically objectionable" and that export taxes were necessary. Langdon worried that exporting states would use export taxes to exploit their neighbors.[68]

[66] *RFC* August 7, 2: 212. James McHenry and General Pinckney proposed to make "All duties imposts & excises, prohibitions or restraints laid or made by [Congress] . . . uniform and equal throughout the [United States]." They also suggested language to retain port states' right to collect duties by prohibiting Congress from forcing ships "to enter or pay duties or imposts in any other State than in that to which they may be bound" (August 25, 2: 417–18).

[67] *RFC* August 31, 2: 480–1. The special committee was established August 25 (2: 418). The Committee of Style recast the language to read "all such duties imposts & excises, shall be uniform throughout the [United States]" (September 14, 2: 614).

[68] Earlier, King complained that "The admission of slaves was a most grating circumstance to his mind, & he believed would be so to a great part of the people of America. . . . At all events, either slaves should not be represented, or exports should be taxable" (*RFC* August 8, 2: 220).

Consistent with his support for national taxes, Madison almost alone among the southerners supported the national power to tax exports as an important tool for managing the economy, one that "might with particular advantage be exercised with regard to articles in which America was not rivalled in foreign markets, [such] as Tob[acc]o." Sherman assumed that the matter had been settled. "The complexity of the business in America would render an equal tax on exports impracticable," he said. Madison moved to require an extraordinary majority of each House to tax exports ("a lesser evil than a total prohibition"), but this proposal lost on a vote of five to six, opposed by Connecticut and the five southernmost states. When King moved to ban *state* export duties, this provision also passed on a six-to-five vote, with North Carolina joining the coalition of the New England and middle states against Connecticut, Maryland, and the South.[69]

Although the convention authorized the national government to levy taxes, it tried to place obstacles in the way of using national taxes to advantage or to harm any state.[70] As North Carolina's delegates later explained this arrangement to their governor, "we were taking so much care to guard ourselves against being over reached and to form rules of Taxation that might operate in our favour" so that "Fifty citizens of North Carolina could not be subject to more taxes for all their Lands than fifty Citizens in New England." Most national revenues would be generated by tariffs, they continued, "but you will find it provided in the 8th Section of Article the first that all duties, Impost and excises shall *be uniform*

[69] *RFC* August 16, 2: 305–8; August 21, 2: 359–65; August 28, 2: 442. Export taxes continued to irritate delegates in the convention's final weeks. Mason moved to permit states to levy the incidental costs of inspecting, storing, and insuring exports. Dayton expressed suspicion that Pennsylvania would use this permission to tax New Jersey unfairly. Mason suggested an additional clause permitting Congress to regulate abuses, and this provision passed seven states to three, with Pennsylvania, Delaware, and South Carolina opposed (September 13, 2: 607). On the last day of the convention, Mason moved to combine and restate the agreements on export and import duties with a substitute, that "No State shall, without the consent of Congress, lay any imposts or duties on imports or exports, except what may be absolutely necessary for executing its Inspection laws; and the net produce of all duties and imposts, laid by any State on imports or exports, shall be for the use of the Treasury of the U– S–; and all such laws shall be subject to the revision and controul of the Congress." A motion to strike out congressional power over these duties lost, and the substitute was adopted over Virginia's opposition (September 15, 2: 624–5). This provision was combined with the prohibition on state tariffs and placed in Article I, Section 10 of the Constitution.

[70] Pinckney proposed to limit national taxing authority, restraining "the Legislature of the U.S. from establishing a perpetual revenue" (*RFC* August 18, 2: 325–6). This restriction was not reported or seriously discussed.

throughout the United States."[71] Although the national government fully controlled tariffs, a vital tool of national sovereignty, the use of tariffs was encumbered by restrictions. Tariffs could not be coupled with the tools of managing the routine economic life of the nation. The delegates found it easier to deal with the national powers that would develop the nation's markets.

NURTURING MARKETS

Like Madison, the delegates accepted that the growth of trade and markets fostered the nation's economic growth. Because expanding markets and trade served the national interest, the national government should set rules to reduce the uncertainty and cost of transacting business. Unlike taxes or other policy tools that could be used to bludgeon their constituents, they did not quarrel over national tools that could nurture markets without threat to specific constituencies. Uniform naturalization laws, for example, would facilitate the immigration of needed craftsmen.[72] Uniform patent laws would make it easier for an inventor to protect the rights to his invention within the United States. A single postal system would integrate commercial transactions across state lines and regions.[73] The Committee of Detail enumerated a number of provisions that facilitated markets. Its report proposed that the Congress be authorized to coin money, regulate the value of foreign money, borrow money and issue national bills of credit, and specify the punishment for counterfeiting. The committee's recommendations for national authority to establish uniform naturalization rules for the country, to fix the standard of weights and measures, to establish post offices, and to coin money were all included in the final Constitution. Madison and Pinckney urged added national authority to grant patents and copyrights, and the convention approved these powers

[71] North Carolina Delegates to Governor Caswell, September 18, 1787, in *RFC* 3: 83–4 (emphasis in original).

[72] On naturalization and citizenship rules in the Confederation era, see Rogers M. Smith, *Civic Ideals: Conflicting Ideals of Citizenship in U.S. History* (New Haven, CT: Yale University Press, 1997), pp. 87–114.

[73] Curtis P. Nettels, *The Emergence of a National Economy, 1775–1815* (New York: Holt, Rinehart, and Winston, 1962), p. 101. On the value of patent law for economic development, see Zorina B. Khan, "Property Rights and Patent Litigation in Early Nineteenth-Century America," *Journal of Economic History* 55:1 (March 1995): 58–97. On the postal service, see Richard R. John, *Spreading the News: The American Postal System from Franklin to Morse* (Cambridge, MA: Harvard University Press, 1995).

without debate. By adding the national power to establish "post-roads," they gave the national government a potentially important tool for building the foundations of an internal transportation network.[74] The requirement that fugitive slaves be "delivered up" to their masters even in other states subtly established slaveholders' property rights nationwide.

Much more important for market-driven economic development, the convention amputated many basic tools of economic sovereignty that states had been using to cope with the effects of the economic crisis. The delegates disarmed the states of the power to use tariffs, import restrictions, currency expansion, and debtor relief policies to mitigate economic stress (and to build internal political support, sometimes at other states' expense). These delegates showed little reluctance to nationalize control of currency, despite the strength of paper money advocates in their states. Sherman notably had no qualms about national power when it came to currency; he thought this "a favorable crisis for crushing paper money." States would be prohibited from coining money or, without Congress's consent, issue bills of credit "or make any thing but specie a tender in payment of debts." Most of these provisions were approved without debate. Madison and Sherman agreed that further restrictions on national and state currency powers would be valuable. Gouverneur Morris received much support for a motion to eliminate Congress's authority to emit bills of credit, and only Maryland and New Jersey opposed it. Similarly, Wilson and Sherman moved to expand the absolute prohibition on states' coining money to include "nor emit bills of credit, nor make any thing but gold & silver coin a tender in payment of debts," eliminating Congress's authority to permit states to print paper money. Again, delegates from all sections approved the restriction. The prohibition of state tariffs prompted a debate only about congressional power to permit state tariffs under any circumstances.[75]

[74] *RFC* August 16, 2: 308; August 18, 2: 325; September 5, 2: 509–10; John Lauritz Larson, *Internal Improvement: National Public Works and the Promise of Popular Government in the Early United States* (Chapel Hill: University of North Carolina Press, 2001), pp. 46–8, 54.

[75] *RFC* August 28, 2: 439; September 14, 2: 619. Rutledge had penciled a prohibition on state tariffs into early drafts of the Committee of Detail report. The final report prohibited state tariffs unless Congress explicitly approved them (*RFC* August 6, 2: 187). When the issue came up for discussion, Madison sought to place this prohibition beyond the reach of Congress, and make the prohibition absolute. "He observed that as the States interested in this power by which they could tax the imports of their neighbours passing thro' their markets, were a majority . . . they could give the consent of the Legislature, to the injury of N[ew] Jersey, N[orth] Carolina &c –" Sherman "thought the power might safely be left to" Congress. When Mason supported Sherman by observing that

The Constitution also prohibited states, but not Congress, from interfering in private contracts. A bit of stealth put this provision into the document. The Northwest Ordinance, enacted in mid-July 1787, had stipulated that no territory in the northwest region could "interfere with, or affect" bona fide "private contracts or engagements." Sherman's plan banned many of the state policies that effectively abrogated contractual debts. King proposed that the Constitution include a similar prohibition on the states. Wilson and Madison spoke in favor of the provision. But Gouverneur Morris objected that contracts were too complex for such a blanket rule and that "within the State itself a majority must rule, whatever may be the mischief done among themselves." Sherman appeared to side with King, Madison, and Wilson by asking Morris, "Why then prohibit bills of credit?" Wilson reassured the delegates that only "*retrospective* interferences" would be prohibited, and the convention settled for a ban on state "ex post facto" laws instead. The Committee of Style, which included King, Madison, and Morris, included a clause explicitly prohibiting states from enacting any "law impairing the obligation of contracts." The delegates apparently approved this additional phrase without dissent. Madison revealed his interest in national power when he failed to record the approval of this language restricting *state* interferences with contracts, while he *did* carefully record the rejection of Gerry's motion that *Congress* be prohibited from impairing contracts. No one seconded Gerry's motion, noted Madison, whose records show that the convention explicitly and almost unanimously refused to limit national government authority to interfere in private contracts. Sherman expressed reservations about authorizing Congress to make laws governing bankruptcy, but the convention added this power with overwhelming support.[76] Meanwhile,

"particular States might wish to encourage by impost duties certain manufactures for which they enjoyed natural advantages, as Virginia, the manufacture of Hemp &c.," Madison warned that this permission would "revive all the mischiefs experienced from the want of a Gen[eral]l Government over commerce." Madison's motion lost, though North Carolina, New Jersey, New Hampshire, and Delaware supported it. Sherman then moved to provide that, even if Congress approved of state tariffs, its revenues would accrue to the national treasury. Sherman's amendment aimed at removing any incentive to gain state revenues from such duties. Madison, from an exporting state, supported this proposition (though complained about its complexity); King, from Massachusetts, objected that it would interfere with the state governments' promotion of manufactures. Sherman's motion carried, nine states to two, with Massachusetts and Maryland voting against it (August 28, 2: 441–3).

[76] *RFC* August 28, 2: 439–40; August 29, 2: 448–9; September 3, 2: 488–9; September 12, 2: 597; September 14, 2: 619; 3: 615–16. Richard Morris attributes the language in the Committee of Style report to Alexander Hamilton; *The Forging of the Union: 1781–1789* (New York: Harper and Row, 1987), p. 246.

the convention was delegating the resolution of some of the Confederation's most difficult controversies to Congress.

DELEGATING AUTHORITY TO POLITICS

The delegates artfully set indefinite boundaries between state and national authority, tacitly delegating the resolution of many divisive issues to future politicians. They provided no definitive guidelines for resolving future conflicts over these boundaries.[77] They never spelled out precisely what kinds of public goods would be provided by the states and which by the national government. Sherman's own list of indispensable national powers was imprecise, and during the deliberations he conceded the need for additional powers, such as direct taxes. Collectively, the delegates were at a loss to define key terms such as "direct taxes."[78] The Committee of Detail's insertion of the "necessary and proper" clause indicates that even Madison's opponents were willing to allow for flexible national authority to cover hard cases and unexpected developments. Sherman's inability to place state police powers beyond constitutional amendment demonstrates the delegates' intention to leave the scope of national authority open to future political negotiation.

The convention evaded three issues that had deeply divided the Confederation Congress – the public debt, the public lands, and the permanent location of the national capital – and turned them over to the reconstituted national policy-making process. In an effort to fend off equal representation in the Senate, Rufus King first suggested that the national government throw "all the State debts into the federal debt." Sensitive to the political implications of the provision, King later noted that those to whom the state governments owed money "would otherwise be opposed to a plan which transferred to the Union the best resources of the States without transferring the State debts at the same time."[79] As late as the Committee of Detail report, however, the convention had made no provision for the financial obligations of the Confederation or the states. Pinckney, Gerry, and Rutledge urged the convention to make a specific provision to ensure the payment of public obligations. Rutledge, representing the state with a larger per capita debt than any other, made a motion to create a committee to "consider the necessity and expediency of the U[nited]

[77] See also Rakove, *Original Meanings*, p. 201.

[78] *RFC* August 20, 2: 350.

[79] *RFC* July 14, 2: 6; August 18, 2: 327–8.

States assuming all the State debts," a proposal that "was politic, as by disburdening the people of the State debts it would conciliate them to the plan." The southern states, along with Massachusetts and Connecticut, supported Rutledge on a six-to-four vote.[80] Sherman, who sought to turn the controversy over to the new Congress, served on the committee, and it recommended Sherman's preference ("The Legislature of the U.S. shall have power to fulfil the engagements which have been entered into by Congress, and to discharge as well ... the debts incurred by the several States during the late war, for the common defence and general welfare"). Butler worried that the provision would provide a windfall to speculators who had purchased state and national securities, "the Blood-suckers who had speculated on the distresses of others, as to those who had fought & bled for their country." Although the delegates dropped the committee provision, the Committee on Postponed Matters (which also included Sherman) added it to the first enumerated power, and it was accepted without dissent.[81]

Similarly, the convention delegated controversial choices on the disposition of public lands and the location of the national capital to Congress. Mason proposed to prohibit the national capital from being located in a city that served as a seat of state government. Mason's motion touched off a remarkably cynical discussion of the likely political games that legislators would play to win this prize. Madison thought that Congress would insist on a central location and proposed that Congress "exercise exclusively Legislative authority at the seat of the General Government" and over a capital district of indefinite size, selected with the collaboration of the affected state legislatures. Madison also proposed to add to the enumerated powers the national authority to "dispose of the unappropriated lands of the U[nited] States," create governments in new territories, and purchase lands for "Forts, Magazines, and other necessary buildings." The Committee on Postponed Matters proposed similar language to cover these matters and the delegates adopted it without disagreement. When Gerry objected that national power over military installations would intimidate the states, the delegates added a requirement that the national

[80] *RFC* August 18, 2: 326–8.

[81] *RFC* August 21, 2: 355–6; August 23, 2: 392; September 4, 2: 493, 499. Gerry was a major debt holder; McDonald, *Novus Ordo Seclorum*, p. 221. In a newspaper essay signed as "The Landholder," Ellsworth in December 1787 accused Gerry of opposing the Constitution because it did not specify national assumption of debts (*RFC* 3: 171–2).

government receive the state legislature's consent for any purchase of land for military installations.[82]

THE CONSTITUTION, POLICY AUTHORITY, AND POLITICAL STRATEGY

Political compromise dominated the design of policy authority in the Constitution. The delegates improvised shared sovereignty as the by-product of a series of issue-by-issue negotiations often played out against the ongoing clash between Madison, Sherman, and their respective allies. In the letter explaining their final product, the delegates told Congress that

> It is at all times difficult to draw with precision the line between those rights which must be surrendered, and those which may be reserved; and on the present occasion this difficulty was encreased by a difference among the several States as to their situation, extent, habits, and particular interests.... the Constitution, which we now present, is the result of a spirit of amity, and of that mutual deference and concession which the peculiarity of our political situation rendered indispensable.... each [State] will doubtless consider, that had her interest alone been consulted, the consequences might have been particularly disagreeable or injurious to others; that it is liable to as few exceptions as could reasonably have been expected, we hope and believe; that it may promote the lasting welfare of that country so dear to us all, and secure her freedom and happiness, is our most ardent wish.[83]

The delegates approved a set of national powers on which all agreed, such as the power to tax, to manage international commerce, and to defend the nation. Madison and other proponents of broad national power got a sort of ersatz national veto vested in the federal courts (through the supremacy clause) and some constitutional language that could be used to justify the expansion of national power on a case-by-case basis. Sherman

[82] *RFC* July 26, 2: 127–8; August 11, 2: 261–2; August 18, 2: 324–5; September 4, 2: 493–4; September 5, 2: 505–6, 509–10. When the delegates debated the admission of new states on August 30, Daniel Carroll of land-deprived Maryland asked for a clause specifically stating that the Constitution did not affect the states' claims to land ceded to the United States by Britain. Gouverneur Morris persuaded the delegates to accept a substitute stating that Congress could "make all needful rules and regulations respecting the territory or other property belonging to the U[nited] States; and nothing in this constitution contained, shall be so construed as to prejudice any claims either of the U[nited] S[tates] or of any particular State" (2: 465–6). This wording was incorporated into Article IV, Section 3.

[83] Letter from convention delegates to Congress, to accompany the signed Constitution, in *RFC* September 17, 2: 666–7.

got a list of enumerated national powers, state control of residual policy authority, and some defensive tools that states could use to fight the aggregation of power by the national government. Slavery, the South's "favorite prerogative," received the nation's tacit consent.

The convention armed the national government with better tools for pursuing national economic sovereignty, but it allowed the states to keep most of the tools of economic management (see Figure 5.1). As Luther Martin put it, "all which relates to the external, and concerns that are merely national, may be granted to the U.S. while all that is internal and relative to individuals of the separate States must continue to belong to the particular States."[84] Despite Madison's efforts, the national government would manage only international and interstate commerce, while the states would govern commerce within their borders. By reducing barriers to interstate trade and the cost of commerce, the delegates in effect established the world's largest free-trade zone.

These arrangements shaped subsequent American political strategies in three ways. First, the Constitution permitted broad authority to the states to manage the land, labor, and capital within their borders, but it removed many of the policy tools they used to inhibit the pace of market-driven economic development or to cushion its impacts on their citizens. State officials could still calibrate state regulations, taxes, licenses, charters, subsidies, and other policies to advance their goals. Most of the big, substantive political controversies of the future – for example, slavery, corporate regulation, social welfare, education, labor, civil rights, and environmental protection – initially would be fought out in the states. But the Constitution denied state officials the use of tariffs, trade restrictions, currency manipulation, and other tools that a sovereign nation would use to manage the impact of markets on citizens. These are the very tools that national policy makers in other countries use to export, conceal, delay, or compensate for the costs of market-driven economic development. States, then, would regulate their economies, but the effects of any policy that inhibited private actors would be much more immediate, evident, uncompensated, and politically painful than the effects for a national government that could use the full range of economic tools. State policy makers would feel unusually strong pressures to facilitate market-driven economic growth and would have strong reasons to exercise great caution in taxing or regulating private enterprise. From the

[84] *RFC* June 27, 1: 442.

start, states placed a priority on the short-term interests of speculators and other private interests in their decisions concerning the distribution of land and the management of physical resources.[85]

Second, the Constitution gave the national government sovereign economic powers such as trade restrictions and tariffs but did not give it the tools to manage the development of the domestic economy. Most of the economic tools delegated to the national government, such as monetary policy, credit, and taxes, were macroeconomic tools that were inherently awkward or were made clumsy by constitutional provisions aimed at preventing geographical redistribution. The provision that direct taxes be levied per capita, for example, made it practically impossible to levy direct taxes.[86] National policy makers eventually would learn to exploit tariffs and other authorized tools for the benefit of particular constituents and regions. They also would exploit the Constitution's ambiguity to expand the tools at their disposal. But the inherent limitations of national authority would skew the politics of national economic policy for more than a century.

Third, by including elastic language that intentionally obscured the dividing line between national and state authority, the Constitution made federalism a central battleground of American politics and made "states' rights" a potent political weapon. Uncertain about the future demands for national power, the delegates also allowed for substantial growth in national authority by adding the supremacy clause, the "general welfare" clause, and the "necessary and proper" clause, and by refusing to shelter state police powers from constitutional amendment. A national government with a restricted set of strong policy tools would vie for control of public policy with states that have a different, but also restricted, set of strong policy tools. The result would be an endless struggle for control. Political interests would utilize the Constitution's unsettled political frontier of federal authority as an expedient tool for achieving substantive policy outcomes. American federalism would channel much political energy into contests over state versus national government authority, a tendency evident almost as soon as the new Congress convened in 1789.

[85] Harry N. Scheiber, "Federalism and the American Economic Order, 1789–1910," *Law and Society Review* 10:1 (Fall 1975): 57–118.

[86] Charles Beard, *An Economic Interpretation of the Constitution of the United States* (New York: Macmillan, 1913), p. 176; Dall W. Forsythe, *Taxation and Political Change in the Young Nation, 1781–1833* (New York: Columbia University Press, 1977), pp. 21–2.

As they became more uncertain about the kinds of policies the new government would produce, the delegates grew more concerned about making government safe for their constituents. While they were limiting the national government's authority, they were building a policy process that made it difficult to use the national authority that remained.

7

How Is the Nation Governed?

Constituting the Policy Process

No matter how cautiously the delegates crafted policy agency and authority, the turbulence of ordinary republican policy making posed an ominous threat to the new government. Any republican policy-making process would nurture vigorous political rivalries. Majorities would rule in the new Congress, as they did in the state legislatures. National lawmakers, just like those in the states, would use all the political methods at their disposal to construct winning coalitions for policies whether good or bad. Because the policy process converted political interests into government action, majority coalitions seeking harmful policy would have to be deterred by the rules for making public policy – if they could be deterred at all. The delegates had to arrange the policy process to make it likely to produce good policies and unlikely to produce bad policies, that is, policies harmful to national interests and their constituencies.

As it grew harder to anticipate the way the new government would work, delegates sought to fortify the institution they believed most likely to defend their particular interests. After the compromise on representation on July 16, the Connecticut delegation and its allies pressed for broad Senate powers because the state-based Senate seemed as likely as the Confederation Congress to defend the economically disadvantaged states. James Madison and his allies, in contrast, pushed for more presidential power because the president seemed the most likely advocate for the nationally minded, forward-looking policy Madison initially envisioned. Step by step, the delegates constructed a balance of political power among national policy-making institutions, increasing the independence of each while blocking their cooperation. In effect, the convention instilled divergent policy purposes in national political institutions, forced them to share power to make policy, and gave them separate powers to defend against policy they opposed. These arrangements made it difficult and costly to use the national policy process effectively for any purpose, good or ill.

THE DILEMMAS OF REPUBLICAN POLICY MAKING

Their hard-won agreements on policy agency and authority could not resolve satisfactorily the convention's central dilemma – to reconstruct the national government to promote national interests without harming interests the delegates considered vital. To be sure, the compromises on policy agency guaranteed their varied interests a seat at the policy-making table. Voters would send U.S. representatives to speak for the nation's regions, state legislatures would select senators to speak for them, and some constituency that spanned a large number of states would choose the president. The national policy table, moreover, offered a restricted menu of policy choices. Limits on national authority seemed to constrain the damage that national policies could do to any region or group of citizens. Compromises had blunted the sharp edge of national taxes, hamstrung the exercise of commercial and military power, and made slavery safe for the foreseeable future.

Yet these provisions appeared insufficient to stop a determined national government from wreaking policy havoc. A seat at the table could not ensure enough power to defend against the malicious schemes of others. History showed that mere declarations of limited power could not in themselves stop resolute national leaders from abusing public authority. Week after week, these smart, experienced politicians hammered home the ways that devious state politicians regularly employed republican tools for ends the delegates considered malevolent. Elbridge Gerry and other skeptics frequently predicted how schemers could bend a given proposal to suit their wicked purposes. As Gouverneur Morris observed, "The most virtuous citizens will often as members of a legislative body concur in measures which afterwards in their private capacity they will be ashamed of."[1] The raw nerves of the states' economic rivalries became more exposed each

[1] *RFC* August 15, 2: 299. Compare *Federalist* 55, probably written by Madison: "In all very numerous assemblies, of whatever character composed, passion never fails to wrest the sceptre from reason. Had every Athenian citizen been a Socrates; every Athenian assembly would still have been a mob." Alexander Hamilton, James Madison, and John Jay, *The Federalist*, ed. Jacob E. Cooke (Middletown, CT: Wesleyan University Press, 1961), p. 374.

time debates on slavery, trade, western lands, and other sensitive issues stripped away another layer of superficial republican consensus.

With a rebuilt Congress at the center of the new policy process, the delegates could expect that rambunctious politics would drive most policy making. Unquestionably, some leaders would find the abuse of power alluring.[2] As politicians themselves, they had few illusions about American legislators. Yet they were entrusting power to address the most controversial American economic problems to the legislators in this new Congress. Congress would levy taxes and mobilize the military, the blood and muscle of governance. Congress could borrow money, assume the debts of the states, run budget deficits, and manage currency. The "necessary and proper," "general welfare," and national supremacy clauses expanded congressional authority in ways that were left for politicians and jurists to define.

The crucial problem was to find ways to organize the tumultuous republican policy process so it would produce acceptable national policies. The delegates did not want to prevent factions, and indeed did not believe they could prevent them. But they did want to make it hard for factions that sought bad policies to succeed. Gouverneur Morris emphasized the importance of the policy process for market-driven economic development when he lamented the lack of obstacles to paper emissions and dwelt on the "importance of public Credit, and the difficulty of supporting it without some strong barrier against the instability of legislative Assemblies."[3] The convention had to create a national policy-making process that would facilitate majority coalitions in favor of national policies the delegates believed beneficial (such as fostering national commerce), while deterring majority coalitions bent on pursuing policies they believed harmful (such as paper money or interference in contracts).

Separating powers seemed the obvious solution to this dilemma. The delegates embraced the abstract principle of separate legislative, executive, and judicial institutions checking and balancing one another. As noted in Chapter 4, though, the separation of powers was a general concept divorced from specific, substantive political issues. None had a

[2] Some delegates anticipated relatively little legislative business for the new government. John Rutledge expected meetings of no more than eight weeks a year (*RFC* July 10, 1: 570). Others, including Roger Sherman, expected that "great extent and varying state of our affairs in general" would entail frequent meetings of Congress (August 7, 2: 199). James Madison's preferences for broad national jurisdiction, a national veto of state laws, national corporate charters, and a national university suggest a very busy legislative agenda.

[3] *RFC* August 15, 2: 299.

comprehensive plan for designing the separation of powers to protect the specific material interests that were provoking so many intense disputes. James Madison and Roger Sherman, better prepared for the debates than most delegates, initially advocated relatively simple blueprints for the policy process, each designed to produce the outcomes they preferred (Figures 3.1 and 4.1).

As the delegates put different policy institutions in the hands of agents of different interests, it became more and more important to defend the policy autonomy, prerogatives, and resources of those institutions that their agents controlled. Madison, Morris, James Wilson, and their allies sought a strong presidency because that institution was most likely to champion the national interests they wanted the government to pursue. Sherman and the economically vulnerable states sought a strong Senate to champion the state interests they wanted to protect. Politics, then, rather than abstract philosophical principles, guided the delegates as they worked out the specific scheme of checks and balances they designed into the Constitution (Figure 5.1). Principles often became rhetorical weapons, used to win a point for a particular institution (as when Rufus King attacked a proposal for presidential impeachment by claiming that it would be "destructive of his independence and of the principles of the Constitution" and claimed to rely "on the vigor of the Executive as a great security for the public liberties").[4] This political jockeying over institutional powers got under way almost as soon as the convention accepted the idea of a House of Representatives.

BUILDING THE HOUSE OF REPRESENTATIVES

The convention swiftly made the popularly elected House of Representatives the cornerstone of the new policy process. Elbridge Gerry expressed qualms about popular election of House members, and Sherman expressed a preference for selection by state legislatures, but the convention approved of the House of Representatives in principle on May 31. No serious resistance to the idea surfaced later. "Our House of Commons," as Edmund Randolph and George Mason referred to it, would approve legislation with a simple majority. Sherman and Rutledge urged the delegates to trust the legislators, and James Wilson, defending "the laudable ambition of rising into the honorable offices of the Government," reminded the convention that "The members of the Legislature have perhaps the

[4] *RFC* July 20, 2: 67.

hardest & least profitable task of any who engage in the service of the state." Apart from the issue of proportional representation, the design of the House generated little debate.[5]

To establish Congress's independence and transparency, the delegates gave familiar legislative prerogatives to the House and then extended them to the Senate. Most important, fixed terms of office and a calendar for elections and meetings would set the tempo of the policy-making process.[6] Congress would meet annually and at a set time to ensure it would not become quiescent. The fixed legislative calendar established a very significant, though underappreciated, check on arbitrary government by precluding executive power to dissolve the legislature and call for new elections. In parliamentary systems, such power gives a prime minister the opportunity to schedule major national elections at politically favorable moments, and it tends to strengthen national political parties.[7]

The delegates fostered politics by refusing to limit the number of terms a legislator could serve. The Articles of Confederation had set term limits on members of Congress, and the Virginia Plan proposed term limits for House members. After the presentation of the Virginia Plan, however, no one "proposed or conceived" of term limits for U.S. representatives or senators.[8] The case for term limits was undermined implicitly every time a delegate insisted that reelection would give legislators a personal self-interest in attending to broader policy concerns. Morris also observed that term limits undermined the very stability that the delegates were seeking to strengthen – "A change of men is ever followed by a change of measures," as the intensely partisan Pennsylvania legislature demonstrated.[9]

[5] *RFC* May 31, 1: 48–9, 53, 58; June 23, 1: 387; June 26, 1: 429.

[6] The delegates quibbled about fixing the date in the Constitution itself and had to take a vote to give Congress discretion to change the day of their annual meeting; Connecticut and New Hampshire voted against allowing Congress this choice (*RFC* August 7, 2: 199–200).

[7] Gouverneur Morris commented that "We should either take the British Constitution altogether or make one for ourselves. The Executive there has dissolved two Houses as the only cure for such disputes. Will our Executive be able to apply such a remedy?" (*RFC* July 6, 1: 545). A month later, Wilson stated the president "here could not like the Executive Magistrate in England interpose by a prorogation, or dissolution" (August 13, 2: 275).

[8] *RFC* July 26, 2: 120. The delegates put off discussion of the Virginia Plan's term limit and recall provisions and did not take them up again (*RFC* May 29: 1: 20; May 31, 1: 50–1).

[9] *RFC* July 25, 2: 112–13; July 26, 2: 120. Sherman and Ellsworth also argued against term limits for the president because, as Ellsworth put it, the president "will be more likely to render him<self> worthy of [reelection] if he be rewardable with it" (*RFC* July 24, 2: 101; see July 17, 2: 32–4).

The delegates struggled a bit with the length of legislative terms as they sought a balance between responsiveness and responsible policy. Madison and Sherman again squared off against each other. Madison argued that representatives should serve for a three-year term, arguing that a longer term would provide greater stability and "knowledge of the various interests of the States to which they do not belong, and of which they can know but little from the situation and affairs of their own." Sherman and Gerry favored annual elections for the House, a common provision in the state legislatures. Sherman maintained that "Frequent elections are necessary to preserve the good behavior of rulers. They also tend to give permanency to the Government, by preserving that good behavior, because it ensures their re-election." The convention initially accepted a three-year term for House members but later shortened the term to two years.[10]

There was little disagreement over other internal rules for the houses of the legislature. Each house would choose its own leadership, including the speaker of the House and the president pro tempore of the Senate. Legislators could speak freely in congressional debates and were protected from arrest (both provisions were drawn from the Articles of Confederation). Congress would keep public journals of all its proceedings, correcting a deficiency that Mason thought had undermined public faith in the Confederation Congress. One-fifth of the members in either house could call for recorded roll-call votes.[11] Each house would make its own rules, including rules for seating and expelling members. A simple majority of the members would constitute a quorum for doing business. Because the sad

[10] *RFC* June 12, 1: 214–15; June 21, 1: 360–2; Sherman quotation, June 26, 1: 423. Both Madison and Sherman objected to the settlement on a two-year term.

[11] Mason, *RFC* June 20, 1: 339. Because they were all too familiar with the use of desultory motions in their state legislatures, the delegates debated the circumstances under which roll calls would be required. Morris and Edmund Randolph moved to permit any individual member to demand a roll-call vote; Sherman and Oliver Ellsworth spoke in opposition to any explicit provision to permit a minority to demand a roll call, on the grounds that they provided little information but did "much mischief." George Mason, a member of the Committee on Detail, viewed the committee recommendation as a middle ground ("the yeas and nays of the members of each House, on any question, shall at the desire of one-fifth part of the members present, be entered on the journal"). Randolph and Morris's proposal was defeated unanimously (August 10, 1: 255). The Committee of Detail also required roll-call votes for overriding presidential vetoes (August 6, 2: 181). Sherman and Elbridge Gerry moved to give each house discretion over publishing deliberations concerning treaties and military operations (Sherman arguing that Congress could be trusted in this case); the provision was finally broadened to provide for legislative discretion over information that required secrecy (August 11, 2: 259–60; September 14, 2: 613). The convention accepted Madison's motion to increase the majority required to expel a member to two-thirds (August 10, 2: 254).

experience of the Confederation Congress caused concern about assembling enough members to do business, the convention permitted Congress to compel attendance.[12] Neither house could leverage power by adjourning for more than three days to a different place, unless the other house agreed.[13]

But with a politically driven House of Representatives at the center of national policy making, how could the delegates be certain that the national policy process would produce acceptable outcomes? James Wilson put the problem diplomatically: "In a single House there is no check, but the inadequate one, of the virtue & good sense of those who compose it." Gouverneur Morris was far more blunt. "The Legislature is worthy of unbounded confidence in some respects and liable to equal distrust in others," he cautioned. "When their interest coincides precisely with that of their Constituents, as happens in many of their Acts, no abuse of trust is to be apprehended. When a strong personal interest happens to be opposed to the general interest, the Legislature can not be too much distrusted."[14] Madison, among others, emphasized the problem of policy stability.[15] Some delegates frankly wanted to make the process less likely to produce any laws. "The excess rather than the deficiency of laws was to be dreaded," said Morris.[16] The design of other policy institutions

[12] If a quorum were merely a simple majority of members (as the Committee of Detail recommended), legislators might abuse the rule by collectively refusing to attend to chamber business. The delegates defeated proposals to lower the quorum below a majority. These debates revealed some delegates' suspicion that the rules would politically advantage states in the geographical center of the country, more proximate to the physical location of Congress, at the expense of the more geographically distant states.

[13] *RFC* August 9, 2: 231, 239; August 10, 2: 251–5; August 11, 2: 261–2. This provision briefly excited anxiety and cynicism. Richard Dobbs Spaight of North Carolina believed it was intended to fix the seat of government at New York; Hugh Williamson and Daniel Carroll agreed. Appalled, Gouverneur Morris responded that "such a distrust is inconsistent with all Gov[ernmen]t." Madison and King argued that the provision would address the problem of the Confederation Congress, whose wartime travels "had dishonored the federal Gov[ernmen]t." The convention adopted this language, though it dropped a clause excepting the Senate when engaged in nonlegislative duties.

[14] *RFC* June 16, 1: 254; July 24, 2: 104.

[15] *RFC* May 31, 1: 50, see also June 12, 1: 218. Hamilton thought "we ought to go as far in order to attain stability and permanency, as republican principles will admit" (June 18, 1: 289).

[16] *RFC* September 12, 2: 585–6. An exchange between Mason and Morris demonstrated that the delegates struggled to calibrate legislative capacity as carefully as possible. After Morris and Hamilton exemplified legislative abuses with New York examples, Mason commented that "The example of New York depended on the real merits of the laws.... But perhaps there were others of opposite opinions who could equally paint the abuses on the other side. His leading view was to guard against too great an impediment

would provide the auxiliary precautions needed to stabilize and restrain the House.

THE RISE OF THE SENATE

There was little doubt that the Senate, a second and smaller legislative chamber, would answer the need for a policy check on the House. No one disagreed when Edmund Randolph observed that "the Democratic licentiousness of the State Legislatures proved the necessity of a firm Senate" and that an effective Senate would check "the turbulence and follies" of a democratic House. Most of the states had bicameral legislatures, so that a Senate was both familiar and politically expedient. Like Madison, John Dickinson, Alexander Hamilton, Charles Pinckney, and others who had thought about reconstituting the government proposed two legislative houses. Sherman implicitly acceded to an upper house on his second day at the convention and later argued that a second legislative chamber was necessary for moving beyond the problem of representation.[17] Little theoretical opposition to a bicameral legislature surfaced at the convention after the defeat of the New Jersey Plan.

The Senate, though, was something of an empty vessel, attractive to many delegates because it served different purposes. Madison, Sherman, and other delegates disagreed on the kinds of interests the Senate would bring to the policy table. Like Madison, many thought that the Senate would serve as a bulwark for protecting property because it would be smaller than the House and its members more privileged. In the early weeks of the convention, for example, Madison thought the Senate "ought to come from, & represent, the Wealth of the nation" and as a "more

to the repeal of laws." Gouverneur Morris "dwelt on the danger to the public interest from the instability of laws, as the most to be guarded against.... Many good laws are not tried long enough to prove their merit. This is often the case with new laws opposed to old habits" (September 12, 2: 586).

[17] *RFC* May 31, 1: 51–2, 59; June 12, 1: 218; June 20, 1: 343; "The Pinckney Plan," in 3: 596; "The Hamilton Plan," in 3: 619; "John Dickinson: Plan of Government," in *Supplement to Max Farrand's "The Records of the Federal Convention of 1787,"* ed. James H. Hutson (New Haven, CT: Yale University Press, 1987), p. 85. The apportionment of the Senate, rather than the need for an upper house, caused the delegates initially to defer this discussion (May 31, 1: 51). Rather than attack the concept of a Senate, for example, New Jersey's William Paterson defended the unicameral Confederation Congress and urged the convention merely to increase some of its powers (June 16, 1: 251). Benjamin Franklin seemed to be the only proponent of a unicameral legislature in principle (July 5, 1: 546). Luther Martin preferred a single house but "was willing to make a trial of the plan" (July 14: 4).

capable sett of men." The Senate would be "sufficiently respectable for its wisdom & virtue, to aid on such emergencies" as excessive popular pressure to redistribute wealth. For this reason, Madison believed that the Senate should have additional policy responsibilities.[18] At the same time, there was no doubt that the Senate would not be and could not be an American House of Lords; its constituents, the state legislatures, themselves depended on voters.[19] Sherman, though, supported special Senate prerogatives less for its elitism than its likely advocacy for state governments' interests. He reasoned that "If they vote by States in the [Senate], and each State has an equal vote, there must be always a majority of States as well as a majority of the people on the side of public measures, & the Gov[ernmen]t will have decision and efficacy." The Senate, he believed, should be the source of energy in this policy system, and its members should serve for no more than five years.[20]

These differences began to surface in negotiations over senators' term of office. The convention initially approved a seven-year Senate term, a period that would keep a senator in office through three House election cycles. Madison hoped Senators would serve for terms as long as nine years. Later, when the convention provided for staggered Senate terms to ensure that a majority would keep office after a given Congressional election, Sherman unsuccessfully moved for a five-year term. Compromise resolved the issue, as it had for House terms. When a proposal for a nine-year term also failed, the convention immediately compromised on a six-year term for senators.[21] The delegates subtly enhanced Senate

[18] *RFC* June 26, 1: 422–3. On May 31, John Dickinson had urged the delegates to consider the Senate as an American House of Lords (see Chapter 5). See also Elaine K. Swift, *The Making of an American Senate: Reconstitutive Change in Congress, 1787–1841* (Ann Arbor: University of Michigan Press, 1996), pp. 9–53.

[19] James Wilson observed that the British "House of Lords & House of Commons" were "less likely to concur on the same occasions" than the two chambers of the U.S. Congress (*RFC* August 27, 2: 429).

[20] *RFC* June 6, 1: 136, 143; June 7, 1: 158; June 12, 1: 218; June 13, 1: 233; July 7, 1: 550, 554. In the committee that produced the compromise on representation, Sherman proposed that all Senate policy votes would have to win not only an absolute majority of the states but also a sufficient number of states to represent a majority of the U.S. population. This proposal aimed to guard against senators representing a minority of the population exercising control in the Senate. He had put forward a similar idea in the Confederation Congress a decade earlier, in the process of framing the Articles of Confederation (July 5, 1: 526).

[21] *RFC* June 12, 1: 218–19; June 25, 1: 409; June 26, 1: 423–6. New York, New Jersey, South Carolina, and Georgia voted against the six-year term. A Senate term three times longer than terms in the House, noted Gerry later, allowed the Senate to make "three successive essays in favor of a particular point" (July 6, 1: 545).

influence by providing that two senators would represent each state, and that they would vote separately as individuals rather than as a state unit. Sherman supported the rule, perhaps because it made it easier for individual states to influence policy even if a single senator were absent. He might also have calculated that the rule would work to the advantage of states with homogeneous policy interests, and that smaller states like Connecticut were more likely to have such homogeneous policy interests than a sprawling, populous state like Pennsylvania or Virginia.[22]

Madison would come to regret that "we had so little direct experience to guide us" as the Senate's policy prerogatives became the central obstacle to his constitutional vision.[23] Once the states enjoyed the same equal representation in the Senate that they had in the Continental Congress, some supporters of Senate elitism (such as John Rutledge) joined with delegates from vulnerable states to expand the Senate's role. The Committee of Detail report made the Senate the dominant legislative branch. By staggering the six-year terms for senators (one-third would be chosen every other year), the committee ensured that two-thirds would retain their seats even if a single election caused large turnover and upheaval in the House of Representatives. The Committee gave the Senate the premier role in foreign policy making by delegating it all the power to make treaties and appoint ambassadors. The Senate would influence the judicial process by appointing the justices of the Supreme Court. As the trial court for impeachments, the Senate's power to remove officials hung ominously over the executive and judicial branches. The committee provided that the Senate unilaterally would make treaties, would appoint ambassadors and the Supreme Court, and would serve as a court for impeachment trials. The president of the Senate would serve as U.S. president if the incumbent could not perform his duties, and the Senate would manage the mechanism for settling interstate conflicts that had been exercised by the Confederation Congress. Rutledge even believed the Senate should

[22] *RFC* July 7, 1: 554; July 14, 2: 5; July 23, 2: 94–5. King recalled how an individual in the Confederation Congress had used the rule that states voted as units to "gratify his Caprice" and unfairly extort concessions (July 7, 1: 554). Sherman agreed to per capita voting after explaining that he cared about protecting not the small states but the state governments, "which could not be preserved unless they were represented and had a negative in the Gen[era]l Government" (July 14, 2: 5). This comment strongly implies that states and senators would share a common antipathy to intrusions on state policy authority despite the substantive policy differences among them. On July 23 Gorham suggested that some of the largest states would be divided; this expectation naturally suggested that per capita voting would further advantage smaller states in Senate votes.

[23] Madison's quotation, *RFC* June 12, 1: 218.

originate revenues and appropriations: "The Senate being more conversant in business, and having more leisure, will digest the bills much better, and as they are to have no effect, till examined & approved by the H[ouse] of Rep[resentative]s there can be no possible danger." Charles Pinckney agreed and thought the Senate also would be the best repository for war-making power as well.[24]

COUNTERATTACK AGAINST THE SENATE

The rise of the Senate's policy influence generated strong resistance. The states' equal representation in the Senate undermined the relative policy influence of the largest states, and its expected parochialism undermined Madison's aspiration for a government that would pursue national interests. Madison now viewed the Senate as a force for policy instability and uncertainty.

> If the H[ouse] of Rep[resentative]s is to be chosen *biennially* – and the Senate to be *constantly* dependent on the Legislatures which are chosen *annually*, he could not see any chance for that stability in the Gen[era]l Gov[ernmen]t the want of which was a principal evil in the State Gov[ernmen]ts. His fear was that the organization of the Gov[ernmen]t supposing the Senate to be really independ[en]t for six years, would not effect our purpose. It was nothing more than a combination of the peculiarities of two of the State Gov[ernmen]ts which separately had been found insufficient. The Senate was formed on the model of that of Maryl[an]d. The Revisionary check, on that of N[ew] York. What the effect of A union of these provisions might be, could not be foreseen.[25]

Several of Madison's expected allies insisted that the House, the president, and the courts be given some of the Senate prerogatives, or supplied with institutional weapons to counter them. These delegates, however, were divided over the best way to counterbalance the Senate.

A key provision of the compromise on representation specified that the House of Representatives would originate national tax and spending measures, and the Senate could not alter or amend them. After the compromise was announced, George Mason, Edmund Randolph, Elbridge Gerry, and Hugh Williamson battled tenaciously to protect this "corner stone of the accommodation," because their states would exercise relatively more influence in the House than in the Senate. But if the House

[24] *RFC* August 6, 2: 177–84; August 8, 2: 224; August 9, 2: 236; August 13, 2: 279; August 17, 2: 318. The convention on July 18 had rejected a proposal to permit the judiciary to try impeachment cases but did not settle on an alternative (2: 46).

[25] *RFC* August 14, 2: 291 (emphasis in original).

alone controlled revenues and appropriations, a simple House majority alone would determine these crucial choices, a prospect Madison and other delegates feared. Madison dismissed the significance of House control of money bills as soon as it was announced. Political games would make the rule ineffective, he said, because "Bills could be negatived that they might be sent up in the desired shape." Pierce Butler, James Wilson, and both of the Pinckneys concurred. Gouverneur Morris thought that if it were not useless it would be "pernicious," stimulating quarrels and extortion between the two houses.[26] The Committee of Detail, faithful to the compromise, provided that the Senate could not alter or amend bills for "raising or appropriating money, and for fixing the salaries of the officers of the Government." Two days after the committee report, though, the convention struck the clause over the opposition of the three New England states and North Carolina.[27]

When Randolph and others fought back to reestablish House control of the national budget, the convention reacted with an expedient solution that bordered on cynicism. Hugh Williamson railed against the Senate as "a House of Lords which is to originate money-bills." He urged the convention at least to prohibit the Senate from amending such bills. Madison warned that the House origination of money bills would either negate the Senate's check on the House or force the Senate to refuse cooperation, making the provision useless. Dickinson, noting that disputes between the houses could not be avoided anyway, argued that the language would make the Constitution more likely to win political acceptance; John Rutledge disagreed that adding this meaningless provision would promote ratification, warning that the people "will be more likely to be displeased with it as an attempt to bubble them, than to impute it to a watchfulness over their rights." Randolph's motion, and a motion to restore the Committee of Detail language, both lost, seven states to four.[28] The

[26] *RFC* July 5, 1: 527–9; July 6, 1: 544–6; July 14, 2: 5. On the first key vote cast on any part of the grand compromise on representation, four of the states that contributed to the New Jersey Plan were joined by North Carolina to vote for this provision. Madison's coalition fractured on this vote. Virginia, Pennsylvania, and South Carolina voted against the provision, while New York, Massachusetts, and Georgia divided their votes (July 6, 1: 547). Gerry had championed the proposal for House control of money bills early in the convention (June 13, 1: 232).

[27] *RFC* August 8, 2: 224–5. Later, the Committee of Detail's mandate that "No money shall be drawn from the public Treasury, but in pursuance of appropriations that shall originate in the House of Representatives" was added to Article I, section 9.

[28] *RFC* August 8, 2: 224–5; August 9, 2: 232–4; August 11, 2: 262–3; August 13, 2: 273–80; August 14, 2: 287; August 15, 2: 297. George Washington determined the Virginia vote

Committee on Postponed Matters resurrected the provision. Sherman, explaining the committee's reasoning, argued that its restoration was purely political: it could facilitate broader agreement among the delegates, giving "immediate ease to those who looked on this clause as of great moment, and for trusting to their concurrence in other proper measures." The convention finally agreed to give the House the power to originate money bills, adding that "the Senate may propose or concur with amendments as in other bills," a proviso that effectively gave the Senate equal budget power with the House.[29] Their failure to win a real fiscal prerogative for the House further soured Mason, Randolph, and Gerry on the Constitution. Madison, meanwhile, was trying to counter the Senate's growing power by enhancing the role of the president.[30]

THE RISE OF PRESIDENTIAL INDEPENDENCE

At first, most of the delegates approached the need for an executive with uncertainty and suspicion. Until the Senate's composition and powers became clear, they dealt with executive power as much a philosophical as a political problem. As Morris said of the president, "Make him too weak: The Legislature will usurp his powers: Make him too strong. He will usurp on the Legislature."[31] Like Sherman, Madison initially imagined that the president would serve the will of Congress. He worried more about limiting presidential power than about the prerogatives of the office. Madison supported a privy council and impeachment for simple "malpractice," for example. James Wilson alone spoke for a stronger executive at the outset, an executive vested in a single person who could exercise the needed "powers of secrecy, vigour & Dispatch."[32] Some delegates distrusted a single individual to serve as executive. Even after July 16, Randolph strongly

by joining Randolph and Mason. This vote indicates that Washington, too, took political considerations into account. Madison noted that Washington "disapproved & till now voted ag[ain]st, the exclusive privilege, he gave up his judgment he said, because it was not of very material weight with him & was made an essential point with others, who if disappointed, might be less cordial in other points of real weight" (August 13, 2: 280).

29 *RFC* September 5, 2: 510; September 8, 2: 552.

30 Madison himself tried to expand House influence by preparing a motion requiring that treaties that affected territorial boundaries or navigation or fishing rights would have to be approved by the House as well as the Senate (September 7, 1787, in Hutson, *Supplement to Max Farrand's Records*, p. 262).

31 *RFC* July 24, 2: 105. For a recent interpretation of the creation of the presidency, see Sidney M. Milkis and Michael Nelson, *The American Presidency: Origins and Development, 1776–2002* (Washington, DC: CQ Press, 2003), chaps. 1–2.

32 *RFC* June 1, 1: 65–7, 70–1, 73–4.

felt that three individuals should share executive power, with each representing a different section of the country. Dickinson and Williamson agreed.[33]

This uncertainty made the delegates indecisive about the critical issue of the appropriate term of office for the president. Sherman and Gunning Bedford proposed a three-year executive term. For most others, the fact that Congress would appoint the executive seemed to require a longer term, to preserve the president's independence. William Davie called for a term lasting eight years, Luther Martin for eleven years, and Elbridge Gerry for fifteen years. Rufus King sarcastically called for a twenty-year term, quipping that "this is the median life of princes." Alexander Hamilton went to the extreme and advocated an appointment for life. Although Hamilton's preference was too extreme by far, even Oliver Ellsworth worried that frequent elections might make the executive less resolute than necessary in confronting those "duties which will make him unpopular for the moment."[34] Early in the convention, the delegates voted for a seven-year term by a narrow five-to-four margin and later rejected it on a vote of three states to five. On July 26, just before they turned their work over to the Committee on Detail, they restored a seven-year term with ineligibility for a second term, on a vote of seven states to three (Connecticut, Pennsylvania, and Delaware opposed).[35] By this time, of course, Madison and his allies viewed the executive's role much more positively than they had in May.

On the heels of the defeat of the national veto on July 17, Madison quickly elevated the executive as the champion of national interests against the parochialism of Congress. Madison drew on his catalog of state misbehavior to emphasize the states' tendency "to throw all power into the Legislative vortex. The Executives of the States are in general little more than Cyphers; the legislatures omnipotent." Republican government required that the national executive be strengthened as an

[33] *RFC* July 24, 2: 100–1; Hutson, *Supplement to Max Farrand's Records*, p. 87. On June 4 the delegates approved the single executive by a seven-to-three vote, over the opposition of Delaware, Maryland, and New York (1: 97). These same three states contributed to the New Jersey Plan, which provided for a multiple executive of unspecified number and powers to "appoint all federal officers not otherwise provided for, & to direct all military operations; provided that none of the persons composing the federal Executive shall on any occasion take command of any troops, so as personally to conduct any enterprise as General or in other capacity" (June 15, 1: 244). The proposal disappeared with the plan and the single executive was approved again without debate on July 17 (2: 29).

[34] RFC June 18, 1: 289; July 19, 2: 59; July 24, 2: 102–3.

[35] RFC June 1, 1: 68; July 19, 2: 258; July 26, 2: 120.

"effectual check... for restraining the instability & encroachments of the latter." The president's independent influence in policy making was vital for national interests: "[T]he collective interest & security were much more in the power belonging to the Executive than to the Judiciary."[36] Wilson, King, and Morris joined Madison in urging stronger presidential prerogatives. "One great object of the Executive is to controul the Legislature," said Morris, "The Executive therefore ought to be so constituted as to be the great protector of the Mass of the people."[37] The Committee of Detail did almost nothing to enhance presidential power, however. It named the executive "President," authorized the president to receive ambassadors and write to state governors, added the power to grant reprieves and pardons and the authority to adjourn Congress if houses could not agree on adjournment, and obliged the president to ensure that the laws "be duly and faithfully executed."[38]

After the Committee of Detail report, Madison and his allies battled insistently to strengthen presidential powers and institutional alliances to offset congressional power.[39] Sherman fought just as hard against Madison's efforts to expand presidential prerogatives.[40] As this struggle

[36] *RFC* July 17, 2: 34–5. Compare Madison's *Federalist* 48 on the way the "legislative department" draws "all power into its impetuous vortex." *Federalist* 48, p. 333.

[37] *RFC* July 19, 2: 52; Jack N. Rakove, *Original Meanings: Politics and Ideas in the Making of the Constitution* (New York: Alfred A. Knopf, 1996), p. 84.

[38] *RFC* August 6, 2: 185. The Committee of Detail seemed divided on the title of the executive office. Early drafts of committee reports allude to a "governor" of the United States (2: 144, 161). The final committee report established the title of "President of the United States of America" (2: 185). The Committee of Style simple vested "the executive power" in a "president of the United States of America," removing the capital "P" (2: 597). The final Constitution capitalizes the title. The Committee of Detail provided for a presidential oath: "Before he shall enter on the duties of his department, he shall take the following oath or affirmation, 'I ——— solemnly swear, (or affirm) that I will faithfully execute the office of President of the United States of America'" and "The members of the Legislatures, and the Executive and Judicial officers of the United States, and of the several States, shall be bound by oath to support this Constitution" (August 6, 2: 185, 188). At Mason's request, they added "and will to the best of my judgment and power preserve protect and defend the Constitution of the U.S." (August 27, 2: 427).

[39] Madison gave nearly unqualified support to executive power after July 16, but there were limits to his support. He moved, for example, to require a two-thirds vote of the Senate for approval of peace treaties, because the president would have so much power from a state of war, he might be tempted to impede a peace treaty (*RFC* September 7, 2: 540). Morris disagreed, saying no treaty should be made "without the concurrence of the President, who was the general Guardian of the National interests."

[40] *RFC* July 25, 1: 110; August 14, 2: 291; August 24, 2: 401–4; September 7, 2: 538; September 8, 2: 551; September 12, 2: 585. Sherman tried to take the initiative, by proposing that the Senate consent to presidential pardons. Sherman's effort to expand the Senate's

played out in specific issues, such as the veto, foreign policy, and appointments, the convention gradually settled on giving the president much more policy independence than either Madison or Sherman had sought at the beginning. At the same time, the convention also refused to create the cross-institutional alliances that Madison hoped would establish a stronger countervailing power against Congress.

The Veto

The Virginia Plan proposed "a council of revision," on which judges and the executive would share the power to veto bills approved by Congress. Throughout the convention, Madison insisted that judges should join with the president in exercising this shared veto. By forming an institutional alliance with the president, the judges, with lifetime appointments, could strengthen the resistance to any rash policies put forward by legislators. Madison drew on a British example to make his case, arguing that "The King of G[reat] B[ritain] with all his splendid attributes would not be able to withstand ye. unanimous and eager wishes of both houses of Parliament." Compared with a hereditary monarch, the president would lack preeminence, property, and "personal interest against betraying the National interest"; if the judges joined him in exercising the veto, they would inject "perspicuity, . . . conciseness, and . . . systematic character" into policy formation. Judges, in short, should be joined with the executive as codefenders of national interests. Such a joint veto did not violate the separation of powers but rather added "an auxiliary precaution" to that maxim.[41]

Several delegates, including some of Madison's allies, disagreed with him. They emphasized the importance of keeping the judiciary strictly separate from the political turmoil of republican lawmaking. Nathaniel Gorham thought that judges "are not to be presumed to possess any peculiar knowledge of the mere policy of public measures" and ought to

prerogatives was beaten back (August 25, 2: 419). Randolph made a last-minute effort to eliminate the president's power to grant pardons for treason, and Madison suggested that the Senate approval be required. Randolph's proposal was defeated, with only Virginia and Georgia in favor. This issue occasioned a disagreement between Johnson and Sherman, who uncharacteristically divided Connecticut's vote (September 15, 2: 626–7).

[41] *RFC* June 4, 1: 99–100, 108; June 6, 1: 138–9; July 21, 2: 77. Charles-Louis de Secondat, Baron de Montesquieu, *The Spirit of the Laws* (New York: Hafner Press, 1948), book 11, pp. 150–60. On the background of the executive veto power, see Charles J. Zinn, *The Veto Power of the President* (Washington, DC: Government Printing Office, 1951).

have "no prepossessions" about the laws they exposited. Charles Pinckney expected that the injection of judiciary into policy making would "involve them in parties."[42] The first time the convention considered the shared veto, Elbridge Gerry successfully moved to take up an executive veto instead. Alexander Hamilton and James Wilson proposed an absolute presidential veto, one that Congress could not override. Sherman, opposed to any presidential independence, objected to giving the president any veto power "to stop the will of the whole" and "overrule the decided and cool opinions of the Legislature." On an eight-to-two vote, the convention gave the president alone a power to veto legislation, while giving Congress the right to override the veto with a two-thirds vote in each house. Two days later, the delegates rejected a proposal by Wilson and Madison to give the veto jointly to the president and Supreme Court justices. Connecticut and New York, though, joined Virginia in support of this shared veto.[43]

After the compromise on congressional representation, Wilson and Madison again proposed that national judges join the executive in vetoing congressional acts. They advanced this argument primarily as a defensive measure against Congress. Gerry, though, still opposed "making Statesmen of the Judges," and fellow Massachusetts delegate Caleb Strong worried that the "Judges in exercising the function of expositors might be influenced by the part they had taken, in framing the laws." This time a fractured convention rejected the proposed shared veto by a single vote, three votes to four, with two states divided. Madison's coalition failed spectacularly. Only Delaware and Maryland joined Virginia to support the measure. Massachusetts and the South voted against Madison; Georgia and Pennsylvania divided. The convention reaffirmed support for the presidential veto and a two-thirds margin required to override it. The Committee of Detail report included this provision, specified that the bills the president refused to sign would become law, and added an end-of-session pocket veto.[44]

Madison and his allies subsequently battled to strengthen the president's veto power. When Madison proposed a modified version of the

[42] *RFC* June 6, 1: 139–40; July 21, 2: 73, 79, 80; August 15, 2: 298.

[43] *RFC* June 4, 1: 97–104; June 6, 1: 138–40. Weeks later, Ellsworth eloquently spoke of judges' ability to provide more "wisdom & firmness to the Executive" (July 21, 2: 73–4).

[44] *RFC* July 21, 2: 75, 80. The pocket veto provided that if the legislature adjourned after sending a bill to the president, the bill would not become law without his signature. With little debate (but with Massachusetts and New Hampshire opposed, possibly because of their distance from the capital), the convention on August 15 extended the period for presidential consideration of congressional bills from seven to ten days, excepting Sundays (2: 302).

shared veto, the convention dispatched it by a vote of three states to eight. Gouverneur Morris, aiming to strengthen the president's hand, immediately responded by pushing to raise the barrier to veto overrides. Hugh Williamson moved to increase the veto override requirement to three-quarters of each house as an alternative "to admitting the Judges into the business of legislation." Although Sherman cautioned that "We have gone far enough in forming the negative as it now stands," Williamson's motion passed, six states to three.[45] After the presidential compromise of early September increased presidential power, however, the delegates retreated toward Sherman's position. Williamson himself moved to lower the barrier to veto overrides back down to a two-thirds majority. The three southernmost states joined Connecticut, New Jersey, and Maryland to vote for the two-thirds requirement.[46] Note that the convention placed no limitations on the circumstances, place, or number of times the president could exercise this veto power.[47]

Foreign Policy

The convention also expanded the president's role in foreign affairs and military policy, where future national interests were most at risk. When the Committee of Detail gave the Congress the power to make war and the Senate the power to make treaties, it vested responsibility for implementing these policies to the president as "commander in chief of the Army and

[45] *RFC* August 15, 2: 298–302. Gunning Bedford and John Francis Mercer opposed any presidential veto, Bedford arguing that "the Representatives of the People were the best judges of what was for their interest, and ought to be under no external controul whatever." In a session already described as "tedious," Madison included this report: Madison, "observing that if the negative of the President was confined to *bills*; it would be evaded by acts under the form and name of Resolutions, votes &c – proposed that 'or resolve' should be added after 'bill' in the beginning of sect 13. with an exception as to votes of adjournment &c. – after a short and rather confused conversation on the subject, the question was put & rejected."

[46] As received from the Committee of Detail, the veto language provided that "Every bill, which shall have passed the House of Representatives and the Senate, shall, before it become a law, be presented to the President of the United States for his revision" (2: 181). The confusing discussion of this "presentment" clause on August 15 and 16 has created considerable difficulties of interpretation. See Seth Barrett Tillman, "A Textualist Defense of Article I, Section 7, Clause 3: Why *Hollingsworth v. Virginia* Was Rightly Decided, and Why *INS v. Chadha* Was Wrongly Reasoned," *Texas Law Review* 83 (Spring 2005). Madison certainly was trying to ensure that the president would influence legislation. The Committee of Style dropped all references to "for his revision" (2: 568, 593–4). The change was not discussed subsequently.

[47] Robert J. Spitzer, *The Presidential Veto: Touchstone of the American Presidency* (Albany: State University of New York Press, 1988), pp. 18–19.

Navy of the United States, and of the Militia of the Several States." After the Committee of Detail report, Madison and his allies fought to expand the president's foreign policy influence and shrink the role of the Senate. Because "the Senate represented the States alone," said Madison, "it was proper that the president should be an agent in Treaties." Gouverneur Morris questioned whether the Senate should have any role in treaties at all.[48] Over Sherman's opposition, the convention accepted Madison's and Gerry's motion to narrow Congress's authority to the power to "declare" rather than "make" war, permitting the president more discretion to deploy the military against immediate threats. The Committee on Postponed Matters transferred the authority to make treaties to the president but, at the same time, required treaty approval by an extraordinarily large two-thirds majority of the Senate. James Wilson suggested that the proportionally chosen House should join the Senate in approving treaties, but Sherman objected to this further surrender of Senate power, and Wilson's proposal was defeated overwhelmingly. In a subsequent discussion that surely exasperated other delegates, Sherman and Madison battled over the rules for a quorum on treaty votes, aiming to better ensure the outcomes they desired.[49]

The Policy Agenda

The convention greatly increased the president's interest in future policy by giving him responsibility to shape the nation's policy agenda. The Committee of Detail explicitly encouraged the president to participate in the initial stages of the policy process by providing Congress information on "the state of the Union" and by recommending "such measures as he shall judge necessary, and expedient." Gouverneur Morris moved to make such recommendations a presidential *duty*, and the convention accepted this change.[50] The president's power to convene either or both houses of Congress on extraordinary occasions implied even more power

[48] *RFC* August 6, 2: 185; August 23, 2: 392–3.

[49] *RFC* August 17, 2: 318–19; September 4, 2: 493–4, 498–9; September 7, 2: 538; September 8, 2: 540–50. The delegates temporarily acceded to Madison's proposal to permit a simple Senate majority for treaties of peace, but further deliberation reminded the delegates of the state interests that even a peace treaty could threaten (September 7, 2: 540–1). The delegates rejected Madison's proposal to give the Senate the power to conclude peace treaties without presidential approval if they could muster a two-thirds vote. Only Maryland and two of the southern states with exposed boundaries, South Carolina and Georgia, voted in favor of this proposal.

[50] *RFC* August 6, 2: 185; August 24, 2: 405.

to shape the agenda; this provision permitted the president to summon the Senate to deal with those issues uniquely in its purview.[51] The delegates understood that the veto power also would shape Congress's policy agenda. James Wilson acknowledged that the veto was "an extraneous" function, calculated not for executive goals but "for collateral purposes." He expected that the veto would force Congress to take presidential policy preferences into account, and that its "silent operation would therefore preserve harmony and prevent mischief."[52]

Appointments

The power to appoint national officers created well-known, tempting opportunities for political patronage. The delegates were wary of vesting this power in the executive. When Madison proposed to give the president the power to appoint judges, unless two-thirds of the Senate disagreed, Ellsworth opposed this transfer of power to the executive because the Senate's "right to supersede his nomination will be ideal only. A nomination under such circumstances will be equivalent to an appointment." Only the three largest states voted for Madison's proposal on July 21. The Committee of Detail report gave the Senate the power to appoint judges, ambassadors, and top executive officials, and gave Congress the power to appoint a treasurer; it gave the president only the power to "commission all the officers of the United States" and "appoint officers in all cases not otherwise provided for." New England and the three southernmost states defeated George Read's proposal to allow the president, instead of Congress, to appoint a treasurer.[53]

As unease about Senate power grew, the convention became more receptive to presidential appointments. Hugh Williamson said he "had

[51] *RFC* September 8, 2: 553.

[52] *RFC* June 4, 1: 100; June 6, 1: 140.

[53] *RFC* July 21, 2: 80–3; Committee of Detail, in 2: 167, 182; August 17, 2: 314–15. The convention refused to inject into the "necessary and proper" clause an explicit statement about Congress's power to establish offices (August 20, 2: 344–5). In late August, Sherman made a motion to ensure that offices would be established by law, but only Connecticut supported the motion. Dickinson suggested that some appointments be delegated to state governments, but this proposal also was defeated, three votes to six, with Connecticut, Virginia, and Georgia voting in favor of the proposal (August 24, 2: 404–6; August 25, 2: 419). Gerry's final effort to ensure that executive positions would be established by Congress failed when it was described as unnecessary (September 8, 2: 550, 553). The convention also approved presidential power to "fill up all vacancies that may happen during the recess of the Senate by granting Commissions which shall expire at the end of the next Session of the Senate" (September 7, 2: 540).

scarcely seen a single corrupt measure in the Legislature of N[orth] Carolina, which could not be traced up to office hunting" and was irritated that Congress was now free "to cut out offices for one another."[54] The Committee on Postponed Matters compromised by permitting the president to pick ambassadors, judges, and executive officers, but requiring the Senate to give its "advice and consent." This compromise gave the president substantial independent power to influence future policy administration and judicial interpretation, while it allowed the Senate to check executive appointments with which a majority of senators disagreed. When the convention discussed the committee's arrangement, Wilson and Pinckney objected to any Senate approval of appointees, seeking to distance the president from the Senate still further. Morris and King were conciliatory, however, and their flexibility helped the convention approve the compromise unanimously.[55] At the end of the convention, Rutledge and General Pinckney moved to strike a remaining provision requiring Congress to appoint a separate treasurer. Despite objections that the move would increase opposition to the Constitution (and Sherman's reiterated support for separate Senate and House votes), eight states voted to eliminate a congressionally controlled treasurer. Only the three largest states voted to retain the office (most likely because their relative weight in the House of Representatives would give them some leverage over the treasurer's selection).[56]

Multiple Officeholding

The delegates walled Congress off from the presidency when they prohibited members from serving in executive offices during their term in the legislature. Britain was evolving a government in which legislators in

[54] *RFC* August 14, 2: 287.

[55] *RFC* September 7, 2: 538–9. The committee also injected the vice president, the only other nationally elected officer, into the policy-making process as the presiding officer of the Senate (removing the Senate's presiding officer as the immediate successor to a disabled president). This decision is meaningful only in the context of Madison's effort to extend executive influence in Congress. Dissatisfied with the compromise giving the president contingent appointment power, Wilson had complained that the president could not "even appoint a tide-waiter without the Senate" (September 6, 2: 522).

[56] *RFC* September 14, 2: 614. To ensure the independence of American policy makers from foreign influence, the convention agreed to Pinckney's provision that "No person holding any office of profit or trust under the U.S. shall without the consent of the Legislature, accept of any present, emolument, office or title of any kind whatever, from any King, Prince or foreign State" (August 23, 2: 389).

Parliament also filled cabinet posts. The admired British authors David Hume and William Blackstone viewed this dual service as essential for the successful implementation of public policy.[57] Some of Madison's allies advocated the creation of similar opportunities for members of Congress. Alexander Hamilton invoked Hume in defending the notion that multiple officeholding facilitated the equilibrium of British institutions. Charles Pinckney and Nathaniel Gorham observed the Constitution would go further than any state or foreign country in separating offices. Like many outside the convention, though, a number of delegates believed that joint officeholding facilitated political corruption.[58] The Virginia Plan banned members of Congress from serving in any other state or national office during their term and for a year afterward, a proposal endorsed without debate. George Mason viewed this disqualification for other offices "as a corner stone in the fabric" and railed against the "venality and abuses" that resulted from multiple officeholding in Britain. Gorham's motion to drop the provision failed on a tie vote.[59] Madison tried to reframe the proposal so that legislators could not fill any offices established during their term or for a year afterward, or for which Congress had

[57] James Bryce, *The American Commonwealth*, 3rd ed. (New York: Macmillan, 1901), 1: 278–81; M. J. C. Vile, *Constitutionalism and the Separation of Powers* (Oxford: Clarendon Press, 1967), pp. 72–3, 106; Gordon S. Wood, *The Creation of the American Republic, 1776–1787* (Chapel Hill: University of North Carolina Press, 1969), pp. 32–3, 143–8.

[58] *RFC* June 22, 1: 376–80; August 21, 2: 284; September 3, 2: 491. By dispensing patronage for the purpose of securing support for his policies, the British king was viewed as corrupting the delicate balance of the British constitution. The ambitious quest for offices undermined the independence of the British Parliament and its resistance to the agenda of the king. The notion that patronage had corrupted British government had strong support at the Constitutional Convention (June 22, 1: 376). The state constitutions produced by the revolutionary governments severely limited, and in some cases destroyed, executive control over administrative and judicial appointments. Virginia banned multiple officeholding explicitly. See further Wood, *The Creation of the American Republic*, pp. 32–4, 148, 156–7. On June 23 Madison, who had not entered into the debate on multiple officeholding previously, now announced that he was concerned that members of Congress would create offices for themselves (*RFC* 1: 388).

[59] *RFC* May 29, 1: 20; June 12, 1: 211, 217; June 13, 1: 229; June 22, 1: 375–7. The next day, General Pinckney moved to permit members of the House to be eligible for state offices. Early on, the delegates narrowly voted against prohibiting members of the House from serving in state offices, four votes to five, with Connecticut, New York, and the Carolinas voting for this exception (June 12, 1: 217). Sherman, who had simultaneously held national, state, and local offices, quickly seconded Pinckney's motion, warning that "we are erecting a Kingdom at war with itself." Eight states voted for this motion, in a vote that brought together most of the smaller states with the South (June 23, 1: 386).

increased pay. The convention, however, decisively defeated Madison's modification.[60]

The Committee of Detail included the ban on multiple officeholding. Charles Pinckney tried to persuade the delegates to allow members of Congress to hold other offices without pay, expressing the hope that the Senate in particular would "become a School of Public Ministers, a nursery of Statesmen."[61] Elbridge Gerry, for one, did not want many ministers and did not "wish to establish nurseries for them." Sherman thought "The Constitution sh[oul]d lay as few temptations as possible in the way of those in power." A motion to consider Pinckney's motion lost on a tie vote.[62] The matter was dropped. In what may have been an explicit compromise, the Committee on Postponed Matters simply banned joint officeholding for members of Congress, without extending the ban past their term in office, and it banned other national officers from holding

[60] Madison conceded to Mason that legislatures were partial to their own members and might abuse a power to serve in multiple offices, but he also noted that the ban on multiple offices had thinned the pool of quality public officials. "The objects to be aimed at were to fill all offices with the fittest – characters, & to draw the wisest & most worthy citizens into the Legislative service" (*RFC* June 23, 1: 388). Wilson and King embraced Madison's qualified proposal, but Rutledge, Mason, and Sherman thought it did not go far enough, and Sherman detailed the imaginative ways corrupt legislators could evade the rule. In perhaps the most puzzling vote of the convention, Madison's motion lost two states to eight, with Connecticut and New Jersey voting for it, Virginia and Pennsylvania voting against it, and Massachusetts divided. Possibly the debate had made it seem a poisonous amendment whose approval would sink the idea entirely. On an eight-to-two vote, the delegates voted to make members of the House ineligible for other offices during the term for which they were elected (Pennsylvania and Georgia opposed and Massachusetts divided). Then they declined to add an additional year of ineligibility by a vote of four to six, with Massachusetts, Connecticut, New Jersey, Virginia, North Carolina, and Georgia against (June 23, 1: 390). The delegates then extended the ban to the Senate (June 26, 1: 429).

[61] *RFC* August 14, 2: 283. Wilson used the occasion to attack state agency in the Congress: "...as one branch of the Legislature was to be appointed by the Legislatures of the States, the other by the people of the States, as both are to be paid by the States, and to be appointable to State offices; nothing seemed to be wanting to prostrate the Nat[iona]l Legislature, but to render its members ineligible to Nat[ional]l offices, & by that means take away its power of attracting those talents which were necessary to give weight to the Govern[men]t and to render it useful to the people. He was far from thinking the ambition which aspired to Offices of dignity and trust, an ignoble or culpable one. He was sure it was not politic to regard it in that light, or to withhold from it the prospect of those rewards, which might engage it in the career of public service" (August 14, 2: 288).

[62] *RFC* August 6, 2: 180; August 14, 2: 283–90. When Charles Pinckney moved to eliminate representatives' and senators' ineligibility for other offices, Mason sarcastically moved to eliminate the whole section to facilitate the development of an aristocracy (August 14, 2: 284).

a seat in Congress.[63] Thus the convention deliberately kept the connections between the president and Congress weak, and their potential rivalry strong.

Collective Advice

Many delegates, including both Sherman and Madison, originally thought that an executive council would benefit the new government by limiting presidential discretion.[64] When the Committee of Detail initially made no provision for an executive council, Ellsworth and Morris each proposed one.[65] Accordingly, the Committee on Detail supplemented its

[63] Pinckney tried one last time to permit members of Congress to hold multiple public offices, as long as other offices offered no pay. Pinckney's proposal was defeated, with only the support of Pennsylvania and North Carolina. King and Williamson then sought to exclude members of Congress only from those offices created during their tenure in Congress. Morris, Gorham, and Wilson supported this amendment; Madison, a member of the committee, did not speak. Sherman opposed this provision but expressed a willingness to permit such appointments if salaries were not increased. Randolph, Mason, and Gerry all spoke against the provision. An amended version preventing appointments to offices "created or the emoluments whereof shall have been increased" won on a narrow five to four vote (Connecticut, New Jersey, Maryland, and South Carolina opposed). Then the clause prohibiting concurrent service in the Congress and an executive office was approved unanimously (*RFC* September 3, 2: 489–92).

[64] *RFC* June 1, 1: 66, 70, 74; June 4, 1: 96–7, 110. Wilson, though, thought a council "oftener serves to cover, than prevent malpractices" (June 4, 1: 97).

[65] *RFC* August 18, 2: 328–9; August 20, 2: 342–3. Gouverneur Morris proposed, with Pinckney's second, an elaborate Council of State to "assist the President in conducting the Public affairs . . . composed of . . . 1. The Chief Justice of the Supreme Court, who shall from time to time recommend such alterations of and additions to the laws of the U.S. as may in his opinion be necessary to the due administration of Justice, and such as may promote useful learning and inculcate sound morality throughout the Union: He shall be President of the Council in the absence of the President 2. The Secretary of Domestic Affairs who shall be appointed by the President and hold his office during pleasure. It shall be his duty to attend to matters of general police, the State of Agriculture and manufactures, the opening of roads and navigations, and the facilitating communications thro' the U.States; and he shall from time to time recommend such measures and establishments as may tend to promote those objects. 3. The Secretary of Commerce and Finance who shall also be appointed by the President during pleasure. It shall be his duty to superintend all matters relating to the public finances, to prepare & report plans of revenue and for the regulation of expenditures, and also to recommend such things as may in his Judgment promote the commercial interests of the U.S. 4. The Secretary of foreign affairs who shall also be appointed by the President during pleasure. It shall be his duty to correspond with all foreign Ministers, prepare plans of Treaties, & consider such as may be transmitted from abroad; and generally to attend to the interests of the U- S- in their connections with foreign powers. 5. The Secretary of War who shall also be appointed by the President during pleasure. It shall be his duty to superintend every thing relating to the war-Department, such as the raising and equipping of troops, the

recommendations with a privy council for the president. This advisory council would include the speaker of the House, the chief justice, and heads of departments. The convention never took up this idea. Instead, the Committee on Postponed Matters simply recommended that the president could require department heads to submit written reports on relevant topics. When Mason tried to resurrect the proposal for a privy council composed of members from different sections of the country, Morris explained that the committee felt that the council would do more harm than good by allowing the president to acquire protection for his "wrong measures" by "persuading his Council – to concur" in them.[66] The president would develop a future national policy agenda without formal input from the chief officer of the popularly elected branch of the Congress or the nation's chief magistrate.

Madison and his allies had more success enhancing independent presidential power than their colleagues who fought to defend the fiscal power of the House. But their success was limited. The president received a qualified veto, qualified appointment powers, and qualified influence over treaty powers, all "aspects of government business that did not fit neatly into the theory of the separation of powers."[67] They persuaded the convention to enhance the president's independent power to shape public policy, but they could not persuade the delegates to build bridges of

care of military Stores – public fortifications, arsenals & the like – also in time of war to prepare & recommend plans of offence and Defence. 6. The Secretary of the Marine who shall also be appointed during pleasure It shall be his duty to superintend every thing relating to the Marine-Department, the public Ships, Dock-Yards, Naval-Stores & arsenals also in the time of war to prepare and recommend plans of offence and defence. The President shall also appoint a Secretary of State to hold his office during pleasure; who shall be Secretary to the Council of State, and also public Secretary to the President. It shall be his duty to prepare all public despatches from the President which he shall countersign. The President may from time to time submit any matter to the discussion of the Council of State, and he may require the written opinions of any one or more of the members: But he shall in all cases exercise his own judgment, and either Conform to such opinions or not as he may think proper; and every officer abovementioned shall be responsible for his opinion on the affairs relating to his particular Department. Each of the officers abovementioned shall be liable to impeachment & removal from office for neglect of duty malversation, or corruption." This intriguing proposal disappeared in the Committee for Postponed Matters.

[66] *RFC* August 22, 2: 367; September 7, 2: 537, 539, 541–3. Franklin seconded Mason's motion, warning against the "caprice, the intrigues of favorites & mistresses," that plagued monarchies unchecked by councils. Dickinson supported a "Council"; Wilson "supported the idea to reduce the influence of the Senate." Madison thought the idea should be returned for further committee consideration. Mason's motion was defeated, three states (Maryland, South Carolina, and Georgia in favor) to eight.

[67] Vile, *Constitutionalism and the Separation of Powers*, p. 156.

institutional collaboration in national policy making. By rejecting collaborative arrangements, the convention increased the independent power and the rivalry of national policy-making institutions. At the same time, the failure of the national veto and other mechanisms for enforcing national interest made the delegates increasingly receptive to *judicial* independence.

THE RISE OF THE COURTS

While the convention added to the president's power to shape future policy, it was expanding the courts' power to defend established policy arrangements.[68] John Rutledge, Roger Sherman, and other judges were disposed to see law and courts as powerful independent forces for protecting established regimes. Many delegates hoped to protect judges from politics as much as possible. Gerry and King thought the presidential veto could insulate the judiciary from ruling on "the policy of public measures." James Wilson thought that "Judges would be in a bad situation if made to depend on every gust of faction which might prevail in the two branches of our Gov[ernmen]t."[69] The Virginia and New Jersey plans offered nearly identical proposals for the national judiciary. Judges would be appointed to unlimited terms "during good behaviour" and would "receive punctually at stated times a fixed compensation for their services in which no increase or diminution shall be made." These provisions won unanimous agreement even after the compromise on representation.[70] The provision for presidential appointment of national judges, with Senate advice and consent, also enhanced judicial independence.

As the delegates fleshed out the rivalries they were building into the policy-making process, the courts' independence made them increasingly willing to extend more authority to national judges. State courts in New York and Rhode Island had recently provided examples of the way an independent judiciary could check the implementation of popular legislation.[71] In three ways, the convention increased the likelihood that the

[68] Jack N. Rakove, "The Origins of Judicial Review: A Plea for New Contexts," *Stanford Law Review* 49 (1997): 1031–64.

[69] *RFC* June 4, 1: 97–8; August 27, 2: 429. John Francis Mercer believed the "true policy" of separating the courts from the legislature "is that legislative usurpation and oppression may be obviated.... He thought laws ought to be well and cautiously made, and then to be uncontroulable" (August 15, 2: 298).

[70] *RFC* May 29, 1: 21–2; June 15, 1: 244; July 18, 2: 41, 44.

[71] Wood, *The Creation of the American Republic*, pp. 453–63; Richard B. Morris, *The Forging of the Union: 1781–1789* (New York: Harper and Row, 1987), p. 128.

courts would influence American public policy independent of the other branches.

First, the convention enhanced the national judiciary's influence by allowing Congress to create a system with several national courts instead of a single Supreme Court. South Carolina's delegates and supporters of the New Jersey Plan instinctively opposed a system of inferior national courts as a threat to state judicial arrangements. Madison and his allies insisted that the inferior courts were necessary for an effective national government. Sherman was conciliatory, easing the way for the delegates' acceptance of inferior courts even though he "wished them to make use of the State Tribunals whenever it could be done with safety to the national interest." After the compromise on representation July 16, the delegates agreed to inferior courts without dissent or discussion.[72]

Second, the convention expanded the national courts' authority to deal with the nation's most politically sensitive issues. The Virginia Plan's authors won approval for their proposal to extend the national courts' jurisdiction broadly, to "questions which involve the national peace and harmony." Even after July 16, the convention agreed to this language without debate. The Committee of Detail limited this jurisdiction somewhat by recommending that the Supreme Court's jurisdiction extend to "all Cases arising under" congressional laws, "to Controversies between States" (except for conflicts over jurisdiction and territory), and to impeachment trials.[73] The national courts' specific jurisdiction expanded thereafter. The delegates explicitly extended the courts' jurisdiction to interstate disputes over territory, some of the most divisive issues in the nation. Sherman received unanimous support for replacing the cumbersome Confederation process for settling land disputes by simply adding this responsibility to the Supreme Court's jurisdiction. They gave national courts responsibility for umpiring the interstate requirements specified in the privileges and immunities clause and the "full faith and credit" clause. They extended jurisdiction to equity cases. Wilson assured the delegates that the Committee of Detail intended national courts to determine questions of fact as

[72] *RFC* June 5, 1: 119; June 15, 1: 244; July 18, 2: 46; August 17, 2: 314–15. James Willard Hurst concluded that Article III "left to Congress unqualified discretion in the creation of inferior courts and in the determination of how much of the allowable jurisdiction should be vested in the federal courts"; James Willard Hurst, *The Growth of American Law* (Boston: Little, Brown, 1950), p. 89.

[73] *RFC* June 13, 1: 232; July 18, 2: 46; Committee of Detail, in 2: 146–7; August 6, 2: 186–7. The Committee of Detail also proposed the allocation of original and appellate jurisdiction between the Supreme Court and lower national courts.

well as law, and questions of common law as well as statute law. Charles Pinckney even recommended that policy makers be permitted to request Supreme Court opinions on proposed laws. When Madison objected to impeachment trials by the Senate, delegates designated the chief justice as the manager of impeachment trials.[74]

Third, the delegates encouraged the courts to exercise judicial review, the power to invalidate state and national legislation when judged inconsistent with the Constitution.[75] Early on, Elbridge Gerry observed that the courts could defend their independence by expounding on the laws, including the constitutionality of laws. In states where courts exercised this power to review laws, Gerry thought they generally were praised. After July 16 the judicial power to review state laws became an increasingly important component of policy making. Morris was the first to suggest outright that "A law that ought to be negatived will be set aside in the Judiciary departm[en]t and if that security should fail; may be repealed by a Nation[a]l law." Luther Martin, a strident opponent of Morris and Madison in most matters, also acknowledged that "the Constitutionality of the laws, will come before the Judges in their proper official character. In this character they have a negative on the laws." Wilson warned that while courts could interpret laws, "this power . . . did not go far enough. . . . Laws may be unjust, may be unwise, may be dangerous, may be destructive; and yet not be so unconstitutional as to justify the Judges in refusing to give them effect." George Mason agreed that judges "could declare an unconstitutional law void." The convention agreed unanimously to expand the supremacy clause to include the Constitution as well as congressional laws (the requirement that national and state officials swear an oath to uphold the Constitution later was placed directly after the supremacy clause). Sherman reaffirmed that the supremacy clause allowed courts to exercise a kind of national veto over state laws.[76]

The delegates tacitly accepted the exercise of judicial review of *national* legislation. John Francis Mercer and John Dickinson criticized the extension of judicial review to national laws, and when Johnson moved

[74] *RFC* August 20, 2: 341; August 24, 2: 400–1; August 27, 2: 428–32; August 30, 2: 465–6; September 8, 2: 551.

[75] Gunning Bedford's notes on the presentation of the Virginia Plan suggest that the national veto could be appealed to the federal judiciary, allowing the federal courts to umpire potential disputes between state and national legislation (Hutson, *Supplement to Max Farrand's Records*, p. 27). Other convention records do not provide evidence that the Virginia Plan actually included this provision.

[76] *RFC* June 4, 1: 97–8; July 17, 2: 28; July 21, 2: 73, 76, 78; August 23, 2: 390–1.

to expand court authority to all legal cases involving "this Constitution" in addition to national law, Madison expressed reluctance to extend judicial power that far. The delegates acquiesced to it unanimously only when reassured that the phrase was limited to "cases of a Judiciary nature."[77] The delegates, then, knew that judicial review of national legislation was a distinct possibility and they knew it was controversial. But they never even considered a proposal to prohibit it. In this way, the convention allowed judicial review to "blossom."[78]

The convention underwrote an independent role for courts as vehicles for shaping public policy in the nation's interest. Congress, of course, retained substantial power over the courts through its power to determine who would serve as a federal judge, how many federal judges there would be, and what the jurisdiction of different levels would include.[79] But the Constitution's provisions for judicial selection, powers, and independence gave the national courts a fundamentally different perspective on national interest than that of Congress or the president. While the delegates increased the president's power to shape policy prospectively, they denied such power to the courts. They refused to involve judges in prospective policy influence, such as the national veto or privy council. The courts were left with the means and motive to judge only after the fact whether public policy was consistent with established conceptions of national interests.

AMENDING THE CONSTITUTION

No one disputed the need to provide for changing the Constitution. The Virginia Plan recommended that "provision ought to be made for the amendment of the Articles of Union" when necessary, and without the "assent of the National Legislature." Early on, some delegates questioned the need to permit the Constitution to be amended without the consent of the national legislature. The Committee of Detail accordingly lodged the initiative for constitutional amendments in the states, mandating Congress to call a Constitutional Convention on the application of

[77] *RFC* August 15, 2: 299; August 27, 2: 430.

[78] Vile, *Constitutionalism and the Separation of Powers*, p. 158; see also William N. Eskridge Jr., "All about Words: Early Understandings of the 'Judicial Power' in Statutory Interpretation, 1776–1806," *Columbia Law Review* 101:5 (June 2001): 990–1106.

[79] The delegates rejected a motion to broaden Congress's discretion ("[i]n all other cases... the Judicial power shall be exercised in such manner as the Legislature shall direct"; *RFC* August 27, 2: 431). Only Delaware and Virginia supported this motion.

two-thirds of the state legislatures. Although Gouverneur Morris suggested that Congress be allowed to call for a constitutional convention at will, the delegates approved the Committee of Detail report unanimously.[80]

In the convention's final week, its provision for constitutional amendment was being attacked from two sides. Gerry, who now distrusted national power worried that two-thirds of the states could use the process to subvert state constitutions. Hamilton worried more about state encroachments on national powers and warned that "The State Legislatures will not apply for alterations but with a view to increase their own powers." Sherman proposed that Congress submit amendments to the states, a procedure that ultimately became the most common method for amending the Constitution. The delegates quibbled over the threshold for ratifying amendments, narrowly rejecting ratification by a minimum of two-thirds of the states (Massachusetts, Connecticut, and New Jersey joined the three southernmost states in opposition) before unanimously accepting a minimum of three-quarters. Madison then moved to include other alternatives for the amendment process and to require a two-thirds vote of the House and Senate for amendments initiated by Congress. The convention overwhelmingly approved Madison's additions.[81] In the end, the delegates had arranged for constitutional changes only if an extraordinary geographical and political majority supported them.

THE CONSTITUTION, THE POLICY PROCESS, AND POLITICAL STRATEGY

The Constitutional Convention used no predetermined blueprint to lay out the national policy process. Republican principles demanded only that the powers to legislate, to execute the law, and to judge legal disputes be separated in some way. Practical experience encouraged a bicameral legislature, an executive with veto power, and courts divorced from the play of politics. The delegates assumed that skilled republican politicians would use the process to advantage themselves and their constituents. Beyond these indefinite guidelines, the convention built the policy process piece by piece. Decisions about the policy process were pushed along by an evolving web of agreements about whom each branch would represent,

[80] *RFC* June 5, 1: 121–2; June 11, 1: 202–3; July 23, 2: 87; in Committee of Detail, in 2: 148–9, 174, 188; August 30, 2: 468.

[81] *RFC* September 10, 2: 557–9.

what powers the national government would have, and what role each institution would play in using this process.

As the delegates grew less certain about the consequences of their choices, political logic dictated that they should arm their favored agents with the will and ability to stop policies threatening to their vital interests. They could not agree on the exact boundaries of national authority, but they could agree that by building separate defenses for their favored institutions, they could reduce the danger that the national government would use its authority to take advantage of their constituents. Their choices in turn forced them to adjust the powers and independence of these institutions to one another. The Senate gained extraordinary powers to ratify treaties, confirm presidential appointees, and try impeachments. The House gained nominal authority to initiate revenue measures. The president gained influence over the policy agenda, major appointments, and foreign affairs. Courts gained more autonomy to interpret state and national laws. The convention rejected efforts to build institutional collaboration into national policy making, including proposals to require the joint exercise of veto power by the president and the Supreme Court, the creation of a privy council, and the eligibility of sitting members of Congress to serve in executive offices.

When their work was done, the delegates found that they had created a policy-making process with more complexity and rivalry of purpose than any of them originally anticipated. They had infused each institution with a different perspective on the nation's interests. They had given each institution the power to block the use of government. By doing so, they made it difficult and costly to make effective national public policy, that is, to use the government for any purpose. Public policy would succeed only if it survived a gauntlet of institutions, each deliberately anchored by different constituencies, calendars, and powers.

Members of Congress would be tied to distinct geographical constituencies, and the interests of these constituents would shape their perception of national interests. Most U.S. representatives would concern themselves primarily with the welfare of regions smaller than a state. U.S. senators would act on behalf of the state governments and statewide constituencies. Representatives and senators could pursue reelection. Each Congress would have a two-year frame of reference, because the political dynamics in each house could change after every national election. Veto points would abound: the Senate and House effectively could veto each other, and the president could veto any bill on which they could agree. It would be relatively easy for one institution to exercise its independent power to stop legislation, but it would be relatively difficult to engineer the institutional cooperation required to enact laws. On the other hand, it would be difficult, costly, and time-consuming for representatives of existing regional interests to construct the political majorities necessary for lawmaking. Only an extraordinarily large geographical majority could win concurrent House and Senate approval for any public policy measure. For example, no law could be passed in the first Congress without, at a bare minimum, the consent of representatives of 55 percent of the American population.[82] No treaty or major appointment could be made without the assent of senators representing nine of the thirteen states.

Compared with Congress, the president and his appointees to the national courts would serve much larger constituencies, and their constituencies would greatly broaden their perception of national interests. The president would represent at least a large number of voters in many parts of the nation. Given a four-year term, the president would serve during two Congresses. The possibility of reelection to additional terms further lengthened his time horizon. The president's agenda-setting, administrative, and foreign-policy powers armed the office with the power to change the path of public policy. Presidents could frame policy agendas aimed at directing policy outcomes and building political support well into the future, and so would define the national interest in terms of prospective achievements that cultivate a chosen national constituency.[83] Presidents could be expected to build new national political orders or to articulate existing ones. The president would tend to pursue national interests more proactively than Congress, more coherently, and for longer time horizons.

[82] For example, a minimum winning coalition of New England and the middle states would require New Hampshire (with three representatives and two senators), Massachusetts (eight representatives and two senators), Connecticut (five representatives and two senators), New York (five representatives and two senators), New Jersey (four representatives and two senators), and Pennsylvania (eight representatives and two senators) and a senator from another state, either Rhode Island or Delaware (each with two senators but only one representative). This coalition of states would represent 54 percent of the House of Representatives, 55 percent of the population of the thirteen states according to the 1790 census, and 56 percent of the October 1786 Confederation requisition. A minimum winning coalition that included all the large states would require the unanimous support of representatives from Virginia (ten representatives), Pennsylvania (eight), and Massachusetts (eight) and, for example, Maryland (six) and the three states with the smallest representation: Georgia (three), Delaware (one), and Rhode Island (one). This coalition represented about 57 percent of the House of Representatives and of the population of the thirteen states according to the 1790 census, and 60 percent of the October 1786 requisition.

[83] Stephen Skowronek, *The Politics Presidents Make: Leadership From John Adams to Bill Clinton*, 2nd ed. (Cambridge, MA: Belknap Press, 1997), p. 20.

While the Senate embodied Sherman's aspiration to protect the interests of the states, the office of the president embodied Madison's ambition to instill in national policy makers the means and motive to pursue national interests, independent of the states.

No institution would view public policy in a longer time horizon than the national judiciary, whose judges would not have to cultivate voters to stay in office. Compared with Congress, and like the president, the national judiciary would have more latitude to define national interests broadly. But judges would lack the policy tools necessary for fine-tuning a future policy agenda. Judges' tools were reactive. They could only respond to disputes about actions already authorized by other institutions. Judges could settle disputes about existing national law and strike down laws inconsistent with the Constitution. Together, these powers would allow judges to defend existing political arrangements rather than to fashion new ones. Judges would have incentives to interpret national interest in the context of the political order in which they had been appointed. The national judiciary would tend to frame national interests more coherently than Congress but more reactively than the president.[84]

The delegates' compromises, in short, produced a policy-making system that would be hard to use. Different institutions with different perspectives on national interest would share responsibility for major steps in the policy process, from setting the policy agenda to implementing law. By providing these institutions with the power to defend against harmful policies, the Constitution made political cooperation extraordinarily difficult by erecting high barriers to national political coalitions bent on any public policy that would harm even a minority of the states. Presidents could clash with Congress over control of the policy agenda and over policy implementation, while courts would clash with other branches over the meaning and enforcement of public policy. Late in August, Madison pointed out that it was safe to permit a simple Senate majority for commercial laws because the delegates already had built so many defenses into policy-making institutions and the selection of their officials. Abuses were improbable, he said, because of "the provision of 2 branches – by the independence of the Senate, by the negative of the Executive, by the interest of Connecticut & N[ew] Jersey which were agricultural, not commercial States – by the interior interest which was also agricultural in the most commercial States – by the accession of Western States which w[oul]d

[84] National courts can and have shaped the outcome of policy disputes and the future path of public policy by invoking one definition of national interest rather than another.

be altogether agricultural."[85] The states' agents could delay, defeat, or extract concessions for the expansion and use of national powers.

To use this government successfully would require extraordinarily large political coalitions and extraordinary effort. Only a large majority could align the interests of the House, the Senate, and the presidency, any one of which could torpedo policies to which it objected. The delegates had negotiated a government that would be hard for anyone to use to impede national economic development driven by markets. It also was a government that would be hard to use to manage economic development.

In *Federalist* 51, published only five months after he signed the Constitution, James Madison made the best of these expedient political compromises and the unexpected constitutional design they produced. Defending the Constitution to New Yorkers, he portrayed them as logical and principled.

> In order to lay a due foundation for that separate and distinct exercise of the different powers of government, which to a certain extent, is admitted on all hands to be essential to the preservation of liberty, it is evident that each department should have a will of its own; and consequently should be so constituted that the members of each should have as little agency as possible in the appointment of the members of the others.... Were the executive magistrate, or the judges, not independent of the legislature in this particular, their independence in every other would be merely nominal. But the great security against a gradual concentration of the several powers in the same department, consists in giving to those who administer each department the necessary constitutional means, and personal motives, to resist encroachments of the others. The provision for defense must in this, as in all other cases, be made commensurate to the danger of attack. Ambition must be made to counteract ambition. The interest of the man must be connected with the constitutional rights of the place.[86]

As a factual description of the framers' intentions, *Federalist* 51 plainly is disingenuous. But as a prediction of the logic of American political development, it is prescient. The framers could not have anticipated the politics that subsequently developed in the United States, but they would not be entirely surprised by the consequences of the political logic they set in motion. America's politicians – including many of the delegates themselves – became skilled, inventive, and creative architects of politics adapted to the constitutional rules the framers bequeathed them.

[85] *RFC* August 29, 2: 452.
[86] *Federalist* 51, pp. 348–9.

8

Our Inheritance

The Constitution and American Politics

> Look through [the Constitution] from beginning to end, and you will not find an article which is not founded on the presumption of a clashing of interests.
>
> – Senator (and former Constitutional Convention delegate) Jonathan Dayton, November 24, 1803

The delegates who came to Philadelphia in the spring of 1787 could not have envisioned the Constitution they signed in September, or the uses to which Americans would put it. Their Constitution was the by-product of unanticipated political compromises. Instead of fully solving their central political dilemma – to ensure satisfactory public policy from a republican national government that would not itself threaten their vital interests – they had narrowed the scope of the problem. They built a partially finished national policy-making process, furnished it with an incomplete set of policy tools, and required extraordinary cooperative efforts to make the government work.

James Madison was among the first Americans to put the Constitution to work. Elected to the first House of Representatives, Madison initially urged his colleagues to interpret national powers and presidential authority broadly, as he had at the Constitutional Convention. But when Secretary of the Treasury Alexander Hamilton proposed economic plans diametrically opposed to his vision for the nation's economic development, Madison began to bring together Hamilton's opponents in a coalition unified by limited constitutional authority and states' rights. As secretary of state and later president, Madison used the Constitution with principled flexibility to achieve his policy purposes.

Madison's experiences illustrate the Constitution's enduring effects on America's destiny. The Constitution has made it difficult – but not impossible – for Americans to use their government to accomplish their policy purposes. The Constitution's authority and its ambiguity have encouraged Americans to employ the Constitution as a weapon to win substantive policy conflicts by arguing about its meaning. Lacking the tools of economic sovereignty, state policy makers have confronted an intense interstate economic competition that has made many of them prone to resist policies that jeopardize private investment. National policy-making institutions have given national officials conflicting policy roles and perspectives on national interest, making it difficult for the national government to pursue a coherent and consistent course of public policy. These institutional incentives, in turn, have influenced the unique way that Americans conduct their politics. American federalism and the separation of powers have made it difficult to build successful, broad-based political parties around a detailed, coherent policy program. The interplay of these institutions and evolving strategies helps explain why American politics became so different from politics in comparable nations.

BRINGING THE CONSTITUTION TO LIFE

Many of the Constitution's signers returned home to fight for it in their states' special ratifying conventions. Gunning Bedford Jr. helped Delaware become the first state to ratify in early December 1787. Several days later at the Blazing Star Tavern in Trenton, David Brearley signed New Jersey's unanimous ratification. In Philadelphia, James Wilson staunchly defended the plan in Pennsylvania's lopsidedly pro-Constitution ratifying convention. Roger Sherman, Oliver Ellsworth, and William Samuel Johnson helped persuade Connecticut's convention in Hartford to ratify overwhelmingly. In Boston, Rufus King, Nathaniel Gorham, and Caleb Strong stood up for the Constitution in a closely divided Massachusetts convention. A political deal secured Massachusetts governor John Hancock's endorsement, in return for a list of recommended constitutional amendments and support for the governor's reelection. In Charleston, John Rutledge, Pierce Butler, and both Pinckneys convinced their fellow convention delegates that the Constitution benefited South Carolina and protected slavery. And in the summer of 1788, while James Madison and his allies effectively beat back former Virginia governor Patrick Henry's efforts to kill ratification in the Richmond convention, Alexander Hamilton took up the battle for ratification against Governor George Clinton and his allies at New York's convention in Poughkeepsie. Virginia and New York narrowly ratified the Constitution, with both states insisting on amendments to protect state powers and individual rights. The Confederation Congress called for national elections and arranged for the new government to start up in the spring of 1789. Despite the tumultuous debates over ratification in 1787 and 1788, nearly all its Antifederalist opponents quickly acquiesced to the Constitution when it took effect.[1]

In all these ratification debates, the Constitution's advocates had promoted it as a safe remedy for the Confederation's obvious economic problems. Edmund Randolph, who supported ratification on the condition that the Constitution be amended, clearly reached out to those Virginians who had been disaffected by the inadequacies of economic policy under the Confederation.

> Candor, sir, requires an undisguised representation of our situation. . . . Many citizens have found justice strangled and trampled under foot, through the course of jurisprudence in this country. Are those who have debts due to them satisfied with your government? Are not creditors wearied with the tedious procrastination of your legal process – a process obscured by legislative mists? Cast your eyes to your seaports: see how commerce languishes. This country, so blessed, by nature, with every advantage that can render commerce profitable, through defective legislation is deprived of all the benefits and emoluments she might otherwise reap from it. We hear many complaints on the subject of located lands; a variety of competitors claiming the same lands under legislative acts, public faith prostrated, and private confidence destroyed.[2]

In South Carolina, John Rutledge's brother Edward asked rhetorically, "Could [the Confederation] obtain security for our commerce in any part of the world? Could it force obedience to any one law of the Union? Could it obtain one shilling of money for the discharge of the most honorable obligations?"[3] Oliver Ellsworth's letters from "A Landholder" reminded New England's farmers that "every foreign prohibition on American trade is aimed in the most deadly manner against the holders and tillers of the land, and they are the men made poor. Your only remedy is such a national government as will make the country respectable, such a supreme

[1] Patrick T. Conley and John P. Kaminski, eds., *The Constitution and the States: The Role of the Original Thirteen in the Framing and Adoption of the Federal Constitution* (Madison, WI: Madison House, 1988); David J. Siemers, *Ratifying the Republic: Antifederalists and Federalists in Constitutional Time* (Stanford, CA: Stanford University Press, 2002), pp. 25–73.

[2] Randolph in the Virginia ratifying convention, June 6, 1788, in *ED* 3: 66.

[3] Edward Rutledge in the South Carolina ratifying convention, in *ED* 4: 274.

government as can boldly meet the supremacy of proud and self-interested nations."[4]

Although the new government enjoyed more power, its leaders would confront most of the same divisive economic problems that had stymied the Confederation. The interests of northerners and southerners, or of manufacturers, merchants, and farmers, were no more compatible than they had been when the Annapolis Convention met in 1786. Congress would need to make politically charged decisions about raising revenues, paying debts, and better defending the nation. Westerners still demanded the right to ship goods on the Mississippi and needed defense against Native Americans. Southerners still sought to improve markets for tobacco and rice. South Carolina and Georgia insisted on importing slaves. New Englanders still wanted trade agreements guaranteeing access to European markets and Atlantic fisheries. Some Americans sought close trading ties to Britain, whereas others sought more trade with France and other British rivals. On top of these issues, the government had to establish its new offices, rules, and routines.

Most of the Constitution's framers helped bring this new government to life.[5] James Madison, denied one of Virginia's U.S. Senate seats by Patrick Henry's partisans, instead won a seat in the first House of Representatives, where he served four terms. Roger Sherman concluded his distinguished career serving Connecticut in Congress, first as a U.S. representative and, in 1791, as a U.S. senator appointed to fill the unexpired term of William Samuel Johnson (Sherman died a senator in 1793). Voters eventually sent eleven of the Constitution's signers to serve in the U.S. House of Representatives. State legislatures selected fifteen to serve in the U.S. Senate.[6] George Washington, elected the nation's first

[4] "The Landholder," Letter 1, November 5, 1787, in *Friends of the Constitution: Writings of the "Other" Federalists, 1787–1788*, ed. Colleen A. Sheehan and Gary L. McDowell (Indianapolis, IN: Liberty Fund, 1998), p. 287.

[5] Of the thirty-nine signers, three died in 1790 (Benjamin Franklin, Daniel of St. Thomas Jenifer, and William Livingston). Almost 90 percent of the surviving signers served in federal government posts. Thomas Mifflin served as governor of Pennsylvania during the 1790s. John Dickinson retired from politics. Jacob Broom became a postmaster. Nathaniel Gorham engaged in land speculation.

[6] James Madison, Roger Sherman, Charles Pinckney, Hugh Williamson, Daniel Carroll, Richard Dobbs Spaight, Abraham Baldwin, Jonathan Dayton, George Clymer, Thomas Fitzsimons, and Nicholas Gilman were elected to the U.S. House of Representatives. Sherman, Gouverneur Morris, Rufus King, Charles Pinckney, George Read, William Samuel Johnson, William Paterson, Pierce Butler, Abraham Baldwin, John Langdon, Jonathan Dayton, William Few, Richard Bassett, Robert Morris, and William Blount served in the U.S. Senate.

president, appointed Alexander Hamilton as secretary of the treasury and Edmund Randolph as U.S. attorney general (and later secretary of state). In time, James McHenry served as secretary of war, Gouverneur Morris and General Charles Cotesworth Pinckney each served as minister to France, Rufus King as minister to Great Britain, and the younger Charles Pinckney as minister to Spain. Oliver Ellsworth became chief justice of the U.S. Supreme Court. James Wilson, John Rutledge, William Paterson, and John Blair served as associate justices on the Court.[7] In 1804 and 1808 General Charles Cotesworth Pinckney unsuccessfully ran for president as the nominee of the Federalist Party, and in 1816 Rufus King unsuccessfully ran as the last presidential candidate nominated by the fading Federalists. James Madison eventually served as secretary of state from 1801 to 1809, and as president from 1809 to 1817.

No one made use of the Constitution more effectively than Madison. He became the unofficial floor leader of the first House of Representatives, where he helped establish new rules and procedures. He steered the House agenda as he had tried to steer the convention, taking up a national tariff as a first order of substantive business for the revenue-starved government. He helped construct political compromises on specific import duties, building the necessary legislative majority for the tariff bill. True to promises he made his constituents as a candidate for the House, Madison proposed a bill of rights and shepherded it through Congress.[8] Behind the scenes, he advised President Washington on titles, appointments, and policy initiatives. He served as a ghostwriter for Washington's inaugural address, then wrote the House of Representative's formal response to Washington's address, and finally wrote Washington's response to the House and Senate.[9]

Madison's policy positions during the first session of Congress in 1789 closely matched his positions at the convention. Madison remained true to the principles of republicanism, market-driven economic development, and Virginia's interests. Still wary of the states, he advocated broad

[7] For a brief period, Rutledge served as chief justice, but the Senate did not confirm his appointment. Gunning Bedford and David Brearley served as federal district court judges, and Jared Ingersoll served as U.S. district attorney for Pennsylvania.

[8] Madison wanted the amendments to be placed in the original wording so that the written document would be altered accordingly, as is done today with the United States Code or state revised statutes. Roger Sherman persuaded the House that the amendments should be appended to the end of the Constitution. *DHFFC* August 13, 1789, 11: 1208–9; August 19, 1789, 11: 1308. The Bill of Rights was ratified in December 1791.

[9] Ralph Ketcham, *James Madison: A Biography* (Charlottesville: University Press of Virginia, 1971), p. 284.

interpretations of national economic authority and executive power. When newly appointed Treasury Secretary Alexander Hamilton asked his advice on raising revenues in the fall of 1789, Madison urged Hamilton to consider direct taxes on liquor and a national tax on land, hoping to preempt the states from establishing a claim to this kind of revenue.[10] He tried but failed to include in the Bill of Rights a provision to protect the "equal rights of conscience ... freedom of the press ... [and] trial by jury in criminal cases" from *state* interference.[11] He persuaded a wary House that the president should remove his appointees at his discretion, rather than seeking legislators' permission to remove them, setting a precedent that permanently enhanced presidential independence.[12] When other representatives objected to Hamilton's proposed authority to "digest and report plans" for improving public revenues and funding public debts, Madison defended Hamilton's request by warning of "the danger and inconvenience of not having well-formed and digested plans."[13]

But Hamilton soon proposed economic policies that threatened Madison's vital interests. Hamilton recommended that the federal government assume responsibility for all the existing state debts, as well as the Confederation government debts. This proposal benefited Massachusetts, Connecticut, and South Carolina, but it stirred deep resentment in Virginia, Maryland, North Carolina, and Georgia, states that had imposed austere measures to reduce their own debts. Hamilton also proposed to pay the investors who held federal debts at the face value of Confederation-era

[10] Madison to Hamilton, November 19, 1789, in *PJM* 12: 450. Virginia had used land taxes in the 1780s; Jackson Turner Main, *Political Parties before the Constitution* (Chapel Hill: University of North Carolina Press, 1973), pp. 250–1.

[11] Madison in the House of Representatives, in *PJM* 12: 202. When South Carolina representative Thomas Tudor Tucker proposed to add the word "expressly" before the word "delegated" in what would be the Tenth Amendment ("The powers not delegated by this Constitution, nor prohibited to it by the States, are reserved to the States respectively"), Madison objected, stating that "it was impossible to confine a Government to the exercise of express powers. There must necessarily be admitted powers by implication, unless the constitution descended to recount every minute." He had also helped remove a similar stipulation from the recommendations of the Virginia ratifying convention. Madison in the House of Representatives, August 18, 1789, in *PJM* 12: 346.

[12] *DHFFC* April 20, 1789, 10: 211–13. Sherman commented that the committee that considered the matter had gone "as far as warranted by the Constitution." See also Jack N. Rakove, *The Beginnings of National Politics: An Interpretive History of the Continental Congress* (New York: Alfred Knopf, 1979), pp. 80–91; David P. Currie, *The Constitution in Congress: The Federalist Period, 1789–1801* (Chicago: University of Chicago Press, 1997), pp. 7–115.

[13] *DHFFC* June 25, 1789, 10: 1072.

securities. This proposal benefited financial investors and speculators who currently owned these notes, but angered many veterans, farmers, and other original owners who had sold off their notes at a fraction of their face value. Madison and others were incensed. The treasury secretary's proposals seemed designed to benefit New England and the urban centers at the expense of the South and rural areas.[14] Madison, Hamilton, and other political leaders settled their policy disagreement with the national government's first major political deal: Madison agreed to permit the national assumption of state and Confederation debts, while Hamilton agreed that the nation's permanent capital could be located on the Potomac River, a location favored by Virginia.[15]

Hamilton next proposed a new national bank, modeled on the Bank of England, and a far-reaching policy for protecting, subsidizing, and promoting manufactures in the United States. Now Hamilton had gone too far. Madison, Thomas Jefferson, and their political allies believed the national economic interest depended on expanding agriculture and commodity exports, not on cultivating manufacturing and centralized finance. Unbridled commercial and manufacturing development in the North and East threatened Madison's political base: small farmers, advocates of western agricultural expansion, and the South. Yet Madison confronted a serious tactical problem in trying to unify these potential allies against Hamilton. Slavery made it difficult to form a policy alliance of southern plantation owners and small farmers in the North and Northwest. It would have been difficult or impossible for these disparate opponents to unify around a comprehensive agenda for using national economic power actively in a way different from that proposed by Hamilton.

[14] Consistent with his position at the Constitutional Convention, Sherman thought it desirable to assume state debts, "But, at the same time, I think the debts to be assumed, ought to consist of those only which were incurred for common or particular defence during the last war; and not those debts which a state may have incurred for the support of its government, the protection and encouragement of its manufactures, or for amending and opening highways – clearing the obstructions in the navigation of rivers – or any other local purpose, undertaken merely for the benefit of one or two states" (*DHFFC* February 23, 1790, 12: 508–9).

[15] E. James Ferguson, *The Power of the Purse: A History of Public Finance, 1776–1790* (Chapel Hill: University of North Carolina Press, 1961), pp. 251–325; Rakove, *The Beginnings of National Politics*, pp. 90–1; Lance Banning, *The Sacred Fire of Liberty: James Madison and the Founding of the Federal Republic* (Ithaca, NY: Cornell University Press, 1995), pp. 311–21; D. Roderick Kiewiet, "Vote Trading in the First Federal Congress? James Madison and the Compromise of 1790," in *James Madison: The Theory and Practice of Republican Government*, ed. Samuel Kernell (Stanford, CA: Stanford University Press, 2003), pp. 264–302.

Instead of uniting opponents of Hamilton's plans around an alternative economic program, therefore, Madison simply used the Constitution's ambiguity to attack Hamilton's claims for national authority. It "was not possible to discover in [the Constitution] the power to incorporate a Bank," Madison advised the House. The Constitution should be interpreted strictly; "[I]f a power was not given, Congress could not exercise it." Hamilton's plans, he argued, exceeded the federal government's constitutional authority and violated the "necessary and proper" clause, which, he asserted, narrowly authorized only specific means to enumerated ends. A national bank would undermine state economic management by interfering with state banks, and "the rights of the States, to prohibit as well as to establish Banks, and the circulation of Bank Notes." If Congress could establish a bank, he warned, it might charter corporations, cut canals (powers he himself had urged the Constitutional Convention to adopt), or "establish religious teachers in every parish."[16] Madison stoked fears of federal intrusion into the most deeply held cultural practices of the various states.

Madison, Jefferson, and their allies had hit upon a policy platform that could unite a political majority while avoiding divisive issues like slavery that could fatally fracture their anti-Hamilton alliance. These politicians began to construct a self-styled "republican party" to oppose Hamilton's positions. They built it on the defense of states' economic authority and on attacking national power to centralize commercial and financial management. Although Congress enacted Hamilton's bank proposal, the bank battle solidified the opposition bloc of legislators representing southern and peripheral agricultural areas. Madison soon instigated the development of opposition newspapers that attacked Hamilton and his political allies. Madison and Jefferson also built alliances with political leaders beyond Virginia, most ironically with Governor George Clinton of New York, an avid opponent of ratification, but an even more avid opponent of Alexander Hamilton.[17]

Thus, the Constitution made it easier for opponents of consolidated national economic power to organize around the defense of states' economic policy prerogatives than around an alternative program for using

[16] Madison in the House of Representatives, February 2, 1791, in *PJM* 13: 375. See also Jack N. Rakove, *Original Meanings: Politics and Ideas in the Making of the Constitution* (New York: Alfred A. Knopf, 1996), pp. 350–5.

[17] Rakove, *The Beginnings of National Politics*, pp. 92–123; James Rogers Sharp, *American Politics in the Early Republic: The New Nation in Crisis* (New Haven, CT: Yale University Press, 1993); Banning, *The Sacred Fire of Liberty*, pp. 321–65.

national power. For them, the defense of "states' rights" remained a winning formula that united diverse, far-flung, and self-governing agricultural constituencies in opposition to the centralizing commercial pretensions of Hamilton's emerging Federalist Party, without directly threatening the distinct political orders constructed in each state. States' rights appealed to farmers and small entrepreneurs, and nurtured coalitions across states with different political economies and at different points of development. By the end of the 1790s, Madison had come full circle, espousing claims of states' rights that his convention opponents easily could have endorsed. His Virginia Resolution of 1798, expressing his state's opposition to the policies of Federalist President John Adams, declared that national authority was "limited by the plain sense and intention" of the Constitution to enumerated powers. Virginia called on other states to join in declaring the actions of the Adams government unconstitutional.[18]

When Jefferson became president three years later, these same Democratic-Republican Party leaders had to readjust their view of the Constitution yet again. Confronted with the unexpected opportunity to purchase the Louisiana Territory from France, Madison advised Jefferson that the government needed no specific constitutional authority to add territory to the United States, even though the Constitution had no specific provision authorizing such an acquisition.[19] When President Madison himself was faced with financial demands of impending war with Britain, he reversed position on the constitutionality of the Bank of the United States and supported its extension.[20] But at the end of his presidency, when Congress sent him a bill authorizing federal road and canal projects across the nation (and a bill believed to be consistent with his wishes), Madison vetoed the bill as a threat to the "definite partition" between the "General and State Governments."[21]

[18] Virginia Resolution, in *PJM* 17: 188–91.

[19] Ketcham, *James Madison: A Biography*, pp. 421, 506.

[20] Ibid. Madison also played a part in establishing the Supreme Court's power of judicial review. When he became secretary of state, Madison refused to deliver John Adams's last-minute appointment as a federal justice of the peace to one William Marbury. Marbury sued Madison to deliver the appointment, and the Supreme Court received the case. Chief Justice John Marshall, himself a Federalist appointed by Adams, wrote an opinion that asserted the Court's institutional prerogative of judicial review, to rule invalid those congressional acts inconsistent with the Constitution. Marshall served as chief justice for over three decades, issuing Federalist interpretations of the Constitution for many years after the Federalist Party itself had passed away. See Mark A. Graber, *Marbury versus Madison: Documents and Commentary* (Washington, DC: CQ Press, 2002).

[21] John Lauritz Larson, *Internal Improvement: National Public Works and the Promise of Popular Government in the Early United States* (Chapel Hill: University of North Carolina Press, 2001), pp. 64–9. Madison's veto message stated that " 'The power to

Madison's principled flexibility never dented his growing reputation as a leading constitutional architect. At a dinner in 1827, Madison was proclaimed the "father of the Constitution," a label that has stuck to Madison ever since. During their dramatic U.S. Senate debate on western lands in 1830, Daniel Webster and Robert Hayne each cited Madison as a preeminent constitutional authority – in support of their *opposite* positions on states' rights. At his death in 1836, Madison had outlived every one of the other delegates to the Constitutional Convention.[22]

USING THE CONSTITUTION: ENDURING FEATURES

The Constitution has set the basic rules for using American government for more than two hundred years. It has shaped not only the behavior, but also the aspirations of those who seek public policy.[23] The political resilience of these enduring institutional features has been remarkable. This basic framework lasted through the many wrenching social and political convulsions triggered by an American economy that has urbanized, industrialized, nationalized, suburbanized, and globalized. Since 1789 the United States has added hundreds of thousands of square miles of land, nearly three hundred million people, and thirty-seven states. The nation's political structure survived the British burning of Washington, D.C., the secession of eleven states and a bloody civil war, various moral panics

regulate commerce among the several States' can not include a power to construct roads and canals, and to improve the navigation of water courses in order to facilitate, promote, and secure such commerce with a latitude of construction departing from the ordinary import of the terms strengthened by the known inconveniences which doubtless led to the grant of this remedial power to Congress"; "Veto Message," March 3, 1817, in *A Compilation of the Messages and Papers of the Presidents* (Washington, DC: Government Printing Office, 1897), 2: 569. In Larson's view, Madison was trying to utilize the warrant of the Constitution to limit the future play of national politics, a view consistent with the use of the presidency to shape future political orders. In a speech in the House of Representatives as early as 1792, Madison complained that a broad definition of the "general welfare" clause would allow for the regulation of funding roads other than post roads (*PJM* 14: 223).

[22] Irving Brandt, *James Madison: Commander in Chief, 1812–1836* (Indianapolis, IN: Bobbs-Merrill, 1961), p. 471; Drew R. McCoy, *The Last of the Fathers: James Madison and the Republican Legacy* (Cambridge: Cambridge University Press, 1989).

[23] Douglass C. North argues that institutions structure incentives in *Institutions, Institutional Change and Economic Performance* (Cambridge: Cambridge University Press, 1990), p. 3. Jack Knight observes that "social actors produce social institutions in the process of seeking distributional advantage in the conflict over substantive benefits.... the development of institutional rules is merely a means for that substantive end. The importance of these institutional rules lies in the constraints that they place on strategic action." *Institutions and Social Conflict* (Cambridge: Cambridge University Press, 1992), p. 126.

and national security alarms, several electoral crises, four presidential assassinations, and the impeachment trials of two presidents. It enabled the government to declare war and engage in undeclared wars, to build the world's most powerful military and an arsenal of nuclear weapons, and to levy numerous tariffs and make various treaties. It allowed the national government to shelter slavery and then to abolish it, to battle Indians and then resettle them on reservations. It enabled national officials to quell riots, put down strikes, and subsidize railroads. It permitted government to initiate a Federal Reserve Bank, a system of national parks, a national highway system, an agricultural stabilization policy, a Social Security Act, a Peace Corps, a War on Poverty, a program for exploring space, and a mass of business, labor, consumer, and environmental regulations.

The Constitution helped enable Americans to use government to achieve goals that were sometimes noble, sometimes divisive, and occasionally appalling. But using American government rarely has been easy, regardless of the goal. The enduring rules for governing the United States, laid out by the Constitution, make it difficult and costly for Americans to employ public policy to accomplish their purposes.

The Constitution as a Political Weapon

Its resilience, utility, and popular acceptance have made the Constitution far and away the most esteemed source of public authority in the United States. The Constitution's political preeminence quickly became plain to all observers. In the nineteenth century, for example, British political scientist James Bryce wrote that "The Constitution of 1789 deserves the veneration with which the Americans have been accustomed to regard it."[24] Today, according to the authors of one of the most widely used American government textbooks, "[t]he Constitution remains a document Americans revere."[25] In a 2002 public opinion poll, three-quarters of American adults viewed the Constitution as a "great document that had some blind spots."[26] The following year, almost two out of three adults expressed

[24] James Bryce, *The American Commonwealth*, 3rd ed. (New York: Macmillan, 1901), 1: 28.

[25] James MacGregor Burns, J. W. Peltason, Thomas E. Cronin, David B. Magleby, David M. O'Brien, and Paul C. Light, *Government by the People*, National Version (Upper Saddle River, NJ: Pearson/Prentice-Hall, 2004), p. 27.

[26] Public Agenda, "Americans Proud of U.S. and Constitution, but Want Children Taught the Bad with the Good," http://www.publicagenda.org/press/press_release_detail.cfm?list=48, accessed June 22, 2004.

the belief that the U.S. Constitution affected their own life "a great deal."[27]

The Constitution's preeminence, combined with its ambiguity, has made it an irresistible weapon in political conflict.[28] Sometimes, Americans use the Constitution as an offensive weapon, a battering ram employed to justify a major change in the current path of public policy. Presidents frequently invoke the Constitution to legitimize their plans for profound changes in political direction. For example, Franklin Roosevelt in 1933 justified the extraordinary policy measures he was preparing to take by explaining that "Our Constitution is so simple and practical that it is possible always to meet extraordinary needs by changes in emphasis and arrangement without loss of essential form," a quality that explained "why our constitutional system has proved itself the most superbly enduring political mechanism the modern world has produced."[29] Advocates for rights for African Americans, for women, for criminal defendants, and for homosexuals have argued that the Constitution necessitates active government protection for the people they champion. More often, the Constitution is employed as a defensive weapon, a shield used to stop government from acting. Opponents of legal restrictions on property, speech, the press, religion, gun ownership, or employer prerogatives unfailingly are attracted to constitutional provisions that allegedly prohibit such laws.

When opponents invoke the Constitution to win a political battle, as they often do, the conflicting parties vie to establish their legitimacy by

[27] ABC News, "U.S. Constitution: Great Impact, but Hold the Details," http://abcnews.go.com/images/pdf/883a28Constitution.pdf, accessed June 22, 2004.

[28] "Social actors become so accustomed to complying with particular rules that they come to accept those rules as the natural way of doing something. Eventually they change the way people view facts and values" (Knight, *Institutions and Social Conflict*, p. 186).

[29] Franklin D. Roosevelt, "Inaugural Address," March 4, 1933, in *The Public Papers and Addresses of Franklin D. Roosevelt* (New York: Random House, 1938), 2: 15. See also Arnold Schwarzenegger's inaugural address, Los Angeles Times website, November 17, 2003: "But for guidance, let's look back in history to a period I studied when I became a citizen. The summer of 1787. Delegates of the original 13 states were meeting in Philadelphia. Our Founding Fathers KNEW that the fate of the union was in their hands – just as the fate of California is in our hands. What happened in that summer of 1787 is that they put their differences aside – and produced the blueprint for our government; our CONSTITUTION. Their coming together has been called 'the Miracle of Philadelphia.'" http://www.governor.ca.gov/state/govsite/gov_htmldisplay.jsp? BV_SessionID=@@@@0830482220.1073144121@@@@& BV_EngineID=eadcjedgmdjjbemgcfkmchchi.0&sCatTitle=Speeches&sFilePath=/govsite/selected_speeches/20031117_SwearingIn.html&sTitle=2003, accessed January 3, 2004.

claiming they are more faithful to the Constitution's true meaning.[30] Candidates repeatedly have invoked constitutional history to gain the upper hand in campaigns. In the 1860 election, Abraham Lincoln famously challenged the constitutional understanding of his Democratic rival, Stephen A. Douglas.[31] Officeholders regularly have used the Constitution to defend their prerogatives and interpretations of public policy.[32] During the Watergate crisis, President Nixon's lawyers warned that the Constitution would be at risk if the Supreme Court ordered him to surrender Oval Office audiotapes; Special Prosecutor Leon Jaworski warned that the Constitution would be at risk if they did *not* do so. Policy battles over constitutional interpretation often displace considerable time, energy, and resources from substantive issues.

As Madison and Jefferson recognized early on, the states' authority itself – "states' rights" – is a particularly attractive constitutional weapon in policy disputes. The Constitution left obscure the boundaries between state and national authority, and delegated these boundary issues to the politicians who would contest them according to the newly established policy-making rules. The delegates left no definitive guidelines about which public goods would be provided by the states and which by the national government. National power could be expanded, but could not be expanded at will. States would influence national public policy, and their agents could delay, defeat, or extract concessions for the expansion of national power.[33] Political opponents have invested much energy into battles over the boundary between state and national government policy authority. "States' rights" has been used regularly to try to win substantive political struggles over taxes, commerce, banking, manufacturing, labor, energy, public utilities, canals, roads, education, social welfare, public health, slavery, segregation, pollution, criminal justice, civil liberties, and

30 Lawrence Lessig and Cass R. Sunstein, "The President and the Administration," *Columbia Law Review* 94:1 (1994): 1–123.

31 Harold Holzer, *Lincoln at Cooper Union: The Speech That Made Abraham Lincoln President* (New York: Simon and Schuster, 2004).

32 Keith E. Whittington, *Constitutional Construction: Divided Powers and Constitutional Meaning* (Cambridge, MA: Harvard University Press, 2001); H. Jefferson Powell, *A Community Built on Words: The Constitution in History and Politics* (Chicago: University of Chicago Press, 2002).

33 Rakove, *Original Meanings*, 201; Herbert Wechsler, "The Political Safeguards of Federalism: The Role of the States in the Composition and Selection of the National Government," in *Federalism: Mature and Emergent*, ed. Arthur W. MacMahon (New York: Columbia University Press, 1955), pp. 97–114.

civil rights.[34] It is almost impossible to imagine American politics without recurring conflict over the boundaries of state and national economic power. Rarely, if ever, though, do American policy makers invoke "states' rights" except as a political weapon to achieve a desired, substantive policy outcome. "States' rights" has been such a politically appealing weapon because policy adversaries expect the state and national governments to produce different policy outcomes.[35]

The Difficulties of Using State Authority

States always and intimately have governed the fundamentals of American life: property, contracts, labor, the natural environment, health and safety, marriage and family. States governed most of the nation's factor endowments – land, labor, and capital – until after the nation was a mature industrial power. State licenses, corporation laws, and economic regulations police many of the nation's most influential economic actors. Tiny Delaware charters half a million corporations, including a large majority of the Fortune 500 companies. States still supervise utilities, transportation, and banking, though national rules now limit state discretion in these areas. States nurture markets by building roadways and by managing natural resources. They fund and manage much of the nation's education, health, welfare, and domestic security. They regulate gambling, liquor, drugs, and other vices, real and imagined. State attorneys general have

[34] See, for example, Forrest McDonald, *States' Rights and the Union: Imperium in Imperio, 1789–1876* (Lawrence: University Press of Kansas, 2000); David Brian Robertson, *Capital, Labor, and State: The Battle for American Labor Markets from the Civil War to the New Deal* (Lanham, MD: Rowman and Littlefield, 2000).

[35] In his study of political development during the American Civil War, Richard Franklin Bensel wrote that "If... the South created in the Confederacy a central state at least as strong as the one that guided the Union war mobilization, we can begin to distinguish between states' rights ideology, on the one hand, as a determinative world view and, on the other, as a pragmatic political program. From the latter perspective, both decentralist opposition to a strong federal government (when the South was in the Union) and support for a strong Confederate state can be viewed as defensive strategies directed against the hegemonic influence of the northern industrial economy in the middle and late nineteenth century.... explanations of the antithetical positions of plantation and industrial elites in American development should assign the primary part to highly divergent regional political economies and only a tactical role to ideological principles." Bensel, *Yankee Leviathan: The Origins of Central State Authority in America, 1859–1877* (Cambridge: Cambridge University Press, 1990), p. 13.

engaged in legal battles with some of the nation's foremost businesses, such as tobacco companies and Microsoft.

State officials have strong incentives to use their authority to favor private investment and market-driven economic development. The Constitution prohibited state policy makers from using the tools of economic sovereignty. They cannot, therefore, use tariffs, currency manipulation, and other policies that nation-states regularly have used to shift policy costs to foreigners or to extract rents from abroad. Unlike national policy makers in even the smaller nation-states in Europe (until the recent growth of coordinated European Union economic policies), American state officials could do little to conceal, shift, or compensate business for the costs of social policy or regulation. States could manage their assets, but could use the most potent of these tools only by putting prosperity and political fortunes at risk. Without the tools of economic sovereignty that national governments use to cushion the effects of social welfare and regulation on business profits, American state governments face intense competition from other states over investment, jobs, and economic growth. The economic costs of these taxes and regulations usually have been immediate, conspicuous, and uncompensated, and they often motivate the affected private interests to oppose the incumbent policy makers who inflict them. The Constitution's distribution of authority, in effect, imposed high political costs on officials responsible for taxes, regulations, and other policies that seem to put the state's enterprises at a competitive disadvantage with enterprises elsewhere. These enduring institutional arrangements generally have biased state policy makers toward policies that favor private investment and economic development and against policies that seem to inhibit it in the short run. This arrangement may be termed competitive American federalism.[36]

Competitive American federalism has made state officials generally resistant to business regulations and social expenditures that lack business support. State policy makers have had relentless reminders of the immediate economic impact of the way they govern people and natural resources. They have had less latitude than national policy makers to treat workers, including female and child workers, as something other than factor endowments. If constituents in some of the more-liberal states give

[36] Robertson, *Capital, Labor, and State*, pp. 17–20, 51–2. State policy makers are willing to pay those costs in the short run. But, compared with national policy makers, state officials are more resistant to policies that inhibit economic development, more responsive to opponents of such policies, more reluctant to implement such policies faithfully, and more unlikely to sustain these policies for the long term.

their lawmakers a warrant to expand regulations and taxes on business, governments in many other states often advertise their more hospitable "business climate" to draw investment away from rivals.

In every state, popular demands for regulation and redistribution have offset these interstate pressures from time to time. When large numbers of voters demand protection against the economic insecurity that naturally accompanies unregulated markets, restrictions on business autonomy and redistributive programs become politically expedient despite competitive pressures. Supportive political cultures, charismatic reform leadership, internal divisions in the business community, and powerful movements for reform all have produced more extensive economic regulation and public provision in some states, and some degree of regulation and social welfare in every state.

The American states are busy policy laboratories, but competitive American federalism restricts the range of experiments these state policy laboratories can conduct. States have used their discretion to build canals, highways, universities, and prisons; to restrict business collusion and to entice business to incorporate and invest within their boundaries; to resist the entry of potential welfare recipients and hazardous waste; to establish pioneering air quality standards; and to invent both Jim Crow segregation laws and civil rights protections, both social insurance programs and punitive workfare programs. Taken together, the states' policy inventions have tilted decidedly in favor of private enterprise. No American state has matched the universal labor or social programs that became common in Western Europe in the twentieth century. No American state could provide the universal access to health insurance available in nearly every other developed nation.

The Difficulties of Using National Authority

For different reasons, the national policy-making process also has remained difficult to use throughout American history. Its hurdles remain rooted in two features of constitutional design: the cumulative impact of its originally restricted authority, and the deliberately unaligned political incentives of national policy makers.

First, the United States national government was given a limited set of blunt instruments for governing the American economy. The Constitution authorized the national government to conduct foreign relations, to regulate economic relations between the states, to lay tariffs, to impose direct taxes (in a way that did not redistribute economic assets among the states), to manage debts, and to provide for a limited national military. It could prohibit states from interfering in interstate commerce and printing currency. To be sure, the calculated ambiguity of specific constitutional provisions made it possible to claim a broader warrant for national policy. Policy makers like Hamilton tried to make the most of the tools the Constitution authorized and battled to institute more-dexterous national economic management. James Madison used the Constitution as a political weapon to put a brake on early efforts to expand these powers, and even Federalist John Marshall's Supreme Court acknowledged the limits of national power and the states' legitimate right to manage many of their own policies.[37] The government exercised much more authority during the Civil War and World War I, but these powers contracted substantially after the end of combat.

Until the late 1930s, the Supreme Court refused to acknowledge broad national authority to regulate commerce. Since then, most Americans have come to accept extensive national regulation of markets and provision of social welfare programs as constitutionally valid. The economy, however, already had become industrially mature by the time national economic authority permanently expanded. Business had become accustomed to its economic autonomy, and states to their economic powers. The national government consequently never assumed full control of most economic sectors, and it never has developed a fully stocked economic toolkit for fine-tuning the economy. National grants and mandates tried to establish national standards while leaving substantial policy discretion in state hands. State control over corporation laws and laws that affect the

[37] The Supreme Court effectively endorsed this understanding of state power to develop economically in *Gibbons v. Ogden* (9 Wheat 1, 1824), which ruled that state inspection laws "form a portion of that immense mass of legislation, which embraces everything within the territory of a state, not surrendered to the general government; all which can be most advantageously exercised by the states themselves. Inspection laws, quarantine laws, health laws of every description, as well as laws for regulating the internal commerce of a state, and those which respect turnpike-roads, ferries, &c., are component parts of this mass." *Gibbons v. Ogden* also recognized that the ambiguous boundary between state and national power would trigger political disputes over policy authority: "In our complex system, presenting the rare and difficult scheme of one general government, whose action extends over the whole, but which possesses only certain enumerated powers; and of numerous State governments, which retain and exercise all powers not delegated to the Union, contests respecting power must arise. Were it even otherwise, the measures taken by the respective governments to execute their acknowledged powers, would often be of the same description, and might, sometimes, interfere. This, however, does not prove that the one is exercising, or has a right to exercise, the powers of the other."

organization of trade unions have had a critically important impact on the balance of political power between business and labor, which in turn has affected the balance of power in American politics as a whole.

Despite the expansion of national policy influence, the Constitution has limited the exercise of national power. The boundary of national authority remains unsettled.[38] The burden of proof generally has fallen on the national government to exercise control over markets, though the difficulty of meeting that burden has been relaxed over the years. Agents of state interests still influence the way the national government uses its authority.[39]

Second, it is still necessary but still very difficult to align the houses of Congress, the president, and the courts behind any national policy initiative. The policy makers in these institutions still have the dissimilar incentives and perspectives originally designed into the Constitution.[40] It is true that the evolution and expansion of the national government would astonish the framers. In Congress, entrenched political parties and a system of permanent committees organize the activities of 535 lawmakers. The executive branch now includes over two and a half million federal civilian employees and a large, permanent military, scattered across the nation and the globe. Hundreds of federal judges deal with over two hundred thousand cases a year.

But the fundamental features of the national policy process have remained intact since 1789. A bicameral Congress still bears the principal responsibility for national lawmaking, and members of Congress have always been motivated to pursue the present interests of local constituencies.

[38] Keith E. Whittington, "Dismantling the Modern State? The Changing Structural Foundations of Federalism," *Hastings Constitutional Law Quarterly* 25:4 (Summer 1998): 483–527.

[39] Wechsler, "The Political Safeguards of Federalism"; Larry D. Kramer, "Putting the Politics Back into the Political Safeguards of Federalism," *Columbia Law Review* 100 (January 2000): 215–93.

[40] This is a more specific formulation of the observation that the separation of powers makes it difficult for a faction to determine public policy outcomes; see Madison's *Federalist* 51 in Alexander Hamilton, James Madison, and John Jay, *The Federalist*, ed. Jacob E. Cooke (Middletown, CT: Wesleyan University Press, 1961), pp. 347–53. Aaron L. Friedberg makes the conventional case effectively: "These institutional arrangements were intended to make it very difficult for one group or one branch of government to increase its power at the expense of the others, or for the federal government as a whole to exercise its authority over the people, without a significant measure of consensus and consent." See Friedberg, "Reinventing the American State: Political Dynamics in the Post-Cold War Era," in *Shaped by War and Trade: International Influences on American Political Development*, ed. Ira Katznelson and Martin Shefter (Princeton: Princeton University Press, 2002), p. 240.

Representatives still are elected for two-year terms by geographical constituencies that represent a small fraction of the nation. Two senators still represent each state (though state voters instead of legislatures now choose senators), and senators still serve six-year terms. Today, California's senators, who represent about 12 percent of the U.S. population, have no more weight in Senate policy making than Wyoming's senators, who represent two-tenths of 1 percent of the U.S. population. The Senate never has provided representation for minorities per se.[41]

To pass a law, a majority of U.S. representatives still must collaborate on equal terms with a majority of U.S. senators. Extraordinarily large geographical majorities are still necessary to enact laws. These concurrent majorities, along with the president's veto, make gridlock common whether or not different political parties control different branches of government.[42] Even when political leaders can assemble winning coalitions, it is difficult to sustain the same coalition from issue to issue. Legislative policy, then, still requires inventive logrolling compromises among a supermajority of diverse regional interests. Tariffs, river and harbor improvements, antipoverty programs, highway programs, economic development initiatives, defense contracts, and even academic research grants all illustrate this logrolling imperative.

While the president's responsibility for the national policy agenda has expanded greatly, presidents still find the original policy-making structure a major impediment to achieving their goals. The president still serves a four-year term that puts him on a different timetable than the lawmakers in Congress. Unlike legislators, the president must build a constituency across many states to win a majority of electoral votes. The president's national constituency and powers still give the office strong incentives to define the national interests in terms of prospective national policy outcomes that also build a national political constituency.

[41] "With respect to race, arguably the most important and enduring political cleavage in American history, Senate apportionment undercuts the protection of political minorities.... Senate apportionment does not function to protect political minorities per se. At most one can merely claim that Senate apportionment, like any other form of geographic districting, enhances the representation of some interests and diminishes that of others, without respect to majority or minority status." Frances E. Lee and Bruce L. Oppenheimer, *Sizing Up the Senate: The Unequal Consequences of Equal Protection* (Chicago: University of Chicago Press, 1999), p. 23.

[42] David W. Brady and Craig Volden, *Revolving Gridlock: Politics and Policy from Carter to Clinton* (Boulder, CO: Westview Press, 1998).

Thomas Jefferson, Andrew Jackson, Abraham Lincoln, Franklin Roosevelt, and Ronald Reagan all pursued public policy with a vision of the national interest partially aimed at forming future national coalitions.[43] The president's veto remains a powerful bludgeon for stopping policy. Along with national government authority and the American role in the world, presidential powers grew in the twentieth century. Some of these expanded powers help the president achieve his goals; examples include executive orders to implement policy, executive agreements to accomplish foreign-policy goals, and the authority to commit troops for a time without a declaration of war. All these powers have their limits, and none can substitute for legislation. Congress still holds power over the president's most fundamental priorities: legislation, taxes, spending, and major appointments.

Courts' powers still independently influence both the design and the implementation of American public policy. The Constitution's eminence has greatly strengthened judicial independence and authority to serve as the final arbiter of policy disputes. Presidents still select judges, generally selecting members of their own political party (although some judicial nominations spark controversy in the Senate, it confirms most presidential nominees for the bench).[44] Courts have tended to defend the political perspectives of the presidents who placed them in office. Chief Justice John Marshall tried to defend Federalist Party principles in the early nineteenth century, for example, and Chief Justice Roger Taney's Supreme Court tried to defend the principles of the Jacksonian Democratic Party until the eve of the Civil War. The Supreme Court tried to limit the definition of national commerce powers until 1937. Some Supreme Court decisions have changed the course of politics, including the Court's decisions on civil rights, criminal rights, and privacy in the mid-twentieth century. The courts, though, remain institutions that can only react to policy disputes that aggrieved parties bring to them after policy has been in place, and they remain filled with judges whose selection reflected past elections instead of present or future ones.

[43] Stephen Skowronek, *The Politics Presidents Make: Leadership from John Adams to Bill Clinton*, 2nd ed. (Cambridge, MA: Belknap Press, 1997).

[44] Presidents usually nominate justices for the Supreme Court who share their political and policy views; Richard L. Pacelle Jr., *The Role of the Supreme Court in American Politics: The Least Dangerous Branch?* (Boulder, CO: Westview Press, 2002), pp. 12–19. See also George L. Watson and John Alan Stookey, *Shaping America: The Politics of Supreme Court Appointments* (New York: Longman, 1995).

Making this national policy process work requires broad political support and sustained, concerted effort.[45] Yet it has been difficult to build and sustain the large political coalitions necessary to make this effort, as the unique development of American political parties shows.

THE CONSTITUTION, INTEREST GROUPS, AND POLITICAL PARTIES

Demands for government action have swept across the American political system repeatedly since 1789. Profound cultural changes have prompted shifts in policies affecting minorities, women, children, the disabled, and criminals. Religious fervor has inspired campaigns against slavery, liquor, drugs, and sexual licentiousness.[46] Economic crises have fueled fear, resentment, and demands for limits on the power of economic elites. Populist farmers in the 1890s demanded the national ownership of telephones, telegraphs, and railroads. Influential legislators and administrators called for national planning in the 1930s and 1940s. Entrepreneurial experts battled for far-reaching regulation of economic activity in the 1960s and 1970s.

The Constitution not only made it hard for such roused political interests to use the national policy process, but it also made public policy a less reliable answer to their problems. New public policies would have to appeal across many geographical areas and groups of voters to survive the institutional gauntlet of the national policy process. In the absence of a crisis or some other arresting event that focuses support, creating this broad appeal in Congress takes considerable time, sustained effort, and substantial resources. Even if Congress is persuaded to enact a law dealing with a problem, the president, public agencies, or courts have exceptional discretion to apply the law in a different way than intended, or even decline to apply the law effectively. Indeed, its disconnection from other parts of the policy process invites Congress to enact ambiguous legislation that masks divisive political choices with heroic but vague platitudes. Such ambiguous statutory language effectively delegates controversial decisions to other policy makers such as the president, public administrators, or the courts. In this sense, the system is more capable of providing the illusion of public policy than reliable policy solutions

[45] Douglass C. North would describe these costs as political transaction costs; see *Institutions, Institutional Change and Economic Performance*, pp. 49, 138.

[46] James A. Morone, *Hellfire Nation: The Politics of Sin in American History* (New Haven, CT: Yale University Press, 2003).

to citizens' demands.[47] The national government can simply respond to policy demands with largely symbolic policies, such as a declaration of "war" on a problem like poverty or drugs, or an underfunded mandate imposed on state or local officials.

These features have made it difficult to build broad-based, sustainable policy coalitions, notably political parties. It is hard for politicians to deliver on policy promises they make in an election campaign. To enact any law, political leaders have to assemble extraordinarily large coalitions of policy makers with different constituencies, time perspectives, and priorities. Even if a coalition is assembled, the slowness and unreliability of the policy-making process makes it easy for potential coalition partners to defect as the process wears on. Party leaders cannot promise that a law will be interpreted and executed as promised; administrators, states, and courts can renege on key parts of a deal by pursuing independent interpretations of the law. Because of the number of access points in the system, individual interest groups sometimes shop around for the best policy outcome, and have less incentive to join a broad policy coalition. The nation's size and its economic and cultural diversity only amplify these problems.

American politicians since James Madison have found it more expedient to build political parties around elections and office seeking, relying on a very few specific national policy priorities to pull the coalition together, leaving great latitude for individual candidates to tailor their election platforms to local circumstances.[48] Because states have controlled the tools of economic management, political leaders found it much easier to organize political parties at the state level where the control of the levers of government had a more direct payoff. In turn, the robust, state-rooted American political parties gave state politicians strong incentives

[47] Theodore Lowi's notion of interest group liberalism resembles this argument; see Theodore J. Lowi, *The End of Liberalism: The Second Republic of the United States* (New York: W. W. Norton, 1979). Lowi's analysis suggests that statutory ambiguity was a distinctive development of the New Deal, but I am arguing that statutory ambiguity is prevalent throughout the history of American public policy. I differ from Lowi in locating the incentive to this ambiguity in the original Constitution rather than a "reconstitution" during the New Deal. The New Deal amplifies the tendency to policy illusion already designed into American government, and evident in such pre-1900 laws as the Interstate Commerce Act and the Sherman Antitrust Act, as well as the delegation of implementation to states in laws such as the Morrill Act of 1862. Policy illusion is a universal temptation in politics, of course, but American constitutional design amplifies it.

[48] John Gerring, *Party Ideologies in America, 1828–1996* (Cambridge: Cambridge University Press, 2001); Richard Franklin Bensel, *The Political Economy of American Industrialization, 1877–1900* (Cambridge: Cambridge University Press, 2000).

to insist on keeping control over policy tools needed to maintain and build party strength. Democratic Party leaders for decades ignored legal segregation in the South because southern Democrats won elections in their home states by supporting these Jim Crow laws. In national government, politicians could gain by colluding with politicians from other states without subordinating themselves to a disciplined party organization. The fragmentation of policy authority rewarded elected officials for creating long-term alliances of officeholding (American political parties) and using short-term, opportunistic coalitions to advance specific policy outcomes.[49]

The separation of public offices, constituencies, and interests severely limited the disciplined cross-state party control of candidates, money, or philosophy that were prerequisites of the more programmatic political parties that emerged in other industrializing democracies a century ago. Instead, the difficulty of using the American policy-making process, along with its unreliability, often encourages interests to pursue narrow, incremental policy changes without building broad policy coalitions. Many observers note that American public policy evolves in small, incremental steps.[50] By focusing on small policy benefits, such as a targeted tax break, a minor grant-in-aid program, or a change in a specific regulation, interest groups can achieve a policy goal without building broad policy alliances with other groups. Thus, the American policy process encourages interests to remain fragmented and pursue their goals independently, a situation that political scientists term "pluralism." It made it easier for businesses, trade unions, and interest groups to lobby for individual gains than to work together in an inclusive, disciplined alliance united by a clear policy agenda.

The Constitution does not determine the tactics employed by political parties and interest groups. These tactics are natural responses to the opportunities and constraints built into the enduring features of American political institutions. Nothing demonstrates the impact of these natural

[49] From this perspective, theories of political parties that assume parties seek offices rather than policy outcomes may draw too heavily on the U.S. experience. See Anthony Downs, *An Economic Theory of Democracy* (New York: Harper, 1957); Wolfgang C. Müller and Kaare Strøm, eds., *Policy, Office, or Votes? How Political Parties in Western Europe Make Hard Decisions* (Cambridge: Cambridge University Press, 1999).

[50] Charles E. Lindblom and Edward J. Woodhouse, *The Policy-Making Process*, 3rd ed. (Englewood Cliffs, NJ: Prentice-Hall, 1993), pp. 23–32. But see James L. True, Bryan D. Jones, and Frank R. Baumgartner, "Punctuated Equilibrium Theory," in *Theories of the Policy Process*, ed. Paul A. Sabatier (Boulder, CO: Westview Press, 1999), pp. 97–115.

responses better than the politics of industrialization, when American politics decisively set out along a unique path of political development.

THE DISTINCTIVE POLITICS OF AMERICAN INDUSTRIALIZATION

Industrialization created political upheavals everywhere it occurred. It uprooted rural populations, relocated people from farms to cities, and established an industrial working class. Emerging political parties that responded to these changes in the working class, such as the Labour Party in Britain and the Social Democratic Party in Germany, profoundly changed the path of politics in their nations. Uniquely among the industrialized nations, no comparable mass-based American working-class party sustained electoral support.[51] Observers usually explain the absence of a working-class political party in the United States as the result of a culture unusually attached to free markets, the unusual mobility enjoyed by American workers, the size and ethnic diversity of the American working class, the conservatism of American trade-union leaders, or the strength of America's patronage-based political parties. All these things played a role in American labor's unique political response to industrialization.

But the Constitution also played a central role in discouraging a working-class political party in America. The enduring political structure of the United States helps explain how several distinctive pieces of the early twentieth-century American political economy interacted to create immense obstacles to the creation of a working-class party. These pieces are antitrust policy; the large, vertically integrated corporation; and relatively weak industrial unions. These developments each followed logically from Americans' response to the irresistible force of industrialization on the one hand and America's hard-to-use political framework on the other.

Antitrust policy – a uniquely American approach to the growth of business collusion in the nineteenth century – followed naturally from the Constitution's restrictions on state and national economic authority. After the Civil War, railroads posed a major challenge to the states' authority to manage their own commerce. With billions of dollars of capital, vast

[51] Maurice Duverger, *Political Parties: Their Organization and Activity in the Modern State* (London: Methuen, 1964), pp. 22–3; see also Werner Sombart, *Why Is there No Socialism in the United States?* (London: Macmillan, 1976); Giovanni Sartori, *Parties and Party Systems: A Framework for Analysis* (Cambridge: Cambridge University Press, 1976), p. 1; Seymour Martin Lipset, *American Exceptionalism: A Double-Edged Sword* (New York: W. W. Norton, 1997).

interstate rail networks, and extensive political influence, the large railroads became industrial behemoths. These national firms set rates that angered merchants, farmers, and other important constituents of state politicians. Illinois and Minnesota legislators created state railroad commissions to regulate railroad pricing policy inside their states, but the Supreme Court struck down Illinois's ban on discriminatory rates as a violation of the Constitution's commerce clause. When the states found themselves largely helpless to deal with the unprecedented price and production power of the railroads, congressional representatives demanded national action to defend their state officials and constituents.[52] Congress created an Interstate Commerce Commission (ICC) and, in collaboration with the courts, gave the ICC the warrant to confront and challenge the prices the railroads set. This strategy nationalized some policing of corporate conduct.[53]

[52] Gerald Berk, *Alternative Tracks: The Constitution of American Industrial Order, 1865–1917* (Baltimore: Johns Hopkins University Press, 1993); Colleen A. Dunlavy, *Politics and Industrialization: Early Railroads in the United States and Prussia* (Princeton, NJ: Princeton University Press, 1994). The Illinois law was invalidated in the case of *Wabash, St. Louis and Pacific Railway Company v. Illinois* (118 U.S. 557, 1886). Writing for the Supreme Court majority in this case, Justice Samuel Miller, an Iowa Republican nominated by Abraham Lincoln, wrote that "It cannot be too strongly insisted upon that the right of continuous transportation, from one end of the country to the other, is essential in modern times, to that freedom of commerce from the restraints which the State might choose to impose upon it, that the commerce clause was intended to secure. This clause, giving to Congress the power to regulate commerce among the States and with foreign nations, as this court has said before, was among the most important of the subjects which prompted the formation of the Constitution.... And it would be a very feeble and almost useless provision, but poorly adapted to secure the entire freedom of commerce among the States which was deemed essential to a more perfect union by the framers of the Constitution, if at every stage of the transportation of goods and chattels through the country, the State within whose limits a part of this transportation must be done could impose regulations concerning the price, compensation, or taxation, or any other restrictive regulation interfering with and seriously embarrassing this commerce.... when it is attempted to apply to transportation an entire series of States a principle of this kind, and each one of the States shall attempt to establish its own rates of transportation, its own methods to prevent discrimination in rates, or to permit it, the deleterious influence upon the freedom of commerce among the States, and upon the transit of goods through those States, cannot be overestimated.... the regulation can only appropriately exist by general rules and principles, which demand that it should be done by the Congress of the United States under the commerce clause of the Constitution."

[53] Stephen Skowronek, *Building a New American State: The Expansion of National Administrative Capacities, 1877–1920* (Cambridge: Cambridge University Press, 1982), pp. 121–62; Elizabeth Sanders, *Roots of Reform: Farmers, Workers, and the American State, 1877–1917* (Chicago: University of Chicago Press, 1999), pp. 179–97.

The Sherman Antitrust Act soon extended the idea of policing corporate conduct to all large interstate enterprises in the nineteenth century. The sheer size of the American economy favored the creation of large-scale national enterprises such as Standard Oil and U.S. Steel, companies that were larger than comparable enterprises abroad.[54] Like European firms, American firms sought to manage competition by making price and production agreements with their competitors. In Europe, governments and unions helped enforce these cartel agreements. But the fragmentation of public authority and competitive federalism made it impossible for governments to enforce such cartel agreements in the United States. State governments were helpless to protect colluding employers from predatory competitors outside the state's jurisdiction. The federal government had no authority to sanction cartels because it had no authority to manage the economy. As the states struggled to cope with out-of-state trusts, twenty-one enacted constitutional or statutory prohibitions on trusts by 1890. As in the case of the railroads, only federal law could reach some of the interstate trust practices that fell between the cracks of these state laws. Congress responded with the Sherman Antitrust Act of 1890, which tried to restrict the conduct of such businesses by declaring illegal "[e]very contract, combination in the form of trust or otherwise, or conspiracy, in restraint of trade or commerce among the several states."[55] Although the U.S. Justice Department at first did virtually nothing to implement the Sherman Act, it marked a singularly American response to the growth of private enterprise. No other industrializing nation responded to the growth of business with antitrust policies and efforts to police business conduct.[56]

Ironically, antitrust fostered the growth of the large industrial corporations that became the most important distinguishing feature of the American economy after 1900. Federalism already had helped induce state political parties to collude instead of merging into centralized national

[54] Alfred Chandler, *The Visible Hand* (Cambridge, MA: Harvard University Press, 1977) and *The Scale and Scope: The Dynamics of Industrial Capitalism* (Cambridge, MA: Belknap Press, 1990).

[55] Hans B. Thorelli, *The Federal Antitrust Policy* (Baltimore: Johns Hopkins University Press, 1955); William Letwin, *Law and Economic Policy in America: The Evolution of the Sherman Antitrust Act* (Chicago: University of Chicago Press, 1965).

[56] "No country has tried more consistently to structure economic competition and supervise marketplace behavior than the United States," according to Richard Lehne in *Government and Business: American Political Economy in Comparative Perspective* (New York: Chatham House, 2001), pp. 234–35.

political parties. Now, at the end of the nineteenth century, it encouraged key American businesses to merge because they could not collude. Antitrust law did not change the fact that states still controlled corporate law. A large "trust" could evade the law simply by transforming itself from an illegal combination of distinct businesses into a single, legal corporation by seeking a state corporate charter. If the state permitted it, a state-chartered corporation could legally absorb its competitors through mergers and thus exercise much more-effective control over production and prices than it could through a trust or a cartel. New Jersey relaxed its corporate regulations and became a magnet for companies seeking to take advantage of this opportunity. Because of competitive federalism, New Jersey's gains put pressure on other states to follow its lead, and New York and other states relaxed their corporate laws as well.[57]

Eleven hundred large industrial firms incorporated in New Jersey during the great merger movement of the turn of the century.[58] Corporations like U.S. Steel and International Harvester came to dominate their markets, and many integrated vertically – that is, they gained substantial control over the supply of needed raw materials and over the distribution of the products they produced. These companies were larger and more dominant in their markets than their counterparts abroad; they unilaterally exercised great control over prices and production in their markets.[59] Well after these companies had established themselves, Woodrow Wilson's New Freedom produced the Clayton Antitrust Act and the Federal Trade Commission, initiatives that elaborated the national strategy of policing corporate conduct and protecting consumers from interstate business predators.[60] The structural logic of the Constitution, then, almost

[57] Christopher Grandy, *New Jersey and the Fiscal Origins of Modern American Corporation Law* (New York: Garland, 1993); Harry Scheiber, "Federalism and the American Economic Order, 1789–1910," *Law and Society Review* 10 (Fall 1975): 57–118; Henry N. Butler, "Nineteenth Century Jurisdictional Competition in the Granting of Corporate Privileges," *Journal of Legal Studies* 14 (January 1985): 129–66.

[58] Naomi R. Lamoreaux, *The Great Merger Movement in American Business, 1895–1904* (Cambridge: Cambridge University Press, 1985).

[59] Alfred D. Chandler Jr., who emphasizes that market conditions caused the growth of American corporations, discusses the distinctiveness of American corporations in *The Visible Hand* and in *The Scale and Scope*. See also Tony Freyer, *Regulating Big Business: Antitrust in Great Britain and America, 1880–1990* (Cambridge: Cambridge University Press, 1992), pp. 23–6.

[60] Marc Allen Eisner, *Antitrust and the Triumph of Economics: Institutions, Expertise, and Policy Change* (Chapel Hill: University of North Carolina Press, 1991), pp. 55–69; Martin J. Sklar, *The Corporate Reconstruction of American Capitalism, 1890–1916: The Market, the Law, and Politics* (Cambridge: Cambridge University Press, 1988).

simultaneously had encouraged confrontational national law, state regulatory laxity, and the growth of the large industrial corporation.

In turn, the rise of the large industrial corporations helped suppress industrial unions and encouraged U.S. trade-union leaders to approach politics much more cautiously than their counterparts abroad. Because few American businesses could collude – as they could in local printing or construction markets, for example – relatively few American businesses needed unions to police their price and production agreements. Because large industrial corporations did not need unions to police agreements, they fought off the unionization of industrial workers in the steel, auto, agricultural implement, and other important industries. Smaller employers fought unions more aggressively than such employers in other nations. This ferocious employer counterattack especially damaged the machinists, coal miners, and other industrial unionists who led the battle for independent labor parties and socialist policy agendas abroad. Instead, the building trades, the printers, and other craft unions grew relatively strong in the American Federation of Labor (AFL), the most politically influential labor organization of the period. Already frustrated by years of ineffective public labor protections, AFL leaders concluded that they had to rely as little as possible on American public policy to protect workers. The AFL narrowed the scope of its policy demands, lobbied for particular benefits, and rejected the idea of an independent political party. AFL leaders made tactical alliances with both Democratic and Republican politicians.

Together, these developments discouraged the emergence of a working-class political party in the United States. The craft-dominated AFL refused to endorse the American Socialist Party, and it opposed public health insurance. In effect, the AFL strategically abandoned much of the field of labor protection to employers just as corporations were coming to dominate the American political economy. Leaders of British and German unions in the 1890s sounded just as skeptical of government as did AFL leaders. In these nations, though, union leaders found that government was easier to use and more reliable. When they faced adversity in the early twentieth century, these leaders were much quicker to embrace independent labor politics. By the time the U.S. national government took up worker protections seriously in the 1930s, employers had gained a position of economic and political dominance, and the Democratic Party had largely precluded independent labor politics.[61]

[61] Robertson, *Capital, Labor, and State.*

OUR CHALLENGE

The Constitution gave American politicians extraordinary responsibilities, while at the same time made it extraordinarily hard for them to fulfill these responsibilities. It gave the Congress the duty to make laws for the entire nation, but has encouraged its members to view public policy primarily through the lens of the short-term, parochial interests of their local constituents. It gave the president a duty to formulate plans for achieving future national interests, but limited his capacity to pursue these interests. It gave the courts the duty to ensure the supremacy of federal law, but insulated courts so they can only react to individual conflicts about public policy long after the policy's initiation. Founded on the principle of rule by the people, the Constitution tacitly gave unelected judges the duty of rising above politics to protect established national interests. Founded on the principle of majority rule, the Constitution has obstructed and complicated the construction of majorities.

While Americans revere their Constitution, its paradoxes have fostered frustration and cynicism about their government. These frustrations are rooted in the way the framers answered the agonizing questions they confronted: how can a popularly controlled government promote national well-being without also being a threat? James Madison, Roger Sherman, and the other delegates who wrote the Constitution understood this question just as well – and even better – than we do now. These politicians crafted an answer that suited both their ideals and their vital political interests. Politicians designed the United States Constitution. Ingenious politicians use it. Altering the U.S. Constitution therefore can offer no panacea for curing America's political frustrations. Changing the Constitution is hard, and the results are unpredictable. There are no guarantees that any politically feasible change in the Constitution today would do more good than harm. No one who reflects on presidents' struggle for power in the past forty years, for example, can be confident that making it easier for presidents to get their way would unambiguously benefit the nation.

Instead of changing their Constitution, Americans must learn to use it better. To repeat: making this national policy process work requires very broad-based political coalitions and sustained, concerted effort. To use this government, Americans must engage in politics. They must build and sustain the large political coalitions necessary to align the House, the Senate, the presidency, the courts, and a large number of states. Building coalitions requires understanding the interests of many different kinds of people, forging an understanding of the common interests of these people, locating a common set of objectives that can motivate their continuing cooperation, and working constantly to anticipate and remedy the endless, inevitable conflicts that threaten their cooperative effort. American history abounds with ingenious, tough-minded leaders who have constructed politics in this way. These leaders have spotted opportunities in the Constitution's structural constraints, and they have learned to mold the ambiguities of American politics into new possibilities for political cooperation.

Abraham Lincoln epitomized these resourceful politicians who have found ways to make American government work. No political novice, Lincoln understood instinctively that the Constitution assumes that Americans will engage in the *political* pursuit of their objectives. No impractical romantic, Lincoln put government to new purposes even while invoking the warrant of the founders. No political innocent, Lincoln learned how to create the politics necessary for advancing inseparable political and policy goals. Americans feared for their destiny in 1862, when it seemed beyond their control. Lincoln defied this fear of insurmountable problems when he reassured Congress that "We – even *we here* – hold the power, and bear the responsibility." When he said, "*we* cannot escape history," Lincoln might just as well have told Americans today that they cannot escape the politics to which their Constitution has condemned them.

The Constitutional Convention produced an American government that is hard to use. Building political coalitions is hard even where government was not designed to obstruct their success, but the designers of the American Constitution made it especially difficult to build coalitions in the United States. Idealists must grasp this reality as a challenge and resolve to develop the politics necessary to make the Constitution work. It invites them, and it needs them, to build the exceptionally broad, strong, and durable coalitions required to overcome its hurdles and resist its frustrations. Making the politics that make this government work is arduous. Frequently, it seems impossible, but it is not. It is not cynical to believe that our well-being depends on how well our idealists make politics. It is the last true measure of idealism.

Index